FOOD LOVERS' SERIES

FOOD LOVERS'
GUIDE TO®
LONG ISLAND

The Best Restaurants, Markets
& Local Culinary Offerings

1st Edition

Peter M. Gianotti

gpp

Guilford, Connecticut

Editor: Tracee Williams
Project editors: Lynn Zelem and Lauren Brancato
Layout artist: Mary Ballachino
Text design: Sheryl Kober
Illustrations by Jill Butler with additional art by Carleen Moira Powell and Mary-Ann Dubé
Maps: Alena Joy Pearce © Morris Book Publishing, LLC

ISBN 978-0-7627-7943-7

Printed in the United States of America

10 9 8 7 6 5 4 3 2 1

All the information in this guidebook is subject to change. We recommend that you call ahead to obtain current information before traveling.

To Rita

Contents

About the Author

Peter M. Gianotti is restaurant critic for *Newsday*, where he also reviews wines and spirits. He has been a Washington correspondent, economics writer, book critic, and New York City reporter for the newspaper. Gianotti is the author of *A Guide to Long Island Wine Country* (2001), *Newsday's Guide to the Wines of Long Island* (1998), *Dining Out with Newsday* (1997, 1998), and co-author of *Eats NYC* (1995). He was a Bagehot Fellow at Columbia University, where he received his MS, and an adjunct instructor at Fordham University, where he received his BA. Gianotti was born in Brooklyn and lives on Long Island. Follow him @PeterMGianotti.

Acknowledgments

I'm grateful to Tad Smith, president of The Madison Square Garden Company and former president of local media for Cablevision, former *Newsday* publisher Fred Groser, editorial director Debby Krenek, editor Deborah Henley, and assistant managing editors Barbara Schuler and Mary Ann Skinner for their support of this work.

My gratitude to Marjorie Robins, *Newsday*'s cross-media and food editor, for her backing, patience, and expertise; and to food-staff members, restaurant reviewer Joan Reminick and food writer Erica Marcus, for their aid and encouragement.

For their help here, and in other areas, credit belongs to *Newsday* colleagues Liane Guenther, Ann Silverberg, Alan Fallick, Tom Beer, Lorina Capitulo, Rebecca Cooney, Shawna VanNess, Jack Millrod, Polly Higgins, Robin Topping, Jayme Wolfson, Ronnie Gill, Jonalyn Schuon, Jessica Damiano, Lynn Petry, Peggy Brown, Alan Wax, Dorothy Edmonds, Pat Brandt, and, now long-distance, Sylvia Carter. Thank you to Herbie Wheeler, who has improved every sentence.

I'm indebted to Globe Pequot Press editors Amy Lyons, Lynn Zelem, Lauren Brancato, Tracee Williams, and her predecessor Kevin Sirois for all they've done to make this project a reality.

And I'm deeply obliged to former *Newsday* editors Anthony Insolia and Anthony Marro for taking the risk and opening a new career for an economics reporter. I owe much to mentor and role model Leonard Levitt.

The book reflects many meals, much tasting, countless miles. I've been fortunate to be aided by family and friends in these adventures: Betty and Jack Maggio, Charles and Marie Maggio, David Fluhrer, Larry Klein, Ellen and Ira Travis, Catherine and Frank Rinaldi, Theresa D'Amore, and particularly Joseph D'Amore—a true food lover.

For their generosity and their skill at keeping me going, my appreciation especially goes to Michael H. Lavyne, Dominic A. Filardi, Margaret M. Ames, and Mitchell R. Berger.

To the chefs and restaurateurs who agreed to contribute the recipes in this book, I offer both my thanks and those of all the home cooks gathering the ingredients.

Recognition also to my ever-ready writing companions, who made sure no leftovers remained beyond midnight: Shadow, Tiger, Bonnie, Clyde, Hayley, Milo, and Nero.

I'm very thankful to my sister, Margaret; my mother, Lillian; and to my daughters, Claire and Teresa, always immeasurably supportive, deserving far more than any page can hold.

And special thanks are due my understanding, wise wife, Rita, without whom this book could not have been written and to whom it is dedicated with love.

Introduction

The distance between Great Neck and Montauk is about 102 miles, or approximately 45,000 pizzas. You can eat your way to the lighthouse and never have the same thing twice—or just have it every day.

Geographically, of course, Long Island is four counties: Kings (or Brooklyn), Queens, Nassau, and Suffolk. It's certainly the largest and longest island in the contiguous United States, as anyone driving east on a summer Friday immediately knows. Shaped roughly like a fish, it ends with two forks.

For this book, however, Long Island is defined as Nassau and Suffolk. Brooklyn and Queens have their own Food Lovers' guides.

Nassau gave the country its first suburb, Levittown; let Charles Lindbergh take off; inspired Robert Moses to build highways to beaches; was home to Theodore Roosevelt; and must have more restaurants serving linguine with clam sauce than any location between Rome and Naples.

Suffolk lured the Puritans to New York, the wealthy to the Hamptons, farmers and winemakers to the North Fork, surfers to Ditch Plains, and is the home of the Long Island Ducks, both baseball team and main courses. It was the birthplace of a certain iced tea, and has sent tons of calamari to their deep-fried destinies. No one will ever be without a lobster roll, either.

Montauk is synonymous with lobster. And the region also brings you Peconic Bay scallops and Blue Point oysters; littlenecks and cherrystones; bluefish and flounder; striped bass and tuna; sweet corn and cauliflower; strawberries and peaches; tomatoes and potatoes.

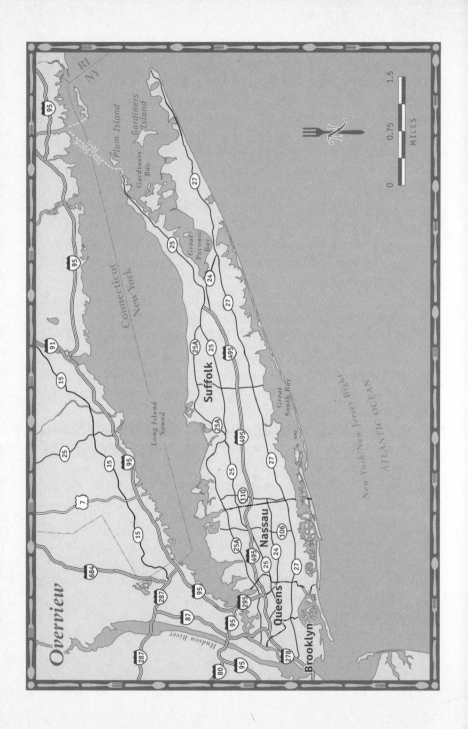

Overview

Connecticut
New York

Long Island Sound

RI
NY

Plum Island

Gardiners Island

Gardiners Bay

Great Peconic Bay

Suffolk

Great South Bay

New York/New Jersey Bight

ATLANTIC OCEAN

Nassau

Queens

Brooklyn

Hudson River

MILES
0   0.75   1.5

Long Island's 13 towns, three cities, and numerous villages and hamlets host thousands of restaurants. The most popular cuisines are Italian, steakhouse, and seafood but the mainstream is ocean-size.

For decades, Nassau and Suffolk's fine-dining establishments were dominated by Italian-continental hybrids and before that by traditional, midcentury American shrimp-cocktail-and-roast-beef houses.

Now, prime steakhouses are expanding into that role, New American establishments are on the upswing, gastropubs are booming, Latin cuisines are more widespread, small plates are big, fusion goes pro and con, and there's clearly a run on sliders, sushi, goat and Gorgonzola cheese, sausages, chimichurri, balsamic vinegar, hanger steak, cupcakes, designer sandwiches, and fries of all kinds.

Nassau and Suffolk contain numerous bakeries, gourmet markets, ethnic food shops, expert butchers, and as many places to purchase fresh fish and shellfish as you'll find on any US coast. Few communities are either short a pizzeria or absent a table for tacos, and you're always within driving distance of a decent bagel or an acceptable sushi stop.

Bring your appetite.

How to Use This Book

Each county is divided by town or towns and, when applicable, by city, going west to east, north to south.

Under each are sections devoted to **Foodie Faves,** or the better, recommended restaurants; **Landmarks,** or places with some history to go with the food; and notable **Specialty Stores, Markets & Shops.** These aren't directories listing each and every spot. They're selective. Some well-known places, for example, just didn't make the cut.

Following these are sections on Long Island wineries and vineyards, breweries and a distillery, farm stands and festivals, and signature recipes from Long Island chefs.

Price Code

The following symbols indicate the price range for a typical three-course meal, including beverages, at restaurants discussed in this guide. They go from the inexpensive ($) to the most expensive ($$$$).

$$$$	$100+
$$$	$50 to $100
$$	$25 to $50
$	$25 or less

Food News & Views

Newsday, the Long Island newspaper, covers Nassau and Suffolk restaurants and food news in print and online at newsday.com. The food section's blog, *feedme*, will keep you informed and up to date.

Edible Long Island is a magazine with food-related, local feature writing. *Edible East End* focuses on the North Fork and the Hamptons; ediblelongisland.com and edibleeastend.com.

Eastofnyc.com and **longislandrestaurantnews.com** are websites that address the region's food and dining.

Longislandfoodcritic.com provides listings of upcoming events and promotions at restaurants, wineries, and more.

Town of North Hempstead

Jay Gatsby ate here.

North Hempstead takes in a large section of what's often called the "Gold Coast" of Long Island. In *The Great Gatsby*, West Egg translates into Great Neck, East Egg into Manhasset. Both are in the basket of North Hempstead, a town enriched by a lot of restaurants and food shops.

One of the local landmarks is Castle Gould, patterned after Kilkenny Castle and finished in 1912, a dozen years after the property was acquired by the son of railroad magnate Jay Gould. After it was sold, the extravagant estate was dubbed Hempstead House.

Its opulence would have appealed to Gatsby, whose tastes are reflected in some of the great houses that remain in the northern part of town. The home of William Cullen Bryant, now the Nassau County Museum of Art, also is a landmark; likewise, Old Westbury Gardens, now open to the public and the former estate of John S. Phipps, the US Steel heir.

North Hempstead originally was part of Hempstead. Hempstead itself sympathized with the Tories during the American Revolution; what would become North Hempstead in 1784 did not. Residents drew up their own version of a declaration of independence about a year before John Hancock's signature became immortal.

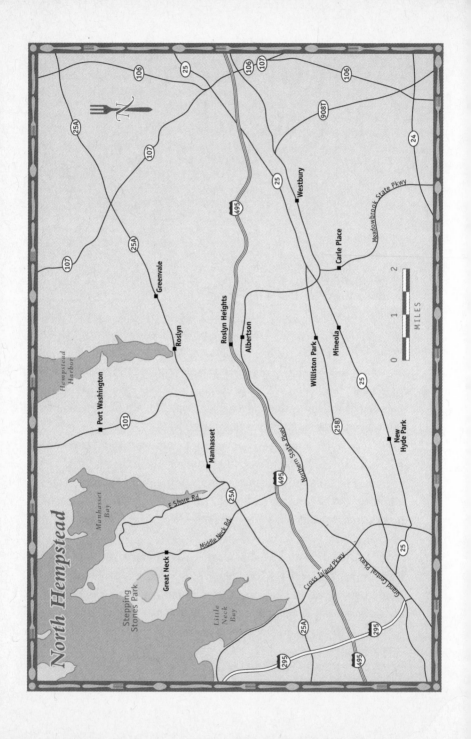

North Hempstead

Among other communities in the town with notable restaurants or markets and shops are Albertson, Carle Place, East Hills, part of Greenvale, Mineola, New Hyde Park, Port Washington, Roslyn, Roslyn Heights, Westbury, and Williston Park. Plate for plate, it has to be among the most appetizing towns around.

To the west of North Hempstead is Queens, one of New York City's five boroughs. North Hempstead is about 15 miles from Manhattan.

The green light at the end of Daisy's dock was a symbol of Gatsby's aspirations and dreams. Of course, it could signal time to eat, too.

Foodie Faves

Abeetza Next Door, 82 Glen Cove Rd., Greenvale, NY 11548; (516) 484-3123; abeetza.com; Italian; $$. How do you resist a place with a name like this? It's the neighboring restaurant to a popular pizzeria and market. And you already have a pretty good idea about what to eat. Maybe *pasta e fagioli* or tortellini in brodo; burrata cheese and heirloom tomatoes; eggplant rollatine or baked littleneck clams. Three savory flatbreads compete, with a Margherita-style number; a duck, caramelized onions, and goat cheese production; and a third capped with prosciutto, arugula, Gorgonzola cheese, rosemary, and fig puree. The fine pastas include rigatoni Bolognese, linguine with white clam sauce, and lobster ravioli in pink sauce. Chicken Milanese and tuna au poivre also stand out, along with the obligatory eggplant and chicken parmigiana. The surprise dessert is a chocolate soufflé.

Bar Frites, 400 Wheatley Plaza, Greenvale, NY 11548; (516) 484-7500; barfrites.com; French, New American; $$–$$$. Bar Frites began with a French bistro theme and played it very well. But French cuisine has faced the guillotine many times in Nassau and Suffolk. The purists usually don't last. Now, even though the appointments continue to wave the tricolor, the kitchen at Bar Frites is more international and, accordingly, the dining room more crowded. Don't expect to hear Piaf or Chevalier as background sound. And feel free to bypass the French wines. In addition to onion soup gratinée, there's chicken noodle soup; pizzettes and pastas vie with coq au vin and hanger steak frites; sliders compete with the croque monsieur. At lunch, the choices comprise a Vietnamese spring roll, fluke crudo, and wok-seared frogs' legs with yellow chives to buttress the *frisée aux lardons*. Whatever route you take, try the pommes frites, even with BBQ-chipotle sauce. Bar Frites is situated in the Wheatley Plaza shopping center. It's a Poll brothers production. They also operate Toku in Manhasset and both Hendrick's Tavern and Bryant & Cooper steak house in Roslyn.

Benny's Ristorante, 199 Post Ave., Westbury, NY 11590; (516) 997-8111; bennysristorante.com; Italian; $$–$$$. Benny's has been highly rated for decades, combining seamless service and primo Italian dishes. It has old-fashioned flair and modern sensibility, on display in an elegantly restrained dining room. You're sure to meet Benny DiPietro himself, the genial embodiment of hands-on management. Easily recommended dishes include eggplant rollatine filled with goat's milk ricotta and capellini pasta; spiedino alla Romana, with caper-anchovy sauce; and beef carpaccio. Visit if only for the Sicilian classic, bucatini con le sarde, with sardines, fennel from Benny's garden, pine nuts, raisins, and toasted bread crumbs. For a wry surf-and-turf affair, consider linguine with clams and sausage. Pasta alla carbonara, grilled polenta topped with melted Gorgonzola cheese and oyster mushrooms, and mushroom risotto also stand out. Consider the herb-and-mustard-crusted rack of lamb, pan-seared diver sea scallops with asparagus risotto, and, to be less traditional, grilled tuna crowned with pineapple-and-tomato salsa. The cannoli are freshly filled with delectable ricotta cream. Continue with tiramisu or Italian cheesecake, and one of the frothiest zabagliones around, on berries. See the recipe for **Pasta con le Sarde** on p. 338.

Ben's Kosher Delicatessen, 140 Wheatley Plaza, Greenvale, NY 11548; (516) 621-3340; bensdeli.net; Delicatessen; $–$$. The three Ben's delis in Nassau are dependable and very good for overstuffed sandwiches, soups, chicken or beef in the pot, kasha varnishkes, hot dogs—basically, the whole line of familiar specialties. The soups include a satisfying chicken, available every day, with noodles or matzo balls. On Friday, sample the sweet-sour cabbage soup or potato soup. Tuesday, it's split pea. Corned beef, pastrami, beef brisket, hard salami, and turkey are recommended sandwiches, on rye or club bread. The hot, open sandwiches also are reliable, especially turkey, brisket, and the corned beef–pastrami combo. There's tasty Hungarian goulash plus omelets, knishes round and square, potato pancakes, and, for the salad and burger set, enough to choose. The Israeli hero, a packed foot-long, is a noble thing. The mix-and-match options allow for outbursts of creativity. Noodle pudding and rugalach count here, too. Lots of take-out orders are made. Ben's in Carle Place is at 59 Old Country Rd., (516) 742-3354; in Woodbury, at 7971 Jericho Tpke., (516) 496-4236.

Besito, 1516 Old Northern Blvd., Roslyn, NY 11576; (516) 484-3001; besitomex.com; Mexican; $$–$$$. Most Mexican restaurants on Long Island are very casual affairs. The two Besitos, here and in downtown Huntington, are the region's high-end representatives of the cuisine. Each "little kiss" has no real competition in the category. This branch, in a commercial strip on the south side of the Roslyn viaduct, is the offspring of Besito Huntington, and it's both equally good and definitely festive. Consider it always party time, so go with a group and please pass the chips. The wall of luminaria adds a visual focal point and the slightest hint of serenity. Go for the tableside guacamole, spiced to whatever level you like; fish tacos with pickled red onion; a plump chile relleno with goat cheese and pine nuts; queso fundido made with Chihuahua cheese; and the *quesadillas de calabaza,* squash blossoms with roasted green chiles, salsa verde cruda, cheese, and mushrooms. Mole poblano is rich stuff. Same for the skirt steak, chorizo, and chicken tacos; short ribs with tomatillo-piquin salsa; and the *budin de mariscos,* a tortilla layered with shrimp and jumbo lump crabmeat with tomato salsa and more. Fried sweet plantains are a necessary accompaniment for any and all. Naturally, sample one of the margaritas. They know how to mix a drink here.

Biscuits & Barbeque, 106 E. Second St., Mineola, NY 11501; (516) 493-9797; Barbecue; $–$$. The little restored-railroad-car diner that houses Biscuits & Barbeque goes back decades. But the food has even more history. This is a haven for superior southern food. Of course, its few booths, lone table, and counter stools are jammed. The flavor of Louisiana shows in fried okra with mustard sauce, blackened catfish, seafood gumbo, and shrimp and grits. You'll want seconds when it comes to the smoky, barbecued ribs and the juicy smoked chicken. Southern fried chicken is the main competition, and it's both crisp and moist. B&B naturally makes a noble shrimp po' boy sandwich; and an even grander Muffuletta, the mega-sandwich that any hungry visitor who at least once spent some time in New Orleans can already taste. Banana pudding, pecan pie, and Key lime pie are fine. And, yes, the biscuits are on par with the 'cue.

Bistro Citron, 1362 Old Northern Blvd., Roslyn, NY 11576; (516) 403-4400; bistrocitron.com; French; $$–$$$. With a pondside perch, Bistro Citron adds a pretty view to its basic appeal. Try to snag a table by the window as the waterfowl provide a sideshow. Inside, it gets noisy in a hurry, with voices bouncing off a lot of hard surfaces. Generally, the appointments keep to the Gallic theme without overdoing it. And so does the kitchen. Check for the night's specials. Mainstays are a satisfying salad of *frisée aux lardons,* niçoise salad, escargots in herb butter, and onion soup gratinée. Have your elemental strip steak frites or spark it au poivre. The tender roast chicken for two, coq au vin, duck à l'orange, and the roasted duck breast with confit of leg in a sour cherry-red wine sauce are Bistro Citron's big birds. Pan-seared striped bass with preserved lemon beurre blanc brightens up the seafood choices. Braised short ribs in a red-wine reduction command Saturday; roasted monkfish with chorizo and saffron risotto, Wednesday. Also consider the lobster club sandwich; sesame seed-crusted tuna on baby bok choy and oyster mushrooms; and the macaroni and cheese with goat cheese, gruyère, and Parmesan. This restaurant is connected to, among others, Bistro Cassis in Huntington and Brasserie Cassis in Plainview.

Bistro Etc., 43-B Main St., Port Washington, NY 11050; (516) 472-7780; bistroetcetera.com; Mediterranean; $$–$$$. The cozy sliver of a restaurant seems slightly wider than a bowling alley. But it has the right mood and no attitude. The winning combination is buttressed by attentive and accommodating service, whether you're here on business or arriving with kids in tow. And when it's crowded, you may end up making new friends in a hurry. It nearly gets elbow-to-elbow. But everyone seems to be having a very good time. The fare is equally understated and appealing, beginning with a plate of mezze that's headed by creamy hummus, and a roasted butternut squash soup that doesn't belong exclusively to autumn. Pan-roasted shrimp and chorizo is a solid pairing. Cavatelli Bolognese rivals the versions at many pricier Italian spots. Duck, with preserved lemon and olives, is a flavorful alternative. The wild striped bass, accompanied by a spinach risotto cake and the rainbow trout with beluga lentil salad keep the regional theme going.

Bryant & Cooper, 2 Middle Neck Rd., Roslyn, NY 11576; (516) 627-7270; bryantandcooper.com; Steak, Seafood; $$$–$$$$. Bryant & Cooper has been contenting carnivores since 1986, with its clubby look and prime beef. It's one of Long Island's best steak houses. And it's crowded. B&C is run by the Poll brothers, whose other restaurants include nearby Bar Frites, Hendrick's Tavern, and Toku Modern Asian in Manhasset. The establishment overflows with regulars, whose favorites seem permanently recorded in the staff's collective memory. Waiters are efficient, moving things along and making suggestions. But, inevitably, the choices are clear: porterhouse, sirloin, rib eye, filet mignon, chopped steak with onions, the full-cut prime rib, maybe lamb chops. If you're here in winter, they may have very expensive but very good stone-crab claws. All year: shrimp and lump crabmeat cocktails, raw oysters, clams oreganata and casino, and the sizable broiled lobster. The Gorgonzola and Caesar salads are well made. And they make a shockingly good linguine with white clam sauce. All the potato side dishes are tasty, as is the creamed spinach. The dessert to have is cheesecake, unless you're irrevocably drawn to rice pudding.

Burton & Doyle, 661 Northern Blvd., Great Neck, NY 11021; (516) 487-9200; burtonanddoyle.com; Steak, Seafood; $$$. It is remarkable how many prime steak restaurants are a mere artery away from North Shore University Hospital. In this neighborhood, Northern Boulevard becomes steak row. One of the main players is Burton & Doyle, which must have wiped out a small mahogany forest, and stays competitive with attentive and accommodating service, a clubby atmosphere, and very good beef. Take the traditional route. Recommended are lobster and crab cocktails, raw oysters, Caesar and iceberg-wedge salads, and for the diner intent on a full supply of red meat, carpaccio. Pick either the porterhouse, filet mignon, sirloin, or rib steak. To complement them, the kitchen prepares professional béarnaise and green peppercorn sauces. Contrarians will be contented with sesame seed–crusted tuna with a soy-ginger accent, the ample seafood plateaus, and especially the 3- or 4-pound lobsters, either steamed or broiled. On the side, it's creamed spinach and potato-bacon hash browns, sweet potato fries, onion rings, and that perpetual lily-gilder, lobster macaroni and cheese.

Centro Cucina, 43-C Glen Cove Rd., Greenvale, NY 11548; (516) 484-3880; centrocucinacafe.com; Italian; $$–$$$. Brick-oven pizzas and panini vie with seafood and pasta at Centro Cucina, an informal restaurant that's good for all of the above. The pace is quick midday and becomes more leisurely in the evening. But if you're in the neighborhood anytime, stop by. The 4-cheese pizza, with Gorgonzola, mozzarella, fontina, and pecorino Romano, and the campagnola pie, with tomatoes, mushrooms, sausage, smoked mozzarella, and olive oil are best, along with the "bisacquino," with fried eggplant, ricotta salata, basil, and tomato sauce. "Bellezza" here means mozzarella, olive oil, and pesto. Trenette with pesto tops the warm-weather pastas; linguine with broccoli rabe, sun-dried tomatoes and sausage, the year-rounders. A special of bucatini all'Amatriciana is in the same category. Seaside: grilled, whole red snapper with lemon and herbs; grilled whole branzino finished with lemon-and-olive-oil dressing; and sautéed shrimp with onions, pancetta, and white wine. Pick a panino at random. Have either cannoli or ricotta cheesecake for dessert.

City Cellar, 1080 Corporate Dr., Westbury, NY 11590; (516) 693-5400; citycellarny.com; New American; $$–$$$. Big and bustling, City Cellar is a major gathering place for lawyers, politicians, or anyone looking for a good, casual meal. Service is brisk and efficient. And the maître or maîtresse d' will be unfailingly polite even if citizens waiting in line seem ready to start an insurrection after the nearby movies let out. If they served more brews, it would seem like an American extension of the traditional brasserie. The joint is big and boisterous on weekend nights, only a little more sedate for a midweek lunch. There's a striking bar that acts as a focal point, but City Cellar actually is more about the eating than the drinking. Sample the lobster or meatball sliders. The assorted flatbreads are pretty good, too. For more sustenance, you'll do well ordering the pork osso buco with cannellini beans or the Moroccan-spiced lamb chops. Good steak frites, hamburgers, and braised short rib rigatoni Bolognese. To go with drinks, linger over a plate of local cheeses and respectable charcuterie.

Eric's Italian Bistro, 70 E. Old Country Rd., Mineola, NY 11590; (516) 280-5675; ericsbistro.com; Italian, New American; $$–$$$. Veteran Chef-Restaurateur George Echeverria's latest spot is a warm, satisfying dining room that balances the traditional and the contemporary with ease. Service also is notably attentive and accommodating. Go for the shrimp-and-chorizo risotto or the penne alla Brooke, which stars with sweet sausage and broccoli rabe. Echeverria also prepares fine eggplant rollatine, a cold antipasto dubbed "Italian sushi" for its design, hanger steak pizzaiola and branzino alla puttanesca. The don't-miss side dish: a goat-cheese-and-potato soufflé. Poached pear tops the desserts.

Heart of Portugal, 241 Mineola Blvd., Mineola, NY 11590; (516) 742-9797; heartofportugalrestaurant.com; Portuguese; $$–$$$. Heart is part of what makes this longstanding restaurant so good. It's a place with a personality, unpretentious ways, and deeply flavorful food, in a countrified dining room that time has ignored. The essentials include pan-roasted bacalhau, or salt cod, with sautéed onions; pork-and-clam stew Alentejana; chouriço pork sausage flambéed at table; shrimp in garlic sauce; fillet of sole with butter sauce and toasted almonds; and paella Valenciana. There's also a tasty sirloin steak au poivre. Flan wobbles and wins the dessert contest.

Hendrick's Tavern, 1304 Old Northern Blvd., Roslyn, NY 11576; (516) 621-1200; hendrickstavern.com; American; $$$–$$$$. What used to be the creaky George Washington Manor has been transformed into a Gold Coast playground, named for the local guy who hosted the first president there. The parking-lot scene is a show unto itself, as Italian sports cars and German sedans compete to see who gets the better space. The remade restaurant itself is very entertaining, exceedingly expensive, and generally excellent. The main dining room takes on a clublike atmosphere as regulars continue the conversations they began elsewhere. Everyone seems to know who's at the adjoining table. The very demanding clientele does put the staff to the test. Hendrick's is festooned with black-and-white photos of celebrities and more. The recommended dishes include an absurdly good Kobe beef hot dog, mighty rich roasted marrow bones, savory deviled eggs, a full slate of first-class steaks, the raw bar's shellfish assortment, the diverting pasta called linguine Zsa Zsa, and seafood from Chatham cod to Maine lobster. Although the imperially slim may skip desserts, you should sample the cheesecake.

Hunan Taste, 3 Northern Blvd., Greenvale, NY 11548; (516) 621-6616; hunantasterestaurant.com; Chinese; $$–$$$. Commendable Chinese restaurants are few on Long Island. Actually, the scene almost suggests abandonment. It's dominated by so-so take-out joints and some kitchens that have decided neither the flavors of Hunan nor Sichuan can rival the Americanized Cantonese stuff. In this environment of chow, Hunan Taste is an exception. First, it looks absolutely contemporary and refined compared with most of the other Chinese eateries in Nassau or Suffolk. Start with steamed dumplings in hot sesame sauce or with the chicken Soong lettuce cups. Tangerine beef does deliver the heat; General Tso's chicken nearly earns its rank. Sesame chicken delivers both crunch and flavor. And the sliced leg of lamb Hunan is a very pleasant surprise. To accompany the main dishes, sample the dry sautéed string beans. If you're a fan of staples such as moo shu pork and lobster Cantonese, Hunan Taste does a good job keeping those traditions going, too.

Iavarone Cafe, 1534 Union Tpke., New Hyde Park, NY 11040; (516) 488-4500; iavaronecafe.com; Italian; $$. Here's the sit-down eatery sprung from the Iavarone Bros. food markets, including one adjoining the restaurant. The temptation is to eat and then go shopping. That's a smart strategy because Iavarone has some of the best take-out around. At table, you may order mainstays such as a hearty *pasta e fagioli* or vegetable-laden minestrone, the tangy beet salad with goat cheese, and the irresistible Mama's Sunday Meatballs. Some of those are likely to make the trip home, too. Of course, there's fresh mozzarella Caprese, a tender osso buco Milanese, orecchiette Barese with sausage and broccoli rabe, generous meat-filled lasagna, and eggplant parmigiana that underscores why the dish is so popular. Pasta al forno, with a well-seasoned Bolognese-style sauce, also is notable. For later, Iavarone prepares excellent sandwiches with cured meats and cheeses and fried eggplant; chicken and tuna salad wraps are good, too.

Il Mulino, 1042 Northern Blvd., Roslyn, NY 11576; (516) 621-1870; ilmulino.com; Italian; $$$–$$$$. The Long Island branch of this constantly expanding empire is much like the others. The food can be very good, the decibels extremely high, the prices absolutely astronomical. Most diners already know what they're getting into. Part of that is the obligatory wait at the door even if you have reservations. It just goes with the turf as cognoscenti linger over their desserts. The theoretically gratis cheeses and meats could comprise an appetizer. Tuna carpaccio, beef carpaccio, seafood salad, and endive salad are good to begin. Then contemplate pappardelle with tomato and basil, gnocchi sauced with pesto, spaghettini alla carbonara, and meat-filled cannelloni with béchamel sauce. The workmanlike risotto is made with porcini mushrooms, Milanese style with saffron, and a light, springy primavera with vegetables. Although you wouldn't think it would be one of the better main dishes, Il Mulino understands the intricacies of chicken parmigiana as well as the essentials of osso buco. You, meantime, will receive a lesson in free-market capitalism.

Kotobuki, 1530 Old Northern Blvd., Roslyn, NY 11576; (516) 621-5312; kotobukinewyork.com; Japanese; $$–$$$. One of the noisiest restaurants on the planet, Kotobuki gives your ears a workout before appealing to your appetite. Even the staff members look weary as the beat goes on. You'll be communicating with sign language. This is one of three Kotobukis raising the decibels on Long Island. The others are in Babylon and Hauppauge. In addition to overdoing the sound, Kotobuki tends to overorchestrate its special sushi rolls, which have about as much harmony as a congressional committee meeting. That said, more restrained selections can be very good. The unadorned sashimi and the familiar nigirizushi, or raw fish on ovals of vinegared rice, lead them. Usuzukuri, or fluke delicately fanned out and accented with citrusy ponzu sauce, also is pleasing to the eye and the palate. If you're adamant about having your food cooked, Kotobuki does offer satisfactory gyoza, or seared pork dumplings; beef negimaki, wrapped around scallions; and a marinated shell steak about as westernized as the greatest dissenter would like.

Kyma, 1446 Old Northern Blvd., Roslyn, NY 11576; (516) 621-3700; kyma-roslyn.com; Greek; $$$–$$$$. Kyma succeeded Trata Estiatorio at this address, keeping it home to a great Greek restaurant, emphasis on seafood. The look is brighter and airier now; the service, more attentive. And the food is consistently excellent. Order perfectly grilled octopus, finished with olive oil, capers, red onion, and vinegar;

outstanding spreads, taramosalata to tzatziki; a delectable appetizer of roasted beets; fried zucchini and eggplant chips; giant Greek lima beans with tomato sauce; zucchini fritters; and Greek salad. Then, go fishing after checking the display on ice: superb red fagri, or pink snapper; royal dorado; red snapper; black sea bass; langoustines. Shrimp saganaki is excellent. Alternatives to the seafood include tender char-grilled lamb chops and a savory braised lamb shank. All the desserts are recommended, from baklava to *ekmek, galaktoboureko* to Greek yogurt.

La Casa Latina, 611 Old Country Rd., Westbury, NY 11590; (516) 280-7795; lacasalatinany.com; Latin; $$. La Casa Latina starts in Spain and then gives you a tour that takes in cuisines from South America and Central America. The results at this amiable, sunny restaurant are flavor-packed. Sip sangria and savor grilled Argentinian sausage, tender octopus with paprika and olive oil, sautéed shrimp in garlic, pork kebabs, and stuffed chayote. Extend the borders with fried calamari and clams oreganata. The ceviche of shrimp is very good, as are tuna tartare, Blue Point oysters, and the charcuterie-and-cheese plate. Fine main courses include the Argentinian barbecue with grilled skirt steak, sweetbreads, sausages, and short rib; the Salvadorean platter of grilled steak, fried pork, yucca, cheese, avocado, rice and beans; a Peruvian seafood stew; and the paella with shrimp, clams, and chicken. Finish with flan.

La Piccola Liguria, 47 Shore Rd., Port Washington, NY 11050; (516) 767-6490; Italian; $$$. No website, no nonsense. That's the approach at La Piccola Liguria, which has been around for decades, preparing generally northern Italian food that has gotten better year after year. This has to be one of the more idiosyncratic Italian spots around. You can't say it's under the radar thanks to an understandably devoted clientele. Steady word of mouth drives the place, which you easily could pass by along this curve of a busy roadway. The menu, as you'd expect, is only a springboard. The market helps decide the rest. The main advice is to go with those specials, which may include ricotta-stuffed zucchini flowers, crisp-skinned suckling pig, grilled sardines, and a delectable appetizer of perfectly fried anchovies. The display of cold antipasti could make you compose a meal of vegetables alone. But you'd miss the professionally fired-up lobster fra diavolo, tender and vinous Barolo-braised beef, deftly done risotti, and a series of impeccably prepared pastas. The dessert trolley is a very serious affair.

Limani, 1043 Northern Blvd., Roslyn, NY 11576; (516) 869-8989; limaniny.com; Greek, Seafood; $$$–$$$$. Limani is a Greek temple where fresh fish is worshipped. It's one of the more opulent dining rooms on Long Island and the prices keep pace with the decor. The display of fresh fish, domestic and imported, is a little ice show unto itself. You may examine your selections before they go to the kitchen to be expertly char-grilled. The whole fishes are sold by the pound, so take a long look at those langoustines and the red fagri. Royal dorado, red snapper, black sea bass, and Dover sole all are very good. Grilled lamb chops and steaks are fine. Taramosalata, skordalia, and other Greek spreads head the starters alongside smoky grilled sardines, cheese-stuffed grilled squid, Kumamoto oysters, saganaki, and spanakopita. Greek yogurt with thyme honey and walnuts leads the sweets, though the baklava and shredded-phyllo-and-custard finale, *ekmek,* also are worthwhile. Brunch is ample and popular, too, and it goes from cereal and carving stations to lobster on ice.

LL Dent, 221 Old Country Rd., Carle Place, NY 11514; (516) 742-0940; lldent.com; Southern; $$. Lillian and Leisa Dent bring the flavors of the American South to a busy section of central Nassau. The sunny, casual joint sometimes seasons the fare with live music. Chef Leisa takes care of the rest with the pleasures of smothered or fried pork chops, southern fried chicken, chicken and waffles, fried chicken livers, shrimp and grits, pulled pork, barbecued beef brisket, and the husky combination of brisket, barbecued ribs, and Cajun sausages. The elemental side dishes include baked macaroni and cheese, candied yams, collard greens with smoked turkey, sweet potato fries, okra and tomatoes, black-eyed peas and rice, hush puppies, and cornbread. And you'll want the coconut-pineapple cake, banana pudding, sweet potato pie, and peach cobbler, too.

Lola, 113A Middle Neck Rd., Great Neck, NY 11021; (516) 466-5666; restaurantlola.com; Eclectic; $$$–$$$$. Michael Ginor, the undisputed king of foie gras, delivers an adventurous, seductive take on fusion cooking and then goes beyond it at this exciting, contemporary restaurant. His cool, stylish dining room entices you by redefining tapas. There are savory "pizza tarts" with smoked duck breast and duck prosciutto or wild mushrooms and caramelized onions; Thai-style mango and papaya salad with Chinese sausage; Sri Lankan shrimp curry with polenta and raita; orange butter-poached lobster with caramelized fennel; Maine lobster rolls on Korean milk buns . . . it goes on. Beijing duck sliders are delicious. So are the Korean fried chicken with a honey-soy-Sriracha glaze and pickled Asian vegetables and the confit of orange-glazed duck leg with creamy, truffled polenta and red cabbage. Hanger steak is sparked with smoked paprika potato puree and Spanish piquillo pepper relish. Go south with barbecue smoked pulled pork with collard greens and pickled watermelon rind. Enjoy the 3 tasting menus. Banana bread pudding, coconut panna cotta, Key lime pie, and the house's Kit-Kat bar are super sweets, just right to conclude the party at chez Ginor.

Mitch & Toni's American Bistro, 875 Willis Ave., Albertson, NY 11507; (516) 741-7940; mitchandtonis.com; New American; $$–$$$. Chef Mitch SuDock's lively cooking suits the setting and the crowd at this more casual and easygoing successor to his departed

Pizzaland

One easy way to start an argument is to compare your favorite pizza with anyone else's. There are pizzerias in almost every part of Nassau and Suffolk except Plum Island. Ten recommendations follow. Let the debate begin and the toppings fly.

Abeetza in Greenvale
Centro Cucina in Greenvale
Emilio's in Commack
Grana in Jamesport
Grimaldi's in Garden City
The Pie at Salvatore's in Port Washington
Pizzetteria Brunetti in Westhampton Beach
Red Tomato in East Norwich
Satelite Pizza in Bayport
Umberto's in New Hyde Park

Bistro M in Glen Head. The seating is tight and the noise level high. And service sometimes lapses under the pressures of an ardent clientele. But the food displays SuDock's ongoing ability to engage your appetite. He's a very focused chef. His specialties range from more modest fish tacos with mahimahi and fish-and-chips made with tempura-battered sole to lush pumpkin ravioli in brown butter and the clever combination of tender roasted duck breast accompanied by a duck-confit egg roll. The grilled pork porterhouse with organic farro, wild mushrooms, and broccoli rabe and the marinated and grilled flatiron steak with parsnip puree, onion rings, and orange-scented braised sweet onions both work. The dark chocolate semifreddo is a solid finale.

Morton's The Steakhouse, 777 Northern Blvd., Great Neck, NY 11020; (516) 498-2950; mortons.com; Steak, Seafood; $$$–$$$$. You may rent your own wine locker at Morton's, an establishment that breeds devoted fans nationwide. Just go along with the show at this big, showy branch and you'll be rewarded with some excellent steaks, especially the porterhouse, a very tender filet mignon, fibrous and minerally sirloin, peppery strip steak, and the hefty bone-in rib eye. The husky pork chop, lamb chops, braised short ribs, and big Maine lobsters are on par with them. And, for the undecided, there are some mixed grills that will keep you busy. Tuna tartare and oysters Rockefeller enrich the proceedings. On the side: horseradish-spiked mashed potatoes, bacon-and-onion macaroni and cheese, and creamed corn. Start with lobster and shrimp cocktails. Assuming you have any room left, Morton's offers upside-down apple pie, chocolate cake, and a Key lime pie that may not take you to Florida but is better than most.

MP Taverna, 1363 Old Northern Blvd., Roslyn, NY 11576; (516) 686-6486; michaelpsilakis.com; Greek; $$–$$$. Chef Michael Psilakis oversees a remarkable Greek restaurant, full of flavor and personality. It's part of a mini-empire. Tight quarters and broad ambition are your first impressions. Savory openers: Cypriot lamb sausage, gyro-spiced beef sliders, octopus with chickpea salad, fried calamari with cauliflower, chickpeas, tomato and yogurt sauce, barrel-aged feta cheese, crisp cod with garlic-potato puree, eggplant, and chickpea dips. Then move on to moist roasted lemon chicken, grilled whole daurade, a Greek version of paella with shellfish and spicy lamb sausage, lamb-sausage dumplings, the juicy lamb shank or lamb burger, and "simply grilled" swordfish, salmon, branzino, or chicken. A bit different: grilled pulled salmon salad with bitter greens, dried fruits, smoked almonds, pistachios, red onion, and manouri cheese. And to go whole hog, so to speak, with 5 days notice, MP Taverna will prepare roast suckling pig, roasted whole lamb, goat, rack of rib steak, and shank of veal.

Pepe Rosso 24, 24 Manorhaven Blvd., Port Washington, NY 11050; (516) 944-9477; peperosso24.com; Italian; $$. Informal and inviting, Pepe Rosso 24 brings you in with pizzas, pastas, and panini, as well as salads, wraps, and heartier courses. The eatery is straightforward and unpretentious. The white pizza with ricotta and mozzarella and the Grandma pie are very good. So are the brick-oven, "ultra thin" individual pies, especially the Margherita and the Gorgonzola pizza. For bigger appetites: the stuffed meat pizza with pepperoni and sausage. Also, consider the baked pastas, especially the meat-laden lasagna and homey manicotti. Pepe Rosso's parmigiana contingent is headed by very good eggplant and chicken. Balance all this with the refreshing fennel salad with orange slices and pistachios and the Gorgonzola number with arugula. They're tasty either as intermezzos or as starters. Minestrone, *paste e fagioli,* and lentil soup are options, too. And the kitchen prepares uncomplicated panini. The Campano includes mozzarella, roasted peppers, arugula, and prosciutto; the Barese, chicken and broccoli rabe.

The Pie at Salvatore's, 124 Shore Rd., Port Washington, NY 11050; (516) 883-8457; salvatorescoalfiredpizza.com; Italian; $$. The fervor with which regulars speak of the pizza here is remarkable. Then again, so are the pies. The preliminaries include a good Greek salad and antipasti such as eggplant parmigiana, a sausage roll, or a meatball parm roll. Then you get to the main decisions. Will your pizza be a 10-, 16-, or 18-inch production? And are you a mozzarella-tomato-basil purist? A mozzarella-garlic-grated-cheese-basil fan? Many toppings will require thoughtful review. The ricotta-and-mozzarella calzone is a necessity whatever else you choose. If there's a pasta advocate in your group, the restaurant does a fine job with baked ziti, especially with sausage or eggplant. The Pie at Salvatore's is one of the best pizzerias in Nassau.

Rialto, 588 Westbury Ave., Carle Place, NY 11514; (516) 997-5283; rialtorestaurantli.com; Italian, Continental; $$–$$$. New management has kept the quality very high at Rialto, where the news almost always is very good or better. The dining room is a cozy, comfortable one, with a small forest of polished dark wood and graceful arches. And the staff knows how to cosset regulars and first-timers alike. This also is an establishment where the specials provide a cue. Rialto is mainly Italian, but it also will remind you of the continental restaurants that for decades meant haute dining in Nassau. Standout dishes include tuna carpaccio, gnocchi with tomato-basil sauce, spaghetti alla carbonara, pappardelle Bolognese, pansotti packed with vegetables, braised pork osso buco, the juicy double-cut pork chop, a nostalgic-infused duck a l'orange, rustic chicken cacciatore, and a definitive Dover sole meunière. The desserts arrive on an old-fashioned trolley that you'll want to stop at your table. The sponge-cake sweet, *zuccotto,* and the wobbly flan are excellent. If all this seems too much, don't be concerned. You'll return to Rialto.

Sarin Thai, 43 Glen Cove Rd., Greenvale, NY 11548; (516) 484-5873; sarinthaicuisine.com; Thai; $$. Sarin Thai prepares very good fare, according to the heat level you request. Attentive service and an easygoing style boost the prettily decorated place, too. It's a good stop for the family. Dishes to try include Bangkok duck finished with chiles and coconut milk; tamarind duck with tamarind sauce, kiwis, and a bed of spinach; mussaman jumbo shrimp sautéed with coconut milk, peanuts, and potatoes; and sea scallops in red curry. Enjoy stir-fried beef with chiles, garlic, onion, and basil; barbecued beef salad; clear shrimp soup; pad Thai; and Panang curry. *Pla larg prig* translates into whole fish or filet, typically red snapper, deep-fried and topped with a zesty chile-pepper-and-garlic sauce; and *pla jearn* means the same fish garnished with ground pork, mushrooms, and garlic sauce. Both work. The pad Thai, with shrimp, egg, bean curd, and bean sprouts; and Siam noodles, with barbecued duck, are good for the table.

Southern Spice, 1635 Hillside Ave., New Hyde Park, NY 11040; (516) 216-5448; southernspice.net; Indian; $–$$. The flavors are as big as the prices are small at Southern Spice. This passage to India is full of good tastes and good feeling. Sample the vegetable samosas, crab cake with coconut gravy, crab vadai finished with coconut gravy; crisp squid with mango chutney, the southern masala omelet with chiles and cilantro, fried golden chile peppers, and the refreshing samosa chaat, with tricolor chutneys. Chicken soup with mint and lime, fiery lamb vindaloo, milder lamb kadai, rack of lamb, and delicate dosas, or rice and lentil crepes with onion, spinach, cauliflower, and peas liven up dinner, too. The Chettinadu curry, fueled by spicy and dark pepper gravy with potatoes, is a snappy way to have your lamb or chicken. The northern curries have less of a kick. For milder spicing: lamb kadai, stir-fried with ginger, coriander, and bell peppers; and *kashimiri murg musalam,* in creamy almond gravy. Lobster masala is diverting, especially sauced vindaloo. Tandoori chicken and prawns, spiced chickpeas, and the Indian breads are mandatory.

SriPraPhai, 280 Hillside Ave., Williston Park, NY 11596; (516) 280-3779; sripraphairestaurant.com; Thai; $$. The terrific, tiny Thai restaurant in Woodside, Queens, juiced up the cuisine in Nassau with this opening. The food tingles. Open your meal with a papaya salad that includes peanuts, long beans, tomato, chiles, and lime juice, or the crisp watercress salad with oyster mushrooms. *Mee krob,* or noodles in a sweet-and-sour sauce, is good, too. Sample fried curry-potato puffs, fried chive dumplings, pad Thai, sautéed "drunken" noodles, and any of the green, yellow, red, mussaman, and Panang curries. SriPraPhai also excels with *tom yum,* the hot and spicy lemongrass-fueled soup with mushrooms and snow peas, and *galangal* soup, with oyster mushrooms, cabbage, coconut milk, lemongrass, chiles, and lime juice. Fried tofu with lemongrass sauce could turn you into a vegetarian, as may the sautéed eggplant with garlic, chiles, and basil leaves and the pan-fried scrambled eggs with red onion, tomato, lemongrass, and basil. The crisp whole sea bass with chiles, garlic, and basil; crisp pork belly; *larb,* a fired-up ground-meat salad; and lychee ice cream point the way, too. Thai iced tea is the right drink.

Steve's Piccola Bussola, 649 Old Country Rd., Westbury, NY 11590; (516) 333-1335; stevespiccolabussola.com; Italian; $$–$$$. Family-style dining makes the ordering easier and Steve's Piccola Bussola is a specialist in the Italian wing. Big groups are the mainstays here. You probably could recite the menu without seeing it. But some of the satisfying options are cold seafood salad, stuffed artichokes, fried peppers, broccoli rabe, and escarole. Pastas include a well-seasoned rigatoni Bolognese, linguine with seafood fra diavolo, and penne with broccoli and sausages. Chicken scarpariello, campagnola, parmigiana, alla cacciatora, and rollatine—all solid. That also goes for the pork chops pizzaiola, veal chop Milanese topped with salad, and veal parmigiana. The seafood is secondary, but the top catches are swordfish oreganata, lobster fra diavolo, red snapper marechiaro, shrimps scampi-style, and shrimps marinara. A tricolor salad or a chopped salad should make it somewhere into the mix. For a similar experience in a fresher space, there is a second Steve's Piccola Bussola at 41 Jackson Ave., Syosset; (516) 364-8383.

Stresa, 1524 Northern Blvd., Manhasset, NY 11030; (516) 365-6956; stresarestaurant.com; Italian; $$$. Italian restaurants dominate dining out on Long Island. And Stresa is one of the best Italian and continental restaurants between Great Neck and Montauk. It's a traditional, elegantly appointed place, with exceptional service and stellar food, under the experienced, ever-attentive, and accommodating Giorgio Meriggi. Chef Ella Rocca's winners include glistening carpaccio of swordfish; rustic and yet sophisticated 4-bean soup "campagnola"; roast duck with rosé wine and semolina gnocchi; sliced bistecca alla King, named for the late comedian and customer Alan King, with peppers, onions, and mushrooms; filet mignon Rossini; and bigoli pasta Latina with pancetta and cabbage. Note the daily specials. They're invariably worth ordering. Stresa encourages you to linger over dessert. The choices include a decadent chocolate cake; superb zabaglione on berries; classic biscotti, which are ideal with a glass of Vin Santo; and unquestionably the airiest soufflés this side of the East River. You'll be partial to the chocolate and Grand Marnier varieties. See the recipe for **Campagnola Soup** on p. 337.

Thyme, 8 Tower Place, Roslyn, NY 11576; (516) 625-2566; thymenewyork.com; New American; $$–$$$. Thyme grows briskly here, in the shadow of the landmark Roslyn tower. The energetic eatery alternates between cozy-quiet and very noisy, depending on the day. The food and the service, however, are consistent. And the mood is very upbeat. Some of the better selections: the generous Fuji apple, stilton cheese, and endive salad; lush butternut squash ravioli finished with a professional sage-infused beurre noisette; the sautéed crab cake balanced with the crunch of jicama-and-apple slaw. And this is the right place to select tender filet mignon with crisp pommes frites; the roseate duck breast with caramelized pear; pan-roasted chicken finished in a Pinot Noir reduction; and a juicy, double-cut pork chop with sweet potato and an apple-cranberry tart. Thyme scores with its hamburgers, too, especially one crowned with applewood-smoked bacon and stilton cheese and another with cheddar cheese and grilled red onions with mushrooms.

Toku Modern Asian, 2014-C Northern Blvd., Manhasset, NY 11030; (516) 627-8658; tokumodernasian.com; Asian; $$$.

Inventive and excellent Asian-themed dishes define Toku, a handsomely appointed restaurant in the Americana shopping center. The decor mixes the antique and the contemporary, from a lit onyx bar to the 19th-century wooden bells that look as if they tolled in a monastery in Shangri La. Toku rivets you with fluke tiradito and lobster taco, chicken lettuce wraps and steamed sea bass rolls, teriyaki sliders and Kurobuta pork dumplings, pork buns and Beijing duck salad. They're eclectic, playful, and make you want to eat more. Salmon tartare, the tuna spring roll pork buns with pickled cucumber and hoisin sauce, and the Kurobuta pork gyoza encourage the same. A grilled skewer of duck and lychees, or another of Kobe beef and shishito peppers, is a good bridge to main dishes. Here are ideal kung pao chicken, crisp hoisin-spiked duck breast, roasted lobster with udon noodles, charred filet of beef with mustard sauce, prawns Sichuan, crisp whole fish, and miso black cod. There's first-class sushi, too, and a Fuji apple tart for dessert, along with fine teas, port, cognac, and dessert wines.

Trattoria Diane, 21 Bryant Ave., Roslyn, NY 11576; (516) 621-2591; trattoriadiane.com; Italian; $$$. Chef John Durkin's emphasis is the regional cooking of Rome, but he's just as consistent when foraying beyond Lazio at this warm restaurant. Try for a table on the first floor. The vegetable appetizers are delicious: roasted beets with ricotta salata, near-candied brussels sprouts with lemon and pecorino Romano; grilled zucchini with orange and mint; radicchio with almonds and balsamic vinegar. Rice balls with mozzarella, meatballs in tomato-rosemary sauce, and burrata with roasted cherry tomatoes also excel. Superb pastas include the spaghetti alla carbonara and bucatini all'Amatriciana; ricotta gnocchi with sausage, fennel, and tomatoes; and fettuccine Bolognese. For "secondi," or main courses, you'll revel over the roasted chicken with mashed potatoes and crisp artichoke;

pot roast with Parmesan-mashed potatoes; short ribs; pan-seared pork chop with broccoli rabe and caponata; and the pan-roasted branzino. The desserts are luscious. That's no surprise. Be sure to visit Diane's Bakery next door whenever you're in the neighborhood.

Vinoco Wine Bar & Tapas, 147 Mineola Blvd., Mineola, NY 11501; (516) 307-8055; vinocony.com; Eclectic, Tapas; $$. Wine bars are a relatively new phenomenon on Long Island, but they've definitely moved in and have found an audience. Vinoco pours away as one of the better ones. And tapas, the great snacks of Spain, take on an international flavor at Vinoco. You'll come across husky duck empanadas, barbecued pulled-duck arepas, and pork-belly buns that would be at home in any restaurant, plus flatbreads, salads and ceviches, quesadillas and taquitos. The samosas filled with peas and potatoes rival those at your local Indian haunt. Also dig into the chickpea puree with roasted peppers and black olive aioli. Go Spanish with paella, or even turn Brazilian with a surprisingly satisfying spin on *feijoada,* the national dish. Also, there are patatas bravas to return you to Barcelona. The wine selections are good, if not great. But they are pleasing enough company for the small plates. The best thing about Vinoco is the simplest: It's fun.

West End Cafe, 187 Glen Cove Rd., Carle Place, NY 11514; (516) 294-5608; westendli.com; New American; $$–$$$. Informal, crowded, and always ready for something new, West End Cafe is an upbeat place to meet, whether you're looking for a business lunch venue or a casual night out. Service sometimes lags, but the staff never loses its enthusiasm. The shopping center location doesn't affect the style much. The Asian-style duck sliders with Sriracha ketchup and the Kobe beef sliders are evenly appealing competitors.

The crab cake with jicama-mango slaw also suggests the way to go. And at lunch, look for the "mile high" salmon club sandwich. You'll like the onion soup, quesadillas, a surprisingly first-rate coq au vin with toasted spaetzle, the grilled bone-in rib eye steak, and the grilled pork chop with whipped potatoes and cranberry-apple chutney. Alternatives: the lean, flavorful bison sirloin, with the curious but tasty company of shrimp mac-and-cheese; roasted chicken with fingerling potatoes; and seared day-boat scallops with mushroom risotto and crisp leeks.

Landmarks

Andel's of Roslyn, 350 Roslyn Rd., Roslyn Heights, NY 11577; (516) 621-5466; andels.com; Delicatessen (Kosher); $–$$. Fressers, unite. Andel's has been mastering matzo ball soup, whitefish salad, chopped herring salad, kasha varnishkes, and overstuffed sandwiches for six decades. There are 5 tables at this revered establishment, and enough take-out each day to feed a small village. In addition to the matzo ball soup, stick a spoon into the potato-leek, green split pea, and chicken noodle soups. Revel in chicken or flanken "in the pot." Have a blintz or potato pirogen with sour cream. Be sure to leave with some Nova Scotia smoked salmon, belly lox, pickled lox, sable carp, and even a few slices of pastrami-treated salmon. The sandwiches: pastrami, corned beef, hot brisket, tongue, and definitely hard salami. Knishes are essential. And you'll be tempted by the fundamental hot dog with mustard and sauerkraut. There's a full line of Dr. Brown's soda.

Chez Noëlle, 34 Willowdale Ave., Port Washington, NY 11050; (516) 883-3191; French; $$$. Chez Noëlle has been expertly torching ducks for decades. The tucked-away restaurant is primarily French, but it has Italian and continental courses, too, all carefully prepared.

The decor hasn't changed in a while but no one seems to mind. The fine service is from an experienced staff. Over the years, some of the better dishes at Chez Noëlle have been Dover sole meunière, seafood salad, warm goat cheese salad, escargots Bourguignonne, coq au vin, rack of lamb, and braised sweetbreads. They make a subtle pumpkin risotto and a lush duck and foie gras terrine. Just when you think it's all very old-fashioned, the kitchen sends out a spirited yellowfin tuna tartare. And that duck with orange sauce is crisp-skinned, tender, and very good.

Hildebrandt's, 84 Hillside Ave., Williston Park, NY 11596; (516) 741-0608; hildebrandtsrestaurant.com; American; $. Hildebrandt's has been scooping ice cream at this corner location since 1927. The popular spot is known for its sundaes. The banana split has 2 flavors; the banana royale, 3; the Hildebrandt's special, 4. Hildebrandt's has more than a dozen flavors. Two that stand out are banana and peach. As for the kind of sundae, well, hot fudge has to be a prohibitive favorite. That said, go with a small group and head into overload. The nouveau-retro destination also lures you for breakfast and lunch. Omelets, burgers, grilled cheese, that sort of listing. But Hildebrandt's can surprise you with a pasta dish that has a Sicilian accent: rigatoni with cauliflower, garlic, onion, pecorino cheese, and bread crumbs, a combo that was more than enough to get Guy Fieri interested. The burger and fries could do that, too, along with the lasagna, manicotti, assorted sandwiches and wraps, and, above all, a heaping side dish of nostalgia.

The Jolly Fisherman & Steak House, 25 Main St., Roslyn, NY 11576; (516) 621-0055; thejollyfisherman.com; Seafood, Steak; $$$–$$$$. The Jolly Fisherman has hooked diners since 1957. It recently was refurbished. But the menu remains familiar and dependable, especially for seasonal fare such as Nantucket Bay scallops and stone crabs. The fans of the Fisherman are very devoted, in part because this kind of restaurant could be listed as an endangered species in Nassau, where the style used to thrive. For the record, the kitchen prepares tender lobsters, dewy shellfish cocktails, and a buttery Dover sole meunière; good grilled swordfish with mustard sauce, shad, and shad roe in season; fine Florida red snapper and Blue Point oysters; fish-and-chips with malt vinegar; broiled Boston scrod; those delectable Nantucket Bay scallops; and fried Ipswich clams. For those wanting to stay landside, the Fisherman knows how to roast Long Island duckling and sear a steak. For dessert: banana cream pie, chocolate cream pie, cheesecake, and, naturally, rice pudding.

La Marmite, 234 Hillside Ave., Williston Park, NY 11596; (516) 746-1243; lamarmiterestaurant.com; Continental; $$$. La Marmite prepares continental cuisine in a setting that embodies old-fashioned style. Nearing 40 years, it's one of the last of its kind, down to the very professional service. Have a shellfish cocktail or onion soup gratinée, a mushroom tartlet or escargots, maybe a seafood crepe or Caesar salad for two. The housemade lobster ravioli is finished with Champagne sauce, and the duckling, of course, comes a l'orange. Veal sweetbreads are expertly flambéed with cognac, and calf's liver is complemented with bacon and onions. Filet mignon: very tender. And the rack of lamb arrives rosy as ordered. Sample Dover sole or soft-shell crabs meuniere. Try the plump crab cakes, accented with roasted red pepper aioli. They're all satisfying preludes to the trolley of desserts, carrying generous quantities of chocolate mousse, napoleon, cheesecake, fruit tarts, and a gateau Saint-Honoré with plenty of cream puffs.

Peter Luger, 255 Northern Blvd., Great Neck, NY 11021; (516) 487-8800; peterluger.com; Steak; $$$$. This is the suburban branch of the 1887 Brooklyn landmark, home to what's still arguably the best steak in New York City. The half-timbered look and clean lines are far different from the vintage Teutonic spareness of the original. There are tablecloths, too. And the waitstaff is genial, not auditioning for a role in the next Woody Allen movie. The porterhouse in Great Neck ranks very high on Long Island's list of essential steaks. As in Williamsburg, the focus is on one great cut. If, for any reason, you're here for something other than the classic steak for two, three, or four, consider the major prime rib, a well-made chopped steak, or the hefty lamb chops. On the side: creamed spinach and German fried potatoes. They also may have a few lobsters in the back, which are prepared as skillfully as the beef. In season, start with sliced tomatoes and onions. A slice or two of extra-thick slab bacon is the right accompaniment. For anyone sticking around for dessert, the obligatory sweet is cheesecake.

Umberto's, 633 Jericho Tpke., New Hyde Park, NY 11040; (516) 437-7968; originalumbertos.com; Italian, Pizza; $–$$. Long Island has as many Umberto's as Manhattan has Ray's. This is where it all started in 1965. When they use the word "original," they mean it. Other operations have appropriated the Umberto name, but the New Hyde Park site is the only one that counts. And for decades, the pizzas have been first-class, whether you're up for a traditional Margherita or ready for all the toppings. The quality hasn't changed much. The dining room is a kitschy venue, almost endearing in its resolute anti-trend look. Those who aren't ready for pizza may bite into serious hero sandwiches, panini, and salads. Also notable are the ready-to-burst cheese-filled calzones, a trademark eggplant rollatine, and the extensive assortment of judiciously red-sauced pastas. Everything is available for take-out. Call ahead.

Specialty Stores, Markets & Shops

Baci Gelato, 591 Willis Ave., Williston Park, NY 11596; (516) 801-1706; bacigelato.com; Gelato. Baci Gelato extols "the art of ice cream," Italian-style. In addition to gelato that's creamy and ultra-smooth, the shop offers superior sorbetti. The list of flavors is big, and includes stracciatelle, panna cotta, dolce latte, pistachio, zuppa inglese, zabaglione, Grand Marnier, tart cherry, extra-dark chocolate, fig, coconut, ginger, ricotta, mascarpone, cassata, chestnut, and the more familiar tastes of Oreo cheesecake and rum raisin. Leading sorbets: limoncello, blood orange, lychee, guava, papaya, and mint. Go with a small group and try as many as you can.

Ceriello Fine Foods, 541 Willis Ave., Williston Park, NY 11596; (516) 747-0277; ceriellofinefoods.com; Italian Market, Take-out. This is a very good shop for Italian specialties, imports, and take-out, all at reasonable prices and of high quality. The pasta sauces are especially worth sampling, whether basil, marinara, puttanesca, or alla vodka. Ceriello makes flavorful sausages, particularly the fennel and hot varieties, chicken sausage, and pork sausage with pecorino cheese and parsley. The steaks are dry-aged. And this is the place to buy both guanciale and porchetta to give your meal an authentic accent. Ceriello also is a major caterer, notable for pastas including lasagna, manicotti, and stuffed shells; chicken scarpariello and chicken parmigiana; fried chicken; sliced pork chops with vinegar peppers, basil sauce, or broccoli rabe; sausage and peppers; eggplant rollatine; and the assorted packages for Thanksgiving, Christmas, Easter, and the Super Bowl. If you have those in mind, order early.

Fairway Market, 1250 Corporate Dr., Westbury, NY 11590; (516) 247-6850; fairwaymarket.com/store-westbury; Gourmet Market. A suburban branch of the Manhattan market, more spacious and equally appetizing, this Fairway is the newest on Long Island. As at the others, the market offers an outstanding selection of cheeses, teas, and coffees. The fish market and the butcher counter are better than almost any independent you'll find in Nassau or Suffolk. For smoked fish, it has little or no competition. The Fairway brand smoked salmon can be a bargain. The bakery department has some of the top bagels east of Manhattan, as well as first-class croissants, scones, baguettes, and ficelles. Breads from Eli's and Tom Cat Bakery make appearances, too. Plenty of prepared foods: pleasing soups, potpies, meat loaf, wraps, sushi, and juicy rotisserie chicken, all ready to go. Usually, the price of the chickens drops at closing time. And there's another Fairway Market in Plainview.

Grace's Marketplace, 81 Glen Cove Rd., Greenvale, NY 11548; (516) 621-5100; gracesmarketplaceli.com; Gourmet Market. Grace's Marketplace has you covered all day, from its cafe to its take-out, the bakery to the grocery. The bleary-eyed can wake up to a good omelet, waffles, pancakes, or oatmeal. Arrive a little later, and you'll be satisfied with pizzas, panini, burgers, sliders, or an extended session at the salad bar. And the bakery ensures that you'll be bringing home something tasty, too. Fruit tarts and Italian pastries, muffins, and assorted breads, including well-made ciabatta and 7-grain, all are worth the investment. There are at least two dozen coffees available, too. Grace's also has a major selection of imports, part of the "international grocery." This Grace's is connected with Grace's Marketplace and Grace's Trattoria in Manhattan. Grace is Grace Balducci Doria, formerly associated with Balducci's, the New York landmark gourmet shop.

Kitchen Kabaret, 409 Glen Cove Rd., Roslyn Heights, NY 11577; (516) 484-3320; kitchenkabaret.com; Gourmet Market, Take-out. Packed with stations for deluxe take-out, from salads and sandwiches to omelets and pastas, Kitchen Kabaret is a daily destination for the hungry heading to or from work, thinking about dinner or just in need of a snack. The prepared foods are well made. Omelets and other egg dishes highlight the morning fare. Lots of burgers with pickles and cole slaw, focaccia sandwiches, vegetarian sandwiches, all the cold cuts you'll need. The bakery includes good cupcakes, brownies, fruit tarts, chocolate chip cookies, and chocolate-covered pretzels. You'll find sushi and pizzas, too, plus a coffee and juice bar. The rush hour scene here rivals the ones on the Long Island Railroad. The catering menu is extensive. There is a second branch of Kitchen Kabaret in Bay Shore, at 87 Saxon Ave.; (631) 328-1440.

Krön Chocolatier, 24 Middle Neck Rd., Great Neck, NY 11021; (516) 829-5550; kronchocolatier.com; Chocolatier. The Krön name evokes memories for New Yorkers, who recall special visits to the Manhattan location. For many, it was the first time to taste chocolate-covered strawberries and wedges of orange, perfectly prepared and sold in little slatted wooden crates. They were remarkable and doubtless caused a lot of double-parking in the neighborhood. In Krön's new life in Great Neck, you still can buy the chocolate-covered fruits, including banana and pineapple, too. Crème truffles are another reason for Krön's reputation and an essential purchase. The chocolate-covered popcorn is more an acquired taste, but an easy one to obtain. The edible chocolate baskets are delightful. You also get to see the chocolatiers at work here, for a sideshow that's guaranteed to add to your purchases. A list of recommendations could follow. But you can pick at random and be happy.

Lazar's Chocolate, 72 Middle Neck Rd., Great Neck, NY 11021; (516) 829-5785; 340 Wheatley Plaza, Greenvale; (516) 484-1987; lazarschocolate.com; Chocolatier. Lazar's specializes in hand-dipped chocolates and the smiles that automatically follow. These decadent mouthfuls include nut patties that alone are worth the visit, thin mints, buttercrunch, toffee, a cashew-and-raisin variation on the Chunkies theme, elemental chocolate-covered pretzels, clusters and break-up chocolate chunks and bark that you'll dig into before leaving the shop, truffles, marshmallows, soft centers, and, of course, creams. The custom-design chocolate bars are understandably popular and clever choices. The Lazar's catalogue includes high-cocoa-content dark chocolate, marzipan, licorice, hard candy, jelly beans, dried fruits and nuts, and cookies. Lazar's has been in business for more than 80 years.

Leonetti Pastry Shop, 82 Glen Cove Rd., #16, Greenvale, NY 11548; (516) 625-8242; leonettipastryshop.com; Bakery, Cafe. Leonetti is a tribute to the sweet life. Have an espresso and either an Italian or French pastry while taking in the variety at this destination bakery and cafe. The irresistible choices include the torta della Nonna with pine nuts, the orange bavaroise and fresh fig tart, a soulful pastiera Napoletana, tarte Tatin to make the sisters smile, apple-frangipane tart, and the Linzer torte. Excellent cakes: 7-layer, opera, praline, dulce de leche, lemon-coconut, tiramisu, cannoli, and Saint-Honoré. The specialty cakes, whether to celebrate weddings or Super Bowls, are winners. The éclairs, napoleons, and cannoli are classic. And Leonetti also produces a big and delicious collection of chocolates, dark and milk. In addition to all this, Leonetti offers some of the best gelati in either Nassau or Suffolk. Although this bakery has been around for less than a decade, it feels like the kind of establishment the community could never do without.

Marzullo Bakery & Cafe, 1586 Hillside Ave., New Hyde Park, NY 11040; Bakery, Cafe. Row after row of artful pastries and cookies are the lasting image at Marzullo, which merits a special trip just to taste the wonderful St. Joseph's Day sfingi and zeppole. The sfingi, filled with cannoli cream, are among the best you'll taste this side of Palermo. Marzullo's Sicilian sweets are headlined by these holiday treats and fabulous cannoli themselves. You'll also find a classic pastiera Napoletana, baba au rhum, and even black-and-white cookies. Cream puffs: delightful. The equal of the pastries: biscotti and all kinds of cookies. Arrive near Christmas or Easter, and the display is like a holiday gift. The coffee is very good, too. You just may stick around for a couple of cups, while pointing to the pastry that you want to try next. It may take a while. Almost no one departs without a box for the road.

Steiner's Pastry Shop, 432 Plandome Rd., Manhasset, NY 11030; (516) 627-2201; Bakery. The stellar coffee cake still exists. Yes, you've looked a long time, but here it is. Steiner's Pastry Shop is situated next to the movies in Manhasset. The bakery puts on quite a show itself, though in a restrained, polite, and traditional way, presenting a *wunderbar* selection of pastries and cakes. The very popular and very good choices include a classic pecan ring and an apple strudel to compensate for all those soggy affairs you've endured. To all who've given up searching for a good jelly doughnut, Steiner's fulfills the quest with a cinnamon-sugar wonder generously filled with raspberry jelly, not one that seems simply inoculated. The Scottish coffee cake, a slightly chewy beauty, contains coconut along with the raisins and nuts. Buttery and delicious: the apple crumb. The apple and blueberry turnovers make you want to order a coffee on the spot. And the "chocolate cigar" will light up the chocolate lover in everyone. Franz Steiner's shop has been in business more than three decades.

Town of Hempstead

Charles Lindbergh's 1927 transatlantic flight began on the runway of Roosevelt Field in Hempstead.

About 25 years later, residents moved into the new houses of Levittown, the nation's first suburb, a hamlet in Hempstead.

And, in 1980–83, Hempstead was the center of the professional hockey universe. The Islanders won four consecutive Stanley Cups. Their home: the Nassau Veterans Memorial Coliseum in Uniondale, part of Hempstead.

This is the biggest town in Nassau. For many years, it was the county's commercial hub. County government and courts are headquartered here, in Mineola. Hofstra University, which hosted presidential election debates in 2008 and 2012, is on Fulton Avenue in Hempstead.

It's a diverse town in almost every way, from the demographics to dining out. Communities with notable restaurants, markets, and/or shops include East Meadow, Floral Park, Franklin Square, Freeport, Garden City, Garden City Park, Hewlett, Island Park, Levittown, Merrick, North Bellmore, Oceanside, Rockville Centre, Uniondale, Valley Stream, Wantagh, and Woodmere.

Before boarding the *Spirit of St. Louis*, Lindbergh ate one of the six sandwiches he'd received for the flight.

There's a lot more variety now.

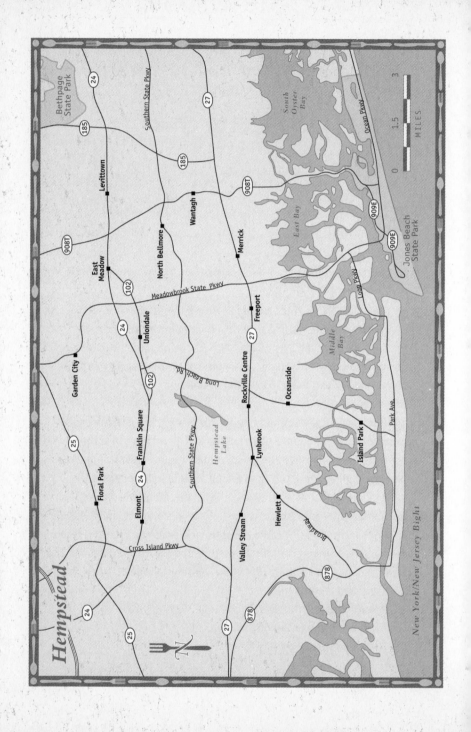

Akbar, 2 South St., Garden City, NY 11530; (516) 357-8300; theakbar.com; Indian; $$–$$$. Akbar may be the fanciest Indian restaurant in Nassau or Suffolk. The appointments are comparatively lavish; the service, very attentive; the food, very good, especially if you're fond of northern delights. The starters of mixed pakoras, or vegetable fritters, and tandoori chicken and lamb are well made. Same for the samosa, a pastry pyramid filled with peas and potatoes. A lively yogurt sauce boosts papdi chaat, or lentil and flour crisps with chickpeas. Mulligatawny soup, with a little heat, also is worth a taste. The tandoor, or clay oven, contributes mightily at Akbar. Sample the tandoori lamb chops, spiced lamb kebabs, and marinated chicken with ginger, cumin, cardamom, and pepper. The house's curries are made with care. Lamb, goat, or chicken vindaloo is for heat seekers. Vegetarians will find plenty. Cottage cheese in creamy tomato curry, yellow lentils simmered with tomatoes and onions, and black lentils simmered in cream are very good, as are the vegetable biryani and basmati rice with carrots and peas. Gobhi paratha, or whole-wheat bread stuffed with cauliflower, and aloo paratha, stuffed with potatoes, top the fine breads.

Aperitif, 242 Sunrise Hwy., Rockville Centre, NY 11570; (516) 594-3404; aperitifbistro.com; French, New American; $$–$$$. Aperitif looks the part, with assorted bistro imagery. But its Gallic appearance is balanced by the reality of the market. You can have either a pasta or risotto du jour here, too. And open with an appetizer of hummus with grilled calamari, deviled eggs, gravlax, or steak tartare. Filet mignon sliders, capped with mushrooms and melted gruyère cheese, would be welcome under any banner. Same for the sirloin burger served at lunch. Steak frites is available via sirloin or hanger steak, prepared au poivre or with a red-wine-and-shallot sauce. Coq au vin isn't overly vinous, but good. Sautéed duck breast has the diverse company of apple-bread pudding and cranberry chutney. Better than either one is the beef Bourguignonne, with pearl onions and mushrooms atop mashed potatoes. Mussels materialize mariniere, which is to say white, or Provençal, meaning red, and with frites that work with everything. Sole Normande is a comparatively delicate addition to the seafood, with a sauce defined by shallots and white wine. Desserts cross borders, raspberry panna cotta to éclair.

Artie's South Shore Fish & Grill, 4257 Austin Blvd., Island Park, NY 11558; (516) 889-0692; Seafood; $$. It doesn't get either fresher or more casual than at Artie's South Shore, a small, exceedingly informal restaurant attached to a retail seafood shop that inspires what's on the table. You can be sure that the local fish were swimming earlier in the day. The specials are listed on a board. Owner Artie Hoerning is a commercial fisherman himself and responsible for what you're eating. On a sunny day, sit outside in a very informal alfresco area that overlooks the parking lot. Among the works of Artie are excellent Peconic Bay scallops, fluke, and striped bass prepared with a minimalist's approach, and sometimes corn on the cob. Bluefish oreganata succeeds with a swimmer often considered a challenge in the kitchen. Deep-fried porgies, sautéed swordfish steak, fried clam bellies, and cod in any preparation are guaranteed. The lobsters are meaty and so are the lobster rolls. For all its modesty and occasional brusqueness, Artie's can bid fair to be one of Long Island's best seafood restaurants. No credit cards are accepted.

Arturo's, 246-04 Jericho Tpke., Floral Park, NY 11001; (516) 352-7418; arturosrestaurant.com; Italian; $$$. Thanks to its torta primavera, you could say it's always spring at Arturo's. This popular restaurant, just east of the border with Queens, has been around for decades but stays remarkably fresh. The dining room has golden hue, dark wood, and a fondness for still-life and landscape paintings. The territory you'll cover is northern to southern Italy, as well as the Italian-American kitchen, all offered by a friendly staff. That torta primavera is a layering of many crepes with cheeses, vegetables, and cured meats. It's husky enough for winter, too. Eggplant rollatine, sweet sausages and broccoli rabe finished with garlic and olive oil, the tricolor salad, spinach salad with mushrooms and crisp bacon, and soups from stracciatella alla Romana to minestrone are good starters. Pastas include fine potato gnocchi Bolognese; rigatoni Siciliana with eggplant, plum tomatoes, basil, and mozzarella; and a respectable spaghetti carbonara rife with pancetta and onions in a creamy Parmesan-cheese sauce. Red snapper bonne femme, baked with white wine and lemon, arrives topped with olives and mushrooms. Chicken scarpariello here means the company of sweet sausage and broccoli rabe. There's a hefty sirloin steak alla pizzaiola and tender osso buco. The essential dessert is zabaglione for two, frothy and vinous, on strawberries and, yes, vanilla ice cream. The rolling dessert cart provides some strong competition.

Brasserie Persil, 2825 Long Beach Rd., Oceanside, NY 11572; (516) 992-1742; persilrestaurant.com; French, New American; $$–$$$. The style is more bistro than brasserie and more American than French. But Brasserie Persil is a friendly local spot with considerable appeal. Steak tartare, escargots with garlic-herb butter, and grilled octopus with chickpeas, red onion, fennel, and tomato are good appetizers. So is a salad of arugula, white beans, cucumbers, and ricotta salata. The chilled lobster salad includes asparagus and hearts of palm. Mussels are competently prepared marinière, with garlic and white wine, or Provençal, with garlic, tomatoes, and basil. Sirloin steak frites and marinated, grilled hanger steak with a red-wine-and-shallot sauce both are tender and to the point, as are the braised lamb shank with white beans and the combination of duck breast and confit of duck leg with sweet cherry sauce. Seaside, go for the sole meuniere and monkfish medallions with sweet-corn-and-crab bread pudding. The Tuesday special is duck a l'orange; the Thursday, coq au vin; and the Sunday, beef Bourguignonne with mashed potatoes, all reasons to visit. End with crème brûlée.

The Capital Grille, 630 Old Country Rd., Garden City, NY 11530; (516) 746-1675; thecapitalgrille.com; Steak, Seafood; $$$–$$$$. The Capital Grille has branches across the country. This one, in Roosevelt Field, provides some local iconography with images of Charles Lindbergh and Jacqueline Kennedy. The style is well beyond clubby, despite the fox-hunt prints. The sprawling dining room could host a small convention. And on a weekend night, the bar is jammed four-or-more deep. Despite the crowds and the demands, the staff stays very friendly and attentive, making sensible suggestions about navigating the menu. Diners may dig into expertly prepared lobster-and-crab cakes and fried calamari ignited with hot cherry peppers. The dry-aged, bone-in, coffee-rubbed sirloin steak is a mouthful. So is the rib eye. And the filet mignon becomes tastier than usual at this address. But the beef is rivaled by some of the seafood. Snowy, crosshatched swordfish is perfectly moist and lightly charred, served with lemon-and-shallot relish. The creamy cheesecake is the best dessert, but the chocolate-hazelnut layer cake is sufficiently rich to suit the restaurant, too.

Ciao Bella!, 1310 Broadway, Hewlett, NY 11557; (516) 569-2654; ciaobellahewlett.com; Italian; $$–$$$. Ciao Bella! merits its exclamation point. The storefront restaurant looks like a miniature trattoria and serves the kind of food you'd expect in a very good one that has an Italian-American approach. It's all done with care, a smile, and an exceedingly homey style. The vintage posters give Ciao Bella! a retro look. Some of the cooking does, too. The menu is changed frequently. But if you're lucky, Ciao Bella! will offer lemon chicken as a special. This is an exceptional, full-flavored production, similar to the much-publicized version prepared at Rao's in East Harlem (and, yes, Las Vegas). The pork osso buco, accompanied by cavatelli, also sharply focuses your attention. The house's cavatelli alla Bolognese delivers an outstanding meat sauce. Any finfish given the Livornese treatment with capers, olives, and tomatoes automatically is a contender. Garlicky shrimp in a white-wine-and-lemon sauce avoids the overcooking that often undermines it. The ricotta cheesecake is the essential dessert here.

Cuzco Peru, 323 Merrick Rd., Lynbrook, NY 11563; (516) 599-4227; Peruvian; $$. The cooking of Peru is a great combination plate, taking in influences European and Asian as well as from native Peru. This restaurant, an offspring of Cuzco Peru in Rego Park, Queens, gives you a little taste of what's offered. You won't find out about every exotic fruit. But it's a quick education about what to eat en route to Machu Picchu. The ceviches are obligatory, especially any with finfish, such as corvina. The shellfish ceviches are led by shrimp. Octopus is better grilled here than served as ceviche. Well-seasoned rotisserie chicken is one of the more popular dishes, and it's juicy, tender, elemental. Try the tamalitos, too, along with the deep-fried potatoes. *Chicha morada,* made with corn, is a popular, distinctive drink in Lima and throughout the country. It may not catch on in Nassau, but it's worth sampling.

Dodici, 12 N. Park Ave., Rockville Centre., NY 11570; (516) 764-3000; dodicirestaurant.com; Italian; $$–$$$. Dodici has the formula down: excellent service, good food, fair prices, with some panache. It's billed as northern Italian, but you'll do some traveling southward here, too. Carpaccio with arugula, Asiago cheese, and lemon vinaigrette will open your appetite. The whole baked clams show some

restraint with garlic. And mussels get a jolt from cherry peppers. The white bean soup arrives hearty and bracing. *Insalata Puglia* may be translated as string beans, red onion, cherry tomatoes, crisp pancetta, and shrimp. Dodici's pizzettes include the Tirolese with spinach, speck, and fontina cheese. The house's panini are highlighted by the Vesuvio, with grilled chicken, smoked mozzarella, and hot cherry peppers, and the Amore, with fresh mozzarella, prosciutto, basil, sun-dried tomatoes, and olive oil. Gnocchi Bolognese is gilded with fresh ricotta; orecchiette Pugliese, with sausage, broccoli rabe, and zesty Gaeta olives. Sweet sausage, red peppers, onions, and roasted potatoes bolster chicken scarpariello. Pine nut–crusted St. Peter's fish has the polite company of asparagus risotto. Finish with Italian cheesecake or tiramisu.

Fortune Wheel, **3601 Hempstead Tpke., Levittown, NY 11756; (516) 579-4700; Chinese; $$.** Fortune Wheel is one of the few Chinese restaurants on Long Island that takes a serious interest in dim sum, those small, savory dishes that amount to a meal of appetizers. You just keep picking from the cart or from a listing of what's available. Typical are steamed pork buns, fried or steamed dumplings, a crisp taro cake, turnip cake, deep-fried shrimp balls, and egg custard. They suit the restaurant, which is sandwiched snugly into a shopping center and not visible to anyone driving on Hempstead Turnpike. But inside, the joint is bright and usually crowded. In addition to the dim sum, Fortune Wheel prepares very good seafood in general. Lobster Cantonese or lobster in black bean sauce, crab with ginger and scallions, shrimp with lobster sauce, and daily specials are all worth sampling. You'll find satisfying lemon chicken, kung pao chicken, and General Tso's chicken; pan-fried noodles; orange beef; shredded beef in garlic sauce; eggplant the same way; sweet-and-sour pork; wonton soup; and hot-and-sour soup.

Frank's Steaks, 54 Lincoln Ave., Rockville Centre, NY 11570; (516) 536-1500; frankssteaks.com; Steak, American; $$–$$$. This is the second branch of Frank's Steaks, situated where the Lincoln Inn used to be. The original Frank's is in Jericho. Their motto is "We Ain't Just Steaks," and each restaurant lives up to it. The two have to rank among the friendlier, less clubby, and more family-oriented steak houses. The major cuts are here, but the memorable steak is the marinated, tender Romanian. The New York strip attracts you for the flavor of the meat but also the crown of melted stilton and fried onions. The broiled filet mignon benefits from sauce béarnaise; and the meat loaf, from brown gravy and mashed potatoes. The prime rib with horseradish sauce and the sautéed calf's liver with bacon also register. Frank's extends its appeal with the sliced filet mignon sandwich, roast chicken, rack of New Zealand lamb with thyme-rosemary sauce and mint jelly, a sesame-crusted tuna steak, the Maryland crab cake, onion soup, and "double Gorgonzola bread," which is precisely that. Cheesecake, rice pudding, and apple cobbler a la mode complete the meal.

George Martin, 65 N. Park Ave., Rockville Centre, NY 11570; (516) 678-7272; georgemartintheoriginal.com; New American; $$–$$$. As the website states, this is "the original," the George Martin that led to a mini-empire of Long Island restaurants, including George Martin's Strip Steak in Great River. This George Martin has been cooking since 1989, adapting to changing tastes and to the economy's gyrations. Visit for onion soup, butternut squash ravioli with brown butter and sage, "rustic meatballs" on garlicky crostini, braised beef short ribs with garlic-mashed potatoes, the pork jaeger schnitzel, and seared tuna Provençal, with zucchini "linguine," tomato, olives, and capers. George Martin also prepares a fine Gorgonzola-crusted filet mignon, a juicy burger with blue cheese and bacon, and filet mignon sliders with onions and crumbled blue cheese. The fettuccine with "Sunday gravy" takes in meatballs, braised short ribs, and sweet sausage. At lunch, the short-rib tacos and the BLT on white toast call. The restaurant is pleasantly lived-in.

Il Luogo, 159 Sunrise Hwy., Lynbrook, NY 11563; (516) 837-9015; illuogoristorante.com; Italian; $$–$$$. Il Luogo gained its initial notoriety because for some Tuesdays last year, actor-chef Joseph R. Gannascoli cooked here. He's no longer associated with the restaurant. But you should come anytime to sample full-time Chef Marco Jara's fare. The dining room has a contemporary look, except for the wax that encrusts candelabras. But the food includes both the old and the new. Winning appetizers include the rice ball with meat sauce; the big, baked stuffed artichoke; tripe with black olives, potatoes, and peas in red sauce, under a blanket of béchamel; and bucatini alla puttanesca, with olives, capers, and anchovies. The main courses feature a fibrous steak au poivre and a tender pork chop inflamed with hot peppers. Chicken al mattone arrives with mashed potatoes and braised escarole for a flavorful alternative. And Il Luogo offers especially fine cannoli. If you're in the mood for some showiness and glitz, know that the flames shoot very high when they're part of the tableside creation of bananas Foster. The staff looks like it's enjoying the performance, too.

Jake's Steakhouse, 2172 Hempstead Tpke., East Meadow, NY 11554; (516) 222-8400; jakessteakhouse.com; Steak, American; $$$. This is the most upscale restaurant near Nassau University Medical Center. Given the amount of beef served on the premises, consider the location a definite plus. Jake's has a modern, American style, friendly and no-nonsense. So, order that slab of thick-cut, applewood-smoked bacon as an appetizer and add a tomato-and-onion salad for balance. The raw bar boasts Blue Point oysters and littleneck clams. Clams casino also are in demand because no meal can have too much bacon. The filet mignon with a blue-cheese crust, frizzled onions, and red-wine sauce underscores the virtues of excess. Purists may stick with the 35-ounce, dry-aged, bone-in rib eye, a mighty plate of red meat. Braised short ribs, off the bone, and the pork shank with mashed potatoes seem like children's fare by comparison, but they're good. Roasted chicken with olive oil–roasted potatoes appears a concession to health food. The obvious side dish with any of the main courses is macaroni and cheese or the spud of your choice. But there's cauliflower with bacon, too. Who needs dessert?

Jimmy Hays Steak House, 4310 Austin Blvd., Island Park, NY 11558; (516) 432-5155; jimmyhayssteakhouse.com; Steak, American; $$–$$$. Jimmy Hays could qualify for landmark status in Island Park, but you should think of it basically as a very good steak house, where the service is good and the quality consistent. It's run by Mr. Hays's grandson. The selections are varied enough to cover the time-capsule likes of steak Diane completed with a cognac-and-mustard demi-glace, Chateaubriand for two, and beef Stroganoff. The filet mignon with onion rings, filet mignon au poivre, and the sliced steak also merit consideration. If you're feeling rebellious, there's pan-seared lobster Jimmy in a cognac-garlic-lemon sauce, shrimp scampi-style, and lump crabmeat au gratin. The double-cut loin lamb chops and broiled pork chops with caramelized Granny Smith apples heighten the competition. Precede these with lobster salad, lump crabmeat cocktail, baked clams, or some applewood-smoked bacon. Follow them with rice pudding, cheesecake, caramelized apples on waffles with vanilla ice cream, or, for old time's sake, white peach Melba.

Jordan Lobster Farms, 1 Pettit Pl., Island Park, NY 11558; (516) 889-3314; jordanlobsterfarms.com; Seafood; $–$$$. Jordan Lobster Farms qualifies as a restaurant because not to include the mainstay on an inlet of Reynolds Channel would be criminal. You're just as welcome to do take-out as to eat in at this operation, which has been selling seafood since 1938. It's the flavor of New England by way of Long Island. Jordan started as Jordan's Lobster Dock in Brooklyn before heading east. You can select raw littleneck and cherrystone clams, oysters, a shrimp cocktail, New England– and Manhattan-style clam chowders, spicy crab-and-corn chowder, a lobster cake sandwich, lobster rolls, and whole lobsters that weigh in at from 1 to 15 pounds. Yes, 15. There's a $3 deposit for the lobster cracker. Fried scallops, fried clam strips, and fish-and-chips made with flounder or fillet of cod add to the decision-making, as do salt cod and smoked eel, if available. Key lime pie is a suitable dessert, assuming your lobster's weight stayed in single digits. The beverage of choice, of course, is Belfast Bay Lobster Ale.

King Umberto, 1343 Hempstead Tpke., Elmont, NY 11003; (516) 352-3232 for reservations and (516) 352-8451 for the pizzeria; kingumberto.com; Italian; $$–$$$. The reigning local monarch for pizzas stuffed with vegetables or meat, as well as the traditional Margherita and the all-white mozzarella-and-ricotta pie, adjoins a very good, formal Italian restaurant. If the daily specials include burrata with melon, figs, and prosciutto, your first decision is simple. "Fire in the hole" means grilled hot sausage on garlic toast, topped with vinegar peppers, onions, and garlic. Hefty mozzarella in carrozza, pan-fried with capers, means business. "Risotto cakes" is the phrase used for rice balls, filled with mozzarella and diced vegetables. Sautéed beef tripe with potatoes and peas in tomato sauce may be listed as an appetizer but it could do double-duty as a main course. There's well-made minestrone, potato-leek soup, and *pasta e fagioli;* fried zucchini, panko-crusted and pan-seared crab cakes, and chicken scarpariello. Eggplant and chicken parmigiana ensure a take-home portion. Sole oreganata, veal piccata, and saltimbocca are solid main dishes. So is cavatelli with braised short rib in red sauce. Six types of pasta are available in a series of different sauces.

La Bistecca, 410 Rockaway Ave., Valley Stream, NY 11581; (516) 341-7177; labistecca.org; Italian; $$$–$$$$. Although the name, which means *steak* in Italian, could make you think this is a beef house, La Bistecca is much more. The understated restaurant, full of polished dark wood and golden tones, is devoted to traditional Italian cooking. That starts with a terrific Bolognese sauce, ready for pappardelle, and gnocchi served any style. The fried calamari are elevated by a genuinely spicy red sauce. The balance of hot peppers and Gorgonzola works with sautéed shrimp on garlic bread. The grilled shell steak is La Bistecca's tribute to beefiness. Osso buco reminds you why it became a menu staple. The tender rack of lamb would be fine on its own, but receives extra flavor from a mustardy bread-crumb crust. This is an easy dining room to linger in. No one is rushed. The second and third espressos go down as easily as the first. The Italian cheesecake has a trace of nostalgia in the recipe. And La Bistecca is one of those establishments that knows how to whip up a vinous zabaglione. It's offered with berries, but you'd be happy with only a spoon.

La Novella, 364 East Meadow Ave., East Meadow, NY 11554; (516) 794-6248; lanovella.com; Italian; $$–$$$. Redesigned and updated, La Novella is a reliable choice for Italian and continental dishes, with an occasional Sicilian specialty to liven up the repertoire. They like to emphasize the "true kitchen" of Italy, which takes on a very broad definition. Here, it apparently includes a tableside Caesar salad for two. The eggplant Salerno, with roasted peppers, tomatoes, and fried mozzarella is a substantial selection, as is the eggplant rollatine. Eggplant elevates penne alla Norma. The linguine with clams, garlic, olive oil, herbs, and some marinara sauce also is good. Naturally, there's crunchy fried calamari. Gnocchi are emboldened by a snappy Gorgonzola-laced sauce. The blue cheese also sparks the filet mignon, which is sautéed with peppercorns and set on portobello mushrooms. Sauteed red snapper is finished with lemon, capers, and white wine. The pork chop stuffed with eggplant, mozzarella, prosciutto, and shallots means business. Cannoli, tiramisu, and Italian cheesecake are the apropos desserts.

Lawson Pub, 3112 Lawson Blvd., Oceanside, NY 11572; (516) 307-8753; lawsonpub.com; New American; $$. Joseph Bonacore's resume includes the upscale, first-rate, and short-lived Tuscany restaurant in Rockville Centre. At Lawson Pub, his approach is more casual but just as flavorful. Here, he prepares lobster sliders with lobster salad, bacon, tomato, and organic greens; a "tuna taco trio" with guacamole, mango ceviche, and Sriracha aioli; "little piggies," or appetizing pigs-in-a-blanket with bacon, ketchup, honey-mustard, and chipotle-apple sauces; and a combo of popcorn shrimp and fried calamari, with cilantro aioli and marinara sauce. Under "LP Classics" is a roast pork sandwich, made with thinly sliced pork butt, duck sauce, and Muenster cheese on garlic bread. His spin on surf-and-turf brings together boneless, braised short rib and grilled, barbecued, and spiced shrimp. One of the house's better specials is the honey-brined and grilled pork chop with mushroom-and-goat-cheese-stuffed sweet potato, caramelized cipollini onions, and *haricots verts*. Pan-seared fluke, with roasted vegetables and red wine-and-basil tinted beurre blanc, also stars.

MoCA Asian Bistro, 1300 Peninsula Blvd., Hewlett, NY 11557; (516) 295-8888; mocaasianbistro.com; Asian; $$–$$$. MoCA stands for Modern Concept Culinary Arts and its goals are as lofty as its design is glitzy. The result is a pretty good variety of dishes that seek to show where the twain meet. The strategy is supposed to unify Chinese,

Japanese, Thai, Vietnamese, and fusion cuisines. While it's not a seamless transition, the food can be good. Sometimes, however, the waitresses do seem stressed and the wait long. MoCA needs a course in crowd management. But patience will earn you a palatable pad Thai, shrimp-dumpling noodle soup, coconut-laced seafood chowder, filet mignon with Chinese greens, and Beijing duck. Veer Japanese with the understandably colorful rainbow sushi roll, beef negimaki, and rock shrimp tempura. The sake-and-miso-spiked black cod and the filet mignon ishiyaki also are in the mix, along with char-grilled Chilean sea bass, Siamese red snapper, and crisp calamari. Faced with these options, the sensible alternative is to focus on the less-orchestrated sushi productions. A second MoCA is destined for Woodbury.

Nick's Pizza, 272 Sunrise Hwy., Rockville Centre, NY 11570; (516) 763-3278; nicksrvc.com; Italian; $$. Nick's specializes in Neapolitan-style pizza and boldly proclaims "No Slices!" at every possible opportunity. It's the suburban scion of Nick's in Forest Hills, Queens. The pies are very good, either red or white, and one that's half-and-half for the undecideds. The tomato sauce at Nick's reins in the acidity that ruins so many others. Toppings of note: prosciutto, sun-dried tomatoes, fresh garlic, extra Parmesan cheese. In addition to the pizzas, Nick's does a professional job with lasagna, manicotti, spaghetti with olive oil and garlic, penne with meat sauce and peas, eggplant rollatine, both chicken parmigiana and pizzaiola, and the playfully named *Morte Fame* calzone, filled with lots of stuffings to deal with your dying-of-hunger appetite—something that will vanish quickly after a few dishes at Nick's. You can precede these with a stuffed artichoke or stuffed mushrooms. The staff sometimes seems distracted, but you'll get out on time. And, once more, for the record, and for posterity: "No Slices!"

Novità, 860 Franklin Ave., Garden City, NY 11530; (516) 739-7660; novitany.com; Italian; $$–$$$. Novità combines wine bar and trattoria. There are more than 100 wines by the glass to accompany your meal in the bustling, modern dining room. Novità has carved out a distinctive niche along this big commercial strip with casual, appetizing fare. Try the mushroom-and-fontina stuffed arancini, or rice balls, with a zesty red-pepper coulis and a chickpea puree. Panini are very good: the breaded eggplant, roasted red pepper, and fontina cheese combo; mozzarella, tomato, and basil aioli; prosciutto, sopressata, provolone, and red wine vinegar among them. The Margherita pizza also is a winner, as are the pies with meatball or sausage, ricotta, and broccoli rabe toppings. "Peasant chicken" enriches the table with white beans, escarole, and mushroom pan jus; caramelized pork chops do the same, with roasted potatoes and cherry pepper marmalade. Bucatini alla carbonara with ramps and peas heads the pastas. Swordfish alla Livornese is the notable catch, with chile-seared ahi tuna, finished with a coulis of sweet pepper, also in the swim. Novità has the right idea with its "street fair" zeppole.

Oak Chalet, 1940 Bellmore Ave., Bellmore, NY 11710; (516) 826-1700; oakchalet.net; German, Continental; $$. Oak Chalet is included in part because it and a few others represent the last stand of German cuisine on Long Island. The establishment certainly is homey and welcoming. And the staff knows how to treat guests. You should treat yourself to the Teutonic specialties. Start with the bracing herring salad or the marinated herring in sour cream, or maybe the smoked trout or the smoked shrimp with creamed horseradish. This also is likely one of the few eateries where you'll see bratwurst listed as an appetizer. More timid appetites can stick with the shrimp cocktail. Then, everyone should head for the sauerbraten with red cabbage and dumplings, bratwurst or knockwurst with sauerkraut, smoked pork chops with sauerkraut, wiener rostbraten with shoestring fried onions, frikadellen with mushroom gravy, or wiener schnitzel à la

Holstein, complete with fried egg and potato pancake. For anyone not up for the house specialties, there's filet mignon with béarnaise sauce. Housemade apple strudel and rice pudding are the noteworthy sweets, unless you're intrigued by peach Melba.

The Palm Court, Eisenhower Park, East Meadow, NY 11554; (516) 542-0700, ext. 1; thecarltun.com; New American; $$$. The Palm Court is the high-end, traditional restaurant in the Carltun catering complex. It's bright, sunny, elegant in its own risk-averse way, and often very good. The very competent dining room staff ensures that you'll be taken care of with skill. Dry-aged steaks highlight the choices, including a porterhouse with sautéed onions and mushrooms and mashed potatoes, and the 28-ounce rib eye, with sautéed onions and baked potato. The Cedar River New York strip steak, with sautéed onions and garlic mashed potatoes, also is juicy. And there's a Wagyu beef burger, festooned with onions, mushrooms, bacon, and cheese, plus fries. The Duroc pork chop makes its mark with polenta rings, *haricots verts* and apple mustard. Roasted chicken arrives with porcini mushroom jus and polenta croutons. The Dungeness crab cakes with Pernod-honey sauce and the roasted halibut with basil-mashed potatoes are tasty alternatives. For a more contemporary spin, cut into panko-crusted yellowfin tuna. The "chocolate chocolate chocolate" dessert succinctly sums itself up.

Pastrami King, 196 Merrick Rd., Merrick, NY 11566; pastramiking .com; Deli; $$. The former monarch of Queens Boulevard in Kew Gardens now rules in Nassau. The reasons to eat at the current location are the same as they've always been: stuffed derma, sweet-and-sour stuffed cabbage, fried kreplach, and overstuffed sandwiches of hot pastrami, hot corned beef, beef brisket, tongue, turkey, and hard salami, plus chicken in the pot and chicken potpie. This time, Pastrami King supplements the traditional menu

Deli & Bagel

The quest for the pristine pastrami, the ideal smoked salmon, even the bagel with absolute integrity can rival Don Quixote's, or at least that of John Wayne looking for Natalie Wood in *The Searchers*. These spots are very reliable and very good.

A & S Bagels in Franklin Square

Andel's of Roslyn in Roslyn

Bagel Biz in Melville

Bagel Boss, 12 locations on Long Island

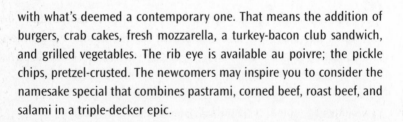

Ben's Delicatessen in Woodbury, Greenvale, and Carle Place

Fairway Market in Plainview and Westbury

Kensington Kosher Delicatessen in Great Neck

Pastrami King in Merrick

Zan's Kosher Deli in Lake Grove

with what's deemed a contemporary one. That means the addition of burgers, crab cakes, fresh mozzarella, a turkey-bacon club sandwich, and grilled vegetables. The rib eye is available au poivre; the pickle chips, pretzel-crusted. The newcomers may inspire you to consider the namesake special that combines pastrami, corned beef, roast beef, and salami in a triple-decker epic.

Pier 95, 95 Hudson Ave., Freeport, NY 11520; pier95.com; Seafood, Portuguese; $$–$$$. Pier 95 is the peak of dining out in

Freeport. And it's not on the very popular "Nautical Mile" of eateries and bars. It also expands the seafood essentials with soulful Portuguese fare, all in a pleasant, relaxed waterside setting. Good beginnings: cod cakes with herbaceous tomato sauce; shrimp sautéed in roasted garlic sauce, steamed clams and mussels, New England–style clam chowder, black bean soup, and caldo verde, with collard greens and chouriço sausage. Then, pick pork tenderloin with clams and sautéed potatoes, baked daurade with caramelized onions, seared sea scallops with sauce Choron, salt cod with roasted peppers, or medallions of monkfish with roasted red potatoes, a julienne of vegetables, and mustard. They make a tasty flan, too.

Polo Steakhouse, 45 7th St., Garden City, NY 11530; (516) 877-9385; gardencityhotel.com; Steak; $$$–$$$$. Ralph Lauren would like the look of the Polo Steakhouse. The restaurant in the Garden City Hotel is full of dark wood and luxe leather, very clubby with an image of instant pedigree and absolutely no sense of irony. There are artsy longhorn images and comfy seats. And the tab reflects all that must have gone into remodeling the space. That said, the crab cake appetizer is good; the baked oysters overcooked; the iceberg salad a tasty still life with blue cheese, bacon, and more. The juicy, dry-aged porterhouse for two is the signature cut, and the filet mignon gives it some competition. Steak Diane has no bearing on the original. It's more like filet mignon *au poivre,* and respectable in its own way. And grilled swordfish arrives moist and cross-hatched with skill. Steak fries, baked potato, hash browns: all fine. Chocolate cake and cheesecake are understandably rich and suitably excessive.

Press 195, 22 N. Park Ave., Rockville Centre, NY 11570; (516) 536-1950; press195.com; Sandwiches; $–$$. Press 195 has a very precise focus: a nice sandwich. The straightforward spot competes well in Rockville Centre, a restaurant hub in Nassau. Before you get between the bread, start with a baby-beet salad with arugula, shaved Parmesan cheese, and lemon-mustard vinaigrette, or with tomato-and-olive bruschetta with goat cheese and basil. There also are good plates of cured meat, with prosciutto, sopressata, and Genoa salami, and a hummus plate with red peppers. The hot sandwiches, on ciabatta bread, are led by the roast pork, ham, swiss cheese, pickle chip, and garlic spread combo; the turkey, smoked Canadian bacon, smoked Gouda, tomato, and garlic spread number; and, for vegetarians, the Press 195 original, with basil, fresh mozzarella, and marinara sauce. For something different: roast beef, Vermont cheddar, sweet onion jam, and spicy brown mustard immortalized between potato knish. The restaurant devotes some attention to hamburgers, too. If you go that route, the cheeseburger with Vermont cheddar is tops.

Prost Grill & Garten, 652 Franklin Ave., Garden City, NY 11530; (516) 427-5215; prostgrill.com; German; $$. Prost takes its cue from German beer halls. And when the weather permits, there are a couple of tables outside that you can turn into a biergarten in your imagination. The cozy, woody spot sports TVs tuned to sports and enough images of Munich to get the point across. The food choices are fairly limited, but they're the right cuisine for the beers. A plate of charcuterie and cheeses will do just fine, as will sauerkraut croquettes and smoked salmon. But Prost knows the value of a husky smoked pork chop and a crisp, greaseless wiener schnitzel. And you can't skip the bratwurst, bockwurst, or knockwurst, three of beer's reasons for being. The less-traditional path: lamb merguez, alligator, venison, and buffalo sausages. German potato salad, potato pancakes, red cabbage, and sauerkraut provide strong support. The Oktoberfest pretzel with mustard sauce is festive all year. Apple strudel, Black Forest cake, and a German pancake-crepe with vanilla ice cream are the finales. There are more than a dozen German brews on tap and a solid selection of bottled beers.

Rachel's Waterside Grill, 281 **Woodcleft Ave., Freeport, NY** **11520; (516) 546-0050; rachelswatersidegrill.com; Seafood; $$–$$$.** Rachel's Waterside Grill is one of the more attractive restaurants situated along Freeport's popular "Nautical Mile." It recovered from Hurricane Sandy, added new floor-to-ceiling windows, and is ready for business. Broiled or steamed lobster is a logical choice. The lobster sliders, on potato rolls, are made with tasty lobster salad and accompanied by warm potato chips. At brunch, there's a lobster potpie, too. Respectable crab cakes, baked clams oreganata, pan-seared local flounder, and sautéed mussels with linguine and tomato sauce are standbys. Sesame tuna salad with baby greens, pineapple salsa, and crushed peanuts with sesame-ginger vinaigrette provides an Asian-themed side trip. Brooklyn Lager steamers also bring a taste of chorizo sausage. Tuna tartare nachos are created with rice paper, chipotle-ginger aioli, and well-seasoned fish. For the carnivore who can't be converted, Rachel's succeeds with a straightforward and juicy Romanian skirt steak, flanked by mashed potatoes and sautéed spinach.

Revel, 835 **Franklin Ave., Garden City, NY 11530; (516) 246-9111; revelrestaurant.com; New American; $$$.** Revel kicks off the partying on Franklin Avenue with a high-decibel bar scene and crowded dining areas. It's a striking, modern design and the set for David Martinez's stylish cooking. The menu changes regularly. But look for Arctic char tartare, veal-and-ricotta salata meatballs, pork-belly sliders, and any of the steaks, which get a boost with horseradish or mustard sauce. Chatham cod with cauliflower-and-green-apple puree and grilled wild Alaskan king salmon with lemon-verbena aioli are flavorful, too. On the side: duck-fat fries, herb-roasted fingerling potatoes, creamy polenta with roasted tomatoes. There's a satisfying crème brûlée to conclude.

Ruth's Chris Steak House, 600 **Old Country Rd., Garden City, NY 11530; (516) 222-0220; ruthschris.com; Steak; $$–$$$$.** Situated near the Roosevelt Field Mall and the hub of Nassau's government and legal establishment, this branch of Ruth's Chris draws a crowd for lunch and for dinner. As at every other Ruth's Chris nationwide, the steaks arrive sizzling on a plate that's as hot as a frying pan that has been working overtime. It's a formula. When the steak house opened, they handed out buttons proclaiming "Sizzling Long Island." And the steaks are predictably good, from filet mignon and New York strip to T-bone and porterhouse. Ruth's Chris also knows how to cook lobsters. They go through a lot of butter here. Suitable appetizers include the shrimp cocktail, shrimp remoulade, and barbecued shrimp; crabmeat-stuffed mushrooms, seared ahi tuna, sliced tomato, and onions; Caesar, chopped, and wedge salads. On the side, potatoes Lyonnaise, au gratin, or baked, and creamed spinach will suffice. For dessert you can stick a fork in the caramelized banana cream pie, the warm apple-crumb tart, chocolate cake, or a high-octane bread pudding with whiskey sauce.

Sage Bistro, 2620 Merrick Rd., Bellmore, NY 11710; (516) 679-8928; bistrosage.com; New American; $$–$$$. They started out waving the tricolor here, but stars-and-stripes now have equal sway at Sage Bistro. Overall, it's a bright, straightforward, satisfying restaurant that provides a periodic surprise. Asian-style duck tacos, with a touch of ginger and plum, are respectable. Likewise, the braised short-rib sliders with barbecue sauce, braised lamb shank with vegetable risotto, and pistachio-crusted rack of lamb accompanied by a blue-cheese-and-potato tart. The Gallic spirit takes over with the basic *frisée aux lardons* and escargots a la Bourguignonne. The whole, roasted chicken for two is backed by roasted potatoes and vegetables and has a hint of garlic. Grilled hanger steak frites also has the right flavors. Mussels marinière, trout meunière, and lobster-enriched macaroni and cheese head the seafood selections. The Tuesday special is duck a l'orange, well-prepared. And the sweets include plump profiteroles and crepes Suzette lit up via Grand Marnier sauce and cooled off with vanilla ice cream.

Sicilia Risturanti, 2715 Hempstead Tpke., Levittown, NY 11756; (516) 731-2538; siciliaristuranti.com; Italian; $$. Sicilian cuisine is a lesson in history. The Mediterranean's biggest island has been a crossroads of cultures and the food reflects almost every influence. Sicilia Risturanti revels in it. The kitchen prepares very good caponata, the eggplant relish; arancini, or rice balls; panelle, the chickpea fritters; and flavorfully stuffed sardines. Pasta con le sarde here is made with bucatini, saffron, pine nuts, golden raisins, fennel, and authenticity. Pasta with eggplant and tomatoes also is recommended, as is ringlets of pasta with meat sauce, peas, garlic, and olive oil. The stuffed pork loin is filled with mozzarella, Parmesan cheese, and prosciutto to good effect. Grilled chicken arrives in a zesty parsley and mint sauce with tomatoes. Baccalà, or salt cod, with garlic and olive oil, and baked swordfish with raisins, onions, green olives, capers, and tomatoes also are a little tour or the island. If you're devoted to osso buco or chicken parmigiana, Sicilia imports those dishes, too. But stick with the specialties.

Snaps American Bistro, 2010 Wantagh Ave., Wantagh, NY 11793; (516) 221-0029; snapsrestaurant.com; New American; $$. Casual Snaps shows off some good cooking from Scott Bradley. In addition to weekly specials that may include fried chicken and hamburgers, he has at least a dozen burger variations, including a Reuben topped with pastrami, sauerkraut, swiss cheese, and Russian dressing; and the "piggy back," with barbecued pulled pork. Bradley prepares a tasty braised short-rib-and-blue-cheese quesadilla with arugula-and-apple salad; an excellent, warm lobster-knuckle sandwich on buttery bread, with a fried egg; a just-as-flavorful lobster "BLT" slider; and "Diablo fries" finished with chili, cheddar cheese, and chipotle aioli. His main courses are wide-ranging: five-spice tuna steak with pineapple rice and soy-ginger lemongrass sauce; grilled pork tenderloin with Granny Smith apple sauce, sauerkraut, and mustard-mashed potatoes; marinated and grilled rack of lamb with multi-flavored couscous; grilled jumbo shrimp in Thai-curry mango broth with calamari and soba noodles; and penne alla puttanesca, sparked with olives and capers.

Sole, 2752 Oceanside Rd., Oceanside, NY 11572; (516) 764-3218; soleny.com; Italian, New American; $$–$$$. Sole cooks with some flair in this section of town. Robert Carmosino's restaurant has a modern look and an old-fashioned approach. The formula work well. He updates the familiar and shows some creativity, too. Veal meatballs, for example, find the company of sun-dried cranberries, shaved pecorino cheese, and toasted almond demi-glace. Basil aioli vies with marinara to boost fried calamari. Tempura-style shrimp benefit from corn relish and guacamole. There are tempting bruschetti: caponata, goat cheese, and chive oil; crab, cherry pepper, arugula, and pesto; ricotta, crushed almonds, and red-wine reduction. For pasta, pick the gemelli Bolognese, cavatelli with chorizo, white beans, and herbs in a Chardonnay-tomato broth. The eggplant and chicken parmigiana are dependable. So are the chicken scarpariello, with sweet sausage, peppers, onions, and roasted potatoes; the crisp duck with caramelized-onion risotto; and the "crusted fish," which may be sun-dried-tomato St. Peter's fish or candied-cashew-and-crab rockfish, each with mashed potatoes and escarole.

Sushi Ko, 2063 Merrick Rd., Merrick, NY 11566; (516) 378-9888; sushikoli.com; Japanese; $$. Sushi Ko is a sharp, reliably fine destination for Japanese cuisine. As you'd expect, sushi itself is the big draw, in different forms. Maguro tuna, scallop, sea eel, sea urchin, red clam, and yellowtail are very good. The banana roll is a curiosity, pairing salmon and cream cheese with fried banana, avocado, and masago in soy paper. The ichiban roll with spicy tuna, avocado, lobster salad, seaweed salad, and mango also stretches things. But tuna-avocado and crawfish-avocado combos are fine. So are pizza, or pancake, with guacamole, tuna, and yellowtail; tuna tataki; and tuna tartare. Seared, peppery tuna also elevates Sushi Ko. But the best route here is to go with two friends and wield your chopsticks in the "super sushi sashimi" combination: 42 pieces and 2 rolls. If you prefer something cooked, first choice is roast duck in a lime-hoisin reduction.

Tennessee Jed's, 3357 Merrick Rd., Wantagh, NY 11793; (516) 308-3355; barbeque.li; American; $$. Bring a few friends to Tennessee Jed's. The informal joint encourages feeding a group. It's an advocate of St. Louis–style ribs and Memphis baby back ribs, Carolina pulled pork, and Texas beef ribs. The restaurant also offers hamburgers and hot dogs, including the Oklahoma State Fair corn dog, fried chicken, and fried shrimp. Tornado Tots are the 'tater variety, made grander with cheddar cheese and smoked bacon. Smoked beef sausage and beef brisket enter the fray, too. The combination po' boy is a multi-level construct of pulled pork, pulled chicken, sausage, cheese sauce, and cole slaw. When you're considering the smoked chicken salad with walnuts and sun-dried cranberries, the char-grilled chicken breast, or the char-grilled rib eye steak, it's like wandering in the general direction of health food. Fresh potato chips, macaroni and cheese, rice and black-eyed peas, collard greens, and creamed spinach are part of the supporting cast. Be assured there are 32 beers to wash down all this. It's highly unlikely that you'll leave hungry.

Thom Thom, 3340 Park Ave., Wantagh, NY 11793; (516) 221-8022; thomthomrestaurant.com; Steak, Sushi; $$–$$$. Thom Thom's name must stem from its initial owner, restaurateur Tom (or Thomas) Schaudel. He has gone on to other enterprises. But the crackling small plates, steaks, and sushi theme now is being played out even better under new ownership. The bar still is very popular and the dining room has a party atmosphere. And the kung pao calamari, with ground peanuts, remains a hit appetizer. Sample the scallop-and-chorizo risotto, too. Additional starters to consider are the Maryland crab cake with red-pepper remoulade, "bang bang" shrimp with a sweet chile glaze and Gorgonzola cheese dip, Thai-curry mussels, and lobster-enriched macaroni and cheese. The elaborate sushi rolls, with names such as Crazy Tuna and Volcano, are colorful and good; and the more familiar sushi with tuna or yellowtail-and-scallion are their equal. Thom Thom sears steakhouse-quality filet mignon, porterhouse, strip, and skirt steaks. The rack of lamb rivals them. Béarnaise, peppercorn, and red-wine sauces are the better complements. Braised pork osso buco and clay-oven roasted chicken lead the specials.

Villa d'Este, 186 Jericho Tpke., Floral Park, NY 11001; (516) 354-1355; villadesterestaurant.com; Italian, Continental; $$$. First, this has nothing to do with the magnificent villa and hotel in Cernobbio at Lake Como. But it is opulent in its own way. And Villa d'Este has been bringing in customers since the year of music at Woodstock and footprints on the moon. The decor has been updated, so Villa d'Este does look more contemporary. But the very good food belongs to decades gone by. Nibble on the seafood salad or the roasted peppers and anchovies. Sample a stuffed mushroom. Order a tricolor salad. Consider the minestrone and the stracciatella alla Romana. Then, pick veal cannelloni marinara or Rossini, saltimbocca, or roast duck with orange sauce. Chicken Pugliese gets its body and soul from sausages and broccoli rabe. The rustic side of Villa d'Este continues with a sizable beef braciola served with rigatoni. The house's mixed grill combines a chicken breast, lamb, and filet mignon. Broiled lamb chops are a mainstay. Red snapper Livornese suits the restaurant, but so does Dover sole Maxim, finished with dry vermouth, lemon, and shallots. The hefty, meat-filled lasagna is made with spinach noodles.

Waterzooi, 850 Franklin Ave., Garden City, NY 11530; (516) 877-2177; waterzooi.com; Belgian, American; $$–$$$. Grand Belgian brews fuel Waterzooi, which bills itself as a bistro but has the style and size of a brasserie. In this buoyant joint, you'll find an assortment of mussel pots. The better ones include a pot with lobster sauce, another with saffron-and-tomato broth, fra diavolo–style, and the Thai-inspired number seasoned with lemongrass, cilantro, coconut, and pineapple. The namesake seafood stew is defined by a tarragon-fennel broth. Carbonnade a la flamande is a beef stew benefiting from brown ale plus caramelized apples and prunes; frikadellen, a relative of meat loaf, well-made, on brioche bread, with fontina cheese. Midday, sliced steak with onions and Gouda cheese on a baguette is an uncomplicated option; and the "bistro burger" a popular alternative. The house's steak frites is very good. The crisp fries themselves are among the best on Long Island, awaiting a dip in mayonnaise. Lobster bisque is a satisfactory appetizer. For dessert, it's hard to resist the Belgian waffles, especially if you have any memories of the 1964–65 New York World's Fair.

Landmarks

Bigelow's, 79 N. Long Beach Rd., Rockville Centre, NY 11570; (516) 678-3878; bigelows-rvc.com; Seafood; $$. Bigelow's has been frying seafood since 1939 and it doesn't seem as if much has changed over the years except the oil. The specialty: the Ipswich clam, also known here as the soft-shell clam. The rest of the menu is about

as no-nonsense as the joint's style. New England and Manhattan clam chowders, lobster bisque, popcorn shrimp, onion rings, shrimp cocktail, salad, cole slaw, fries, mini-crab cakes, clam strips, the Ipswich stars, a burger. Are you ready for a beer yet? Bigelow's also offers swordfish, salmon, whiting, cod, scallops, and sandwich versions of almost everything. No subsititutions, of course.

Blue Moon, 26 N. Park Ave., Rockville Centre, NY 11570; (516) 763-4900; bluemoonpizzeria.com; Italian; $–$$. The coal oven sends out pizzas large and small, smoky and superior. This is no slice joint. Blue Moon is packed with pizza lovers and parmigiana enthusiasts. The restaurant has been in business since 1937, ensuring that the right amount of ricotta, onions, meatballs, anchovies, olives, sweet red peppers, or, yes, extra cheese makes it onto your pie. Before settling in for the pizza, sample the good calzone, with ricotta, mozzarella, and prosciutto; the Caesar salad; or the *pasta e fagioli.* Panini are a specialty here, too. The "classico" means prosciutto, fresh mozzarella, olive oil, and basil; the "campagnola," grilled chicken, onions, sweet and hot peppers, smoked mozzarella, and basil; the "salsiccia con broccoli rabe," exactly that. Pasta wouldn't be the first or second choice at Blue Moon. But if that's what you want, the penne with escarole, hot cherry peppers, and grilled chicken and the rigatoni with sausage, broccoli rabe, and red pepper should satisfy, along with housemade lasagna and manicotti with meat sauce.

Plattduetsche Park Restaurant, 1132 Hempstead Tpke., Franklin Square, NY 11010; (516) 354-3131; parkrestaurant.com; German, Continental; $$. The biggest ompah going on Long Island, Plattduetsche Park is headquarters for Oktoberfest, beer garden, and German celebration. It stands on a site bought by a German-American club from Brooklyn decades ago. The dining room is from another era, with Rhine imagery and a mini-print of Klimt. Visit for the roasted pork shank, a knockout main dish on mashed potatoes and sauerkraut; flaky sauerbraten with red cabbage and potato dumplings; the Bavarian platter of smoked pork, pork loin, and bratwurst; and the *zweibel rostbraten,* or sirloin steak with fried onions. The preliminaries should include smoked trout with horseradish crème fraîche, a Bavarian pretzel, and that carnivore's delight, steak tartare, made with care and sent out with rye toast. Lots of schnitzels are available. The "Bohemian" means a sautéed pork cutlet enriched with bacon and mustard sauce. There's rice pudding, but the obligatory dessert is Black Forest cake. Accompany your meal with one of the German beers on tap.

Specialty Stores, Markets & Shops

A Taste of Home, 1992 N. Jerusalem Rd., North Bellmore, NY 11710; (516) 486-1670; atasteofhomeli.com; Bakery, Cafe, Sweet Shop. This combination bakery, cafe, and sweet shop has ardent fans. You may join them after nibbling on the traditional cassata, the strawberry shortcake, Black Forest cake, or chocolate mousse. The carrot cake, dotted with raisins, inspires loyalty, as do the "shadow" cake, a vanilla and chocolate alliance under a hard chocolate dome, and the assortment of flavorful cheesecakes. A Taste of Home naturally bakes a full line of butter cookies. The cafe offers breakfast and lunch dishes, including omelets, frittatas, egg sandwiches, pancakes, French toast, Danish, panini, and wraps; hot chocolate, cappuccino, and espresso. The sweet shop's attractions include rock candy, Gummi Bears, and malted milk balls. Chocolate bark with almonds could turn you into a steady customer, if the nonpareils haven't already done that. Popcorn aficionados have a quintet of choices, including cheddar and caramel. The candy and caramel apples are well worth the challenge posed to your teeth.

Dortoni Bakery, 3264 Hempstead Tpke., Levittown, NY 11756; (516) 796-3033; dortonibakery.com; Bakery. Dortoni is a master at theme and special-occasion cakes, hand-decorated cookies, and especially the full array of Italian pastries. This is the best local stop for cannoli, sfogliatelle, and company. Napoleons take a sweet Italianate turn here, too. The Black Forest cake and German chocolate cake also are notable, along with the fruit and Chantilly cream crostata. The specialty cakes come in as many designs as you can conjure, from boxing ring to Monopoly board, pyramid to law books, all carefully constructed and detailed. The sister bakery to Dortoni is La Bonne Boulangerie, with locations in East Norwich and Port Jefferson. But this branch has a more easygoing manner. And on the weekend, it draws a big crowd.

Front Street Bakery, 51 Front St., Rockville Centre, NY 11570; (516) 766-1199; frontstreetbakery.com; Bakery. More than 60 years of baking experience is well invested in Front Street, which has a very loyal following that goes beyond the neighborhood. It shows with the entertaining, colorful 3-D cakes shaped like a baseball cap or a teapot, an airplane or a shopping bag. But they're experts when it comes to crumb cake, the popular blackout cake, cheesecakes, and cannoli cake. There are plenty of layer cakes to take care of the sweetest tooth, plus fruit pies for the health-conscious. The black-and-whites and brownies increase the competition. And children usually receive a free cookie somewhere along the line. Speaking of lines, you may have to wait a while before either placing or picking up an order. But consider it time well spent. You may overhear conversations about what extra sweets should be purchased today to avoid a second trip tomorrow.

Iavarone Bros., 1166 Wantagh Ave., Wantagh, NY 11793; (516) 781-6400; ibfoods.com, Gourmet Market. With branches here as well as in Woodbury, Lake Success, and the original in Maspeth, Queens, Iavarone Bros. is an all-purpose market, with fresh fruits and vegetables, plus outstanding Italian specialties. In addition to the major deli counter and butcher shop, Iavarone has an excellent section of prepared foods, from sandwiches to the main course at tonight's dinner. Maybe pasta al forno, or ringlets of pasta in a savory meat sauced flecked with nubbins of carrot; salmon or crab cakes; or tender roast pork. Not that many establishments have caponata to go. The number of fresh and dry pastas, housemade or imported, is big and good. The cheese selection also is notable. You'll never be short of mozzarella, fresh or smoked. The bakery turns out some of the better Italian breads in Nassau and Suffolk, from seeded semolina to brick-oven "lard" bread studded with pork, and loaves loaded with olives. The pastry counter guarantees you're leaving with dessert. The cannoli and sfogliatelle are especially good, along with éclairs and fruit tarts.

Itgen's Ice Cream Parlour, 211 Rockaway Ave., Valley Stream, NY 11580; (516) 825-7444; Ice Cream. Walt Itgen's ice cream emporium has a 1950s quality, even though it opened in 1967. The effect is less "summer of love" than *Happy Days*. It's the land of sundaes in numerous permutations, borne on waves of hot fudge. And Itgen's is one of those places to which you instinctively gravitate once the weather warms. The Sock It to Me sundae, with 15 flavors, deserves to be shared. The Titanic threatens to sink you with a mere 8 flavors. Death by Chocolate pretty much tells you what it is in the title. So does the Banana Skyscraper. You won't go wrong with any selection. In 2012, *Saveur* discovered Itgen's and put it on the magazine's list of 100 favorite things. Yours may be either the strawberry or butterscotch sundae, the wonderful malteds and shakes, ice cream sodas, or the simple magic that comes with an extra scoop just when you need it. If you want something heartier, there's a full menu that includes hamburgers and breakfast items that would be the envy of your local diner.

Marvel Dairy Whip, 258 Lido Blvd., Lido Beach, NY 11561; (516) 889-4232; Ice Cream. In summer, you'll spot the line from almost any vantage point. For decades, Marvel has been a source of soft-serve ice cream and, more recently, frozen yogurt. Post-beach, it will remind you of an oasis near the sand. Soft-serve may prompt lengthy discussions about its provenance, texture, and degree of refreshment. But Marvel does shorten the chatter after a taste or two. Just keep licking. Vanilla, chocolate, strawberry, and especially coffee are the elemental flavors. Pistachio has its fans, too. Heretics may ask for sprinkles or crunchies, chocolate chips or cherries. The too-much-isn't-enough group may call for a brown bonnet or a swirl cone. But the unadorned soft-serve works like a time machine, evoking memories of warm, lazy days when the big decision was whether to unfold a beach chair, sprawl on a blanket, or be an activist and open the umbrella at noon or 1.

Riesterer's Bakery, 282 Hempstead Ave., West Hempstead, NY 11552; (516) 481-7636; riesterers.com; Bakery. August Riesterer, a German immigrant, opened his namesake bakery in 1931. It has been a family operation for succeeding generations, too. Riesterer's makes at least 75 types of cupcakes, and a major selection of big ones. Chocolate addicts will gravitate toward the point-blank blackout cake, the chocolate fudge devil's food cake; and a rich cake based on the classically chocolate Sacher torte that may not totally transport you to the grand hotel in Vienna but gets you near enough. They're equaled by a luscious Boston cream layer cake, red velvet cake, Grand Marnier cake, and tres leches cake. And you should at least have a slice of the house's cheesecake. The birthday and wedding cakes also stand out if you're thinking ahead. There's no table service, but you may have coffee and pastries on the premises.

Town of Oyster Bay

A two-and-one-half-ton bronze statue of Theodore Roosevelt, on horseback and in full Rough Rider regalia, welcomes visitors to downtown Oyster Bay.

The 26th president's home was in Oyster Bay from 1885 until his death in 1919. Sagamore Hill National Historic Site, which includes his Victorian house, is one of the town's major landmarks. And the triangle of land where TR's equestrian statue stands includes five trees, representing Oyster Bay residents who died in World War I. One is for Roosevelt's son, Quentin.

Oyster Bay was first mentioned as such in a diary that dates to 1639. Europeans arrived here in the 17th century. The bivalve lives on, in history, at table, and in Cole Porter lyrics. Native American Matinecocks first settled the region. For centuries, it was primarily an agricultural area.

Roosevelt, who was born in Manhattan, brought Oyster Bay new notoriety. Sagamore Hill was Roosevelt's summer White House. And his office during those years was on the northeast corner of South and Main Streets. Now, it's a restaurant.

In addition to downtown Oyster Bay itself, communities in the town that have notable restaurants include Bayville, Bethpage, East Norwich, Farmingdale, Glen Head, part of Greenvale, Hicksville, Jericho, Locust

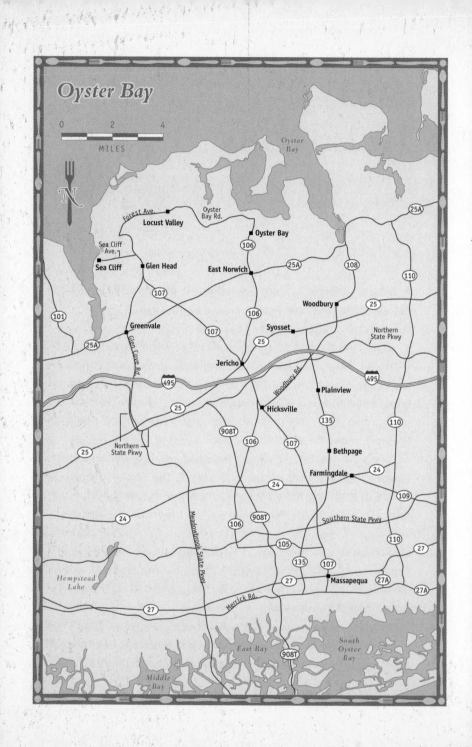

Valley, Massapequa, Massapequa Park, Plainview, Sea Cliff, Syosset, and Woodbury. There also are major food markets, gourmet shops, and bakeries.

Roosevelt, who loved to explore, would approve.

Foodie Faves

Allison's Amalfi, 400 Glen Cove Ave., Sea Cliff, NY 11579; (516) 656-4774; allisonsamalfi.com; Italian; $$–$$$. The sunny and dramatic Amalfi Coast is the inspiration for the hues of this colorful, welcoming Italian restaurant. Although the ambience isn't entirely transporting, Allison's Amalfi is a comfortable, local getaway with reliably good food. Air-cured beef, or *bresaola,* is a tasty beginning, finished with lemony dressing. Roasted peppers are a fine accompaniment. Clams oreganata and clams casino: standard. But there's fine *pasta e fagioli,* with tender beans; and warming *stracciatella alla Romana,* the spinach-egg drop soup. *Penne alla Allison* translates into chopped fresh tomatoes, garlic, and basil, though it's not as spicy as advertised. *Malloreddus alla Bolognese,* penne with four cheeses, and gnocchi in pesto are savory alternatives. Branzino in white wine sauce, tinted with tomato and bolstered by mussels and clams, is a please-all course. Best, however, is orata, similar to snapper, sautéed with fennel and Pernod for a hint of the French Riviera. Lobster oreganata and fra diavolo arrive moist and good. The carnivorous should sample chicken with rosemary sauce.

Arata Sushi, 18 Cold Spring Rd., Syosset, NY 11791; (516) 921-8154; Japanese, Sushi; $$–$$$. Arata Sushi moved into the address Tsubo occupied for many years, transforming the dining room and the cuisine. Chef Jimmy Lian's creative sushi puts this restaurant near the top of Japanese spots on Long Island. His Maguro Invictus with wasabi and daikon dressing makes you taste the red tuna in a new way; his Invincible Sandwich does the same for salmon. The best way to eat at Arata is simply to go with the chef's choice menus, Lian's picks of what's fresh and what he's got in mind for it. Salsa verde all of a sudden makes sense with tuna; Maui onion salsa tastes right complementing fluke. An order of 10 pieces is about right, and so vivid that you might skip anything before or after. While the uncooked and barely cooked fish are the primary reasons to put Arata on your map, the restaurant does nearly as well with leek-and-potato soup and delicately steamed shumai shrimp dumplings. Desserts rarely matter in Japanese restaurants, especially after one too many scoops of red bean or ginger ice cream. But the caramelized banana with pecans offered here could change your mind.

Barney's, 315 Buckram Rd., Locust Valley, NY 11560; (516) 671-6300; barneyslv.com; New American; $$$. The great belt of the namesake Barney Burnett extends about 7 feet. He was a fireman, owned a hotel and bar, and apparently had a very large appetite. The building that houses the restaurant is late 19th century; the restaurant that occupies it now, clearly 21st. It's a cozy, New England–style spot, fireplace ready. Sample the plump crab cakes, served on baby greens and accented with lemon-caper mayonnaise; or the tuna tartare, accented with a mango-and-red-chile emulsion; the arugula salad with feta cheese, tomatoes, olives, and cucumber; ricotta gnocchi with broccoli rabe, pancetta, and Parmesan cream; or the seared diver scallops with braised bok choy and a saffron-tinted sauce. Duck two ways, with confit of leg and seared breast; roasted rack of lamb, with an herbaceous crust and compote of leeks, mushrooms, and artichoke; and teriyaki-roasted salmon with black lentils are worthwhile main courses. Fruit tarts, gelati, and cheeses provide happy endings.

The Basil Leaf Cafe Ristorante, 7b The Plaza (Birch Hill Road), Locust Valley, NY 11560; (516) 676-6252; thebasilleafrestaurant .com; Italian; $$$. In its long history at this address, Basil Leaf has grown in many directions. It finally has taken root in Italian cuisine with a light touch. And service has gotten better over the years, with a more accommodating dining room staff. The restaurant is located a bit south of the railroad tracks. It almost looks like two restaurants, the casual and the more formal, separated by a walkway. The informal venue with the bar seems a magnet for area residents; the other, a destination for diners from all points. Grilled octopus with white beans and baked clams oreganata are familiar and flavorful ways to start your meal. So are the individual pizzas. Pizza piccante, driven by spicy sausage, deserves its name. A ragu of sausage and porcini mushrooms emboldens a platter of pappardelle. Grilled lamb chops, pink and amply herbed, are very good. Branzino, the ever-present and versatile fish, favorably makes its entrance here on escarole. For dessert: crème brûlée and chilled zabaglione with berries.

Ben's Kosher Delicatessen, 7971 Jericho Tpke., Woodbury, NY 11797; (516) 496-4236; bensdeli.net; Delicatessen; $–$$. This is the newest of the Nassau Ben's, spacious and well designed. The menus are identical. Please see the listing in the North Hempstead chapter.

Big Daddy's, 1 Park Lane, Massapequa, NY 11758; (516) 799-8877; bigdaddysny.com; Cajun, Creole, Southern; $$. It's always Mardi Gras at Big Daddy's, a New Orleans festival on a plate. The corner establishment off a main road is festooned with Big Easy images. Wear your beads and fit in. The best advice is to order the day's specials, which are many. Broiled Blue Point oysters are very good; so are "ghost wings," chicken wings ignited with an incendiary pepper. The gumbos are outstanding, from andouille sausage and smoked pork to tasso ham and chicken. The smoked prime rib and "ragin' Cajun" spicy lobster should be regulars. Gutsy Creole jambalaya is seasoned with authenticity, as are the blackened catfish and chicken-fried steak. Barbecued chicken also is recommended. Same for pulled pork and smoked beef brisket, a Muffuletta that's a long-distance visit to Central Grocery, Lady Day crab cakes spiced with care, and chicken Metairie, which means the tasty company of andouille sausage and jalapeño cornbread dressing. Anyone finding all this too exotic can be contented with the Caesar salad, raw oysters, shrimp cocktail, or chicken wings with mango-chipotle-pepper barbecue sauce. Drink beer.

Blue Fish, 828 S. Oyster Bay Rd., Hicksville, NY 11801; (516) 605-0655; bluefishjapanese.com; Japanese, Sushi; $$–$$$. This must be among the least likely locations for a major Japanese restaurant. From the road, it looks like an attachment to a motel. But once inside, you're in for a barrage of color, in the appointments and on the plate. There's a blue room and a red one, a backlit onyx bar, and enough frou-frou for a movie set. The show starts with a 5-piece sushi sampler that suggests a city skyline, each fish with a different topping. The now-familiar union of yellowtail and jalapeño almost tastes new. Peppery tuna tataki also goes beyond the usual, with definite spark. Refresh yourself with seaweed salad and then proceed to ornate sushi rolls with names such as Fallen Angel, Komodo Dragon, Scorpion, and the obligatory Sexy on the Beach. They're all good. Blue Fish prepares the basic tempuras and teriyakis and lights up the hibachi grill, too. But they're sideshows. Instead, pick the crisp tuna dumplings and the tuna-topped pizza. Crisp duck fajitas work their way into the proceedings, too. Still, the elemental, glistening nigirizushi has more allure.

The Brass Rail, 107 Forest Ave., Locust Valley, NY 11560; (516) 723-9103; thebrassraillocustvalley.com; New American, Gastropub; $$. What had been the more formal Heirloom was gingerly and successfully transformed into this first-class gastropub. The eye-catching look remains, especially with the grand bar that dates to the 1880s. Kent Monkan's approach is easygoing. Easily recommended are the grilled pork chop with cherry peppers, vinegar sauce, mashed potatoes, and escarole and the tuna steak au poivre, with a biting peppercorn crust, tomatoes, and onions. The sirloin burger au poivre rivals them. And this is a spot where you may contentedly order a Cuban sandwich with pork loin, ham, pickles, and mustard on a baguette, or fish-and-chips made with cod and finished with shoestring fries. Tuna tartare, fried oysters, lobster dumplings, and  the shrimp-and-oyster po' boy add to the fine choices. The seared Long Island duck breast materializes rosy and flavorful, with sweet-potato gnocchi, broccoli rabe, and a diverting vanilla-citrus reduction. Mascarpone cheesecake, profiteroles with chocolate sauce, and Key lime pie highlight the desserts.

Brasserie Cassis, 387 S. Oyster Bay Rd., Plainview, NY 11803; (516) 653-0090; brasseriecassis.com; French, New American; $$–$$$. The brassiest member of the Bistro Cassis group, Brasserie Cassis definitely looks the part. The playful, antique-filled establishment manages to evoke some authenticity in a shopping-center location. There's ample buzz. And the beverages flow. To accompany yours, start with raw oysters or littleneck clams, a shrimp cocktail, onion soup gratinée, sautéed frogs' legs with garlic and butter, or the frisée salad with bacon and a poached egg. The crab-and-endive salad also is good. Specials change daily. On Tuesday: coq au vin. On Thursday: duck a l'orange. Other times, consider the roasted chicken for two with french fries and vegetables; sirloin steak frites; steak au poivre; grilled hanger steak with spinach and fingerling potatoes; trout amandine; or mussels, prepared mariniere, Provençal with tomato, garlic, and basil, or with Pernod and cream. If you're in the mood to cross borders, or at least be near Basque country, Brasserie Cassis makes respectable paella with shrimp, squid, mussels, chicken, and chorizo.

Cafe Testarossa, 499 Jericho Tpke., Syosset, NY 11791; (516) 364-8877; cafetestarossa.com; New American, Italian; $$–$$$. When Cafe Testarossa careened onto Jericho Turnpike years ago, the decor included an oversize image of the namesake Ferrari in vivid red shooting across the main dining room wall. Things have calmed down a lot since that early *vroom vroom*. For a while, it was as if speed bumps were added. But the cafe has settled comfortably into a style that combines the original Italianate with New American. Consider the pan-seared sea scallops matched with a sweet-corn risotto, or the veal meatball sliders. Recall the old days with a tender osso buco on risotto seasoned with sage, and the mezze-rigatoni with a savory Bolognese sauce, peas, and a dollop of ricotta. A light horseradish crust boosts seared grouper, which is gilded with sautéed spinach and lobster-enriched polenta. Tuna tartare, shiny with ginger-lime vinaigrette, and the poached-pear-and-red-beet salad are worthwhile starters. The cafe prepares good little pizzas, headed by a 3-cheese, roasted garlic, and sun-dried tomato number. The pear, raisin, and strawberry cobbler, with vanilla ice cream, now suits the place.

Chennai Dosas, 128 S. Broadway, Hicksville, NY 11801; (516) 681-5151; chennaidosasny.com; Indian; $–$$. The savory vegetarian cuisine of southern India defines Chennai Dosas, a modest restaurant with a grand appetite. Spices and fillings turn the house's crepes and doughnuts into little stars, elevating the lentil to headliner status. The dosas arrive as long and cylindrical vehicles for potatoes, onions, cheese, lentils, and more. They're uniformly delicious. But before nibbling on one, start with *rasam*, a zesty tamarind-lentil soup, or a fired-up mulligatawny soup. *Uthappam* also are delectable: lentil pancakes, some seasoned with cilantro, others holding cheese. Chennai Dosas' dishes may at first seem a bit monotonous, but they're deftly made variations on a theme. In addition to the southern Indian fare, the kitchen does a good job with the curries of northern India and juices up any dish with coconut chutney and spicy lentil broth. The breads to accompany the curries and other choices include puffy poori with spicy chickpeas and others packed with potatoes or cauliflower. A mango or lychee shake both refreshes and acts as a dessert.

Chichimecas, 169 Main St., Farmingdale, NY 11735; chichimecas restaurant.com; Mexican; $$. The scion of Oaxaca and Quetzalcoatl in Huntington, bright and casual Chichimecas takes some of each and adds smoke, as in smoked barbecue. The smoked chicken is juicy and good, as are the mesquite-smoked pork ribs, pork chops, pulled pork, and spicy pulled pork. Before you get to those, have choriqueso, or chorizo, jalapeños, refried beans, pico de gallo, and either beef, chicken, or pork. Sautéed shrimp with peppers and tequila sauce, cheese-and-chicken quesadillas, and housemade guacamole also are recommended. Savory black bean soup, tortilla soup, and pozole with a tostada on the side are fine year-round; gazpacho, a summer refresher. Arroz con pollo, carne asada, chicken chimichangas, mole chicken enchiladas, and *pepian de porco,* or pork cooked in pumpkin-seed sauce, are hearty and welcome choices, along with pork tamales and soft-corn tortillas with grilled chicken or chorizo. The fried ripe plantain, rice pudding, flan, and tres leches cake all are fine.

CoolFish Grille & Wine Bar, 6800 Jericho Tpke., Syosset, NY 11791; (516) 921-3250; tomschaudel.com; New American; $$–$$$. Although it's buried in a windowless space, CoolFish sees the light. It's popular for business lunches, but just as inviting for social dinners. Notable dishes include the pulled-pork quesadilla, yellowfin tuna tartare, grilled octopus with black bean vinaigrette, crisp duck tacos, and the roasted-beet-and-goat-cheese salad. Well-made flatbreads, topped with goat cheese or taleggio cheese, should be shared by the table. CoolFish is equally at ease with steaks, sirloin to filet mignon to rib eye. The marinated hanger steak, however, is the one to remember, full-flavored and juicy. The cinnamon-chipotle-pepper-marinated, double-cut pork chop also is excellent, flanked by whipped sweet potatoes and apple compote. The 2-pound "lobster boil" is a match for any steak. There are several significant sweets. But you should focus on the "chocolate bag," an irresistible construct that updates the sundae just enough.

Diwan, 415 S. Broadway, Hicksville, NY 11801; (516) 513-1057; Indian; $$. Diwan is the right spot to be introduced to Indian cuisine, and veterans of the Indian kitchen will be satisfied, too. Better appetizers include samosas, the pastry pyramids filled with potatoes and peas; pakoras, or vegetable fritters; and aloo tikka chaat, potato cakes with chickpeas. The clay oven, or tandoor, sends out moist, smoky yogurt-marinated chicken, tender tiger prawns seasoned with ginger, salmon with yellow chiles, and tender lamb chops. For some heat, sample the vinegary chicken, lamb, or goat vindaloo. Rogan josh, the crimson curry, is excellent, with either lamb or goat. Tomatoes, onions, and bell peppers boost the chicken tikka masala; spinach, ginger, and tomatoes do the same for chicken tikka saagwala. Vegetable curries of note: chole Peshawari with chickpeas and potatoes; aloo Gobi with potatoes and cauliflower; and bhindi masala with crisp okra, onions, tomatoes, and cilantro. The Diwan bread basket sampler includes naan, onion kulcha, and parantha. The garlic naan and mint paratha also are well made.

Fanatico, 336 N. Broadway, Jericho, NY 11753; (516) 932-5080; fanatico-restaurant.com; Italian; $$. Fanatico is the Nassau counterpart to Emilio's in Commack. They're both very good, casual

Italian restaurants with super pizzas. Try the Grandpa pie: a thick-crust Sicilian pie with mozzarella, red onion, marinara sauce, and a snowfall of crunchy, seasoned bread crumbs. The basic pizza Margherita is exactly what you want in this pie, then gilded with some prosciutto di Parma. Ham-and-cheese calzones are first-class, too. The Old School spaghetti and meatballs, rigatoni alla Bolognese, rigatoni Calabrese, baked manicotti, lasagna, baked ziti, and linguine with baby clams head the pastas. To get into the rhythm of the place immediately, try the Mamma Mia meatball appetizer with ricotta, the crisp and savory rice balls, and the fresh mozzarella starters. Midday, they make panini, wraps, and salads. If you're up for something that's not pizzeria fare, the red snapper alla Livornese is a savory option. The chicken scarpariello with sausage also falls into that category. When the weather warms, conclude your meal with gelati and ices.

Franina, 58 W. Jericho Tpke., Syosset, NY 11791; (516) 496-9770; franina.com; Italian; $$–$$$. It's easy to drive by Franina, on the busy south side of the turnpike. Once you're inside, everything changes. The look is traditional continental/Italian, with considerable charm. Moreover, the staff is attentive. And the food often is very good. Good openers included the splashy seafood salad, grilled octopus with white beans and a drizzle of olive oil, and baked Blue Point oysters. Ravioli are complemented with a walnut-and-Parmesan cheese sauce; cannelloni, with a caponata and tomato-basil sauce. Pappardelle Bolognese is an ample, savory version. Continue the northern route with a refined osso buco alla Milanese, which here means the company of butternut squash risotto. Herb-crusted rack of lamb with a ragout of lentils and the grilled, double-cut Berkshire pork chop with vinegar peppers and caper sauce are generous and full-flavored. Wild striped bass swims in via a slightly spicy tomato broth. End with frothy zabaglione with seasonal berries, mascarpone-rich cheesecake, and an apple tart with vanilla gelato.

Frank's Steaks, 4 Jericho Tpke., Jericho, NY 11753; (516) 338-4595; frankssteaks.com; Steak, American; $$–$$$. The original Frank's Steaks is tucked into a small shopping center that at first seems an unlikely site. But Frank's is a populist kind of steak house, defined neither by brusque waiters nor ridiculous prices. It's unpretentious, generous, and very good for the whole family. The menu is similar to the Frank's Steaks in Rockville Centre. The marinated Romanian steak remains the restaurant's signature cut, well seasoned, tender, and packed with flavor. The broiled filet mignon is a fine, straightforward alternative, enriched with béarnaise sauce. New Zealand rack of lamb, spiked with thyme and rosemary, also is very good. Frank's roasts a tender English-cut prime rib and offers a juicy New York strip steak capped with melted stilton cheese. The more-modest main dishes are a tasty meat loaf platter and sautéed calf's liver with bacon. The whole roast chicken heads the alternatives. Before cutting into the red meat, try the crab cake, onion soup, or a salad, Gorgonzola bread on the side. Cheesecake, rice pudding, and apple cobbler a la mode key the desserts.

Ginza, 45 Carmans Rd., Massapequa, NY 11758; (516) 882-9688; ginzali.com; Japanese, Sushi; $$–$$$. Ginza rises on a grand scale to match the ambition of its sushi bar. It's a monument to raw fish, situated near a big mall and not far from fast food joints, and, accordingly, has a mirage quality. But the first taste of the exceptional sushi brings you to reality. The sushi includes fish flown in from the Tsukiji market in Tokyo. They make elaborate sushi rolls here. And you can march westward with rack of lamb or Kobe-beef meatballs. But the extraordinary quality of several types of tuna, sweet shrimp, and yellowtail dwarfs the rest. The key to appreciating Ginza is to let the sushi chefs make the important decisions and just enjoy the results. The restaurant itself is a production number with appointments that shimmer. An oversize photo of Tokyo's Ginza district adds to the imagery. There are model warriors on display to suggest the terracotta armies of Xian, too. Even the seating in the bar near the entrance is unusual, sort of *Jetsons* by way of *2001: A Space Odyssey*. Nothing about Ginza is unadorned—except the lustrous seafood.

Heirloom Tavern, 32 Railroad Ave., Glen Head, NY 11545; (516) 686-6633; heirloomtavern.com; New American, Gastropub; $$–$$$. If you're in the vicinity of the Glen Head railroad station, make Heirloom Tavern your stop. Kent Monkan's classic gastropub, related to his other, The Brass Rail in Locust Valley, has excellent food, much variety, and the right sense of what you want to eat today. The joint draws a crowd for beers on tap, cocktails, and wines. And it is a comfortable local hangout, even if the seating is tight and the noise level rapidly rising. The staff knows how to navigate narrow channels and you'll learn the route, too. The eclecticism in the kitchen takes in steak au poivre and a meatball hero; pastas Bolognese and carbonara, the latter gilded with lobster; and array of small plates that ensure plenty of imbibing. Nutty bay scallops receive the tempura treatment and come through both crunchy and sweet, awaiting a dip in spicy aioli. For a bigger plate, there's the generous Berkshire pork chop, accented with sherry vinegar for a touch of sweet-tart flavor. Gelati and cheesecake are first-class. But the big dessert is the flourless chocolate cake.

House of Dosas, 416 S. Broadway, Hicksville, NY 11801; (516) 938-7517; houseofdosas.com; Indian; $$. House of Dosas stars with the vegetarian cooking of southern India. And if you have one meal among Hicksville's Indian restaurants, this casual, straightforward kitchen should be where it's prepared. The 50-seater opened in 1999. The dosas, or fragile and crisp rice crepes, are delicious, filled with seasoned potatoes, onions, cheese, and spices. The selection is broad enough so diners won't have too much overlap. *Uthappam,* or rice and lentil flour pancakes, also are easily recommended. Curries: terrific, especially potato-and-cauliflower, eggplant, and spinach productions. Begin with pakoras, or chickpea fritters; dumplings; or puffed-rice bhel puri. Traditional sweets such as rasmalai, gulab jamun, and carrot halwa are as well made as everything else.

J. Michaels Tuscan Steakhouse, 160 Mill River Rd., Oyster Bay, NY 11771; (516) 628-2800; jmichaelstuscansteakhouse.com; Steak, Italian; $$$–$$$$. The second J. Michaels is just as ambitious as the first. This is an excellent steakhouse, situated in the former site of Serata and the Mill River Inn. And it is a destination restaurant, skillfully retooled and refurbished. The outstanding steaks include an epic tomahawk rib eye for two, bone-in filet mignon, Kansas City cut, T-bone, and porterhouse. The whole branzino, 2 pounds' worth, is a meaty main dish, too; and pan-seared scallops in a sun-dried-tomato beurre blanc are nutty, sweet, and superb. Top appetizers include savory lobster meatballs in a delicious marinara sauce, baked crabmeat-stuffed prawns, shellfish cocktails, raw oysters, and salads. As in Northport, the desserts are first-class, reflecting Vincent P. Michaels' expertise. Cheesecake, chocolate mousse pie, white-chocolate mousse flavored with Frangelico, and double-ganache rainbow cookies are highlights.

Jack Halyards American Bar & Grill, 62 South St., Oyster Bay, NY 11771; (516) 922-2999; jackhalyards.com; New American; $$–$$$. Jack Halyards is in its second life at the ex-address of Fiddleheads seafood house. The focus is on more creative, New

American cooking, and the style is looser, seasoned with some whimsy. That alone makes it rare in downtown Oyster Bay. The plump crab cake is revved up with a sauce remoulade that has a hint of smoked onion; the nachos are enriched with ahi tuna, guacamole, and pineapple–red onion salsa. Avocado relish adds some snap to grilled swordfish. And a mushroom risotto that any Italian restaurant would be glad to offer becomes the accompaniment for the crisp-skinned pork shank. Homey American fare is represented with a bracing shepherd's pie made with beef and lamb, under a creamy coverlet of mashed potatoes. There are a few tasty desserts, but the one that gets your attention is a visual tour-de-force that looks like a meat loaf with mashed potatoes, peas, and carrots. It stars banana bread pudding, vanilla ice cream, and a mincing of kiwi and cantaloupe. More important, it tastes very good.

Luce, 1053 Oyster Bay Rd., East Norwich, NY 11732; (516) 624-8330; luce-ristorante.com; Italian; $$–$$$. This summery, sunlit space used to host Cafe Girasole and, many years ago, the Black Walnut. If Luce isn't as warm as its predecessors, it's frequently as good, with an emphasis on familiar Italian cooking. They prepare a tasty cavatelli alla Bolognese, vegetable ravioli with fresh tomato and pesto sauce, and the leaf-shaped pasta called strascinate with tomatoes, garlic, and ricotta. Rigatoni alla Norma, with roasted baby eggplant, ricotta, and plum tomatoes is more than their equal. Precede these with a refreshing seafood salad, full of shrimp, squid, and octopus. And follow with the grilled branzino, finished with herbs, olive oil, and lemon juice, and accompanied by baby arugula. Potato-crusted halibut with caramelized onions and baby broccoli gets some verve from a balsamic-vinegar reduction; the pepper-crusted ahi tuna, from cucumber, red onion, and dill sauce. Lobster sauce is the foil for crabmeat-crusted grouper. If you're not set for seafood, try the roast duck breast with orange sauce or the double-cut pork chop with caramelized cipollini onions and butternut squash.

Luigi Q, 400 S. Oyster Bay Rd., Hicksville, NY 11801; (516) 932-7450; Italian; $$$. Luigi Q is defined by its owner, Luigi Quarta. He oversees the kitchen and the dining room, and is the embodiment of hands-on management. And the results are exceptional. From the outside, Luigi Q just fits into this commercial stretch as any other restaurant would. To look at the menu, you'd think it's one in a series of traditional Italian spots. But Quarta's daily specials make Luigi Q a destination for anyone seeking meticulously prepared Italian dishes. Once, it might be a perfectly roasted quail, nesting on risotto that has a hint of truffle. Maybe loin of venison in a bracing, slightly sweet red-wine sauce; tender wild boar chops with chard; rabbit paired with polenta flavored with Gorgonzola cheese; a refreshing salad of lemon-and-olive-oil-dressed cuttlefish; or snowy cod alla Livornese. The pastas may take in paccheri, similar to oversize rigatoni, stuffed with shrimp, in a vibrant tomato sauce. Take your host's recommendation for wines, too. Tiramisu tastes new and cheesecake delectably old-fashioned. And the house's biscotti are superior with Vin Santo. A little grappa completes the experience.

Mara's Homemade, 236 W. Jericho Tpke. (Muttontown Plaza), Syosset, NY 11791; (516) 682-9200; marashomemade.com; Cajun, Southern, American; $$. Mara's moved to Syosset from Manhattan, bringing big flavors with it. Informal, spirited, and invariably good, Mara's Homemade is where you'll find a savory crawfish boil and an oyster po' boy, 'gator bites with remoulade sauce, hush puppies with flair, blackened redfish, and a lobster roll. Mara's also prepares a zesty jambalaya, the delectable Creole rice dish, and addictive Arkansas barbecue, especially chopped brisket and pulled pork. The tour continues with southern fried chicken and chicken-fried steak, delicately simmered crawfish étouffée, and

THE BIG DUCK

Long Island's contribution to roadside architecture is situated in Flanders, at Reeves Bay. It immortalizes the white Pekin, also known as Long Island duckling. Some restaurants give the mascot what it's due.

Chachama Grill in East Patchogue: Barbecued duck empanadas with white-bean salsa, daikon sprouts, and romesco sauce is featured on "Latin night."

Lola in Great Neck: Smoked duck breast and duck prosciutto join Gorgonzola, scallions, and fig jam for a "pizza tart."

Mirabelle Restaurant and Tavern in Stony Brook: A 2-course duck production, with seared duck breast and confit of duck leg, is offered. (Please see the recipe for **The Duck Mirabelle** on p. 341.)

Monsoon in Babylon: An outstanding version of Beijing duck is featured, with tender meat and parchment skin.

Orto in Miller Place: Sautéed duck in farro, with cherry agro-dolce, may be a special.

Topping Rose House in Bridgehampton: Roast Rohan duck is paired with spigarello, a wavy-leaf broccoli from southern Italy.

tender baby back ribs. Rainbow trout amandine and smoked duck add to the party, too. For the still uncommitted, Mara's has hamburgers and hot dogs. But stick with the specialties and you'll be rewarded. And be sure to order the chocolate cream pie. Mara's Too, a tasty offshoot, is at 3261 Merrick Rd., Wantagh; (516) 785-5300.

Market Bistro, 519 N. Broadway, Jericho, NY 11753; (516) 513-1487; marketbistroli.com; New American; $$–$$$. The shopping-center location masks a dining room that would be at home in the upscale quarters of an urban downtown. It has a buzz. As you'd expect, much of the food is seasonal. Local sea scallops find a partner with wild mushroom risotto; skillet-roasted chicken has its foil in spaetzle. Spinach-and-ricotta ravioli also are commendable. The lamb sliders are jump-started with harissa-spiked aioli and calmed down with chickpea salad. The pan-seared sirloin steak arrives with good fries. The well-made meat loaf calls for an extra scoop of mashed potatoes. The house's obligatory burger appears to be everyone's second choice. Appetizers include flatbreads with toppings such as duck liver mousse, roasted fennel, and tomatoes. And Market Bistro may be the lone restaurant around here where "market pickles" are an opener.

Mill Creek Tavern, 275 Bayville Ave., Bayville, NY 11709; (516) 628-2000; millcreekny.com; New American; $$. Bayville is a cozy community on the water with plenty of bungalows that have been turned into year-round residences. Mill Creek Tavern fits in as a local hangout with good American and New American dishes, and a welcoming way about it. The restaurant is suitable for all members of the family, too. Bacon-cheeseburger sliders with cheddar vie with an assortment of mussel pots, a shrimp BLT wrap, and chopped cobb salad for an eclectic approach. The mussels are commendable, whether prepared with white wine, fra diavolo, or with Belgian wheat beer. For huskier appetites: braised pork osso buco with Parmesan cheese–infused risotto and pine-nut gremolata, the 16-ounce sirloin steak, the rib eye steak, very tender filet mignon, and chicken alla parmigiana. Mill Creek is associated with Mim's, the casual restaurants in Syosset and Roslyn Heights. The Mim's meat loaf makes the transition to these quarters, too, with onions, potatoes, and gravy. The seafood potpie, seasoned with thyme, heads the seafood selections, followed by lemon sole oreganata.

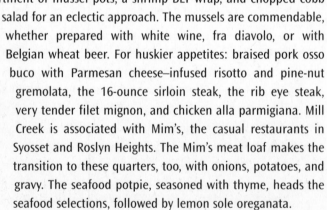

Mio Posto, 600 W. Old Country Rd., Hicksville, NY 11801; (516) 605-2365; mioposto-ny.com; Italian; $$–$$$. Innumerable squid meet their fate at Mio Posto. And if there's a mozzarella shortage on Long Island, this restaurant may be to blame. Hicksville's Mio Posto is the offspring of the Oceanside original and its equal in devotion to Italian-American cooking. The house's "Sunday Sauce" is a mega-plate of braciola, sausage, and meatballs in tomato sauce that's ready for pasta. Lobster fra diavolo, spiced to high levels if desired, also is reason to come here. Be sure to have a side or order of well-oiled and garlicky escarole or broccoli rabe, particularly if you're intent on cutting into the hefty, dry-aged sirloin steak. Of course, the kitchen is adept at all things parmigiana, especially the eggplant and the chicken versions. And the serving of pork chops with peppers, onions, and roasted potatoes understandably feeds two. The pastas are best when they go to Rome and points south. Rigatoni all'Amatriciana and linguine with clam sauce, red or white, are good selections. Cannoli are ahead of the other desserts.

Morrison's, 430 Woodbury Rd., Plainview, NY 11803; (516) 932-8640; New American; $$–$$$. Morrison's, a busy gastropub, enlivens dining out along this patch of Woodbury Road. The style is casual and the results are good, from the beer selection to the menu. Very good sandwiches include the pastrami Reuben on marble rye and the pan-fried, grilled-cheese number with chèvre, Muenster, and smoked bacon on slightly sweet milk bread. The kitchen also makes satisfying shrimp and grits and an assertively spiced jambalaya, balanced with plantains. There are specials each day. On Wednesday, that means fried chicken and waffles, so mark the calendar. Morrison's sends out a husky burger with sweet-onion marmalade, fried pickles, and a "fairground" hot dog, which will ensure you sample one of the craft beers. The desserts continue the sudsy theme with a Guinness stout float. You might go for the lemonade pie or, if available, a pie imported from Briermere Farms.

Nagashima, 12 Jericho Tpke., Jericho, NY 11753; (516) 338-0022; nagashimali.com; Japanese, Sushi; $$–$$$. Calm and businesslike, Nagashima almost seems retro compared with the temples of sushi that have been built in recent years. And it's a very good spot for a business lunch. Families and couples arrive later. Pan-fried pork gyoza dumplings and steamed seafood-and-vegetable shumai dumplings are pretty good. But shrimp-and-vegetable tempura, fried chicken, and beef negimaki have more to them. Steamed salmon with vegetables is the risk-averse diner's choice. Instead, try the lobster tempura, miso black cod, tuna or yellowtail jalapeño, and the grilled yellowtail collar. Sushi and sashimi samplers are carefully put together, but you should order your fish by the piece. Recommended: tuna, yellowtail, Spanish mackerel, fluke, jumbo sweet shrimp, eel, red clam, salmon roe, and, if available, toro. The house's sushi rolls feature yellowtail-scallion, salmon-cucumber, and eel-avocado pairings. Udon and soba noodle soups also are notable here.

The Orient, 623 Hicksville Rd., Bethpage, NY 11714; (516) 822-1010; theorientonline.com; Chinese; $$. The appeal of The Orient rises dramatically if you're known by the owner and the staff. When that happens, dishes other diners haven't heard about make their magical appearances and this becomes the finest Chinese restaurant in either Nassau or Suffolk. Otherwise, it can be a chaotic, overcrowded, wait-in-line experience marked by erratic service, and good but not great fare. That said, you still should go for the weekend dim sum. Pick the roasted pork bun, pan-fried leek dumpling, or whatever suits you. And at other visits, remember specials such as crunchy fried chicken with roasted garlic, crisp shrimp with walnuts and mayonnaise sauce, cubed flounder with yellow leeks, steamed sea bass with ginger and scallions, and the crisp fried flounder. Better items from the standard menu include cold noodles with sesame sauce, tangerine chicken, Hunan beef, shredded pork with Chinese eggplant, pork chop with chiles and spiced salt, shrimp with lobster sauce, oysters with ginger and scallions, and clams in black bean sauce.

Rare650, 650 Jericho Tpke., Syosset, NY 11791; (516) 496-8000; rare650.com; Steak, Seafood; $$$–$$$$. Rare650 is an Anthony Scotto production in the extravagant tradition of Blackstone Steakhouse in Melville and Insignia in Smithtown. The quality is very high and so are the prices. Rare650, formerly Sagamore Steakhouse, has a bold, multilevel design and enough noise to reach every nook. But the main dining area is conducive to conversation. Wherever you sit, sample the shellfish cocktails, either lobster, crab, or shrimp, and consider the mini-burger flight, with Asian spicing such as wasabi-ginger mayonnaise. The smoked-salmon BLT, with applewood-smoked bacon and goat cheese, is good, too. All the steaks are excellent, especially the porterhouse for two, three, or four; the New York strip; and the filet mignon. Rare650 also stars with major lamb chops. Whole fish, from Dover sole to branzino, are flawlessly prepared and they do a good job on the grilled salmon, too. In addition to the cooked, the chefs know how to fashion the raw, with deftly crafted sushi rolls and nigirizushi, fatty tuna to sea urchin. Profiteroles, cheesecake, and the appropriately extreme "chocolate wow" are the coda.

Red Tomato Artisanal Pizza, 6245 Northern Blvd., East Norwich, NY 11732; (516) 802-2840; redtomatopizza.com; Pizza; $–$$. In a strip where La Bonne Boulangerie and Messina Market are among its neighbors, Red Tomato ripens accordingly. The pizzas are very good and come in styles classic and whimsical. Yes, there's an excellent Margherita. But stop in for the Positano, with sun-dried tomatoes, mozzarella, and pesto; the four seasons, with prosciutto cotto, olives, mushrooms, and artichokes; and the Napoletana, with ricotta, smoked mozzarella, fennel sausage, and broccoli rabe. Consider the puttanesca, with tomatoes, fresh mozzarella, cracked olives, and capers. The parmigiana: fresh mozzarella, "savory Neapolitan sauce," roasted eggplant, and, naturally, Parmesan cheese. The white clam pizza will have ardent advocates and fired-up foes; ditto the macaroni-and-cheese pizza, with American cheese. But the one sure to elicit the biggest reaction has to be the "ballpark pizza." To complement the fresh mozzarella: Hebrew National hot dogs.

Rothmann's Steakhouse, 6319 Northern Blvd., East Norwich, NY 11732; (516) 922-2500; rothmannssteakhouse.com; Steak, American; $$$. The Rothmann's name has been associated with this site for decades. Even when it was Burt Bacharach's, locals referred to it by the old name. The name now applies to a good and often better steak house, known for its lively socializing and dependably flavorful red meat. The look is clubby, but not overly so. And the service is both knowledgeable and attentive. At table, the Maryland crab cake with chipotle-pepper aioli and the grilled octopus with white beans and tomatoes are adroitly prepared openers. Yellowfin tuna tartare and the tuna taco with chile-spiked aioli rival them. You can continue the tuna theme with sesame-crusted ahi tuna, flanked by Thai-peanut soba noodles and bok choy. But Rothmann's really gets going with the porterhouse, strip steak, rib eye, and filet mignon, prepared as ordered. The Chas. Burger, as in Chas. Rothmann's, is a more modest way to enjoy the beef here. The steaks receive strong competition from sizable Maine lobsters, 2 to 4 pounds and professionally steamed. On the side: sautéed onions, creamed spinach, hash browns, potato croquettes.

Sergio's, 5422 Merrick Rd., Massapequa, NY 11758; (516) 541-6554; sergiositalianrestaurant.com; Italian; $$–$$$. Sergio's is closing in on 30 years as a neighborhood favorite. Notices about local events seem like part of the decor. It's an old-fashioned spot where the emphasis is on southern Italian and Italian-American specialties. Perciatelli with sardines and fennel, a homey version of the Sicilian specialty, is an essential choice. The kitchen prepares very good spaghetti with olive oil and garlic, lasagna, stuffed shells, and baked ziti. Begin with a fat stuffed artichoke, baked clams oreganata, or eggplant rollatine. The Sicilian salad of sliced oranges is a refreshing opener or intermezzo, too. Beef braciola with rigatoni, tripe marinara, the combo of sausages and meatballs, and eggplant parmigiana top the main courses. You'll do well with chicken alla cacciatore, pork chops or steak alla pizzaiola, pork chops with vinegar peppers, broiled red snapper, broiled striped bass, and lobster fra diavolo. The top desserts are freshly filled cannoli and Italian-style cheesecake.

Wansuapona Musu, 304 Sea Cliff Ave., Sea Cliff, NY 11579; (516) 671-2493; wansuaponamusu.com; Japanese, Sushi; $$–$$$.
The unusual name is a spin on that of the restaurant that previously occupied the stylish corner space, Once Upon a Moose. Musu has a vaguely SoHo look, suitably distressed and reflecting the urban archaeology mix of images and textures. More important, however, Musu is a very good spot for sushi, creative and traditional. The nouveau Japanese approach is an echo of Nobu, picking and choosing from other cuisines. The fluke tiradito suggests Peru, with a zesty update of ceviche. Fried plantain brings a tropical touch to what's dubbed Asian guacamole, with peanuts and ginger. Miso black cod, fried pork dumplings, and steamed shrimp shumai also are fine, as is the tuna pizza with sun-dried tomato and guacamole. But better is nigirizushi, especially the striped bass, maguro tuna, salmon, yellowtail, red snapper, fluke, and striped bass. You also may ignite your palate with spicy miso ramen, or wheat noodles with

either pork or scallion. Musu is a compact establishment and fills up fast, so consider going off-peak.

West East All Natural Bistro & Bar, 758 S. Broadway, Hicksville, NY 11801; (516) 939-6618; westeastbistro.com; New American; $$–$$$. This is the streamlined and updated heir to the popular West East Bistro, now emphasizing sustainable farming and hormone- and antibiotic-free meats. The result is wide-ranging. And along this stretch of South Broadway, the restaurant is a beacon. Sample the pot stickers, made with pork and shrimp. And nibble on the well-seasoned chicken lettuce wraps. West End highlights beef from Painted Hills and the grass-fed steaks are excellent, from filet mignon to skirt. The kitchen comes up with a rich rendition of macaroni and cheese loaded with lobster meat. It's tasty enough to turn your steak dinner into a surf-and-turf affair. The eastern component of West East is represented with panache by curries. The Kerala-style rainbow trout, which gets its personality from coconut curry, is light and fine, with a hint of sweetness. The better seafood choices extend to sashimi, notably the beef-red maguro tuna. The service throughout is attentive.

Wild Honey Dining & Wine, 1 E. Main St., Oyster Bay, NY 11771; (516) 922-4690; wildhoneyrestaurant.com; New American; $$–$$$. This building once housed the summer offices of President Theodore Roosevelt. In recent decades, restaurants have been the primary occupants. Wild Honey is one of the better ones, with very good service and food to fit the compact space. Start with grilled, Moroccan-spiced lamb sliders, accompanied by caramelized onions, spinach, and feta-tzatziki sauce, or the crab-and-lobster cake, with charred corn salsa, roasted red pepper, and mustard aioli. The competition comes from goat-cheese ravioli in a roasted yellow tomato sauce with basil oil and Parmesan cheese and the napoleon of roasted beets and brussels sprouts, with goat cheese and candied walnuts. Wild Honey excels with the Cape Cod lobster hot pot, which takes an Asian turn with Thai red-curry coconut broth. Pan-roasted local flounder with mashed potatoes and a white-wine-lemon-caper sauce also is a good choice. Roosevelt himself might have picked the grilled filet mignon with blue cheese mashed potatoes, grilled broccoli, and a red-wine reduction. Grilled, double-cut pork chops with bourbon-mustard glaze also star. Try banana bread pudding for dessert.

Landmarks

All American Hamburger Drive-In, 4286 Merrick Rd., Massapequa, NY 11758; (516) 798-9574; allamericanhamburger.us; American; $. The name says it all. And on a summer night, the line is long. All American Hamburger Drive-In already has been featured on TV for its more than respectable spin on fast food and the dollop of nostalgia that goes with it. In its own weird way, the scene does offer its own entertainment. That said, to be precise, order the double cheeseburger or, if you feel that restraint is necessary, the quarter-pounder. There are all-beef franks, too. Occasionally, you'll find a child nibbling on a grilled-cheese sandwich. Almost everyone is decimating a serving of french fries. The thick shakes come in vanilla, chocolate, and strawberry. Parking can be an adventure around here, especially when a few softball teams converge on the place for post-game analysis and refreshment. The outdoor tables fill quickly, so you're as likely to be making a take-out order as an eat-in. The burger flippers, however, are young and energetic and they do try to move things along before too many customers get restless.

Canterbury's, 46 Audrey Ave., Oyster Bay, NY 11771; (516) 922-3614; canterburyalesrestaurant.com; Seafood, American; $–$$. It's always an oyster festival at Canterbury's, which began as an English-style pub but has evolved into an American restaurant. The decor includes images from Oyster Bay's history and the life of Theodore Roosevelt. The raw bar is a big attraction, as is the beer selection. Oysters Lobsterfella means the addition of spinach, cheese, anisette, shallots, and lobster sauce; "Buffalo-style oysters," chicken-wing sauce, plus celery, carrots, blue cheese, and toasted bread crumbs. Canterbury's erects a sizable chilled seafood tower of shellfish and tuna sashimi, and a very good sampler of the day's oysters. The fried oysters, with "Creole mustard remoulade" have crunch and flavor. Blue-claw crab cakes are complemented by a yellow-pepper coulis and mango slaw. Crisp, macadamia nut–crusted soft-shell crabs, with toasted coconut basmati rice, and the pork shank osso buco with red cabbage and sweet maple mashed potatoes may be specials.

Hicksville Sweet Shop, 75 Broadway, Hicksville, NY 11801; (516) 931-0130; Luncheonette, Ice Cream, Sweet Shop; $. The original location of the Hicksville Sweet Shop was at South Broadway and West Marie Street. It started in 1925. The current ownership at the latest address dates to 1974. So, tradition continues to reign with an extra serving of whipped cream. Service is warm and inviting; the effect, equal to time travel. The spot is open for breakfast, lunch, and dinner. Come for a grilled-cheese sandwich, peanut-butter-and-jelly, chili, a Reuben, eggplant parmigiana, Greek salad, spinach salad, and similarly eclectic fare, all infinitely better than they would be at a local diner. And be sure to have ice cream, which is made on the premises, as are the syrups. The root beer float and all the sundaes are generous. This definitely is where you go for the extra scoop, in any preparation.

Cardinali Bakery, 14 Cold Spring Rd., Syosset, NY 11791; (516) 937-5402; cardinali.net; Bakery, Cafe. Cardinali is an outstanding bakery, both for bread and for sweets. In addition, it's a popular little cafe and source for gelati. It can be very crowded and the staff may not be all smiles when the lines are long. But you'll be tempted to nibble all day. The seeded semolina twist, stuffed escarole bread, onion and olive loaves, ficelles, and brick-oven productions are among the essentials. Delectable pastries: cannoli, sfogliatelle, cream puffs, napoleons, éclairs, St. Joseph's Day zeppole, and sfingi. And the gelati could make you stop in regularly. Winners include stracciatelle with chocolate chips, coconut, zabaglione, chocolate, blackberry, blueberry, strawberry, hazelnut, and vanilla. They make very good cappuccino and espresso, so linger at one of the cafe tables. Maybe start with a pastry and follow with an apropos gelato and cookies.

The Chocolate Duck, 310 Main St., Farmingdale, NY 11735; (516) 249-0887; chocolateduck.com; Chocolatier. The Chocolate Duck merits a visit just for the collection of hard candy and chocolate molds. The chocolate you'll use to create Easter bunnies and everything else also is sold. Clasens, Callebaut, and Merckens chocolate are among those available. Cake and pastry supplies, fondant and sugar pastes, melting chocolate—all are here. The shop conducts cake-decorating classes, too.

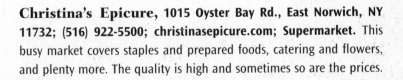

Christina's Epicure, 1015 Oyster Bay Rd., East Norwich, NY 11732; (516) 922-5500; christinasepicure.com; Supermarket. This busy market covers staples and prepared foods, catering and flowers, and plenty more. The quality is high and sometimes so are the prices.

There usually are, however, a lot of specials that may not fall into the bargain category but are worthwhile deals. You can stock up on olive oil, dry pastas, and tomato sauce while deciding which of the day's wraps will be your lunch; peruse the meat counter and select a steak while figuring out how much cheese your refrigerator will hold and which fruits clearly are in season. There is an extensive catering menu covering Asian, Italian, Greek, regional American, and Caribbean selections. The staff, while sometimes besieged, is often very helpful. In an earlier life, this was the home of Blueberries market, which was more limited in its offerings and frequently in its assistance.

Curds & Whey, 20 Birch Hill Rd., Locust Valley, NY 11560; (516) 399-2800; curdsandwheylocustvalley.com; **Gourmet Shop.** Curds & Whey emphasizes local products, from raw wild flower honey to cheeses, baked goods and mixed nuts to nut butter, gourmet snacks and fudge to sauces and marinades. There's also fine, organic olive oil, plus cooking stocks and charcuterie, and those celebrated meatballs from Maroni Cuisine in Northport. You have the potential for a spontaneous picnic.

Fairway Market, 50 Manetto Hill Rd., Plainview, NY 11803; (516) 937-5402; fairwaymarket.com; **Supermarket, Gourmet Shop.** This was the first Fairway on Long Island and it has changed the shopping  habits of thousands. It's a destination market, with an extraordinary selection of cheeses and breads, a fish market better than almost any local, a prime butcher shop, and easily the most impressive array of smoked salmon and other smoked fish anywhere around. The quality is very high for all. And the prices are fair, too, even in the realm of extra virgin olive oil and real balsamic vinegar. In addition to the specialties, you'll find a superior selection of prepared foods, especially soups. Carrot-and-ginger, Italian wedding soup with meatballs, chicken noodle, and corn chowder are among the mainstays. The take-home chicken potpie and meat loaf are understandably popular. There's a fine section devoted to sushi. Good pasta and a broad range of jarred sauces, too.

Jericho Cider Mill, 213 Rte. 106, Jericho, NY 11753; (516) 433-3360; Apples, Cider. You'll know it is autumn when the line of parked cars along Route 106 gets longer and longer. By Thanksgiving week, it will be an invigorating walk to reach this monument to the apple. The apple cider itself is the best on Long Island. You'll also store up on many varieties of apples, not just the basic red and golden delicious, Granny Smith, and McIntosh. Enjoy the winesap and the empire, the Crispin and the Ida red, the gala and the honey crisp, and basically whatever else has come in. Fruit pies are very good: apple crumb, apple-blueberry crumb, apple-cranberry, apple-peach, blueberry, and, when the leaves turn color, pumpkin. Jericho Cider Mill has pumpkins and gourds, sunflowers and cornstalks when fall arrives, too. A cup of the warm apple cider will brace you for anything. Candied apples and caramel apples may challenge your dental work, but they're obligatory purchases, too. And they make tasty place settings for your holiday table. Cider has been made on this site since the 17th century and probably before.

Messina Market, 6255 Northern Blvd., East Norwich, NY 11732; (516) 624-6800; messinamarket.com; Cafe, Gourmet Market, Caterer. Midday at Messina Market reflects everything the popular place does: dining in, ordering takeout, shopping for the next party, and more. Messina, which is connected with La Bonne Boulangerie bakery next door, is a magnet for baked good, salads, wraps, panini, sandwiches, pastas, smoothies, juices, coffees, and 3 meals a day. The Gold Coast sandwich is grilled chicken, pesto, lettuce, roasted peppers, fresh mozzarella on focaccia; their version of a Philly cheesesteak, grilled steak, sautéed onions and peppers, and provolone cheese on a toasted hero. The Napoli burger is finished with mozzarella and marinara; the St. Tropez, with Brie, smoked ham, and tomato. If you're here for breakfast: French toast, pancakes, crepes, Belgian waffles, all very good. There's another branch of Messina Market at 1482 Northern Blvd. in Manhasset; (516) 470-0414.

Patel Brothers, 415 S. Broadway, Hicksville, NY 11801; (516) 681-0091; patelbros.com; Supermarket. Patel Brothers is a major supermarket, part of a national chain specializing in spices, other seasonings, and produce that are essential to Indian and Pakistani cooking. To anyone unfamiliar with the cuisine, a visit to Patel Brothers is like a short road trip, north to south and west to east. You'll find grocery items, dairy, snacks, ethnic foods, fine produce, a huge selection of rice, legumes, and pulses, and an education.

Post Wine & Spirits, 510 Jericho Tpke., Syosset, NY 11791; (516) 921-1820; postwines.com; Wines and Spirits. Post has been the equivalent of a wine cellar for buyers across Long Island. It has an extraordinary selection of new releases and great vintage wines. The choices are especially strong in Bordeaux, Burgundy, Alsace, Champagne, Piedmont, and Tuscany, as well as California Cabernet Sauvignon. The shop, which has been selling wine and liquor since 1965, also offers a fine selection of wines from Long Island's major wineries and vineyards. Post's prices compete favorably with most of the discount shops, too, and when they hold a sale, it's something any wine lover should note. The staff is friendly and very knowledgeable; the website, informed and informative. "Education is our goal" is a motto here. Post will ship via UPS to anywhere in the United States where legal. It's situated on the south side of Jericho

Turnpike (Route 25), just west of the Seaford-Oyster Bay Expressway (Route 135).

Prime Time Butcher, 8045 Jericho Tpke., Woodbury, NY 11797; (516) 921-6519; orderprimetime.com; Butcher. It is prime time and choice time at this excellent shop for dry-aged beef, all-natural poultry, American lamb, and Kurobuta pork. The shop also is a source for very good hamburgers and hot dogs, and prepared fare such as a marinated turkey "London broil," roast chicken with a variety of seasonings, assorted soups, and side dishes. Very good service is a hallmark. There's also a branch of Prime Time Butcher at 382 Jericho Tpke., Roslyn Heights; (516) 625-0032.

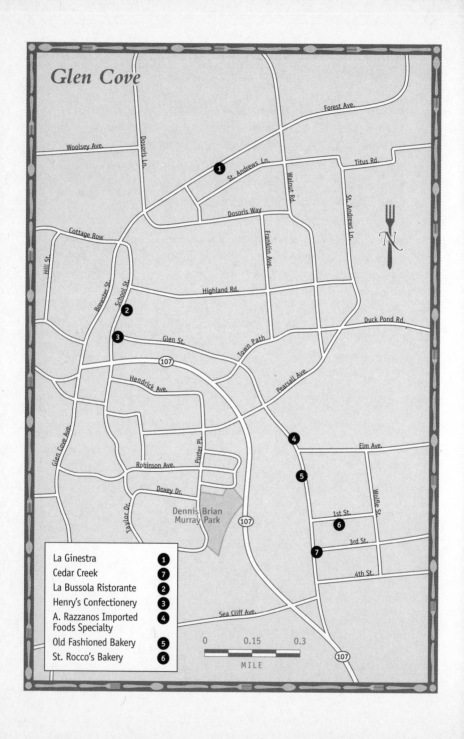

City of Glen Cove

The Feast of St. Rocco, held in late July or early August, celebrates a saint, a spirit, church, a community, a heritage. And the food is fabulous, too.

This is a feast in every way. From sausage and peppers to cannoli, it bids fair to be the most edible outdoor event on Long Island. You'll eat more zeppole than ever before. Last time, they were going six for $4 well spent. Don't be distracted by fried Oreos and fried Twinkies. This feast is about the real thing, pasta restaurant to pastry pavilion.

The Church of Saint Rocco is a city landmark and a very active part of local life in Glen Cove. The church reflects the Italian roots of many city residents. Glen Cove's "sister city" is Sturno, Italy. Many Sturnese came to Glen Cove starting in the 19th century.

Glen Cove's origins may be traced to 1668, when five guys bought about 2,000 acres northwest of Oyster Bay from the Matinecocks.

The quintet was successful setting up a sawmill. More than a century later, the region would be home to a clay-mining site, the location of a major cornstarch plant, and a busy waterfront district for commercial shipping and transportation to New York via steamboat.

How it came to be named "Glen Cove" is uncertain. But one story goes that someone figured that a pretty Scottish-sounding name, something like "Glen Coe," might work. And eventually it became Glen Cove.

The area would become part of the Long Island "Gold Coast," location of many mansions owned by industrialists from companies such as Standard Oil and F. W. Woolworth. Now, it is the city as suburb, combining elements of both. In the 1970s and 1980s, it also became a little hub for very good Italian and continental restaurants.

The feast continues.

Foodie Faves

Cedar Creek American Bar & Grill, 75 Cedar Swamp Rd., Glen Cove, NY 11542; (516) 656-5656; cedarcreekli.com; New American; $$–$$$. Bustling, buoyant Cedar Creek American Bar & Grill is an all-day affair, popular for lunch, dinner, and drinks. The sprawling spot is upbeat, sporting a menu of small and large plates, sandwiches, and 5 nights of specials. Those small plates include housemade kettle potato chips with a Maytag blue cheese fondue, which will vanish fast with a beer or two, and Chicago-style hot dog sliders, with peppers, pickles, onions, tomatoes, and spicy mustard, which require the same beverage. Tasty fried oysters, onion rings, and a salad of goat cheese, beets, and almonds also are good openers. Cedar Creek offers a commendable Cuban sandwich, layered with roasted Berkshire pork, ham, swiss cheese, pickles, and mustard, and respectable fish tacos with pico de gallo and cilantro-lime aioli. Better main dishes are the fish-and-chips, chicken potpie, braised short ribs with whipped potatoes and root vegetables, and steak frites starring a sirloin and hand-cut fries. Monday's blue plate special is southern fried chicken; Tuesday's, a turkey "TV dinner." Banana Betty parfait and apple crisp for dessert.

La Ginestra, 50 Forest Ave., Glen Cove, NY 11542; (516) 674-2244; laginestrarestaurant.com; Italian; $$–$$$. La Ginestra is a comfortable, versatile, and very good restaurant. The 2-level establishment used to be the home of Restaurant Zanghi, a landmark.

Rooms with a View

Restaurants close to the water or with a water view give you some perspective on Long Island as well as something to enjoy between bites.

A Lure in Mattituck: A window on Peconic Bay.

East Hampton Point in East Hampton: Three Mile Harbor glistens.

Louie's Oyster Bar & Grille in Port Washington: Manhasset Bay beckons.

Navy Beach in Montauk: Sit at a table on the beach facing Fort Pond Bay and Gardiner's Island.

Prime in Huntington: Arrive by boat via Huntington Harbor.

View in Oakdale: Accurately named, it offers Great South Bay.

WAVE in Port Jefferson: See the ferries set off to cross the sound.

La Ginestra, a veteran itself, keeps the quality high. Visit for the salmon carpaccio; beef carpaccio; the salad of grilled calamari and beans; another of fennel, endive, and orange; and the union of calamari and shrimp in spicy red sauce. La Ginestra's pastas include savory gnocchi alla Bolognese, enriched Sicilian-style with pine nuts and currants; penne with garlic, tomato, beans, and escarole; and fired-up rigatoni with sausage, broccoli rabe, and hot cherry peppers. The house's risotti also are good, particularly the mushroom and seafood versions. Sauteed red snapper with onions, raisins, pine nuts, and white vinegar emboldens the usually mild fish. Heartier appetites will find an excellent calf's liver alla Veneziana sautéed with vinegar, chicken scarpariello with peppers and potatoes, or housemade sausages with sautéed peppers, onions, broccoli rabe, and polenta. Tartufo tiramisu and cheesecake are the special sweets.

Riviera Grill, 274 Glen St., Glen Cove, NY 11542; (516) 674-9370; rivieragrillrestaurant.com; Italian; $$–$$$. A sunny, gold hue and dark woodwork give Riviera Grill a more inland look. But the emphasis was, and is still, on seafood Italian-style. Try the sautéed mussels, clams oreganata, and the crab cake with a caper-fueled sauce remoulade. Seafood salad is refreshing, full of octopus, calamari, shrimp, and scallops. The tuna carpaccio glistens. Red snapper marechiaro is a good catch here, as is sautéed shrimp with garlic and white wine. Pappardelle in pesto receives what's described as the Portofino treatment with the addition of potatoes and string beans. Spaghetti Toscana for reasons unknown includes capers, anchovies, garlic, and cherry tomatoes. But it tastes pretty good. The rigatoni Bolognese will allow you to go from sea to land without guilt. Black pepper–crusted filet mignon is juiced up with red-wine sauce. Alternatives: veal chop parmigiana and chicken piccata. The desserts are tiramisu, Italian cheesecake, and, another outlier, the apple tart with ice cream.

Sopah Thai Kitchen, 11 Cedar Swamp Rd., Glen Cove, NY 11542; (516) 945-3688; Thai; $–$$. Modest in every way except flavor, Sopah Thai Kitchen is like a hot pepper waiting to ignite your meal. The moderate prices and satisfying take-out also make this a popular stop. Sopah's specials include Volcano Jumbo Shrimp, fired up with chile paste, fresh pepper, and ginger; and Squid in Love, a ménage a trois featuring squid, shrimp, and chicken spurred by lemongrass and Kaffir lime leaves. The kitchen prepares a fine satay of either chicken or beef, zesty curry puffs with potatoes, a crisp spring roll, and tasty *meek rob,* the rice noodles here boosted by tamarind sauce. The Thai curries are green, red, yellow, Panang, mussaman, and "jungle," with fresh basil and Kaffir leaves. They're uniformly recommended, with either shrimp or chicken. Red curry duck, with coconut milk, chiles, and fresh basil, also heightens the competition. Deep-fried whole fishes deliver crunch, sweetness, and heat. Basil–hot pepper chicken, shrimp in ginger sauce, beef with cashews and roasted chiles, and pad Thai all work, too. Precede any of these with a papaya salad or a spicy beef salad. Dessert: mango with sticky rice.

Sweet Tomato, 170 Forest Ave., Glen Cove, NY 11542; (516) 671-4481; mysweettomato.com; Sandwiches, Soups; $–$$. Sweet Tomato, a very casual venue for take-out with a few tables for dining in, has a relaxed approach. But in prime time, there will be a line. Soups change daily. Some of the winners: Caribbean red lentil, white bean and escarole, spicy jerk chicken, broccoli-cheddar, and, of course, sweet tomato bisque. Cobb and Caesar salads merit a mouthful. They make a good lobster roll supported with field greens, and a grilled chicken quesadilla with spicy feta and tomato. Panini include grilled chicken with blue cheese, caramelized onions, and mustard, and the combo of marinated grilled chicken, prosciutto, provolone, sliced tomato, and sun-dried tomato pesto. For a richer choice, there's the crab cake on a Kaiser roll. Grilled cheese with tomato on either rye or sourdough is a mainstay. The little kitchen offers a peanut butter, toasted walnut, banana, and honey wrap, too.

Tappo, 284 Glen St., Glen Cove, NY 11542; (516) 759-1913; tappony.com; Italian; $$–$$$. "Sunday supper" at Tappo is a major meal: salad, hot antipasto, paccheri pasta in meat sauce, and a "misto di carne" that includes pork ribs, meatballs, and braciola in hearty, Neapolitan-style gravy. Inexplicably, the dessert with this is strawberry shortcake. It's all right, just unexpected. Tappo will attract you for a lot of other things, too. Panini are very good: mozzarella and prosciutto; tomato, basil, and mozzarella; and chicken parmigiana among them. Appetizers include the comparatively contemporary union of yellow and red beets with goat cheese; beet-and-goat-cheese ravioli with butter and sage; and the alliance of arugula, pear, candied walnuts, dried cranberries, and Parmesan cheese. Veal meatballs with ricotta and broccoli rabe, osso buco with saffron risotto, chicken Milanese capped with tomato-and-arugula salad, and sliced shell steak with mashed potatoes highlight the carnivore's corner. Gnocchi in pesto brings a taste of summer. Entertaining images of Italian movie stars decorate the place.

Landmarks

La Bussola, **40 School St., Glen Cove, NY 11542; (516) 671-2100; labussolaristorante.com; Italian; $$–$$$.** La Bussola has been a fixture for diners for more than 30 years, serving traditional fare in an Old World–style setting. Service is very good and so's the cooking. Try the housemade mozzarella wrapped with prosciutto, then baked in marinara sauce; bruschetta with caponata; grilled octopus with pesto, butterbeans, and fingerling potatoes; baked clams oreganata; and the cold seafood salad. La Bussola's pastas are essential: linguine with white or red clam sauce; pappardelle alla Bolognese; rigatoni all'Amatriciana; squid-ink spaghetti with seafood and cherry peppers; and orecchiette with broccoli rabe and sweet Italian sausage. Broccoli rabe is the bed for double-cut pork chops, finished with prosciutto and smoked mozzarella. A Gorgonzola-cheese-and-bread-crumb crust complements tender filet mignon. Lush osso buco arrives with fine saffron risotto. A risotto with leeks accents fat, pan-seared scallops. Calf's liver alla Veneziana, with onions and an edge of balsamic vinegar, is very good. Pizzettes are available at lunch; fruit tarts and Italian cheesecake, regularly.

Stango's at The Orchard, 19 Grove St., Glen Cove, NY 11542; (516) 671-2389; stangos.net; Italian; $–$$. The Stango's name dates to 1919. It has been a source for hearty Italian-American specialties in big portions at modest prices. "The Orchard" refers to the city's Italian neighborhood and the reborn restaurant's evocative decor, which includes black-and-white photographs providing history and nostalgia. Former Nassau County executive Tom Suozzi and his wife Helene are among the lead investors here and they operate the establishment with friendly, open-handed style. You visit for mozzarella and tomatoes, baked clams oreganata, fried calamari, clams Posillipo, *pasta e fagioli*, escarole and beans, and a salad before getting to the pasta Bolognese, hefty meat lasagna, stuffed shells, crepes Fiorentina, or penne with sausage and broccoli rabe. Main dishes are highlighted by the pork chops with vinegar peppers, hot or sweet, eggplant parmigiana, and an assortment of other parmigianas, piccatas, Marsalas, and française preparations. Stango's also prepares tasty and popular pizzas. St. Rocco's Bakery is the source of the excellent bread. Enjoy any dessert and an espresso or two.

Specialty Stores, Markets & Shops

Henry's Sweet Shoppe, 8 Glen St., Glen Cove, NY 11542; (516) 671-3222; henryssweetshoppe.com; Sweet Shop, Luncheonette, Soda Fountain. Nearing Easter, Henry's Sweet Shoppe is an ode to chocolate bunnies and chocolate eggs. By Valentine's Day, it's all hearts. Henry's dates back to 1929. In addition to being a fine confectioner, Henry's is popular for breakfast and lunch. Come early for omelets, pancakes, French toast, muffins, and a Belgian waffle with ice cream and hot blueberry or hot strawberry sauce. Arrive later for a turkey club, or maybe one with Virginia ham or roast beef. The obvious dessert is pie a la mode. The fountain always is busy, making very good malteds ("all flavors"), ice cream sodas, milk shakes and milk floats, egg creams, and sundaes, sundaes, sundaes. They require a comparative analysis: strawberry versus pineapple, butterscotch versus caramel, hot fudge versus sprinkles. The Banana Monster is a major split; the fudge brownie sundae, easily shared. Henry's Crowd Pleaser contains 5 scoops; the Olympic soda, merely 2.

Old Fashioned Bakery, 10 Cedar Swamp Rd., Glen Cove, NY 11542; (516) 759-1141; Bakery. In the morning, numerous espressos and cappuccinos are served here, to take out or to drink in at one of the small tables near the window. Bring your newspaper and stay a while. You could write a short story while watching the scene change customer by customer. The regulars don't even have to ask. The first-timers point and request several explanations about what this or that is and whether it must be eaten immediately or can travel. They do so occasionally to the annoyance of the very efficient staff, which does like to move things along. The Italian pastries are excellent, especially the cannoli and the sfogliatelle. Biscotti and cookies also are recommended; focus on the biscotti with nuts and the rainbow or pignoli cookies. And, as if to underscore its name, Old Fashioned Bakery makes crusty, satisfying bread and rolls. By the time you're ready to leave, it's almost guaranteed that you'll have made an investment in on-the-road edibles.

Razzano's, 286 Glen St., Glen Cove, NY 11542; (516) 676-3745; razzanos.com; Gourmet Market. This salumeria has been slicing the prosciutto for decades. The current owners have operated the market since 1968, expanding and updating it, but never losing the lived-in look and the hands-on style. The store is crowded, jammed with customers as well as shelves of imported jars and cans, limitless pastas, and much more. If you want a 100-plus-pound provolone, this is your stop. Same if you need housemade sausages, pastas, and cheese. There's take-out and local delivery, too. You'll look for a long time before coming upon the sandwich with a Calabrian approach that includes hot sausage, hot soppressata, and hot peppers. The Napoli, with hot capocollo, fresh mozzarella, and roasted peppers, gives it some competition, along with the Palermo, which contains prosciutto, fresh mozzarella, roasted peppers, tomatoes, and lettuce. How the lettuce got in is anybody's guess. If this seems too complicated, stick with the meatball hero and, if available, the fennel gratin.

St. Rocco's Bakery, 4 St. Rocco's Place, Glen Cove, NY 11542; (516) 427-5333; Bakery, Cafe. St. Rocco's Bakery was ruined by fire twice. It has been rebuilt and expanded since the 2011 blaze and is an essential stop in this city. Definitely buy bread, stuffed or not. The brick-oven loaves are great. After all, the bakery is subtitled "panetteria" as well as "pasticceria." The *pitone fritto* filled with escarole, mozzarella, and tomato is irresistible. Likewise, the prosciutto-packed bread. So are the pastries. You can transition to them via a croissant jammed with whipped cream and Nutella. Bombolini loaded with cannoli cream or custard also are delightful. And you must buy the cannoli themselves. Before going into sweets overload, nibble on a first-class pizza. St. Rocco's also offers fine coffee. If you're here during Christmas or Easter season, the bakery looks ready to burst with celebratory breads and desserts. The staff is welcoming and the prices are eminently fair, too.

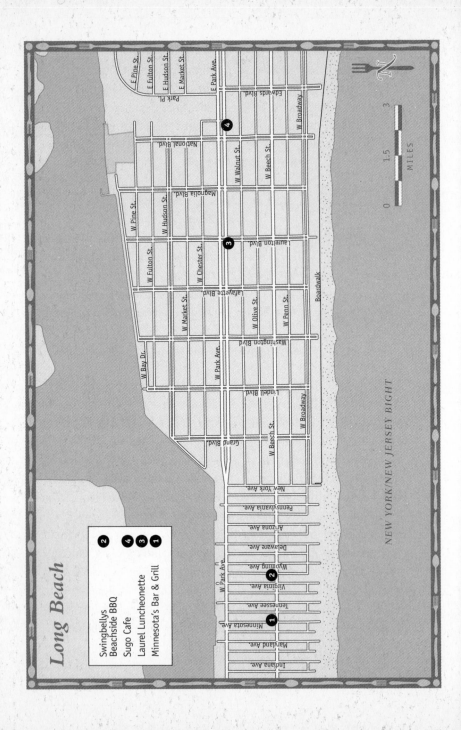

Long Beach

Swingbellys
Beachside BBQ **2**

Sugo Cafe **4**

Laurel Luncheonette **3**

Minnesota's Bar & Grill **1**

NEW YORK/NEW JERSEY BIGHT

0   1.5   3
MILES

E Pine St.
E Fulton St.
E Hudson St.
E Market St.
E Park Ave.
Park Pl.
Edwards Blvd.
W Broadway
National Blvd.
W Walnut St.
W Beech St.
Magnolia Blvd.
W Pine St.
W Hudson St.
Lauriton Blvd.
W Fulton St.
W Chester St.
Lafayette Blvd.
W Market St.
W Olive St.
W Penn St.
Washington Blvd.
W Bay Dr.
W Park Ave.
Lindell Blvd.
Grand Blvd.
W Beech St.
W Broadway
Boardwalk
New York Ave.
Pennsylvania Ave.
Arizona Ave.
Delaware Ave.
Wyoming Ave.
W Park Ave.
Virginia Ave.
Tennessee Ave.
Minnesota Ave.
Maryland Ave.
Indiana Ave.

City of Long Beach

The motto of the City of Long Beach is "Civitas ad Mare," or City by the Sea. It is 3.9 square miles: 2.1 are land; 1.8, water.

On October 29, 2012, Hurricane Sandy reached Long Island as a "superstorm" and devastated Long Beach, which is a barrier island in southwest Nassau County—the ocean on one side and the bay on the other. Its boardwalk, more than 2 miles long, was wrecked. Businesses and residences were flooded.

But by summer 2013, the rebuilding of the boardwalk was almost complete and many of the shuttered restaurants reopened, or were planning to reopen.

Seated on a beach chair in a TV ad, Billy Crystal said, "Just another day in paradise." The comedian encouraged viewers to visit his hometown. They did.

More casual restaurants and shops dominate the main commercial strips. Long Beach began as a resort community, established in 1880. The railroad arrived two years later. The Long Beach Hotel was a major attraction. It was destroyed by a fire in 1907.

Long Beach was incorporated in 1913 and became a city in 1922. The first written description of the area, in the 17th century, referred to it as the "Great Sand Beach." It was and is.

Abe's Pitaria, 32 W. Park Ave., Long Beach, NY 11561; (516) 897-3582; abespitaria.com; Mediterranean, American; $–$$. Abe's covers major food groups such as gyros, falafel, and souvlaki, to eat in or take out, all served with informal efficiency. You're not here for the decor. The chicken gyro is a husky specialty, sliced, grilled, filled out with lettuce, onion, tomato, and feta cheese, finished with yogurt sauce. The falafel pita, with falafel balls, hummus, and tahini, also is good. So is the pita with baba ghanoush, or eggplant salad. The Moroccan Red wrap is eggplant salad, Israeli salad, feta, and hot sauce. Abe's platters range from spinach pie and moussaka to a hummus-and-tahini number and gyro combos. They all go with the mushroom-barley and tomato-vegetable soups. Desserts highlight Greek pastries. You can buy stuffed grape leaves, feta, and Greek olives, bring a beach blanket, and daydream about the Aegean. There's also an Abe's Pitaria in Wantagh at 3045 Merrick Rd., (516) 221-8110.

Chaba Thai Cuisine, 12 W. Park Ave., Long Beach, NY 11561; (516) 897-2888; chabalongbeach.com; Thai; $–$$. Sweet, spicy, and salty arrive in varying degrees and sometimes all at once at Chaba Thai Cuisine, a sleek and subtle taste of Southeast Asia in southwest Nassau. Savor the Thai basil rolls, with roasted chicken, shrimp, bean sprouts, and a spark from basil leaves, or *kanum jeeb,* a dumpling filled with ground chicken, water chestnuts, carrots, and spices. Chicken satay is tender and good, with peanut sauce and cucumber salad. Crisp rice noodles with shrimp, scallions, and tofu also are tasty. The raw papaya salad, spurred by chiles and peanuts, will refresh your appetite. Mint leaves, cilantro, scallions, and onions boost the beef salad; chile paste, cashews, pineapple, and green apple do it for the duck salad. Main courses include the mix-and-match selections for seafood, meat, or tofu, which are best with sautéed hot sweet basil, sautéed ginger, and tamarind sauce. Curries red, green, yellow, masaman, and Panang-style also go with the choices of meat, tofu, shrimp, or squid. Crisp whole snapper and sea bass, scallops with Thai basil sauce, and *kao soi,* curry with noodles, stand out.

The Currywurst Company, 10 W. Park Ave., Long Beach, NY 11561; (516) 665-3150; the-currywurst-company.com; German; $$. Did you know there's a currywurst museum in Berlin? The currywurst is a sliced sausage topped with a mix of tomatoey sauce, not far removed from ketchup, and curry powder. The restaurant bills itself as "Oktoberfest year round." Your choice of wurst may include veal currywurst, Kobe beef currywurst, buffalo bratwurst, elk bratwurst, venison bratwurst, and wild boar bratwurst. There are 6 curry choices. The seasoning, however, may leave an after-burn. You'll have much draft beer to cool down. The wursts make the *leberkäse* on a roll seem like health food. On the side: Belgian fries, curry fries, pretzels, Swabian potato salad, sauerkraut, macaroni and cheese.

Fresco Creperie & Cafe, 150 E. Park Ave., Long Beach, NY 11561; (516) 897-8097; frescocreperie.com; Crepes, Breakfast; $–$$. Crepes savory and sweet, plus salads are the obvious essentials at Fresco, an informal venue for something light or lighter. The smoked salmon salad includes crumbled goat cheese, chives, and cucumber; the bresaola-and-Brie production is an Italo-Gallic combo that's not quite harmonious but will do, bringing together the air-dried beef, lush cheese and sliced almonds, onion, olives, and roasted peppers. The cast of crepes stars ham-and-gruyère cheese, smoked salmon with mascarpone cheese and chives, spinach with shallots and goat cheese, fruit preserves, orange and caramel, banana and Nutella, apples with brown sugar and cinnamon, and "hedgehog style," with coconut, almonds, and dark chocolate that might have puzzled Isaiah Berlin. There's usually a housemade soup to precede any of these.

Long Beach Bagel Cafe, 757 E. Park Ave., Long Beach, NY 11561; (516) 432-2582; libagelcafe.com; Sandwiches; $–$$. This is one of the better branches of the chainlet, which started in 1986. The bagel is the vehicle for enjoying hand-carved Nova Scotia smoked salmon, belly lox, sable, chopped chicken liver, and almost all that follows. The chopped herring and herring fillets also are appetizing. Plenty of egg dishes, too. At lunch, the sandwiches include The Soprano with salami, capocollo, pepperoni, provolone, and roasted peppers; and the Pastrami Supreme, with pastrami, melted swiss cheese, sauerkraut, and mustard. The Brooklyn Bomb detonates with pepper turkey, ham, capocollo, provolone, roasted peppers, and fresh mozzarella.

Minnesota's Bar & Grill, 959 W. Beech St., Long Beach, NY 11561; (516) 432-4080; American; $$–$$$. Minnesota's has enough variety to be the envy of your local diner. Kung pao calamari vies with chicken parm dumplings. The informal eatery gives you a little tour with Shanghai calamari, sweet-hot style; Buffalo meatball sliders, chicken on toasted brioche; tostada scallops, Cajun blackened; Parmesan truffle fries with Cajun aioli; a Big Sur taco with fish; a Santa Fe chicken taco; West Coast lobster roll with avocado; New England lobster roll with Old Bay fries; Korean kimchee salad with seared tuna; Anjou shrimp salad with pear; California cobb salad with flavor; and Prince Edward Island mussels with provenance. Add Bourbon Street rigatoni, with grilled chicken, and New York strip steak to complete the trip. The "butcher block" burger is a sensible alternative.

Sugo Cafe, 62 W. Beech St., Long Beach, NY 11561; (516) 431-7846; sugocafe.com; New American; $$–$$$. Contemporary and creative, Sugo Cafe likes to cross borders and cuisines to come up with its own style. It works with the tender, grilled octopus salad, crisp

Keeping Cool

Ice cream and gelati refresh you when the temperatures are high and taste just as good when the degrees drop. Here are 6 destinations for superior scoops.

Baci Gelato in Williston Park: A big selection of flavors to test your decision-making.

Itgen's Ice Cream Parlour in Valley Stream: A sundae star with old-fashioned flair.

Magic Fountain in Mattituck: When you're way beyond van-choc-straw.

McNulty's in Miller Place: Nostalgia as a topping.

Sant Ambroeus in Southampton: Luxurious gelati.

Snowflake in Riverhead: Sundaes, malteds, shakes, waffle cones, great flavors, peerless soft-serve, brown bonnets, flying saucers.

oysters with a Cajun-inflected sauce remoulade, and the tuna tartare with avocado mousse. If this seems overorchestrated, the chicken meatballs will suffice. The kitchen adds sausage-and-pea "risotto" poppers, which are fine with drinks. In season, look for the crunchy soft-shell crabs paired with jicama slaw and spicy cilantro aioli. The braised short ribs and the grilled branzino should satisfy argumentative purists, while the seared halibut with "Sicilian eggplant ragu," is sure to upend them. The roasted pork chop is juicy and finds a match with pea-and-Gorgonzola-cheese risotto and *haricots verts*. The pistachio-and-Dijon-mustard crust gives a tasty edge to pink, baby lamb chops.

Swingbellys, 909 W. Beech St., Long Beach, NY 11561; (516) 431-3464; swingbellys.com; Barbecue; $–$$. The reopening of

Swingbellys inspired immediate celebration among Long Island's barbecue enthusiasts. The ultracasual eatery always ranks among the top destinations for 'cue fueled with cherry, hickory, and apple wood. Pulled pork and beef brisket are the smoky lures, but the St. Louis ribs and baby back ribs will make you spend on take-out, too. And chicken wings expand the menu, with many sauces, including one overheated affair dubbed "insanity." Mango-habanero and mustard barbecue are more even-tempered alternatives in the messy-hands, multi-napkin competition. Swingbellys also prepares a snappy "burnt ends" chili. Try the pickle chips and fried onions, smoked andouille sausage, and smoked chicken, and the house's versions of a Cubano and a cheesesteak. The Big Dawg means andouille with chopped pickles, cheese, chili, and onion strings. And there's very good cornbread to go with any of it.

Landmark

Laurel, 300 W. Park Ave., Long Beach, NY 11561; (516) 432-7728; laureldiner.com; Luncheonette; $–$$. In full, this is the Laurel Luncheonette & Restaurant. It has been serving the city since 1932. Breakfast is your main meal here, with omelets and other egg dishes, Belgian waffles, pancakes, French toast, and sandwiches. Eggs a la Laurel: poached, on an English muffin, with smoked bacon and melted American cheese, served with spuds. Lunch and dinner are more eclectic, but they do have deli sandwiches, triple-decker clubs, panini, Greek pitas, wraps, hamburgers, and weightier fare, including roast turkey, steaks, and chops. There's also a beach menu, and your selections may be delivered to you at the shore. Laurel notes that it's the birthplace of the cherry lime Rikki soft drink, named for an early owner before it became a Rickey.

Town of Huntington

Downtown Huntington is a drizzle of balsamic vinegar from the Nassau border. But it's Suffolk's epicenter of eating out.

The entire town has an extensive menu of restaurants and cuisines, shops and markets, and a variety of price points. And it has been a destination since 1867, when the Long Island Railroad first pulled in.

But the history of Huntington begins with Native Americans and with English settlers who arrived in the 17th century. Originally, it took in what's now Babylon, too. The British occupied the town and established headquarters following the Battle of Long Island during the American Revolution.

Plaques "in everlasting remembrance" to honor patriot Nathan Hale are on the sides of a boulder north of downtown, welcoming visitors to the community of Halesite. You know the story.

Blue-and-yellow signs identify notable and historic sites in Huntington. The region was an agricultural area and a major transport hub because of its five harbors. They're situated close to downtown Huntington, and in Lloyd Harbor, Centerport, Northport, and Cold Spring Harbor, which became a whaling port.

The town's communities known for restaurants and food shops today include Huntington, Huntington Station, Greenlawn, Northport, East Northport, Melville, Cold Spring Harbor, and part of Commack.

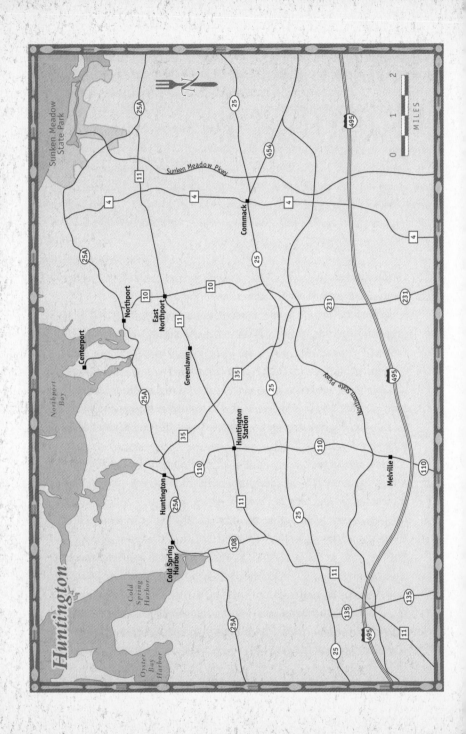

Huntington has been home to Walt Whitman, Booker T. Washington, and John Coltrane. Antoine de Saint-Exupéry wrote *The Little Prince* while in Northport. Otto H. Kahn built one of the country's biggest homes, the chateaulike Oheka in Cold Spring Hills. Orson Welles filmed part of *Citizen Kane* there. Philanthropist and industrialist August Heckscher contributed the art museum that carries his name and the bucolic adjoining park. And, a long time ago, Alexander Gardiner operated a pickle works.

It has stayed a very appetizing place.

 Foodie Faves

Acacia, **371 New York Ave., Huntington, NY 11743; (631) 923-2299; acaciali.com; New American; $$–$$$.** Acacia brings both restaurant and music scene to downtown Huntington, and succeeds at both. The dimly lit spot brightens the whole avenue. Mandatory are mussel pots, especially those with Thai and Provençal seasonings and another that includes the equivalent of a cheese fondue. Seared dry sea scallops, crab cakes with lemon aioli, and fennel-crusted yellowfin tuna also are recommended. If you're not feeling particularly marine: filet mignon with scalloped potatoes. Desserts are skippable. Know that the noise level skyrockets three days a week when a DJ works very hard. An acoustic guitarist plays another night, as if to provide some balance. This is a lively addition to dining out along a street of many fine meals.

Ariana, **255 Main St., Huntington, NY 11743; (631) 421-2933; arianacafe.com; Afghani, Vegan; $$.** Ariana, named for the east end of Alexander's empire, reaches far itself, with vegan specialties to go with its savory Afghan fare. The restaurant is warm and in its own way refreshing. Pick *bolanee,* similar to knishes, filled with potatoes and leeks, accented with yogurt-mint sauce; or *aushak,* the herbaceous leek dumplings with meat sauce and yogurt dressing. *Mantoo,* the steamed lamb-and-beef dumplings, also are good, as is *sambossa,* a pastry full of chopped meat, onions, and chickpeas, with that popular yogurt-mint sauce. There's a tasty vegetarian sampler with eggplant salad, hummus, falafel, olives, and baba ghanoush. Vegetarian soup, made with mung beans and black beans, and golden lentil soup are soothing starters, too. One house special is dubbed Salmon Rushdie, freed from hiding under falafel. Lobster-and-shrimp risotto expands the Ariana map, as does the marinated skirt steak with onion rings. The roasted lamb shank, assorted kebabs, and lamb cooked with nuts, raisins, and vegetables round out the selections. Notable vegan options: mung-bean risotto with brown rice, herbed spinach with basmati rice, and curried vegetables.

Be-Ju Sashimi & Sake Bar, 400 Broadhollow Rd., Melville, NY 11747; (631) 755-0555; Japanese; $$–$$$$. Be-Ju is the extraordinary sushi and sashimi bar situated in a quiet dining room that's part of Jewel restaurant. In this space, Chefs Shigeki Uchiyama and Hiroki Tanii put on a show. Be-Ju seats fewer than 30 fortunate diners. Sample the superb fatty tuna and medium-fatty tuna, Japanese mackerel, and whatever else the chefs suggest. Wild bluefin tuna, with green-olive tapenade; tuna tataki with black truffle; and shrimp–and–sea urchin risotto are their contemporary competition. Also, try steamed monkfish liver, with sea urchin and ponzu sauce, a terrific dish akin to pâté that hints of nouvelle cuisine. Tea-smoked salmon and star-anise smoked local duck breast continue the tour de force. A yuzu-white chocolate semifreddo and a chocolate-wasabi bombe provide exclamation points. Be-Ju is overseen by Tom Schaudel, Jewel's chef, who periodically may be seen working on the sushi, too. Toast the whole crew with one of the bar's excellent sakes.

Besito, 402 New York Ave., Huntington, NY 11743; (631) 549-0100; besitomex.com; Mexican; $$–$$$. The original Besito is the cornerstone of Mexican restaurants on Long Island and a spirited destination that contributes to one of the busiest downtowns. It avoids the clichés and emphasizes genuine flavors, attracting diners since 2006. The excellent guacamole, prepared tableside, is spiced to order, served with a side of jicama. The house's tortilla soup with pulled chicken also stars, fueled with cilantro pasilla chiles, avocado, and Chihuahua cheese. Besito prepares fine ceviche, served with plantains; fish tacos with pickled onions and salsa; stuffed poblano peppers; and *queso fundido,* baked with chorizo sausage. Savory tacos with chicken, skirt steak, or both, and another with braised short rib and a tamarind–chipotle pepper glaze are recommended, as are the pork carnitas in jalapeño–black bean salsa and the tortilla pie filled with shrimp and crab in a poblano cream sauce. The day's catch prepared Vera Cruz–style, with sweet peppers, tomatoes, olives, and peppers stands out, too. There's an exceptional selection of tequilas, blanco, reposado, and anejo; the restaurant is much more than margarita central. Besito in Roslyn is at 1516 Old Northern Blvd.; (516) 484-3001.

Bistro Cassis, 55B Wall St., Huntington, NY 11743; (631) 421-4122; bistrocassis.com; French; $$–$$$. Cozy, handsome, and always welcoming, Bistro Cassis heads the list of Gallic restaurants in Nassau and Suffolk. The bistro-and-brasserie style overtook the grander approach on Long Island years ago. Bistro Cassis, which spawned others including Brasserie Cassis in Plainview and Bistro Citron in Roslyn, is the original, marked by attentive service and a consistent kitchen. Sample the *frisée aux lardons, salade niçoise,* onion soup gratinée, garlicky escargots, and the tart of goat cheese and caramelized onions. The mussels mariniere and Provençal also call. Main dishes: grilled hanger steak Bordelaise, steak au poivre, duck breast and confit of leg with raspberries and cassis, and the juicy roasted chicken for two.

Arrive Tuesday for duck a l'orange, Thursday for coq au vin. The lobster club sandwich on brioche and the hamburger Lyonnaise with gruyère cheese and onion rings informally and tastefully cross the border. At lunch, order the croque monsieur or pan bagnat. Anytime, dip a spoon into the chocolate mousse.

BiVio, **1801 E. Jericho Tpke., Huntington, NY 11743; (631) 499-9133; bivioristorante.com; Italian; $$–$$$.** Locals always associate this site with Fred's, an informal restaurant that had the look of a diner and sauerbraten as a specialty. A couple of cuisines and establishments later, BiVio brings in a well-tailored Italian menu and a dining room that reflects it. Baked eggplant is homey and very good. Tender clams casino, a sizable crab cake, dependable shrimp cocktail, and mozzarella Caprese with tomatoes and basil make the selection process easy. Cavatelli with pesto and pappardelle Bolognese top the pastas, each tastefully sauced. Chicken scarpariello, on the bone, is supported by sausages, peppers, and garlic. The juicy skirt steak makes an Argentinean turn with zesty chimichurri. The rack of New Zealand lamb is panko-crusted and rosy. Shrimp scampi-style and sole BiVio both are mild and fine. Desserts include cannoli, tiramisu, and Italian cheesecake.

Black & Blue Seafood Chophouse, **65 Wall St., Huntington, NY 11743; (631) 385-9255; blackandbluehuntington; New American; $$$.** Black & Blue specializes in surf and turf, at ease with each. The dining room is tucked into the small shopping center that includes Fiorello Dolce. But once inside, you're definitely in a separate place, stylized and kitschy. There's some whimsy here. But they're serious about what you're eating, from snappy sliders and tuna tartare to clams casino and oysters Rockefeller. The watermelon salad with feta works in summer; the "Caesar spears," 12 months. The shrimp and crabmeat cocktails, raw oysters, and the seafood platter for two head the appetizers. Then, pick a steak: bone-in New York strip, bone-in rib eye, or porterhouse for two, with compound butters. The cornflake-crusted fried chicken lightens things up. You can balance it with macaroni-and-cheese, offered in 4 guises, including truffle and lobster. Lobster-crusted salmon continues the gilding. On the side: creamed spinach, whipped potatoes, shoestring fries, and, of course, the "loaded" baked spud.

Blackstone Steakhouse, 10 Pinelawn Rd., Melville, NY 11747; (631) 271-7780; blackstonesteakhouse.com; Steak, Seafood; $$$–$$$$. Blackstone is the big-ticket dining room off Route 110 for expense accounts, high-end lunches, and the dinnertime splurge. The look is vaguely Frank Lloyd Wright, prairie edition; the effect, very polished. Service is both attentive and accommodating, midday or evening. And the food is excellent, whether you're here for raw fish or rare beef. Shellfish cocktails and raw bar platters are ideal. The lobster-and-crab salad is refined and carefully composed. Sushi and sashimi quality: very high, from multicolored rolls to the pristine. The Blackstone embodiment combines Kobe beef, king crab, spicy tuna, avocado, and spicy eel sauce in a single pricey package. Main courses include adroitly steamed or broiled lobsters; superior steaks, from porterhouse and sirloin to filet mignon and rib eye; artichoke-encrusted halibut; Tasmanian head-on prawns; and whole fish. Finish with chocolate blackout cake, cheesecake, crème brûlée. Blackstone is under the same management as the similar Rare650 in Syosset and Insignia in Smithtown.

Bravo! Nader, 9 Union Pl., Huntington, NY 11743; (631) 351-1200; bravonader.com; Seafood, Continental, Italian; $$–$$$. Complete with exclamation point, Bravo! Nader is a little industry that includes restaurant, cooking classes, and a take-out spot. It's a busy enterprise, this 12-table center of energy. Stop here for *pasta e fagioli*, fat crab cakes, good eggplant rollatine and eggplant parmigiana, baked clams, and the "pyramid mozzarella" layered with marinated and grilled eggplant, sun-dried tomatoes, and roasted peppers. The shrimp fra diavolo, shrimp scampi-style with lemon-garlic sauce, chicken scarpariello with sausage and pepperoncini, grilled flounder, lemon sole amandine, gnocchi marinara, and whole-wheat pasta primavera also count. Sometimes, there are enough daily specials to merit a separate menu or at least a memory exam. The general idea is to sample whatever fish or fishes made it from the waters to the kitchen on the day you visit.

Cafe Buenos Aires, 23 Wall St., Huntington, NY 11743; (631) 603-3600; cafebuenosaires.net; Argentinean, Spanish, Tapas; $$–$$$. Hugo Garcia oversees a distinctive and enticing dining room, with vibrant food, popular entertainment, and a social scene that underscores the restaurant's overall appeal. It's a colorful, engaging, and essential part of a busy downtown. The kitchen excels with eclectic tapas: grilled chorizo; skewered beef with bacon, onions, and peppers; empanadas; sautéed sweetbreads with leeks and beans; octopus with smoked paprika; oxtail-stuffed piquillo peppers; short-rib sliders; stuffed oysters; ceviche; Serrano ham with manchego cheese; white anchovies with olives; more. Enjoy the baby octopus salad with pears and feta cheese; grilled seafood skewers; grilled strip steak with zesty chimichurri and potatoes; steak with melted blue cheese and red wine sauce; roasted pork chop with pistachios, caramelized bananas, bacon-and-fruit chutney, and mashed potatoes; and a grand mixed grill for two, with sweet sausage, chicken, sweetbreads, short rib, and blood sausage. The cafe also serves good pastas, outstanding Argentinean wines, very good cheeses, and desserts such as churros, flan, and dark chocolate cake.

**Cook's Scratch Kitchen & Bakery, 1014 Fort Salonga Rd.,
Northport, NY 11768; (631) 651-5480; cookskitchen.com; Breakfast,
Lunch; $–$$.** Cooking from scratch is the delightful theme at this
address, where you'll have some of the best breakfast
fare in either county. The buttermilk waffle
with maple butter; French toast made
with *pain de mie,* vanilla custard,
and cinnamon; and the fluffy
buttermilk or blueberry pancakes
are great ways to begin the day. Steel-cut
Irish oatmeal, house-made oat granola, and Greek-style yogurt also
are standards. Essentials include applewood-smoked bacon, chicken-
apple sausage, red bliss potato home fries, the house-made buttermilk
biscuits, and the muffins. At lunch, enjoy the Cubano; gruyère, cheddar,
and havarti with bacon on griddled sourdough; and "dueling Reubens,"
including the "traditionalist" with corned beef, sauerkraut, and melted
swiss, pressed on rye, and the "hipster" with house-cured smoked pork,
gruyère, fennel kraut, and mustard on grilled sourdough. Return trips
guaranteed.

**Crew Kitchen & Bar, 138 New York Ave., Huntington, NY
11743; (631) 549-3338; crewli.com; New American; $$$.** Collegial
and cozy, Crew Kitchen & Bar has gracious style, good service, and
a very balanced menu. It's not entirely like dining at the yacht club,
but members doubtless would feel at ease. You will, too, tasting the
braised baby back ribs with their bourbon glaze, the crab cake accented
with a lemon-caper emulsion, or the Mediterranean salad, with feta
cheese, cucumber, tomato, and olives. The filet mignon comes with a
fine potato gratin. And Crescent Farm duck 2 ways is a satisfying main
course, pairing seared breast and confit of leg in a preparation that
changes regularly. Braised spare ribs, off the bone, make a fine, cool-
weather course, with garlicky mashed potatoes and root vegetables.
Seaside, try the pan-seared red snapper with crisp polenta chips. Or

go surf-turf with the paella, this one bringing together chicken, clams, shrimp, and andouille sausage. Crew is an easygoing place to linger over coffee.

Doppio Artisan Bistro, 24 Clinton Ave., Huntington, NY 11743; (631) 923-1515; doppiohuntington.com; Italian; $$–$$$. Doppio in Huntington is the offspring of the Greenwich, Connecticut, casual Italian spot. It's a good choice for individual pizzas, small plates, salads, pastas, and panini. They're all served by a genial staff in a pleasant, modern setting. From the red pizzas, sample the disc topped with prosciutto, fresh mozzarella, arugula, Parmesan cheese, and tomato; from the whites, the Bel Haven, with mozzarella, Gorgonzola, grilled pear, and truffle oil. The salad of endive, with Bosc pear, pine nuts, and goat cheese croquettes, is a tasty bridge to panini, such as the grilled chicken number with roasted peppers, pesto, arugula, and mozzarella and the eggplant, mozzarella, and pecorino combo. Better pastas: gnocchi alla Sorrentina with tomato sauce, basil, and Parmesan; the housemade, meat-filled lasagna; and fusilli in cartoccio with porcini, mascarpone, and tomato. Chicken scarpariello and grilled branzino also are good.

Fado, 10 New St., Huntington, NY 11743; (631) 351-1010; fadohuntington.com; Portuguese; $$. The sangria keeps pouring at Fado, as you prepare to dive into the flavorful, shredded salt cod with potatoes and olives, the tender grilled octopus, and the smoky, grilled Portuguese sardines. The chorizo sausage, flamed tableside, must be rescued quickly and, if it is, this becomes a savory appetizer. Fado brings downtown something long missing: a taste of Iberia. Actually, it has been gone since The Iberian restaurant itself departed decades ago. Fado cheerfully makes up for the time with fine striped bass finished with almonds, mushrooms, and baby kale, in a lemony beurre blanc. Braised pork shank, tender and tasty, arrives with a spinach-and-artichoke-heart risotto. You'll also want the stuffed squid, cod croquettes, seafood paella, the tuna and salmon tartare, the grilled rib steak, and the pork chops any style. Good, warm bread stays that way, offered in a cloth holder. Flan for dessert.

Faz's Tex-Mex Grill, 38 Gerard St., Huntington, NY 11743; (631) 271-4333; Tex-Mex; $–$$. Faz's is a small, spare, and no-frills restaurant that looks as if it does more take-out than eat-in. During prime time, you may find a short line. The perpetual-motion kitchen makes zesty chili, both beef and vegetarian, which customers take home with bags of soft, fresh flour tortillas. Burritos are heavy-duty, with 2 cheeses, rice, black beans, lettuce, and tomato supporting the chicken, chicken stew, steak, and combos. Good quesadillas, especially the Monterey Jack cheese, chorizo and cheese, and jalapeño, and hard-shell tacos with chili, black or pinto beans, guacamole, chorizo, or steak. The fajitas can be uneven. You're better off with chicken than beef. The house's specials may take in chili and rice with onions and cheese or grilled chicken atop rice with peppers and onions.

Four Food Studio & Cocktail Salon, 515 Broadhollow Rd., Melville, NY 11747; (631) 577-4444; fourfoodstudio.com; New American; $$$. It's impossible to miss Four, a bold and entertaining enterprise that has contributed to the ongoing transformation of dining out along the Route 110 business corridor. Designed to suggest the four seasons (lower case), Four includes an igloo-look ode to winter and a bar that pulsates like summer; a green lounge for spring; and a woody main dining room for fall. The waiters and waitresses are in year-round black. The four-cheese flatbread is good shared while the rest of the decisions are made. Depending on your season of attendance, there may be light gnocchi in a braised short rib ragu, jumbo shrimp and grits with chorizo and charred scallion, roast chicken with fingerling potatoes and baby artichokes, and a meat loaf with potatoes, peas, carrots, and gravy. They're all worth it. Chicken lettuce wraps with cashews bring in an Asian aside as do the spicy sambal chicken lollipops with cucumber kimchee. Beef brisket tacos with hot sauce and the grilled skirt steak are good. Four has a whimsical way about it but it's as commendable for a business lunch as it is for a dinner date. Everyone gets cotton candy.

Gold Mine Mexican Grill, 99 Broadway, Greenlawn, NY 11740; (631) 262-1775; Mexican; $. Gold Mine seems equal parts eat-in and take-out, very casual and just as friendly. The prices are reasonable, too. That means it's time for the "burrito grande," a copious construct packed with diced chicken, refried beans, rice, shredded lettuce, and more. Wraps are popular here and they range from basic to surprising. You wouldn't ordinarily associate Gold Mine with, for example, Cajun chicken. The cheese nachos deluxe are all you'd expect them to be, and as these things go, quite good. Steak fajitas deliver sufficient char and more than a little sweetness. And you'll join a list of advocates on behalf of the crisp taco salad bowl, a production laden with greens, Monterey Jack cheese, and enough ingredients to feed the entire middle school softball team. Maybe the coaches, too.

Grasso's, 134 Main St., Cold Spring Harbor, NY 11724; (631) 367-6060; grassosrestaurant.com; Italian; $$–$$$. Grasso's has lived several lives along Main Street, going through themes from trattoria to New American. Through it all, the restaurant has maintained lighthearted style and a loyal following. These days, visit for cavatelli Bolognese, with a rustic beef, pork, and veal sauce; pappardelle with mushrooms, leeks, garlic, and cream; roasted Long Island duckling with rhubarb-strawberry sauce and mushroom risotto; and New Zealand lamb chops crusted with mustard and pistachio nuts. The watercress, fennel, and beet salad emboldened with feta cheese is a savory opener; ditto the combo of crabmeat, white beans, and red onion, glistening from lime juice and mint oil. Grasso's turns out a satisfying burger, too.

Honu Kitchen & Cocktails, 363 New York Ave., Huntington, NY 11743; (631) 421-6900; honukitchen.com; New American; $$$. Honu Kitchen & Cocktails boasts one of the town's more dramatic dining rooms, with its high ceiling, contemporary artwork, and extra-long bar. The cocktail half of the name is earned, with some creative and appealing drinks that fuel the buzzing establishment. Once you're focused, or unfocused, on the menu, the show continues, with small plates and larger ones. The charred-beef flatbread with onion marmalade, crumbled blue cheese, and arugula sounds several notes at once. Pumpkin tortelloni with goat cheese and roasted pepper sauce take you contentedly west; Beijing duck, with scallion, cucumber and hoisin sauce, happily east. "On a stick" comes Thai chicken, bolstered by crushed peanuts and peanut sauce. Sage-roasted, French-cut chicken translates into a tasty main course, with whipped potatoes and pan juices. The snowy spuds also accompany a tender filet mignon au poivre. And the burger improves either gruyère or cheddar, herb mayo, or applewood-smoked bacon. Cheesecake and chocolate fudge cake suit Honu.

House of India, 256 Main St., Huntington, NY 11743; (631) 271-0059; houseofindiarestaurant.com; Indian; $$. There are almost no surprises at House of India and pretty much everyone likes it that way. The dining room veers toward genteel these days. The food is livelier. Easy calls are the professionally reddened tandoori chicken and the moist lamb kebab marinated in yogurt and spices. *Rogan josh,* the crimson-hued lamb stew, also is good, with notes of ginger and garlic in the yogurt-and-tomato mix. Lamb vindaloo has the necessary kick, though the approach can be too strong for lobster and shrimp.

But if you want heat, these are the right dishes. Vegetarians do well here, especially with biryani and the fine lentil productions. Aloo gobi, with cauliflower, potatoes, and peas, similarly attracts you. Breads are uniformly commendable, with standout onion kulcha and whole-wheat aloo paratha. Mint and mango chutneys provide refreshing company. The sweet lassi, a yogurt drink, and both mango ice cream and rasmalai effectively cool things off.

Ichiz, 301 Main St., Huntington, NY 11743; (631) 470-0210; Japanese; $$–$$$. Ichiz stresses small plates and the sakes that make them seem to grow larger. This narrow, stylish storefront is equal parts for diners and imbibers. The front seating area and the bigger space in the back come across like private hangouts. The bar and the tight seating opposite it will test your devotion. Ichiz's food is fairly straightforward. Baked oysters and deviled eggs suit the quick-bite mood. Scallops wrapped with maple wood-smoked bacon and spicy tofu with red rice up the competition. Tempura-fried shrimp has crunch and orange-glazed pork ribs sweetness. Fried squid with chile sauce guarantees a second round of beverages. Grilled hamachi collar arrives with spiced-up ponzu sauce for a diverting alternative. The filet mignon sliders are tender and flavored with wasabi-laced mayo. Creamy wasabi sauce is a good accent for the seared tuna. There are several more desserts than you'd expect: crème brûlée, poached pear, chocolate mousse, warm peach pie. Have your sake chilled.

J. Michaels Tuscan Steakhouse, 688 Fort Salonga Rd., Northport, NY 11768; (631) 651-9411; jmichaelstuscansteakhouse .com; Italian, Steak; $$$–$$$$. J. Michaels Tuscan Steakhouse likes to describe its food as New World and Old World. Either way, it's excellent. The steak-house theme is reinterpreted here and becomes more expansive. It's a good-looking dining room, refurbishing the vintage restaurant building long occupied by La Capannina. Super starters include lobster meatballs, shrimp and crabmeat cocktails, spicy sautéed calamari, and "Tuscan tuna tacos," a rich variation on bruschetta. The blackboard will list steaks, dry-aged for 28 days, among them the New York strip, Kansas City cut, T-bone, and porterhouse for two. Tuna St. Francis with lobster and broccoli rabe is a solid alternative. Side dishes are exceptional: escarole and white beans, sautéed broccoli rabe with cherry peppers, whipped potatoes, hash browns, creamed spinach. Outstanding multilayer chocolate cake and cheesecake continue the party. There is a second J. Michaels Tuscan Steakhouse at 160 Mill River Rd., Oyster Bay; (516) 628-2800.

Jewel, **400 Broad Hollow Rd., Melville, NY 11747; (631) 755-5777; jewelrestaurantli.com; New American; $$–$$$.** Jewel glitters on the south service road of the Long Island Expressway. The extravagant establishment showcases a bubble theme and delivers some pop. There are party rooms and cozier niches and a main dining room that could be a stage. It's restaurateur Tom Schaudel's high-profile addition to the Route 110 business strip. The food is a something-for-everyone combo plate. Very good yellowtail crudo with yuzu, mint, and olive oil competes with a taleggio-fig-prosciutto pizza; butter-poached lobster vies with a juicy "5-napkin" hamburger. The short-rib-and-taleggio sandwich is, too. Tuna with red curry; octopus with olives, capers, and fingerling potatoes splashed with "local Merlot vinaigrette"; and beets, roasted, poached, and pickled, keep the action going. And that's what Jewel is about. Nobody will be bored, whether busy with business lunches or date-night dining.

Jonathan's Ristorante, **15 Wall St., Huntington, NY 11743; (631) 549-0055; jonathansristorante.com; Italian; $$–$$$.** In a town rife with Italian restaurants, Jonathan's inspires loyalty. The dining room shows some whimsy in the artwork, with its images of dogs and monkeys in chef's garb. And the kitchen takes an expansive view of Italian cooking, appealing to purists and heretics alike. The union of sautéed wild mushrooms and soft polenta works all year. Cucumber and radish salad perks up with white anchovies. A drizzle of wasabi dressing nudges yellowfin tuna tartare and avocado salad beyond standard. They make an excellent fritto misto with squid, shrimp, and zucchini, complemented by tomato and anchovy sauces. Strozzapreti Bolognese is delicious, as are the spaghetti with spicy lobster and the light gnocchi with tomato, basil, and mozzarella. *Pollo al mattone,* or "under a brick," materializes juicy and crisp. A tasty double-cut pork chop benefits from cipollini onions. Very good steak frites, too. The mascarpone cheesecake and the panna cotta lead the desserts.

Kabul, **1153 E. Jericho Tpke., Huntington, NY 11743; (631) 549-5506; kabulny.com; Afghani; $$.** Kabul is in a small commercial strip, packing plenty of flavor. The cuisine has few major representatives in Nassau and Suffolk. But Kabul does its part with *aushak,* a pasta with leeks and spring onions finished with meat sauce, yogurt, garlic, and mint. Leeks also star in *bolani gandana,* a turnover. *Bolani kadu* is packed with pumpkin; *bolani kachalu,* with seasoned, minced meat and spiced potato. Baba ghanoush is very good, as are the house's hummus; and mantu, or dumplings with meat and onions, in a savory sauce hinting of coriander. Kabul prepares a tasty rack of lamb with rice and vegetables, lamb kebab with dried grape leaves, and lamb tenderloin with rice, carrots, and raisins. In addition to the lamb specialties, Kabul does well with marinated and broiled chicken, stir-fried chicken with vegetables, and tandoori-style Cornish hen. *Dahl chalaw* is beef cooked with yellow split peas, tomatoes, onions, and garlic for a hearty stew. Sultani kebab: filet mignon, sliced, marinated, skewered, charbroiled, and very good. The wild salmon kebab and shrimp in cauliflower stew also are noteworthy, as are all the vegetarian main courses. Baklava, rice pudding, and firnee, an almond-and-cardamom cream pudding, are fine sweets.

Legal Sea Foods, 160 Walt Whitman Rd., Huntington Station, NY 11746; (631) 271-9777; legalseafoods.com; Seafood; $$–$$$. This is the lone branch of the national chain currently moored on Long Island. Ordinarily, you'd say that on a seafood-centric island, such an establishment would be rammed and sunk by competitors. But Legal remains a convenient restaurant at the south end of the Walt Whitman Shops. The New England–style clam chowder, the lobster roll, and fried oysters with seaweed salad are satisfying. They know how to steam lobster, bake Boston scrod, and wood-grill haddock, too. The officially designated lobster bake includes the starring shellfish plus steamers, mussels, corn on the cob, and chouriço sausage. The fried cod and fried haddock are crunchy and sweet, and the baked shrimp with crabmeat stuffing, a dish that usually announces itself as if with a warning label, tastes fine. For dessert, you'll be contemplating Boston cream pie and Key lime pie. Not bad.

Los Compadres, 243 Walt Whitman Rd., Huntington Station, NY 11746; (631) 351-8384; Mexican; $. Just off Route 110 and close to the Walt Whitman Shops is this ultracasual, bargain-priced burrito-size spot. There are a few tables, a TV usually tuned to a soccer game, a refrigerator that keeps the Jarritos sodas cold, and a tiny kitchen that's invariably in overdrive satisfying a diverse clientele that has in common true affection for flavorful and homey Mexican cooking. The noise level is very low because everyone seems focused exclusively on his or her plate. The chunky corn tortilla with sausage and potatoes and the mellow tamales inspire loyalty. You'll have more than one taco with chorizo or chicken and are guaranteed to dive into empanadas, enchiladas, quesadillas, flautas, and chiles rellenos. Juicy chicken with rice and beans, too. And try the guacamole and/or the salsa with thick, crunchy chips. Los Compadres does a brisk take-out business.

Mac's Steakhouse, 12 Gerard St., Huntington, NY 11743; (631) 549-5300; macssteakhouse.com; New American, Steak, Seafood; $$$. A stylized steer is the mascot for Mac's. It's on almost everything. If new owners wanted to change either the image or the name, they'd need an extra line in the budget. The spacious dining room has abundant western-themed visuals, too. But the main part of the decor for hungry diners is the blackboard, overflowing with specials; and the very solid menu, for carnivores and the not-always meat-eaters. For example: *arancino di risotto,* an oversize rice ball with tomato-cream sauce, and the warm pear salad with spinach, Gorgonzola cheese, and pecans. Mac's prepares excellent shellfish cocktails and a big-deal seafood plateau for four. The short-rib dumplings surprisingly work and the Maryland crab cake with napa cabbage coleslaw and tartar sauce predictably does. The serious will focus on the dry-aged steaks from grass-fed cattle. The 60-day bone-in New York strip steak is exceptional; the 30-day, not far behind. There's a very good porterhouse for two or four, and a bone-in rib eye coming in at 28 ounces. The pork chop "porterhouse," filet mignon, and grilled lamb chops add to the turf; grilled swordfish, halibut, and tuna, the surf.

Maroni Cuisine, 18 Woodbine Ave., Northport, NY 11768; (631) 757-4500; maronicuisine.com; Eclectic; $$$$. Chef Michael Maroni gained national publicity with his victorious meatball "throwdown" versus celebrity chef and Food Network star Bobby Flay. It was entertaining. But anyone who has eaten here knows that Maroni's

Mondo Parmigiana

In the city of Parma, Italy, where prosciutto and Parmesan cheese are pillars of the local cuisine, a dish of eggplant parmigiana doesn't include a blanket of melted mozzarella. But the familiar Italian-American rendition is an ode to it.

"Parmigiana" is the magical adjective at red-sauce specialists and pizzerias. It modifies eggplant, chicken, veal, meatball, shrimp, sausages, and just about anything the kitchen wants to cover in the molten mozza. All versions, however, aren't the same. Order it at one of these five restaurants and you'll find out fast why it's so popular. Stick with chicken or eggplant.

Centro Cucina in Greenvale

Eric's Italian Bistro in Mineola

La Tavola in Sayville

Matteo's in Huntington

Mio Posto in Hicksville

meatballs and spaghetti sauce and his take-home pots are a small part of the package. The chef's creative, international repertoire shows in exceptional tasting menus that change frequently. Sashimi, lobster bisque, Kobe beef sliders, duck with Grand Marnier syrup, a lobster roll, linguine with clams, barbecued ribs, eggplant parmigiana, Thai spring rolls, deluxe hot dogs, chicken Milanese, clams casino, ice-cream sandwiches, and pretty much whatever Maroni feels like making ensure a memorable experience each time he pops in from behind a curtain, dish in hand. The restaurant is vise-tight. There are some tables that squeeze in 4. Maybe 5 can squeeze into the window space. Duets dominate. The tab is high. But it's quite a show. Reserve early.

Matteo's, 300 W. Jericho Tpke., Huntington, NY 11746; (631) 421-6001; matteosristorante.com; Italian; $$–$$$. Family-style Italian restaurants are among the rigatoni-shaped pillars supporting dining out in Nassau and Suffolk. They earn their popularity with generosity and consistency. The Matteo's group is the most reliable, with portions big and medium depending on your appetite. Service: brisk and friendly. Style: streamlined and efficient. Your table's order should include fried zucchini and baked clams, maybe a shrimp cocktail, and definitely the stuffed artichokes. Chicken Angelina, all white meat and on the bone, with peppers, peas, and potatoes, and chicken scarpariello, on the bone, with roasted peppers, onions, broccoli, and sausage, both are major deals. Chicken parmigiana, veal Milanese, and shrimp marinara are their rivals. Everyone must taste some pasta, whether in white clam sauce, Bolognese-style meat sauce, marinara, or with meatballs and sausage. You'll be full before dessert. Other Matteo's branches are at 88 Mineola Ave., Roslyn, (516) 484-0555, and 416 Bedford Ave., Bellmore, (516) 409-1779.

Mill Pond House, 437 E. Main St., Centerport, NY 11721; (631) 261-7663; millpondrestaurant.com; American; $$$. Mill Pond House has a pretty, waterside setting as a backdrop for its often partylike scene. The dining room can be serene and charming; the outdoor bar, well, different. At table, sample the roasted cauliflower oreganata with béchamel sauce, which could turn you vegetarian. But then you'd miss the very good raw bar, the crab salad tacos, and filet mignon "burnt ends," with caramelized onions, mushrooms, and barbecue sauce. The Kobe beef sliders and Blue Point oysters Rockefeller enrich the proceedings. Linguine with white clam sauce, pappardelle Bolognese, and penne with tomato sauce and ricotta lead the pastas. Steamed lobster, roasted Chatham cod, grilled jumbo "Margarita" shrimp, and fine sushi do the same for seafood. Chicken parmigiana, the grilled sirloin, filet mignon, and porterhouse steak for two also are recommended, with sides of home fries, mashed potatoes, and creamed spinach. The banana cream tart and chocolate layer cake are good.

Oaxaca, 385 New York Ave., Huntington, NY 11743; (631) 547-1232; oaxacamenu.com; Mexican; $–$$. Oaxaca is a sliver of a restaurant, a casual spot, subtitled "Mexican food treasure," keeping the tacos at a high level and the prices affordable as it nears 20 years downtown. The nachos deluxe and the stuffed jalapeños informally get things started. The chicken and chorizo quesadillas do, too. Pozole, gazpacho, tortilla soup, and black bean soup are respectable choices, as are the avocado and taco salads. Better main courses include ropa vieja, or shredded beef with onions in hot sauce; the familiar arroz con pollo; tamales with chicken and mole steamed in banana leaves; the husky chicken chimichanga; mild pork burrito; and the carne asada, or steak with grilled vegetables, rice, beans, and tortillas. Just as good are the shrimp enchiladas with green sauce and melted cheese and the mole Oaxaca, or broiled chicken with a mellow mole sauce and rice. The fajitas do sizzle. And the Mexico City tacos are especially tasty when made with baked pork, grilled pork, or chorizo. Empanadas, either chicken, beef, or vegetable, compete, too, rice and beans alongside.

Old Fields Restaurant, 81 Broadway, Greenlawn, NY 11740; (631) 754-9868; oldfieldsgreenlawn.com; American; $$. Old Fields Restaurant used to be known as Old Fields Inn. There have been many other changes here over the decades, most notably some refurbishing of the dining area and a major overhaul of the cuisine. The style remains certifiably traditional, even old-fashioned, from the dark wood to the brick fireplace. But the choices have gone well beyond the marinated steak that had been the centerpiece. You can sample the flatiron and skirt steaks with their 1956 marinade, or cut into the even better bone-in rib eye or filet mignon. The house's hamburgers include the Greenlawn, with bacon, cheddar, and crisp onions, and the 56, with the marinade, swiss cheese, and sautéed onions, both good. Grilled loin of pork with apples, turnips, and sweet potatoes; roasted chicken; and a cobb salad also are recommended. Begin with the short-rib-and-potato croquettes, the gumbo-stuffed pepper, fried Ipswich clams, or pulled-pork sliders on pretzel bread. Old Fields has a well-chosen list of beers in bottles and cans, and a respectable wine list to accompany the fare.

PG Steak House, 1745 Jericho Tpke., Huntington, NY 11743; **(631) 499-1005; Steak; $$$.** PG has been cooking since 1985, when Paul Grewenig, a Peter Luger veteran, established the restaurant. It's still a family operation. The spare, rustic look remains unchanged. And the menu hasn't varied much, either. There's an instant familiarity to PG. Most diners already know what they want before they see the terse menu. Waiters politely make recommendations, steering you to the standards. You begin with a shrimp or crabmeat cocktail, herring in cream sauce, maybe tomatoes and onions. Then, depending on your entourage, it's porterhouse steak for two, three, or four, crusty and juicy. The filet mignon and the rib steak compete for solo honors with the lamb chops. The chopped steak also appeals. If, for some reason, a member of your group starts talking about the virtues of seafood, fish oil, and the like, you can safely and politely suggest poached salmon with dill sauce. On the side, the basics: creamed spinach, onion rings, and your favored potato. Apple strudel, pecan pie, chocolate mousse cake, and ice cream are the unsurprising desserts.

Piccola Bussola, 970 W. Jericho Tpke., Huntington, NY 11743; **(631) 692-6300; piccolabussolarestaurant.com; Italian; $$.** Piccola

Bussola is a member of the group that includes La Bussola in Glen Cove. This family-style, Italian restaurant is good from antipasti to dolce. Portions are hefty but the tab isn't. Some fried peppers, fried zucchini, the stuffed eggplant, and the stuffed artichoke generously begin dinner. Share a roasted beet salad or the Caesar salad. Decide on either rigatoni Bolognese or linguine puttanesca. Then start slicing the well-seasoned steak alla pizzaiola, rustic chicken scarpariello, or ever-faithful chicken parmigiana, all good. If you're adamant about seafood, they'll deliver a respectable order of shrimp marinara and, if you're feeling expansive, lobster fra diavolo. The key sides with anything at Piccola Bussola are escarole and beans and sautéed broccoli rabe. The desserts are cannoli, Italian cheesecake, tiramisu, and that ball of ice cream that has been termed a tartufo.

Piccolo, 215 Wall St., Huntington, NY 11743; (631) 424-5592; piccolorestaurant.net; New American, Italian; $$$. Piccolo's transition from mainly Italian to largely New American went smoothly and the restaurant has retained loyalists. In part, that's because of the service. Regulars are revered. Whatever your status, refresh yourself with the summery watermelon-and-feta salad and the yellowfin tuna tacos. Figs stuffed with goat cheese, wrapped in prosciutto, and finished with balsamic vinegar also appeal. Braised beef short ribs, minus the bones, get a spark from horseradish cream sauce. Pork chop Milanese, sirloin steak or filet mignon au poivre, and the husky chicken parmigiana with linguine point in the restaurant's different directions, each good. Among the pastas, one of the better choices is tagliatelle Bolognese. Littleneck clams, either casino or oreganata, and either the tricolor or Greek salad are respectable openers. Desserts wander from crème brûlée and tiramisu to bread pudding and chocolate cake. Sometimes, the gelati supersede them.

Porto Vivo, 7 Gerard St., Huntington, NY 11743; (631) 385-8486; porto-vivo.com; Italian; $$–$$$. Splashy, exuberant Porto Vivo lights up what had been one of downtown Huntington's quieter streets. The multilevel showcase pulsates on weekend nights and attracts a crowd most weekdays, too. The sleek, modernist look is balanced by largely traditional fare with some contemporary twists. "Chianti-stained" pappardelle Bolognese and the untinted capellini with clams, garlic, lemon, and white wine lead the pastas. Precede them with the grilled artichoke or veer toward Iberia with skillet-roasted octopus paired with chorizo and finished with sherry. Pan-seared scallops are enriched with a braised-leek-and-lobster sauce with crisp speck. Turrets of seared ahi tuna get their gilding from a black truffle puree and caponata. Olive oil–poached fingerling potatoes go with the filet of branzino, accompanied by broccoli rabe and brightened with lemon and basil. Porto Vivo also presents a very good version of chicken parmigiana. Desserts: a lush cheesecake, the espresso panna cotta "coffee cigarette," and a crackling crème brûlée.

Prime, 117 New York Ave., Huntington, NY 11743; (631) 385-1515; restaurantprime.com; New American, Steak, Sushi; $$$–$$$$. Prime time is now. The sharp, waterside restaurant attracts you with its view, style, service, and the stellar food of Executive Chef Ben Durham, who previously cooked at Four Food Studio. Prime is part of the Bohlsen Restaurant Group, which includes Monsoon in Babylon and Tellers in Islip. Come by car or by boat, since there's dockside dining as part of the experience. Dinner highlights include superior shellfish cocktails and the raw bar plateau; crab cake with caper-driven sauce remoulade; pan-seared potato gnocchi with Parmesan cheese–white truffle sauce; and terrific steaks. The dry-aged New York strip, porterhouse for two, and Tellers rib eye are ideal. Be sure to accompany them with whipped potatoes, macaroni and cheese, and/or the housemade version of Tater Tots. Prime deftly steams or broils lobsters, matches local swordfish with Sicilian eggplant and black olive vinaigrette, and boosts black bass with pistachios, dates, quinoa, and balsamic vinegar. The very good sushi rolls emphasize harmony and flavor while providing the expected flashes of color. So does Prime.

Primo Piatto, 138 E. Main St., Huntington, NY 11743; (631) 935-1391; primopiattorestaurant.com; Italian; $–$$. The first plate at Primo Piatto is Sicilian: *bucatini chi sarde,* or pasta with sardines. But before that, you should try the *arancino,* or rice ball, packed with a savory, meaty ragu. They're rich ways to enjoy this informal spot, where diners dabble in brick-oven pizzettes, salads, and lots of Italian-American favorites. Someone at your table should ask for the *salumi* platter within seconds of seating. The cured meats are very good, backed by Sicilian olives and caponata. Eggplant rollatine, mozzarella in carrozza, and roasted tomato soup with a drizzle of basil aioli also are definites. In the mix are spaghetti with meatballs, ravioli in creamy pesto, bucatini all'Amatriciana, and orecchiette Barese, with sausage, broccoli rabe, and, here, tomatoes. From the pizzettes, pick the arugula-prosciutto-Parmesan and the anchovy-caper-olive pies. For main dishes, consider pan-seared swordfish and chicken alla pizzaiola.

Red, 417 New York Ave., Huntington, NY 11743; (631) 673-0304; redrestaurant.com; New American, Italian; $$–$$$. Red comes in a range of hues. Here, it can be bold and subtle, soothing and spirited. It's a comfortable, modern restaurant with broad appeal. Sautéed calamari with spicy tomato sauce, pine nuts, capers, and black olives is matched by mussels steamed in yellow curry broth, as if to underscore the range. Carpaccio, with arugula and a lemon vinaigrette, also is right. Spinach-and-ricotta ravioli show up in pesto that has some tomato, too. Pan-seared yellowfin tuna takes the Asian route with a soy-ginger glaze. Paella with seafood, chicken, and chorizo brings the saffron trade back west with flair. Tender steak frites and braised beef rib with red wine are good, too. Red is part of the restaurant group that includes Osteria da Nino, which is more Italian, at 292 Main St., Huntington, (631) 425-0820, and Cafe Red, more eclectic, at 287 Main St., Kings Park, (631) 673-0051.

Roast Sandwich House, 827 Walt Whitman Rd., Melville, NY 11747; (631) 629-4869; roastsandwichhouse.com; Sandwiches; $. Few places to eat have been welcomed more warmly on Route 110 than Roast Sandwich House. It's exactly what a business corridor needed as expense accounts and martini lunches shrank faster than the collective 401k. Roast stars with its housemade fare, from soups to salads, sandwiches, panini, wraps, and sides. Among the favorites: chilled local corn soup with lump crabmeat and cilantro oil, poached lobster salad, a lobster roll panino on grilled focaccia, and a Waldorf chicken salad sandwich with red grapes, celery, apples, and arugula. Also recommended are the New England–style clam chowder, roasted beet salad with goat cheese and greens, the obligatory grilled chicken Caesar, and a roast turkey cobb salad. The notable sandwiches are many. As a sampler, consider BBQ roast pork with roasted poblano aioli on ciabatta, braised-brisket grilled cheese on sourdough, meatballs on a garlic-toasted hero, and the Cuban roast pork panino. Roast carries bottled sodas, waters, and teas.

Ruvo, 63 Broadway, Greenlawn, NY 11740; (631) 261-7700; ruvorestaurant.com; Italian, New American; $$–$$$. Ruvo balances old and new with dexterity at this restaurant and its second branch in Port Jefferson. Crab-and-corn cakes benefit from chipotle-spiked aioli;

diver scallops, from a porcini crust and arugula pesto. Fennel sausage enriches the arborio rice balls. A plum-tomato-and-basil broth backs cavatelli with lobster, spinach, and white beans. Crisp roast duck finds its foil in a peach-apricot gastrique, plus a blend of farro and wild rice. And rack of lamb is complemented by a risotto of mushrooms and, unusually, Gouda cheese. The lushness of seared Montauk tuna is cut by a caper-honey vinaigrette. Ruvo succeeds with the familiarity of flounder oreganata, cavatelli and meatballs, spaghetti with littleneck clams, and the full quartet of parmigianas, chicken and veal, shrimp and eggplant. Solid desserts, especially mascarpone cheesecake and tiramisu.

Sapsuckers, 287 Main St., Huntington, NY 11743; (631) 683-4945; sapsuckersli.com; Gastropub; $$. Slide into Sapsuckers for some casual, well-made pub fare that's more refined and better conceived than those beer nuts and the hard-boiled egg that may have been your last bar's cuisine. Here, enjoy the housemade hummus with pita bread, fries with truffled aioli, marinated olives with Parmesan cheese, and a butter-baked pretzel with spicy mustard that guarantees another drink. Sapsuckers' hard-boiled eggs are devilled with care and have real flavor. Potato pierogies, crisped in a pan, are boosted by caramelized onions and sour cream. "Three little pigs" means pulled Berkshire pork and housemade slaw on brioche rolls, and it's very good. Baby back ribs are, too. And Sapsuckers prepares a deluxe Cubano on ciabatta. Have macaroni and cheese with any of the "hops and grub." The bread is excellent and the microbrews complement the food start to finish. That finale may include desserts from Huntington's Fiorello Dolce.

Show Win, 325 Fort Salonga Rd., Northport, NY 11768; (631) 261-6622; Japanese, Sushi; $$. Show Win is one of those local, all-purpose Japanese restaurants, the type of dining room that you return to automatically. It's a popular destination for the familiar sushi and sashimi. And you can have good renditions of tuna tataki, salmon

teriyaki, soba noodles served chilled, broiled yellowtail collar, beef negimaki, baked eggplant, fried bean curd, and *tonkatsu,* the deep-fried pork cutlet that has more to it than a lot of those you've endured. That goes for the shrimp-and-vegetable tempura, too. The rainbow roll is a colorful union starring tuna, salmon, fluke, and crab. A lot of diners know what they want before seeing any menus.

Spice Village Grill, 281 Main St., Huntington, NY 11743; (631) 271-4800; spicevillagegrill.com; Asian; $$. Get your kebabs here. Spice Village Grill attracts you with samosas and naan breads filled with meat and potatoes. Lentil dumplings with yogurt, tamarind, and chaat masala also are good. You can try Burmese coconut-chicken soup and the more familiar mulligatawny "pepper water," too. The house's grilled chicken, beef, and lamb kebabs are mainstays here. The grilled lamb chops and the mixed grill of beef, chicken, and lamb with peppers and onions are bracing main courses. So are coriander chicken and ginger chicken, chicken with cashews and yogurt, and the trio of curries, with beef, lamb, or chicken. If all this seems too meaty, Spice Village Grill evens things with a savory selection of vegetarian options, led with chickpeas cooked with onions and Indian spices; potatoes and cauliflower stewed with tomatoes and similar spices; and simmered red lentils, also deftly spiced. At lunch, consider the tandoori chicken roll and the tandoori naan loaded with ground beef, herbed and spiced.

Sri Thai, 14 New St., Huntington, NY 11743; (631) 424-3422; srithaihuntington.com; Thai; $$. All you need is some Thai basil and lemongrass to revive your appetite. Sri Thai knows the technique and makes a complex cuisine instantly accessible. Moreover, it's a friendly little restaurant, where you sometimes feel you're eating chopstick-to-chopstick. All the more reason to bite into those savory, deep-fried curry puffs; sesame noodles with shredded cucumber; drunken noodles with basil leaves and hot chiles; and steamed dumplings filled with marinated pork and shrimp. Pad Thai and chicken satay: well done. So are the snappy vegetarian yellow and red curries and the whole, deep-fried fish of the day in a sweet-spicy chile sauce. Thai salads are refreshers, to start the meal or as a side dish. Nam, or ground chicken ignited with chiles, ginger, onions, lime juice, and peanuts, is a wake-up call. There's good fried chicken with ground peanuts and tamarind sauce and soft-shell crabs with either basil or fish sauces. Enjoy soups such as tom kah kai, with chicken, mushrooms, baby corn, and coconut milk; and tom yum kai, with a blast of lemongrass, to jump-start dinner, too.

Swallow, 366 New York Ave., Huntington, NY 11743; (631) 547-5388; swallowrestaurant.com; New American; $$. James Tchinnis brought big-time small plates to downtown, in the quarters that used to house Kozy Kettle, the much-missed soupworks. He immediately endeared himself to despondent Kettlers with a delightful butternut squash cappuccino, a soup squared with a hint of truffle in the foam. His Malbec-poached figs with goat cheese, prosciutto, and balsamic syrup also star. A drizzle of local honey heightens the flavor of roasted beets with housemade ricotta. Pickled jalapeño, citrus mayo, and salsa fresca do likewise for roasted beets. Housemade tomato jam spurs the spiced lamb sliders. Braised and shredded beef short ribs match neatly with curried sushi rice. Spaghetti is sauced with style via a pulled-pork-and-tomato ragu. It's all fun, now in an expanded setting. If you're headed east, there's the seasonal Swallow East, on West Lake Drive in Montauk; (631) 668-8344.

Ting, 92 E. Main St., Huntington, NY 11743; (631) 425-7788; tingrestaurant.com; Asian; $$–$$$. Ting combines Chinese, Japanese,

Thai, New American, and more in a modern mix that's satisfying in every way. Service is excellent. And the dining room has sleek good looks. Start mainly Chinese with Ting's lettuce wraps holding diced chicken, peppers, and, updating chicken Soong, pine nuts and jicama. Chicken and beef satays are enriched with a fine peanut sauce while the flatbread, *roti canai*, is equally spurred by curry sauce. Crisp rock shrimp tempura is complemented with spicy aioli; crunchy fried calamari, with tomato salsa. Roasted corn-and-crab soup and creamy butternut squash soup are flavorful surprises. From the sushi bar: translucent yellowtail with jalapeño, tuna carpaccio with mango salsa, red snapper carpaccio with spicy yuzu dressing, and traditional sashimi, all sharp. Enjoy the "signature rolls," including Spring of Paris with king crab, tuna, and salmon; and the Huntington with lobster tempura. Kung pao chicken with cashews, shrimp in green curry, beef with Japanese eggplant, and standout Beijing duck and rack of New Zealand lamb keep the tour first-class.

Toast & Co., 62 Stewart Ave., Huntington, NY 11743; (631) 812-0056; toastandcompanyeatery.com; Breakfast, Lunch; $$. Toast & Co. fills a big niche downtown, serving the morning and midday crowd with very good dishes at respectable prices. The style of the joint plays on the nostalgia theme, suggesting a time when people did eat breakfast out without necessarily conducting business at the same moment. Ricotta-lemon pancakes are commendably rich, vying with the bananas Foster variety, stuffed French toast, eggs Benedict, omelets to order, Belgian waffles, and, for the diner needing early decadence, the chocolate waffle under a cloudlet of whipped cream. Steel-cut oats with maple syrup are homey enough. And if your company is the right age, it's hard to pass up green eggs and ham. A skillet of scrambled

eggs with caramelized onions, tomato, and chorizo sausage definitely will keep you full till lunch. At that point, consider a segue to the barbecued short-rib sandwich. The staff tries to keep the mood light, but impatient, waiting customers sometimes don't go along with them. Bring some reading material during prime time.

Vitae, 54 New St., Huntington, NY 11743; (631) 385-1919; vitaeli .com; New American, Continental; $$–$$$. Vitae always is hosting wine dinners, offering specials, pushing promotions, and generally making things livelier along New Street. Vitae sprouted on the former site of Abel Conklin's steak house, which seared beef for more than 25 years. Vitae overhauled the entire place, brightened and lightened it, and improved on the food. The marinated and grilled Portuguese octopus with Moroccan chickpea salad is a full-bodied starter. Scallop escabeche, with mandarin orange salsa and pink grapefruit granita, and Australian lamb "lollipops" with rosemary-garlic pesto and green apple salsa are diverting options. But try braised short-rib meatballs with pickled red onions and lemon-horseradish cream. The marinated and grilled Cedar River flatiron steak and the pan-roasted Berkshire pork chop with sautéed onions, hot and sweet cherry peppers, artichoke hearts, and roasted potatoes are fine main courses. Angel-hair pasta and crabmeat "oreganata" works, with lump crabmeat, roasted tomatoes, basil, green onion, and seasoned panko. End with the "falling down" chocolate cake, clever play on banana cream pie, or the house's doughnuts with malted chocolate sauce.

Landmarks

Mediterranean Snack Bar, 360 New York Ave., Huntington, NY 11743; (631) 423-8982; medsnackbar.com; Greek; $–$$. The Mediterranean Snack Bar is one of downtown Huntington's popular, casual eateries. It has been slicing the gyros and sending out the moussaka and pastitsio since 1975, all at moderate prices. Souvlaki, either chicken or veal; gyros, lamb or beef; kebabs, beef and lamb; and openers such as saganaki and Greek salads are acceptable. More ambitious appetites may turn to the whole broiled flounder, grilled lamb chops, braised lamb shank, or the marinated octopus. Sooner or later, you'll have the stuffed grape leaves and the taramosalata. And you can be sure that someone will be ready for the cheeseburger or the hot dog. The restaurant has expanded the selections. But no one would mind if the Ford Administration menu had remained untouched.

Munday's, 259 Main St., Huntington, NY 11743; (631) 421-3553; mundays.kpsearch.com; Luncheonette, Soda Fountain; $. When they refurbished Munday's years ago, modernizing the sign and upgrading the appointments, you could hear a collective sigh from Main Street regulars. Not that it was exactly remodeling Monticello or turning the Taj Mahal condo, but any change seemed inappropriate, particularly since so many have reshaped downtown. To anyone who has dined there since, most fears were washed away with an egg cream. The ice cream soda and the floats do the same thing. Munday's is open for breakfast, lunch, and dinner. Depending on the hour, visit for an omelet or a short stack, hot dog or hamburger, Reuben or turkey club sandwich, maybe the pot roast or fried chicken. None is immortal. But Munday's is only partly about the food. Anyway, a banana split sounds good right about now.

Pumpernickel's, 640 Main St., Northport, NY 11768; (631) 757-7959; German, Continental; $$–$$$. It's impossible to estimate how much sauerbraten and wurst have been served in this establishment, where a beer stein fits into the logo and the German food expands your waistline. Suffice it to say that the house specialties include bracing stuff: pig's knuckle with sauerkraut, frikadellen with mushroom gravy and mashed potato, smoked loin of pork, wiener rostbraten with onions, wiener schnitzel a la Holstein, Hungarian beef goulash, beef roulade, that sauerbraten with potato dumplings and red cabbage, and your choice of bratwurst, knockwurst, or weisswurst. Start with head cheese vinaigrette, herring with sour cream and onions, gravlax, or, if you want to dive in early, a bratwurst appetizer. The competition comes from roast duckling, filet mignon, and sautéed calf's liver with bacon and onions. Drink beer.

Specialty Stores, Markets & Shops

A Rise Above Bake Shop, 333 Main St., Huntington, NY 11743; (631) 351-9811; Bakery. The heir to The Well-Bred Loaf continues the departed little bakery's tradition at this central address. A Rise Above makes good breads and rolls, particularly Irish soda bread and soft dinner rolls ready to be buttered; and a collection of major-league muffins. The carrot cake definitely emphasizes the carrot; and the cookies call for coffee on the spot. But the real winners here are the scones, buttermilk variety, unadorned or fruit-topped; and the triangular Scottish scones, with the texture of crumbly shortbread, which could satisfy an army of Highlanders. On the cookie front: lemon or raspberry bars, apricot squares, chocolate chip cookies with walnuts, pecan puffs, oatmeal-raisin cookies, and almost any item made with peanut butter. For the bargain-hunter, there are a couple of shelves devoted to day-old stuff.

Bon Bons Chocolatier, 319 Main St., Huntington, NY 11743; (631) 549-1059; bonbonschocolatier.com; Chocolatier, Candy. It's easy to know when Valentine's Day, Easter, or any other holiday even remotely associated with chocolate has arrived. Just check the line at Bon Bons. If you haven't checked the calendar, you'll think there's a convention under way. Bon Bons offers fine handmade chocolates, bittersweet and milk. They do a very good job with chocolate-dipped strawberries and wedges of orange, and with chocolate truffles. Creams include orange and raspberry. And the chocolate-covered orange peel, glazed ginger, and glazed apricot turn first-timers into devoted fans. That goes for the mint meltaways, peppermint thins, salty peanut-and-caramel clusters, and housemade marzipan, too. Bon Bons has a full range of Jelly Belly jelly beans. Some items are prepackaged so you don't always have to wait for the customer in front of you to complete interrogating the staff about the content of every sweet in the case. They have some witty greeting cards and related products to go with the chocolates.

The Chicken Coop, 44 Gerard St., Huntington, NY 11743; (631) 423-2667; chickencoophuntington.com; Take-out. There's curbside pickup to speed things up at the Chicken Coop, the "grilltisserie" scion of Fado, the Portuguese restaurant a few blocks away. They have 4 preparations of the juicy bird: garlic-lemon butter; spicy piri piri, which means Tabasco; a tomatoey barbecue sauce; and creamy spinach and walnut pesto. A fifth may pop up, too. The dissenters can choose a shrimp po' boy, a burger with onion rings, and a shredded chicken with blue cheese and hot sauce sandwich. Side dishes include cream-cheese-and-chive mashed potatoes, jalapeño-and-cheddar macaroni and cheese, a potato-and-bacon salad, shoestring skin-on fries, buttered corn niblets, garlic-and-Parmesan spiked creamed spinach, and rice with lentils and beans. Spinach salad, with shrimp, feta cheese, onion, olives, peppers, and apricots, fits in as a refresher. The full-meal choices include buttermilk biscuits.

Clipper Ship Tea Company, 80 Main St., Northport, NY 11768; (631) 651-2764; clippershipteaco.com; Tea. The Clipper Ship Tea Company carries more than 200 loose-leaf teas. They include about 20 seasonals, which in autumn may be pumpkin patch, candy apple, caramel apple, harvest spice, and hot buttered rum; in spring-summer, coconut, pineapple, passion fruit, and lemon. The warm-weather teas may be available year-round, too. There are informative, flavorful tea tastings, for example, a session on Ceylon black teas from Sri Lankan gardens. While at the shop, you can sample teas hot or iced. Clipper Ship also sells tea-infused chocolates, raw honey, and assorted gluten-free and vegan products.

Copenhagen Bakery & Cafe, 75 Woodbine Ave., Northport, NY 11768; (631) 754-3256; copenhagenbakery.net; Bakery. The symbol of Copenhagen Bakery is a kringle, the pretzel-shaped pastry, light and luscious, best strewn with sliced almonds. Come if only for one of them. You'll wonder what the fuss is all about when someone starts jabbering datedly about "cronuts." And contemplate eating the whole thing yourself. Relish the assorted Danish and the apple-cranberry-walnut tart; the strawberry-rhubarb pie and the Granny Smith apple crumb; and a selection of cheesecakes. The "special event" cakes are serious affairs, too, and will take the edge off any birthday. There are well-made breads and rolls, Tuscan to sourdough, even low-carb for the contrarian. Copenhagen attracts regulars for breakfast specials, sandwiches, juices, and soups, too. But it's hard to concentrate on an omelet or French toast, crepes, or egg sandwiches once you start looking at the sweets.

The Crushed Olive, 278 Main St., Huntington, NY 11743; (631) 675-6266; thecrushedolive.com; Specialty Market. This is one of three Crushed Olive stores in Suffolk County. They specialize in, yes, plenty of olive oil and have a large selection of vinegars to finish your dressing. The Nocellara del Belice organic olive oil from Sicily is fruity, fairly mild, and pleasing all around. The early-harvest Arbequina extra-virgin olive oil and lightly peppery Manzanilla from Spain, and the more peppery Chemlali from Tunisia, also are notable. You can dip into a fair amount of flavored oils and vinegars, too, including chipotle-pepper infused olive oil and balsamic vinegar with a maple accent, though these are definitely in the acquired-taste category. Other branches of the Crushed Olive are at 133 Main St. in Stony Brook, (631) 675-6266, and 31-A Main St. in Sayville, (631) 256-5777.

Fiorello Dolce, 57 Wall St., Huntington, NY 11743; (631) 424-0803; fiorellodolce.com; Bakery. The appeal of Fiorello Dolce is year-round. This exceptional shop makes delicious pastries, cakes, cookies, breads, and other baked goods. And it's the source for outstanding gelati, too. You'll be partial to the Sarah Bernhardts, macaroon and chocolate ganache creations that fit neatly in a gift box. And when the trendlet took hold, chocolate or caramel drizzled "cronuts" appeared. At Christmastime, the star is an exemplary *croquembouche*, an evergreen of caramel-glazed pastry puffs filled with vanilla or chocolate cream. Anytime, sample the croissants and brioche, 7-grain bread and olive bread. Then, take home the pine nut, Linzer, or blueberry tarts; Italianate napoleons and lush éclairs; superior cannoli and flourless chocolate cake; a professional Paris Brest; Black Forest cake; opera cake; strawberry shortcake; or carrot cake. The almond biscotti also are essential, along with rainbow cookies. Relax with an espresso or cappuccino while your sweets are packaged. Order enough and you'll be able to slip in an extra gelato.

Forest Pork Store, 380 E. Jericho Tpke., Huntington Station, NY 11746; (631) 423-2574; forestporkstore.com; Butcher. The wurst capital of Long Island, Forest is the offspring of the Ridgewood original. It also is one-stop shopping for German imports, from mustards and preserves to red cabbage and sauerkraut. But buy Forest's own terrific 'kraut. And start putting together your own choucroute garnie. The krainerwurst, or smoked sausage, is addictive; the peppery Fourth of July special kielbasa, a mouthful of fireworks. Excellent bratwurst, bauernwurst, weisswurst, pinkelwurst, blood sausage; pork chops, smoked or not; and frankfurters. The shop's sauerbraten, leberkase, liverwurst, Westphalian and Black Forest hams, ham salad, meat cakes, and bacon also are irresistible. Be sure to get some of the bacon-rich, vinegary potato salad. Forest mandates an investment in steaks, hamburgers, pot roast, crown roast, and other beef specialties, too. You'll want to purchase pretzel rolls and onion rolls to go with everything. The whole place just says "Eat!" Fine German beers available.

Ideal Cheese & Wine Cafe, 308 Main St., Huntington, NY 11743; (631) 923-3434; Cheese. The question is whether to list Ideal as a shop or a restaurant. The main appeal, finally, is as a very good cheese store, so this is the category that determines placement. It's also the north shore source of excellent coffee, in bean or beverage form, from Georgio's Coffee Roasters in Farmingdale. Ideal houses a bar and a take-out operation, too. The dining part of the equation allows for some seriously cheese-themed dishes, plus chicken wings, fries, and plenty of sauces to dip both.

Mr. Sausage, 3 Union Pl., Huntington, NY 11743; (631) 271-3836; mrsausagefinefoods.com; Butcher, Italian Market. Mr. Sausage is *molto salumeria,* from the Baldanza brothers of Calabria. Go for the housemade pastas and sauces, Italian cheeses including fresh ricotta, fresh mozzarella and well-aged provolone, savory spreads, terrific caponata, seafood salad, cured meats, olives, lots of imported olive oils and vinegars, and especially the namesake links. The red-pepper-tinted hot sausage and the chicken sausage with broccoli rabe are among the standouts. There's a fine selection of steaks and chops, plus baked rolls with spinach or broccoli and cheese, and outstanding bread. Mr. Sausage also is popular for lunch. Heroic sandwiches, indeed, including the combo of prosciutto, provolone, and hot cherry peppers; the union of eggplant, arugula, roasted peppers, and goat cheese; and any one surnamed parmigiana. The sauces are led by the meaty Sunday special and a spirited sun-dried tomato number with singular flavor.

The Purple Elephant, 81 W. Fort Salonga Rd., Northport, NY 11768; (631) 651-5002; purpleelephant.net; Caterer, Specialty Market. In addition to being a full-service caterer, the Purple Elephant specializes in vegan and vegetarian fare, carefully prepared. Owner David Intonato formerly was chef at Jamesport Manor Inn in Jamesport and Mill Pond House in Centerport. His menus here do include dishes such as grilled, grass-fed sirloin steak and tuna tacos, plus fine soups.

Town of Babylon

The first house to go up here apparently was built near a tavern. That prompted the early homeowner to question whether she was about to settle in a "new Babylon."

Whether the tale is partly or not quite true, downtown Babylon still has no shortage of destinations where you can have a drink and some food to accompany it.

The village is a spirited draw on weekend nights and doesn't turn too sleepy the rest of the time, either. The neighborhood near the Copiague railroad station is distinctive, too, for its concentration of Polish food shops.

Babylon was settled in 1653, bought from Native Americans including the Massapequa and the Matinecock. Most of the land was used for farming; homes generally were in Huntington.

By 1867, the railroad arrived. The Town of Babylon itself was established five years later; the village incorporated in 1893. Babylon's southern border is the Great South Bay, a lure for anyone set on sailing, swimming, or fishing.

Communities that are in the town include Amityville, which is more than an adjective preceding horror; Amity Harbor, which isn't where Quint and company started their search in *Jaws*; Babylon itself, Copiague, Deer Park, Lindenhurst, West Babylon, and Wheatley Heights.

Fire Island Inlet and Robert Moses State Park are in Babylon.

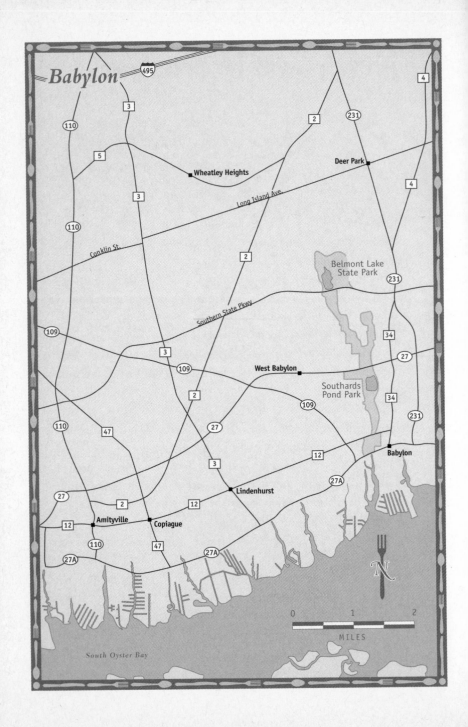

Babylon Carriage House, 21 Fire Island Ave., Babylon, NY 11702; (631) 422-5161; babyloncarriagehouse.com; New American; $$–$$$. A bar and grill, almost in equal parts, Babylon Carriage House stays popular with casual food and good drinks. The restaurant is multilevel and a balance of traditional and contemporary. The "Thai calamari bowl" heads appetizers, with squid and sweet peppers, peanuts, cilantro, lime, and a sweet chile glaze. Yellowfin tuna tartare comes close, in sesame-ginger vinaigrette. Sirloin steak topped with Maytag blue cheese, filet mignon with truffled macaroni and cheese, and the marinated skirt steak with mashed potatoes and sautéed spinach give you an idea of what's best. The burger with bacon and cheddar and the "prime rib melt" with havarti cheese are alternatives. The renegades can pick penne Bolognese or rigatoni alla vodka. The better seafood main course is sesame-crusted seared tuna.

Barrique Kitchen & Wine Bar, 69 Deer Park Ave., Babylon, NY 11702; (631) 321-1175; barriquekitchenandwinebar.com; Small Plates; $$. Barrique serves 30 wines by the glass and enough half-bottles to spur an impromptu tasting. Wine stuff is part of the decor at the welcoming, brick-and-beams dining area. The emphasis is on sharing all around. You may hold onto the octopus salad longer than usual. Or nibble a little more on the panzanella salad and the shrimp ceviche. The cheeses and cured meats are fine with an opening glass or two. And the pressed sandwiches are, too: grilled chicken with pesto and goat cheese, mozzarella-tomato-basil with pesto, and the Italiano with capocollo, speck, and soppressata plus mozzarella and red peppers. For the pizza-focused, there are a few thin-crust pies, a Margherita, and a meatball-and-ricotta disc among them. Worthwhile small plates include clams with chorizo, grilled bratwurst, braised short ribs with mashed potatoes, and pan-roasted chicken. The "mini desserts" range from carrot cake and cheesecake to Key lime pie and tiramisu. Raise a glass.

Bay Vue, 854 S. Wellwood Ave., Lindenhurst, NY 11757; (631) 991-3370; bay-vue.com; Seafood; $–$$. Bay Vue does give you a waterside setting, a casual approach, and some tasty, moderately priced fish and shellfish. They go through a lot of clams here, baked, fried, and steamed. And endless amounts of calamari fry before showing up with marinara and Thai-style dipping sauces. Pine Island oysters are fine on the half-shell. Main dishes: fish-and-chips, made with ale-battered cod; linguine with either white or red clam sauce; sea scallops with a roasted corn emulsion; and definitely the steamed lobster with corn on the cob, a baked potato, and coleslaw. It's not all seafood. The roasted chicken with potato pancakes and the New York strip steak with fried onions and garlic-mashed potatoes are straightforward alternatives. On a sunny, summer afternoon, you wouldn't want much more. Well, maybe an extra hour.

Bozena Restaurant, 485 Montauk Hwy., Lindenhurst, NY 11757; (631) 226-3001; polishdinner.com; Polish; $–$$. Kielbasa and pierogi bring you to Bozena, a spare and genuine place for bracing food. The smoked and fried kielbasa with sautéed onions; combo platter of fried kielbasa, stuffed cabbage, pierogis, and potatoes; and boiled beef with horseradish sauce will prepare you for the next blizzard. The Hungarian pancake, a potato pancake with spicy pork goulash, a shot of paprika, and sour cream, is almost as husky and full-flavored. Likewise, roast pork in brown sauce and the smoked loin of pork with applesauce. *Bigos,* a sort of hunter stew with cabbage, and roast duckling with apples have an autumnal accent, too. If all this seems too heavy-duty, Bozena ably fries trout and sautés veal schnitzel, and starts dinner with herring in cream sauce and smoked salmon. A

Greek salad also makes a cameo appearance. The mandatory pierogies are filled with potato, sauerkraut, mushrooms, or meat. And you may enjoy a blueberry-filled one with sweetened sour cream sauce for dessert. Apple cake and cheese blintzes with raspberry sauce are just as good.

Fancy Lee, 101 W. Main St., Babylon, NY 11702; (631) 422-6505; fancyleeny.com; Asian; $$. A vintage diner was transformed into Fancy Lee, a lively and upbeat place for Asian-fusion dishes in downtown Babylon. You can go through a few countries here, starting with tasty wonton and hot-and-sour soups, miso soup, and tom kha gai. The chicken lettuce wraps, duck roll, and Thai vegetable rolls also are good. From the sushi section, pick toro, sweet shrimp, Spanish mackerel, or bonito, which are all fine. The Spring Breeze roll brings together tuna, pineapple, and avocado for some seasonal refreshment. Crazy Friday is all-purpose, with shrimp tempura and spicy lobster. You can turn westward with Grand Marnier prawns. Fancy Lee prepares pleasing pad Thai and mee fun noodles as well as pan-seared duck breast and rack of lamb. Vegetarians will enjoy the eggplant with garlic sauce.

Horace & Sylvia's Publick House, 100 Deer Park Ave., Babylon, NY 11702; (631) 587-5081; horaceandsylvia.com; American; $$–$$$. Horace & Sylvia's manages to be both homey and sophisticated. The design takes the same approach. The more casual fare takes in southwestern macaroni and cheese, with chorizo, onions, and cherry tomatoes, and southern fried chicken, with buttery biscuits and sautéed spinach. The Kap't Krunch chicken is crisp strips with mustard dipping sauce. Grouper stars in the fish taco, with pico de gallo and chipotle-spiked sour cream. There's heat in the chicken-and-shrimp jambalaya, which includes chorizo and sautéed onions and peppers on rice. For lunch, look for the hummus platter with warm pita bread, the pulled pork sandwich on a brioche roll, lobster salad on pita, and the "publick house" salad with romaine lettuce, feta cheese, olives, diced tomato, and cucumber. The sirloin burger and grilled chicken with bacon, apple, and gruyère on ciabatta are the big sandwiches.

Kotobuki, **86 Deer Park Ave., Babylon, NY 11702; (631) 321-8387; kotobukinewyork .com; Japanese, Sushi; $$–$$$.** This is the most modest of Long Island's Kotobuki restaurant group. While it's short on the special effects and the noise level isn't lethal, the food is largely the same and the service is better. They prepare good tuna and Spanish mackerel tataki, broiled or fried yellowtail collar, and gyoza, the pan-fried pork dumplings. There's the full range of tempuras and teriyakis, chicken yakitori, and sautéed soft-shell crab. Tuna nuta, with a zesty mustard sauce; fluke usuzukuri with ponzu sauce and ground daikon; and the "rainbow tartare" of chopped tuna, salmon, yellowtail, and onion, are well done. In the roll department, where Kotobuki is at its most extravagant, there are enough selections to keep you busy for a week if not longer. McRoll with Spanish mackerel, ginger, scallion, and cucumber, and the Crazy Tuna combo with avocado, scallion, and cucumber, are good.

Monsoon, **48 Deer Park Ave., Babylon, NY 11702; (631) 587-4400; monsoonny.com; Asian; $$$.** Monsoon, a bold and often brilliant restaurant, is housed in a remade Bank of Babylon building that's as dramatic as the creative cuisine on display. The high-ceiling, 2-level dining area is a sharp design. And Chef Michael Wilson's food almost always is exceptional. The steamed pork and steamed duck buns, pork gyoza, Vietnamese summer rolls, crisp pork belly, kimchee pancake, and yellowtail sashimi are outstanding. Remarkable main dishes: kung pao monkfish, "millionaire's curry crab," sea scallops with ginger-coconut sauce, caramel pork with shallots and garlic, shaking beef made with filet mignon and shishito peppers. And the Beijing duck for two is simply Long Island's premier version of the classic dish. Pork fried rice, pad Thai, and wild mushroom chow fun add to the treats. Before you revel in the cooking, pick one of the excellent house cocktails. Cheesecake or chocolate torte for dessert. Monsoon is part of the Bohlsen Restaurant Group, which includes Prime in Huntington and Tellers and Verace in Islip. See recipe for **Kung Pao Monkfish** on p. 345.

The Park Bistro & Restaurant, 1635 Great Neck Rd., Copiague, NY 11726; (631) 464-4445; theparkli.com; Polish; $–$$.

Homey and authentic, the Park Bistro & Restaurant is a Polish-cooking sampler nestled in a small shopping center. It's under the same ownership as the essential Kabanos Polish Deli. The dining area is tight. But it attracts families with an assortment of very husky, satisfying dishes that can seem transporting to Warsaw and Krakow, Lodz and Gdansk, with a hint of juniper in the air. There's a steam-table selection that, if you're here on the right day, may include stuffed cabbage, fried pork, chicken cutlets, chicken meatballs, cheese crepes, potato pancakes, and assorted pierogies. Sauerkraut-and-mushroom croquettes, meat-filled dumplings, herring salads, roasted pork, duck with apples, and especially kielbasa with sauerkraut are typically flavorful choices. Soups may be a vividly red borscht, bean, cauliflower, and better-than-bracing beef tripe.

Ristorante Gemelli, 175 E. Main St., Babylon, NY 11702; (631) 321-6392; gemellirestaurant.com; Italian; $$–$$$. The look

is Tuscany by way of trompe d'oeil. But the food often is good and the reception friendly. Split a hot or cold antipasto for two. The latter has tasty cured meats, cheeses, olives; the former, baked clams, fried calamari, grilled artichokes. Marinated and grilled octopus also is worth it. Pastas generally are recommended, with top selections that include spinach-and-ricotta gnocchi in Bolognese sauce; linguine with white clam sauce; cavatelli tossed with sweet sausage, smoked cheese, and tomato sauce; and fettuccine with meatballs. Follow them with filet mignon in a red wine reduction, with mashed potatoes and asparagus with Parmesan cheese, or the broiled grouper with braised lentils and caramelized carrots in a white-wine-and-tomato sauce. Roasted branzino in lemon-white-wine sauce, accompanied by risotto with vegetables, also subtly swims in. Tiramisu or flourless chocolate cake should precede your espresso.

The Rolling Spring Roll, 189 Main St., Farmingdale, NY 11735; (631) 609-5182; therollingspringroll.com; Vietnamese; $–$$. This is the sole Vietnamese restaurant on Long Island and, as such, should be celebrated. It started as a food truck and became this storefront. There aren't too many selections early on. Better openers include the crisp spring rolls, and rice-paper-wrapped summer rolls are very good, with an undercurrent of mint. Beef satay also is flavorful, with peanut sauce. The Vietnamese sandwich, *banh mi,* stands out. Choose the sliced pork belly, lemongrass chicken, or grilled beef versions, in that order. They arrive with pickled carrots and radishes, plus cucumber and freshly picked herbs, on toasted French bread. *Pho,* the bracing noodle soup, is available with either chicken, beef, or tofu. The beef production, a combo of sliced brisket and meatballs, is best. Basil and lime boost it.

Roppongi Sushi Restaurant, 348 Merrick Rd., Amityville, NY 11701; (631) 598-7189; roppongisushiny.com; Japanese, Sushi; $$. The successor to Sakura has kept to traditional Japanese cuisine and presentation. But the real appeal here is in the name. The uncooked fish is prepared with care and very good. Select from the a la carte listing: tuna, salmon, yellowtail, fluke, striped bass, mackerel, assorted roes, bonito, and fresh scallop, depending on what's available when you visit. Equally tasty are sliced octopus in a sweet-tart vinegar sauce, spicy tuna tartare served with a quail egg, tuna tataki, and tuna carpaccio finished with wasabi sauce. The now ever-present yellowtail jalapeño also is worth considering at this restaurant. The summer roll includes spicy shrimp, cucumber, and caviar; the spring, tuna, avocado, asparagus, and caviar. If you're averse to seafood, try the chicken tempura roll. Roppongi's cooked choices are led by gyoza, or fried pork and vegetable dumplings; *kyoage,* or deep-fried tofu; and deep-fried soft-shell crab. Banana tempura and ice cream are the acceptable sweets.

Shiki, **233 E. Main St., Babylon, NY 11702; (631) 669-5404; shiki-longisland.com; Japanese, Sushi; $$.** Shiki is a dependable, raw-and-cooked Japanese restaurant, spare in its decor and generous on the plate. Soba noodles in soy broth are tasty as a starter. The seaweed salad and spicy tuna-and-avocado salad similarly are fine. Refresh with *hiyayakko,* or chilled bean curd; and *age-dashi* tofu, the deep-fried variety. Gyoza are workmanlike, as are the shumai, steamed crab dumplings, and the shrimp and vegetable tempuras. The cooked main dishes to remember are the grilled yellowtail or tuna, sautéed scallops in lime sauce sparked with horseradish, grilled eel on rice, and *tonkatsu,* the deep-fried pork cutlet. Shiki prepares pleasing nabeyaki udon, of thick noodles with chicken, tempura shrimp, and vegetables. Shiki has very good usuzukuri with whitefish, tuna with sesame sauce, maguro tuna, salmon, mackerel, and Spanish mackerel, and the rolls that include yellowtail and scallion, eel and cucumber, and salmon skin. Kakimaki features deep-fried oysters, spicy mayo, cucumber, and scallion, well packaged inside-out.

Tres Palms, 16 East Ct., Babylon, NY 11702; (631) 482-1465; trespalms.com; Seafood; $$–$$$. Tres Palms is named after a point break in Rincon, Puerto Rico, beloved by surfers including those gliding in with this casual, waterside restaurant. A few palm trees actually would fit in at the eatery, a "coastal dining" establishment situated by the Hi-Hook Fishing Station. Pan-roasted local fish, such as fluke, is a sensible selection. Fish tacos with pico de gallo, the seared tuna version of a BLT, fish-and-chips, and tuna tartare all fit in. You'll like the crisp, fried oysters; fried calamari with coconut, peanuts, scallions, and Sriracha-seasoned aioli; and the New England–style clam chowder, too. Tres Palms segues easily with a Cubano sandwich full of roast pork, ham, pickles, gruyère cheese, mustard, and company; the cheddar-and-chorizo quesadilla; and chili made with beef, pork, and more of the spicy sausage. The restaurant is a fair distance from Ditch Plains in Montauk, but they have the idea.

Vittorio's Restaurant and Wine Bar, 184 Broadway, Amityville, NY 11701; (631) 264-3333; vittorios.biz; Italian, American; $$–$$$. Steaks used to be the big attraction at Vittorio's, a convivial joint where you'll continue to find an excellent T-bone and sirloin. But the pork chop with sautéed pepperoncini, cipollini onions, and red wine vinegar sauce and the chicken scarpariello with sausage, peppers, onions, and potatoes can rival them. There are a few good pastas, too, especially garganelli in a veal-and-sage ragu and the bucatini with a pulled short-rib ragu. Begin with fried calamari marinara, braised short ribs paired with polenta, a wedge salad with bacon and blue cheese, or an assortment of cured meats and cheeses. At lunch, you can have a tricolor salad with goat cheese; seafood salad with garlic-lemon dressing; and a surf-and-turf salad that contains sliced marinated steak and grilled shrimp. The char-grilled burger and the panino of prosciutto, provolone cheese, and roasted peppers are sensible options, too.

The Argyle Grill & Tavern, 90 Deer Park Ave., Babylon, NY 11702; (631) 321-4900; theargylegrill.com; New American; $$–$$$. The site of The Argyle has been a gathering place since the 1940s, living several lives over the decades. The name itself stems from a big hotel that once drew travelers to Argyle Lake. Now, it's an acceptable restaurant-tavern, popular for American food and libations of all kinds. It's all served in a striking dining room, full of vintage photos and dark wood. The New England–style clam bake stars steamed lobster and is a Monday special. Wednesday is devoted to steak, specifically sliced sirloin, skirt steak, and shell steak. Better selections recently: kung pao shrimp and calamari, sesame-seared tuna, Buffalo chicken wings, Caesar salad, Kobe beef sliders, Black Angus burger with bacon and cheese, onion-crusted chicken, and the happy hour.

Post Office Cafe, 130 W. Main St., Babylon, NY 11702; (631) 669-9224; lessings.com; American; $$. Post Office Cafe has left its stamp on Main Street for more than three decades. It's a hub for happy hours, "lifeguard night," and "tap & app" Tuesday, and a gathering place for casual American food. Lots of Buffalo wings fly out of here. And there are Buffalo chicken empanadas for a variation on the theme. The hummus plate with pita bread, spicy popcorn shrimp, and mini-Reuben sandwiches are right with the beverages, as are Bavarian pretzel bites and very loaded nachos. Chicken potpie, fish-and-chips,  marinated skirt steak, a pulled pork sandwich, grilled cheese with bacon and tomato, and the "Tuscan tuna club" with grilled yellowfin are about as formal as it gets. There are many mix-and-match choices in the official hamburger category, including the fancier "rustica" with fresh mozzarella, basil aioli, and roasted red peppers, and the "bistro" with arugula, blue cheese, pesto, and bacon. The "food truck tacos" stand out with the spicy Asian pork and mahimahi productions. At least 10 beers are available on tap.

The Village Lanterne, 143 N. Wellwood Ave., Lindenhurst, NY 11757; (631) 225-1690; thevillagelanterne.com; German, Continental; $–$$. The Village Lanterne becomes a landmark for its years and its cuisine. So, get your ompah on and visit. The restaurant is suitably old-fashioned, too. The sauerbraten is pretty good, served with red cabbage, sauerkraut, and ginger snap gravy. The Bavarian platter adds either a schnitzel or a sausage to the dish. The main course of bratwurst, weisswurst, bauernwurst, and knockwurst automatically mandates an order. Veal a la Holstein, a breaded cutlet with a fried egg and anchovies, and beef rouladen, with smoked bacon, pickles, and onions have long-time fans. And there are meat-stuffed cabbage in brown gravy and Hungarian-style goulash for the cold weather. Start with a stuffed pretzel roll, packed with a brat and Muenster cheese, or creamed herring salad. The cold cut platter, with liverwurst and *leberkase* in the mix, and the fried wurst and kraut should dissuade you from stuff such as browned mozzarella triangles and Buffalo chicken wings.

Specialty Stores, Markets & Shops

Babylon Cheese Cellar, 51 Deer Park Ave., Babylon, NY 11702; (516) 983-8804; Cheese. Babylon Cheese Cellar has to be the most aromatic shop in the downtown area. Babylon Cheese keeps at least 70 different varieties in stock. French, Italian, Swiss, Spanish, English, American, all are well represented. There are good selections of blues and the creamier cheeses. And Babylon Cheese Cellar carries chutneys and assorted accompaniments. For the fromage/formaggio-deprived: an oasis.

Dudek Polish Bakery, 1635 Great Neck Rd., Copiague, NY 11726; (631) 789-1945; and 1907 Great Neck Rd., Copiague, NY 11726; (631) 841-3465; Bakery. Dudek Polish Bakery is your basic babka source, whether with cheese or fruit. The two Dudek shops are little outposts of authenticity whether you're a fan of apple-crumb, plum, or blueberry cakes; softball-size cream puffs; spongy and yeasty fried doughnuts; coffee cake; cheesecake; gingerbread; poppy-seed rolls; or sweets associated with Christmas and Easter. The rye breads and still-darker loaves have the soulful flavors of eastern Europe. Gilded and blond *chalka* is good today, French toast tomorrow. Dudek also features birthday cakes and other specialty orders. Ordering on the spot may require pointing a finger at the item you want to buy. Dudek bills itself as the "first Polish bakery in town." After a few bites, you'll have no doubt about the claim.

Gemelli's Fine Foods, 115 E. Main St., Babylon, NY 11702; (631) 321-4515; gemellis.com; Gourmet Market. Gemelli's is associated with the ristorante nearby. The "oven ready" fare includes stuffed pork roast, Italian-style beef meat loaf, chicken meat loaf, chicken sliders, meat or vegetable lasagna, pork chops stuffed with cornbread or prosciutto and provolone cheese, a lamb roast, and rib roast. They sell dinner specials for two such as eggplant parmigiana, spaghetti and meatballs, and turkey with mashed potatoes and broccoli. The hero sandwiches make Gemelli's one of the obligatory midday stops. The Don includes Genoa salami, soppressata, roasted peppers, and provolone; the Godfather, mozzarella, roasted peppers, cold cuts, tomato, olive oil, and vinegar. Somehow, the Brooklyn Bridge means turkey and swiss cheese; the

Battery Park, turkey with provolone, pesto, and sun-dried tomatoes. Continuing the curiosities is the chicken Cubano. Why not?

Georgio's Coffee Roasters, 1965 New Hwy., Farmingdale, NY 11735; (516) 238-2999; georgioscoffee.com; Coffee. Georgio's is your source for beans from Latin America, Africa, Indonesia, and Arabia. Georgio Testoni previously was the coffee king at Fairway Market. Sample the specials, and look for Sumatra Madheling, Ethiopia Yirgacheffe, Uganda Mount Elgon Water Decaf, maybe Sulawesi or Papua New Guinea beans. And have an espresso. It's excellent. The motto here is "passion for coffee." Georgio and Lydia Testoni have it, caffeinated. Their coffee also is available at Ideal Cheese & Wine Cafe in Huntington.

Hahn's Old Fashioned Cake Co., 75 Allen Blvd., Farmingdale, NY 11735; (631) 249-3456; crumbcake.net; Bakery. Hahn's is a very focused operation. There are fewer than 10 items to choose and they're outstanding. First is the great plain crumb cake that's a testament to extra-large, handmade crumbs. These crumbs are so good that you'll buy a bucket of them to snack on their own or to boost your latest adventure in baking. You won't easily find this flavor elsewhere. The apple crumb cake, chocolate crumb cake, raspberry crumb cake, and the crumb cake "variety pack" are excellent. In addition to the crumb cakes, Hahn's makes rich, chocolate brownies and a sugar-free brownie. The crumb cakes and brownies are sold in sheets and they're suitable for coffee or tea with your best friends. But a lot of them will be gone at breakfast.

Jacqueline's Patisserie, 199 E. Main St., Babylon, NY 11702; (631) 893-5334; jacquelinespatisserie.com; Bakery. This is a custom-cake shop, so you'll have to go elsewhere for the morning's croissants and brioche. But if you're up for cakes that look like iPhones, flower baskets, painter's palettes, boats, guitars, racing cars, sneakers, high heels, or oversize numbers, here's your local destination, full of fondant and butter cream. It's enough to make you want them to get back into pastries, cupcakes, and cookies.

Kabanos Polish Deli, 515 Oak St., Copiague, NY 11726; (631) 842-3999; and 1635 Great Neck Rd., Copiague, NY 11726; kabanosdeli.com; Delicatessen. Rings of kielbasa seem like part of the decor at the Oak Street branch of Kabanos. Thick and thin, they dangle behind the counter and behind the glass. There are at least a dozen varieties, including juniper, smoked, and grilling-style. The selection of other smoked, cured, and prepared meats mandates a party pegged to celebrating Kosciuszko. Smoked ham, top-round ham, veal hot dogs, stuffed duck, and the selection of Polish imports are impressive. Kabanos Polish Deli is under the same ownership as the Park Bistro & Restaurant in Copiague. If two rounds of Kabanos haven't filled you, nearby is the popular and packed with flavor corner-side store, Euro Deli, 1650 Great Neck Rd., Copiague, NY 11726; (631) 842-5084.

Torta Fina Bake Shoppe & Patisserie, 80 Deer Park Ave., Babylon, NY 11702; (631) 669-0824; tortafina.com; Bakery. Torta Fina has been sweetening downtown Babylon since 1998. It's situated near the Argyle Grill. The small bakery prepares its share of wedding and special-occasion cakes with artful expertise, but you'll be content with the well-made cannoli, the mini-cheesecakes, and the fruit tarts. The breakfast winners go from muffins and scones to croissants and assorted Danish. Torta Fina also enters the local competition with fudge, very good biscotti, rainbow cookies, cupcakes, and a fine plum cake. There's another Torta Fina at 11 Vanderbilt Motor Pkwy., in the Bonwit Shopping Center in Commack; (631) 858-1940.

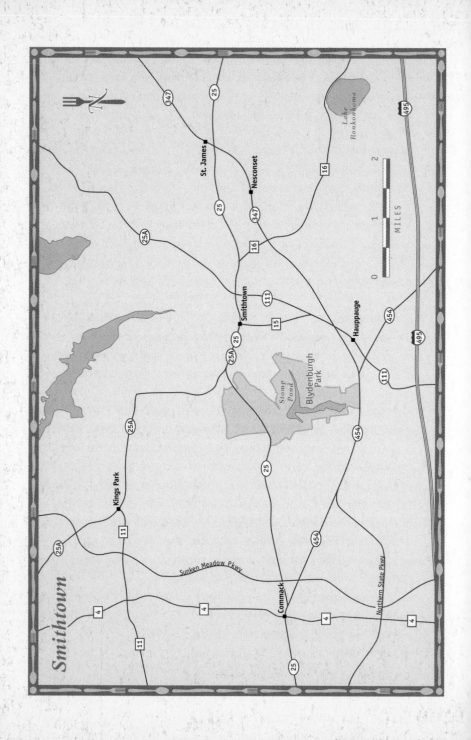

Town of Smithtown

The story of Smithtown almost always begins with the bull.

At the intersection of Routes 25 and 25A, in Head of the River Park, is a five-ton statue of a bull named Whisper. The legend is that Richard Smythe, or Smith, acquired the land that's now within Smithtown's borders in a wager with Native Americans, the Nissequogs. Smith would receive the acreage that he could circle in a day while riding a bull. If he lost, the Nissequogs got the bull.

He apparently did very well.

Historians question this bull story and say that Smith got the property from a friend, Lion Gardiner, whose name pops up elsewhere in Long Island history.

But the saga of the statue, commissioned in the early 1900s, is far more fun. It didn't arrive in Smithtown, however, until 1941 after a stint at the Brooklyn Museum while the sculptor waited to be paid. Charles Cary Rumsey's daughter presented it to the town.

Within the Town of Smithtown are the communities of St. James, Kings Park, Hauppauge, Nesconset, part of Commack, and Smithtown itself.

Smithtown includes Caleb Smith State Park and Blydenburgh State Park, named for patriots during the American Revolution and beyond, and Sunken Meadow State Park facing Long Island Sound. Baseball fans know Smithtown as the birthplace of Craig Biggio and Frank Catalanotto.

There's at least one good steak house in town, too.

Aji53, 1 Miller Pl., Smithtown, NY 11787; (631) 979-0697; aji53 .com; Japanese, Sushi; $$. Here's the glitzy offspring of Aji53 in Bay Shore, filled with elaborate sushi rolls and nigirizushi, plus a series of westernized dishes. It gets crowded; you may have to wait and then experience very speedy service, so be prepared. Good appetizers include the crisp duck salad, seaweed salad, fluke usuzukuri, and the increasingly widespread tuna pizza. Fried oysters, beef negimaki, pork gyoza dumplings, and fried soft-shell crab with hot chile sauce also taste fine. From the a la carte sushi, consider striped bass, fluke, red snapper, yellowtail, scallop, sweet shrimp, and sea urchin. The signature rolls work their way in with the Bay Shore, made with ahi tuna, avocado, spicy salmon, and spicy miso sauce, and the Fire Island, with shrimp tempura and spicy tuna ignited with wasabi sauce. The Aji King makes its claim with deep-fried king crab, avocado, and shrimp, crowned with spicy tuna and yellowtail. Grilled black cod with yuzu-orange-miso sauce and King of the Sea with shrimp, scallops, and lobster in honey-lemon butter sauce head the less-Japanese fare. There's a full contingent of teriyakis and tempuras, fried rice, and hibachi combos.

Butterfields, 661 Old Willets Path, Hauppauge, NY 11788; (631) 851-1507; butterfieldsrestaurant.biz; New American, Italian; $$. Butterfields has had a few lives, the latest being a bit more casual. The spacious restaurant sometimes seems as if it could be one big party room. And there are evenings when it feels that way, too. Overall, it's an upbeat joint and a good night out. At table, the cooking can be as basic as meatballs-and-ricotta and chicken parmigiana. The spread of kung "pow" calamari reaches Old Willets Path with a sweet-spicy accent. Pepper-crusted ahi tuna is a respectable take on an increasingly familiar pairing. Yellowfin tuna becomes the lead player in a remade BLT, emphasis on "T." The porterhouse steak is tender and comes with roasted-garlic whipped potatoes and caramelized onions. Bouncing back to the Italian side: linguine with white clam sauce and rigatoni with sausages, tomato sauce, and melted mozzarella, both pleasing.

Cafe La Strada, 352 Wheeler Rd., Hauppauge, NY 11788; (631) 234-5550; cafelastradarestaurant.com; Italian; $$. They squeeze molto flavor into this little restaurant off the highway. The looks are modest but the food isn't. Devotees make the pilgrimage just for the pasta e fagioli and the escarole and beans, both of which fill lots of take-out containers, too. But stay for the baked clams oreganata and the steamed cockles, the spinach salad with onions and bacon, spaghetti with meatballs and sausage, and any pasta Bolognese. Chicken parmigiana has heft and taste to equal it. Scungilli marinara or with hot sauce benefits from the company of plump clams and mussels. Take the countrified route with tender tripe, accented with prosciutto and plum tomatoes. Shrimp fra diavolo can turn as fiery as you like. Just ask for the extra heat. The New York strip steak turns very pizzaiola with garlic, tomato, oregano, and mushrooms. Italian cheesecake and tiramisu lead the cafe's desserts.

Cafe Red, 107 W. Main St., Kings Park, NY 11754; (631) 544-4500; caferedli.com; New American, Italian; $$. From the owners of Red and Osteria da Nino in Huntington comes Cafe Red. The dining room is a streamlined affair, with minimal artwork and a blackboard of specials. From the Italian side, there's very good eggplant parmigiana, light gnocchi with basil-flecked tomato sauce, spinach-and-ricotta ravioli Bolognese in veal sauce; and *paglia e fieno*. Fettuccine with veal meatballs and tomato sauce refines the familiar dish. Saltimbocca alla Romana is a balanced version, reining in the sage. The flaky, tender beef short rib becomes slightly vinous in a red-wine reduction. Cafe Red ventures into the spice trade with a diverting main course of shrimp in coconut curry sauce, with spicy mango chutney. Tempura-style shrimp does the same with a wasabi-honey vinaigrette. Seared sea scallops provide an east-west contrast with a ginger-lime beurre blanc. The desserts are western: moist tiramisu, husky bread pudding, and a not-too-dense flourless chocolate cake.

Casa Luis, 1033 W. Jericho Tpke., Smithtown, NY 11787; (631) 543-4656; casa-luis.com; Spanish; $$–$$$. The comfort level is high at Casa Luis, where the fare is mostly Spanish and the customers largely regulars. They come to the homey spot for gazpacho and caldo gallego, garlic soup and black bean soup, shrimp with green sauce, and chicken Villaroy. There are practical side trips via fajitas, baked clams, clams Posillipo, and broiled veal chops. Veer back to Spain with paella Valenciana and mariscada in green sauce. Octopus tinted with paprika, broiled chorizo sausage, and shrimp with garlic similarly bring the right tastes to your table. It's all served with generosity, no pretense, and enough warmth to make up for any unpleasantries you may have encountered earlier in the day.

Casa Rustica, 175 W. Main St., Smithtown, NY 11787; (631) 265-9265; casarustica.net; Italian; $$–$$$. For nearly 30 years, Casa Rustica has been one of Long Island's best Italian restaurants. The decor is subtler now, the food still flavor-packed at Mimmo and Benedetto Gambino's establishment. Service continues to be first-class. A memorable dining experience could start with the house's impeccable antipasti, from grilled vegetables and cured meats to fine cheeses, and the refreshing orange-and-fennel salad. The grilled polenta cake with crumbled goat cheese and sausage; rice balls with meat, peas, and cheese; *fritto misto* of calamari, shrimp, and artichoke hearts; and grilled octopus salad are excellent. The superior pastas include veal-and-chicken agnolotti with cream sauce and notes of nutmeg and Parmesan cheese, classic ravioli in pink sauce, and a vivid lasagna Bolognese, rich and meaty. Lobster risotto is expertly made, as are lobster oreganata and fra diavolo. Pasta with sardines is a special, deservedly so. Whole fish baked in a salt crust leads the school, with either red snapper or branzino. Swordfish Livornese also stands out. Enjoy the generously stuffed beef braciola on rigatoni, pancetta-wrapped filet mignon in Barolo sauce, the stuffed pork chop, and chicken scarpariello on the bone with sausage, cherry peppers, and potatoes. Terrific pastries and zabaglione for dessert. See the recipe for **Whole Fish Baked in Salt Crust** on p. 334.

Chop Shop Bar & Grill, 47 E. Main St., Smithtown, NY 11787; (631) 360-3383; chopshopbarandgrill.com; American; $$–$$$. Although it goes under the general category of American cooking, Chop Shop opens a pretty big umbrella in its upbeat, modern dining room, full of brick and hardwood. So, the Buffalo-chicken spring roll seems all right preceding the baked clams oreganata; the crisp sushi roll and rock-shrimp tempura do well close to the steamed mussels with tomato sauce. The cheeseburger is juicy; the barbecued and pulled short rib flavorful in a 3-cheese melt on focaccia. The grilled, Tuscan panino fills with chicken, marinated eggplant, fresh mozzarella, and roast garlic. All satisfy. Sesame-seared tuna and the "panzanella steak salad" seem preludes to the steaks and chops that matter. Try the grilled, double-cut pork chop, which doubles down with the grilled bacon macaroni and cheese, and the rack of lamb, with a hint of garlic and more of rosemary. Filet mignon, shell steak, and skirt steak are dependable. The bar: busy.

Emilio's, 2201 Jericho Tpke., Commack, NY 11725; (631) 462-6267; emilios-restaurant.com; Italian; $$. Emilio's is a quintessential Long Island restaurant, visited for very good, fairly priced Italian cooking, pizzas included. The take-out business always is brisk, mirroring the efficient, genial service at table. The best dishes include an appetizer of meatballs with ricotta, roasted peppers, and garlic bread; fat rice balls; eggplant rollatine; pasta e fagioli; calamari Calabrese; stuffed artichokes; and the items in a separate category devoted to parmigianas. "Old school" spaghetti and meatballs; rigatoni with ricotta, tomato sauce, basil, and meatballs; meatball and burger sliders; and the baked pastas are essential. Pizzas are in all shapes and sizes. The Grandpa pie, Sicilian and topped with mozzarella, red onion, marinara sauce, and seasoned bread crumbs, is especially good. They have fine Italian ices. And you'll be departing with some garlic knots, too. Emilio's spawned Fanatico in Plainview and Passione in Carle Place.

España Tapas & Wine Bar, 655 Middle Neck Rd., St. James, NY 11780; (631) 656-1564; espanatapasny.com; Spanish, Tapas; $$. There aren't many tapas restaurants on Long Island, so España is like a little gift. Sip sherry and spend an evening making a lot of choices. Daydream about Barcelona. The Serrano ham with a tomato-garlic spread is a very good beginning, as are the marinated, white anchovies and the seafood salad. Paprika-tinted octopus, Galician-style, rivals them. Sauteed chorizo delivers its own sparks and may spur a request for sangria. Shrimp and mussels with garlic sauce, deftly spiced *patatas bravas,* and beef meatballs also encourage sharing. You'll find ample salads: Spanish potato salad with eggs, carrots, and green peas; the La Mancha with grilled asparagus and manchego cheese; and the Mediterranean, with tuna. Soups to warm you include lentil, with sausage, carrot, and potato; and *caldo Gallego,* the Galician soup with white beans, chorizo, and Serrano ham. And España's garlic soup will ward off any vampire within miles. The restaurant broadens its offerings with generous paellas.

Five.Five 2, 552 N. Country Rd., St. James, NY 11780; (631) 584-4600; fivefive2restaurant.com; New American; $$$. Crowded and convivial, Five. Five 2 is an address to remember for its party atmosphere and very good food. The restaurant is composed of a few small dining areas, each a distinctive niche. In any of them, sample the Wagyu beef sliders on brioche rolls. The better toppings are caramelized onions, Vermont cheddar, and manchego cheese. Gloucester deviled eggs are fine starters, gilded with lobster and lemon aioli, especially with a beverage or two. The peekytoe crabcake gets a boost from horseradish aioli and fennel-jicama-carrot slaw. Likewise, hand-cut pommes frites with pecorino cheese and kung pao calamari, in a soy-chile sauce. Macaroni and cheese enriched with Maine lobster is one of those rare versions where the ingredients harmonize and the result is worth the effort. Catapano Dairy Farm cheese enriches the ricotta gnocchi in a pork ragu. Seared Montauk swordfish, snowy and moist, swims in on a wavelet of tomato-and-eggplant caponata. The thick, Kurobuta pork chop partners well with sage-flecked risotto. The banana spring roll is a dessert surprise.

The Grill Room, 160 Adams Ave., Hauppauge, NY 11788; (631) 436-7330; thegrillroomrestaurant.com; New American; $$–$$$. The Grill Room is off the main road, situated among the squat buildings of an industrial park. You have to look for it. But the search is worth the effort. This is a dependable spot for lunch and dinner. And there's live music on some nights. Start your own with the barbecued duck tostada, with black beans, mango salsa, Monterey Jack cheese, and a corn tortilla, or with the chicken quesadilla with 3 salsas. Fried oysters offer crunch and a crust with cilantro and jalapeño flavors. Midday, the panini satisfy, especially the Cubano-style sandwich and the grilled chicken-and-roasted-peppers combo. Black peppercorn-crusted duck breast and sweet-potato-apple hash, seared ahi tuna with wasabi and teriyaki sauces, pan-seared swordfish with mango pico de gallo, a version of paella alla Valenciana, and thick steaks are typical of dinner. The warm apple crisp and pecan pie are solid desserts.

H2O Seafood Grill, 215 W. Main St., Smithtown, NY 11787; (631) 361-6464; h2oseafoodgrill.com; Seafood; $$–$$$. The updated version of classic New England seafooder goes in several directions at once, adding some Hampton to Nantucket, some sushi to the lobster specials. Good choices include the spiced Millennium Lobster, grilled swordfish with yellow-tomato salsa, beer-battered flounder, lobster sliders with matchstick potatoes, and lobsters either steamed or stuffed. The sushi is consistently fresh and fine. Consider the "tornado" rolls, the first of which gets you airborne with king crab and the second with spicy tuna. For the record, there's also a lobster tornado. H2O prepares excellent clam chowder. And for dessert, the hard choice is between goat-cheese cheesecake with a hazelnut crust and the coffee pot de crème with warm cinnamon doughnuts. H2O definitely is bubbling on weekends.

Hotoke, 41 Rte. 111, Smithtown, NY 11787; (631) 979-9222; hotokejapanese.com; Japanese; $$–$$$. Hotoke combines sushi restaurant with hibachi house, handling both with flair. If you're not a fan of the clanging and kitsch, you'll be more than satisfied with the uncooked fish here. The tuna pizza, made with a scallion pancake and tofu-wasabi aioli for that added dimension, is tasty. So are the green papaya salad and the cuttlefish salad sparked by a tangy vinaigrette. Fried oysters with mustard sauce are flavorful, too. The Red Sox sushi roll means mango lobster salad; the Yankee, shrimp tempura. Godzilla merely refers to spicy tuna and avocado in a sauce of moderate heat. And the Party Roll brings in spicy lobster salad and shrimp tempura, for a cool-hot contrast. Hotoke comes up with a diverting duck teriyaki and warming udon noodle dishes. Purists should consider investing in the *omakase,* the chef's choice of sushi. But it does begin at $75.

Insignia, 610 Nesconset Hwy. (Rte. 347), Smithtown, NY 11787; (631) 656-8100; insigniasteakhouse.com; Steak, Seafood; $$$$. Everything is over-the-top at Insignia, without question Long Island's most extravagant steakhouse and among the most expensive. The high-ceiling affair is bisected by a dramatic wine-storage section. The bar has its own hard-edge social scene; the restaurant, a high-roller quality. The dry-aged steaks are excellent; the sushi rolls, almost as rich. Insignia makes a $40 surf-and-turf roll that combines lobster, king crab and Kobe beef, just in case. The juicy, 7-spice, Kobe beef burger flight starts you in the right direction. The steaks include a dry-aged New York strip, a Kansas City cut, thick filet mignon, a bone-in rib steak, and the porterhouse for two. Colorado lamb chops add to the competition. Seaside, there's a grilled whole fish of the day and steamed 2-pound lobsters, each as carefully prepared as the steaks. Side dishes are uniformly recommended. If you're ready for more, the warm cinnamon doughnuts with raspberry sauce, the cookies-and-cream cheesecake, blondie banana cream pie, and the S'mores brownie should suffice.

Kitchen A Bistro, 404 N. Country Rd., St. James, NY 11780; (631) 862-0151; kitchenabistro.com; French, Mediterranean; $$$. Relocated to the building that used to house the stellar Mirabelle, Kitchen A Bistro lightens and expands the choices. It's a very good restaurant with an ever-changing menu that's seasonal and refreshing. Roasted golden beets with honey yogurt may be among the openers. Potato gnocchi with tomato confit brings in a tasty Italian side, along with the risotto of ramps and fava beans. The potato gnocchi with kale and heirloom beans has a hearty cross-borders flavor. Braised short ribs with spaetzle and kale richly find their own territory. Duck breast with wild rice, and a gastrique for balance, is tender and rosy. And duck rillettes with pickled vegetables is a Gallic delight. The pan-seared bavette steak with potatoes is typically fine. Weakfish with lentils and farro, and hake with squid and heirloom beans: both excellent. Any dessert is just gilding.

Lobster Rolls

The history of the lobster roll usually begins with a warm one in Connecticut and a cool one in Amagansett. Both versions are summertime treats, from the Maine coast to the South Shore and beyond. It seems as if there are as many versions as there are advocates. Lobster rolls are found with garlic bread and croissants, kaiser rolls, and heros. But more than likely yours will be on a hot dog bun. That bun is best top-split, buttered, and toasted on the sides. But a toasted baguette is a crunchy alternative. Some of the better lobster rolls are found at these summer places.

Clam Bar in Amagansett

Duryea's Lobster Deck in Montauk

Jordan Lobster Farms in Island Park

The Lobster Roll in Amagansett

The Lobster Roll Northside in Riverhead

Red Hook Lobster Pound in Montauk

Silver's in Southampton

Luso, 101 E. Main St., Smithtown, NY 11787; (631) 406-6820; Portuguese, Rodizio; $$. How's your cholesterol? Luso is a protein provider, devoted to meat, specifically the all-you-can-eat, skewered and grilled variety that's paraded around the dining room while you decide which cuts to consume. The meats are served with a salad, greens, and housemade potato chips. To say it will be a hearty and filling meal minimizes the experience. From those brandished skewers, better choices include bacon-wrapped turkey, top sirloin, and fat sausages. But this isn't the only option at Luso. The whole, barbecued chicken is juicy and popular. That applies to the pork loin, spare ribs, and grilled swordfish, too. Grilled calamari is a smoky opener; clams steamed with white wine and garlic, an aromatic one. *Caldo verde,* the husky soup with collard greens, chorizo, and potatoes, makes any winter chill vanish. The desserts are visible at the counter when you enter Luso. Flan is a good selection. Just pace yourself. Be assured that by the time you pick a sweet, still more skewers will be making the rounds.

Mario, 644 Vanderbilt Motor Pkwy., Hauppauge, NY 11788; (631) 273-9407; restaurantmario.com; Italian; $$–$$$. The image of Romulus and Remus and the wolf that nursed them is Mario's symbol. It's fitting, since this is the start of Vanderbilt Motor Parkway's restaurant row, Italian division. The 2-level restaurant is popular for business lunches and for evenings out. Regulars point to the mozzarella in carrozza as well as the smoked trout and bresaola as appetizers. The house's notable pastas include ravioli with meat sauce, meat-filled cannelloni, *paglia e fieno,* trenette with pesto, and a trio of very traditional spaghettis—alla carbonara, all'Amatriciana, and alla Bolognese. Stay with dishes such as calf's liver Veneziana with onions, hearty tripe Napoletana with red sauce, veal parmigiana, beef mignonettes finished with Marsala, and the rack of lamb for two. A salad of arugula and endive or the spinach salad for two should be fit in somewhere, too. Better desserts are cheesecake, zabaglione, and the showy crepes Suzette for two.

Mosaic, 418 N. Country Rd., St. James, NY 11780; (631) 584-2058; eatmosaic.com; New American; $$$–$$$$. The motto at Mosaic is "change is good." So, this cozy restaurant specializes in 5-course tasting menus, the contents of which change frequently. They're always very good, often excellent. Your choices could include Bloody Mary gazpacho with a horseradish-poached prawn and celery sorbet; cedar-plank-grilled ocean trout matched with a feta-pecan baklava; caramelized sea scallops with bourbon-braised pumpkin, brussels sprout leaves, and maple-sage syrup; 2-day roast pork shoulder with blue-cheese smashed potatoes; or grilled lamb chops with truffled parsnips, cocoa nibs, and a pepper-blueberry gastrique. The dessert might be a chocolate tasting, a dark chocolate brownie with espresso gelato, or a white chocolate cornmeal pupusa. The dishes are typically creative, stylishly presented, and the topic of conversation the next day. Mosaic is made with many intricate parts, carefully put together. The result is charming, and very tasty.

Nisen Sushi, 5032 Jericho Tpke., Commack, NY 11725; (631) 462-1000; nisensushi.com; Japanese, New American, Sushi; $$–$$$. Splashy and glitzy, Nisen Sushi is a magnet. Although it's in a shopping center, this is no blend-in-with-the-rest kind of place. That holds for the food, too. Nisen Sushi makes very good lobster tacos and a crisp tuna tortilla, a king crab pizza with guacamole and a black cod lettuce wrap, Kobe beef meatballs and rack of lamb with grilled asparagus. The crunchy soft-shell crab with spiced aioli and apple slaw takes the New American path with confidence as readily as the roasted chicken veers traditional. If you're here for sushi, you won't be disappointed, either. There are the expected, colorful, imaginative rolls. But it's worth considering *omakase,* the chef's choice sushi selection. Entry level for this is $75, a sum that's not hard to reach in any configuration. The Nisen group expands with Nisen 347 in St. James and Nisen 110 in Melville.

Pace's Steak House, 325 Nesconset Hwy., Hauppauge, NY 11788; (631) 979-7676; pacessteakhouse.com; Steak; $$$. This traditional, clubby steakhouse adds some Italian fare to expand the appeal. But you'll still be oriented toward beef, starting with tomatoes and onions. You can pick a good shrimp cocktail and either oysters or clams on the half shell. Then focus on the main event: New York shell steak, untouched or marinated; the porterhouse for one or two; filet mignon; or rib eye. They're all recommended. So are the rack of lamb, the double-cut pork chop, roast chicken, and roast duck. Pace's also steams, broils, and stuffs lobsters with considerable attention. They stay moist. On the side, the basics count. Baked potato, mashed potatoes, home fries or steak fries, creamed or sautéed spinach, and macaroni and cheese are husky accompaniments. Stay with cheesecake for dessert. There's a second Pace's on Wynn Lane in Port Jefferson; (631) 331-9200.

Perfecto Mundo, 1141-1 Jericho Tpke., Commack, NY 11725; (631) 864-2777; perfectomundoli.com; Latin, Fusion; $$–$$$. Tucked in a shopping center from which it's visible only from the east, Perfecto Mundo is in its own little world. The sunny restaurant combines Caribbean and South American dishes with Mexican and New American fare. On some nights, there's live entertainment to go along with the show on the plate. You can have better-than-most nachos grande and guacamole before getting into the bigger dishes. Lobster-and-corn chowder and black bean soup both are very good choices. Fried calamari boosted with ancho chiles will go with that second margarita. Pan-seared sesame tuna is complemented by chorizo-saffron summer creamed corn and an invigorating slaw of pickled fennel, red pepper, and carrot. The coriander-crusted pork tenderloin with grilled linguica sausage, a roasted corn and Monterey Jack cheese cake, and spicy coconut broth also is commendable. Have fried plantains on the side. But the real standout main course here is one that's routinely wrecked at many restaurants: paella. The seafood paella includes lobster, shrimp, mussels, clams, calamari, and enough flavor to make up for all the bad ones. Churros are the apropos dessert.

Relish, 2 Pulaski Rd., Kings Park, NY 11754; (631) 292-2740; **relishkingspark.com; American; $$.** Relish serves breakfast until 4 p.m., benefiting the latest riser and anyone in need of day-long oatmeal. This flavorful eatery prepares good omelets, including the Mexicali with chorizo, Monterey Jack cheese, and green chiles as well as the Philly with, yes, sliced steak, caramelized onions, and American cheese; French toast made with challah bread; and light ricotta pancakes that could be enjoyed at lunch or dinner. During the course of service, you may be attracted to the meat loaf with mashed potatoes and brown gravy, maple-glazed chicken, and chicken-and-chorizo tacos. The dinner burgers include one capped with braised short rib and, at the other extreme, a chicken-bacon-avocado burger, neither of which should deter you from ordering the "classic cheeseburger," as in American cheese, lettuce, tomato, pickle, onion, and, of course, "special sauce." This is an instantly likable restaurant.

San Marco, 658 Vanderbilt Motor Pkwy., Hauppauge, NY 11788; (631) 273-0088; **sanmarcoristorante.com; Italian; $$–$$$.** Although it probably has more in common with Marco Island than the Piazza San, the kitchen reliably prepares Italian and Italian-American dishes at this big, old-fashioned restaurant. San Marco has been frying calamari and baking clams since 1987, as one of the three Italian eateries that still dominate this section of the highway. The gilded squid and the stuffed clams are good. Other satisfying appetizers include eggplant rollatine with spinach and ricotta, mussels marinara, and the torta San Marco, similar to a layer cake of cold antipasti. You can go a different way with the crabmeat-stuffed avocado, coconut shrimp, or grilled ahi tuna with a jolt of wasabi. Pappardelle San Marco means the wide, housemade noodles with tomato and basil. Also good are the penne with tomato, basil, and ricotta; gnocchi Bishop with meat sauce; and rigatoni alla vodka. "Tre moschettieri" arrives as grilled filet mignon, chicken breast, and shrimp oreganata. Cheesecake and flan are well made.

Sempre Vivolo, 696 Vanderbilt Motor Pkwy., Hauppauge, NY 11788; (631) 435-1737; semprevivolo.com; Italian; $$–$$$. Sempre Vivolo is the easternmost of the threesome of Italian eateries along the parkway. It's also the most businesslike and restrained, from the decor to the service. The cold antipasto is as welcome in spring and summer as the eggplant rollatine and mozzarella in carrozza are in fall and winter. Baked clams are tender. And the tricolor, Caesar, and arugula salads are focused and fine. There's a lively spaghettini with garlic, anchovies, capers, and olive oil with toasted bread crumbs; sturdy rigatoni Bolognese; and a savory ravioli all'Amatriciana. A sirloin sautéed with onions, peppers, mushrooms, and tomato sauce is the house's pizzaiola. Gorgonzola cheese enlivens the cream sauce for broiled filet mignon. Vinegar peppers do that for Sempre Vivolo's chicken scarpariello. Calamari marinara and salmon in a creamy mustard sauce are the better seafood courses.

Spezia, 645 Middle Country Rd., St. James, NY 11780; (631) 265-9228; spezianewyork.com; Italian; $$–$$$. Spezia brings together the good from casual and more formal Italian restaurants, from the service to the cuisine. The place has a little glow, a familiar repertoire, and an ambience that makes you want to return. Recommended appetizers include arancini, or rice balls; the combo of burrata cheese and polenta; an Italianate rendition of oysters Rockefeller; hearty meat lasagna; pasta Bolognese; a double-cut pork chop stuffed with prosciutto, crumbled Italian sausage, and fontina cheese; on-the-bone chicken scarpariello with sweet peppers, roasted potatoes, and sausage; pan-seared sea scallops; and lobster any style, but especially fra diavolo or oreganata. Creamy tiramisu heads the desserts.

Thai House, 53 W. Main St., Smithtown, NY 11787; (631) 979-5242; thaihousesmithtown.com; Thai; $$. All the basics are covered at Thai House, an easygoing introduction to the cuisine that has eclipsed Chinese on Long Island. The unpretentious restaurant keeps the prices in check and the flavors unfettered. Both chicken and beef satays are recommended, served with peanut sauce and cucumber salad. Ground chicken, vegetables, and thin noodles are packed into crunchy Thai spring rolls. A broth heady with lemongrass and Kaffir lime heightens the appeal of the steamed mussels. Refresh yourself with larb, a well-seasoned salad of ground chicken or beef spiked with lime juice and invigorated with mint leaves; or the shredded papaya salad with shrimp and ground peanuts. Marinated and spiced beef in chile sauce, grilled pork chop in ginger sauce, and lobster medallions in red curry with coconut cream are satisfying main dishes. Whole red snapper in either red, green, or Panang curry also is a vibrant entree. There are many mix-and-match chicken, beef, or pork dishes with sautéed basil, cashews, ginger, or sweet-and-sour sauce. And very tasty pad Thai, too.

The Trattoria, 532 N. Country Rd., St. James, NY 11780; (631) 584-3518; thetrattoria.com; Italian; $$$. What used to be Kitchen A Trattoria was renamed The Trattoria late last year, when it was sold by Eric Lomando to Chef Steven Gallagher. Gallagher had been creating the menus at Lomando's place for years. Now, it's his, and the creative, full-flavored Italian cooking that drew crowds to the tight, little restaurant still is the attraction. Enjoy the housemade ricotta; sun-dried tomato tapenade; butternut squash soup with almond crostini; meatballs braised in tomato sauce over polenta; mushroom arancini with porcini béchamel sauce; lamb and eggplant stew; bucatini alla carbonara; fennel risotto with goat cheese; spaghetti all'Amatriciana; orecchiette with roasted cauliflower, golden raisins, and bread crumbs; red wine brasato; pork loin with squash puree and grape mostarda; and lasagna Bolognese. The chef's tasting menu is a highlight.

Vintage Prime Steak House, 433 N. Country Rd., St. James, NY 11780; (631) 862-6440; vintageprimesteakhouse.com; Steak, Seafood; $$$. Vintage for sure, you'll think after having grilled baby lamb chops for an appetizer. No errant slice of sashimi here. Vintage revels in the old-fashioned, from the decor, which has shown affection for taxidermy, to the cuisine, which is mostly straightforward. The shrimp and crabmeat cocktails are dewy and good; the crab cake has body; and the prosciutto di Parma comes with mozzarella di bufala. Vintage kicks up the calamari with ginger dressing, the barbecued shrimp with Cajun-spiced sauce, and the clams casino with lemon butter. The Caesar salad and the Gorgonzola number are well made. On to steaks: porterhouse for two or three, T-bone, New York strip, filet mignon, and rib eye, best in that order. To roll back, or move forward, the calendar, there's filet mignon Oskar with crabmeat, béarnaise sauce, and asparagus, a little nod to veal Oscar. Seared yellowfin tuna is the big fish. New York cheesecake vies with crème brûlée and a warm apple cobbler.

Landmarks

Ciao Baby, 204 E. Jericho Tpke., Commack, NY 11725; (631) 543-1400; ciaobabyrestaurant.com; Italian; $$. The message is nostalgia, as in Rat Pack and red sauce, delivered with some humor and a lot of old-time flavors. Just go along with it and hum a couple of Sinatra tunes in your head. Meatballs and rice balls both are good. The pork sauce that goes with rigatoni and ricotta definitely suggests another decade, if not century. Beef ragu gives ravioli added heft. And the Sunday beef ragu would be welcome every day. Eggplant lasagna seems a bridge between the old and new. In the middle of all this, one can order a combo of tuna tartare and pan-seared tuna. Panini and wraps are available. The timeless tiramisu is your sweet. There is another full-bodied branch of Ciao Baby at 5074 Sunrise Hwy., Massapequa Park; (516) 799-5200, because one simply could not be enough. A few Dean Martin songs come to mind.

Kurofune, 77 Commack Rd., Commack, NY 11725; (631) 499-1075; kurofunerestaurant.com; Japanese, Sushi; $$. Kurofune has been slicing uncooked fish for more than a quarter century. The approach hasn't changed dramatically over the years, so much so that the dining room suggests a time capsule. It's a place where you order shrimp and vegetable tempuras without a second thought, look for beef teriyaki, and aren't the lone diner who has decided on beef sukiyaki, either. Even the special rolls have a certain restraint to them in this era of steroidal sushi. Taste the familiar yellowtail-and-scallion roll, the toasty salmon-skin one, and maybe a New York roll, with crab and cucumber. The "Kurofune for 2" production takes in a dozen pieces of sushi and 3 rolls. It's all pretty sedate, flavors included.

Specialty Stores, Markets & Shops

Alpine Italian Bakery and Pastry Shop, 59 Rte. 111 (Hillside Shopping Center), Smithtown, NY 11787; (631) 265-5610; alpinepastryshoppe.com; Bakery. Easily the top bakery in town, Alpine peaks with the classic Italian pastries: cannoli, sfogliatelle, pasticciotto, cassatini, pignoli tarts. The cassata is first-class, too. They also excel with éclairs and napoleons. The rainbow and pine nut cookies are mandatory, along with macaroons and almond crescents. As if to show that the bakery isn't limited by geography, you'll enjoy the German chocolate cake, Black Forest cake, lemon meringue pie, and banana cream cake. And, maybe on your second visit, leave room for cream puffs and Linzer tortes. Alpine has been a mainstay in Smithtown for more than three decades.

Uncle Giuseppe's Marketplace, 95 Rte. 111 (Hillside Shopping Center), Smithtown, NY 11787; (631) 863-0900; uncleg .com; Supermarket, Italian Market. This is the "flagship" in the fleet of Uncle Giuseppe's, a Disneyland for Italian food fans. Basically, they have everything. Terrific cheeses, fresh pasta, fresh produce, a professional butcher shop and seafood market, condiments, olive oils, vinegars, a solid bakery, many Italian imports, and a fine gelati counter, too. The prepared foods are good and better. Come here near Christmas or Easter and you're in for a major production. The catering is on a grand scale. Pick up your order at the separate tent set up at the end of parking lot. Uncle Giuseppe's also is at 364 Port Washington Blvd., Port Washington, (516) 883-0699; 2330 Hempstead Tpke., East Meadow, (516) 579-1955; 37 Hicksville Rd., Massapequa, (631) 308-7377; and 1108 Rte. 112, Port Jefferson Station, (631) 331-1706.

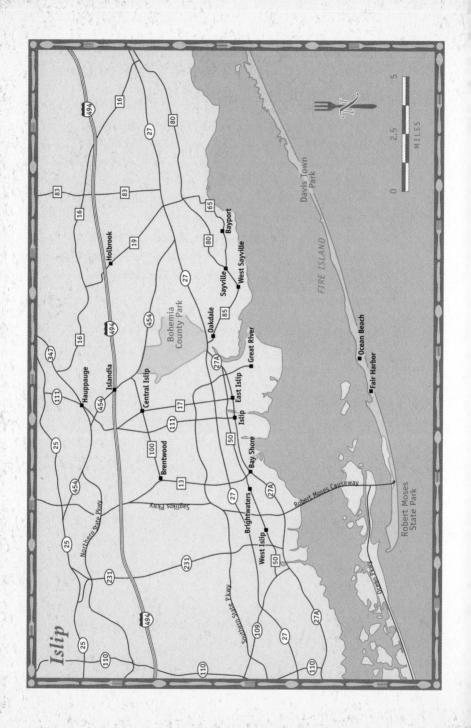

Town of Islip

The Town of Islip welcomes you at the ocean and the bay, at the lake and the canal. It's far removed from the English village 5 miles north of Oxford that inspired the name.

In 1683, a fellow from Oxfordshire purchased land that's now within the town from Native Americans and called his plantation Islip Grange. Islip became a town in 1790, with an economy based on shipping and fishing. The Blue Point oyster is from Great South Bay, a fact of enough consequence to find its way into state law. So many oysters were harvested that their shells were used to pave the streets.

George Washington did sleep here once, in what's now West Bay Shore. He doubtless ate in Islip, too, and may have enjoyed a few bivalves along the way.

The communities in Islip include Islip, Bayport, Bay Shore, Brentwood, Brightwaters, Central Islip, East Islip, Hauppauge, Holbrook, Islandia, Ronkonkoma, Sayville, West Islip, and West Sayville.

The town also includes several sections of Fire Island, among them Atlantique, Fair Harbor, Kismet, Ocean Beach, and Saltaire.

Beaches abound. So does seafood.

Foodie Faves

Da Noi, 301 Main St., Islip, NY 11751; (631) 650-6468; danoiislip .com; Italian; $$. There are few surprises at Da Noi and that may be part of the attraction. The well-appointed "our place" also features dining on the patio during spring and summer. Inside or out, some of the better selections include baked oysters and baked clams, the tricolor salad, saltimbocca, broiled filet mignon, and oven-roasted branzino finished with lemon, garlic, and white wine. And you'll never be short of fried calamari here. Infinite amounts of squid are consumed. Chicken scarpariello comes with sausages and cherry peppers, the tender rack of Australian lamb with a rosy hue. Gnocchi with plum tomato sauce and mozzarella di bufala heads the pastas. Ricotta cheesecake, cannoli, tiramisu, and crème brûlée underscore the kitchen's continental drift.

Fatfish, 28 Cottage Ave., Bay Shore, NY 11706; (631) 666-2899; fatfish.info; Seafood, Tapas; $$–$$$. Fatfish, subtitled "wine bar and bistro," delivers views of Great South Bay and Riley Creek. Overall, the ambience suggests things marine. But many of the notable dishes at the restaurant could be categorized as tapas: patatas bravas, well seasoned; chorizo and peppers, deftly paired; olives and Marcona almonds, a natural. Serrano ham is essential and the empanadas are good, too. Clams oreganata and tuna carpaccio also are commendable, as are almost all the items from the raw bar. Char-grilled swordfish, whole branzino, and lobster any style similarly boost the place. Fish-and-chips, made with cod, is a reliable main course. If you're not set on seafood, the Cedar River filet mignon and the Giannone organic roast chicken with mustard sauce are fine. For lunch: a lobster BLT, tuna niçoise, pan-fried sea scallops with clams and Serrano ham, a panino of cured meats plus mozzarella and arugula, and the beef tenderloin on a baguette.

George Martin's Strip Steak, 60 River Rd., Great River, NY 11739; (631) 650-6777; georgemartinsstripsteak.com; Steak,

American; $$$. This is the most opulent member of the George Martin Group. Stylish, clubby, with very good service, it's also a refined destination near Great South Bay. Consider the place a steakhouse updated. The jumbo crab cake, accompanied by a red-pepper sauce remoulade, is a solid opener. Likewise, the shrimp cocktail, chopped salad, Caesar salad, and clams and oysters on the half shell. The New York strip steak for one and the porterhouse for two are the major cuts, facing competition from the filet mignon with chimichurri sauce, the hefty rib eye, and the molasses-soy marinated skirt steak. Pick a sauce for your steak, béarnaise or au poivre, Gorgonzola or red wine. Sesame-crusted ahi tuna is nearly as beefy, balanced with a cucumber-Sriracha noodle salad. Mashed potatoes and creamed spinach highlight the side dishes; a hot apple turnover and a brownie sundae, the sweets.

Jackson Hall American Bar & Grille, 335 E. Main St., East Islip, NY 11730; (631) 277-7100; jacksonhallbarandgrille.com; American; $$–$$$. Jackson Hall is a casual restaurant for an informal meal. No fireworks, no showstoppers. But it's a modest, relaxed spot and the service is both earnest and good. Better selections: fish tacos, the shrimp cocktail, chicken wings, Bavarian pretzels with cheese sauce and spicy mustard, and the basket of sliders, filet mignon, and fried chicken BLT at the top. The full-size burgers are cooked to order and sandwiches such as the skirt steak and corned beef Reuben fit well into the whole affair. For something more substantial, stick to the herb-roasted chicken, fish-and-chips made with cod, Gorgonzola-crusted filet mignon, or the marinated skirt steak. Sweet potato fries, mashed potatoes, onion rings, coleslaw, and "loaded french fries" are about right. So are cheesecake and the root beer float.

The Lake House, 240 W. Main St., Bay Shore, NY 11706; (631) 666-0995; thelakehouserest.com; New American; $$$. The water view contributes to the popularity of the Lake House. But this handsome, bright restaurant is all about the exceptional cooking of Matthew Connors, who, with spouse Eileen, owns the elegant establishment. Standout starters: braised duck and light gnocchi with chanterelles, pancetta, golden raisins, and pine nuts; littleneck clam chowder with shiitake mushrooms, Yukon Gold potatoes, bacon, and chive oil; roasted golden and baby candy beets with fresh goat cheese, candied hazelnuts, and blood orange; and smoked salmon with horseradish crème fraîche on a crisp potato cake. The masterful main courses include crisp-skinned Long Island duck breast and duck-and-fruit sausage with smoked bacon, lentils, and a cherry–port wine sauce; pan-seared local tilefish with truffle-smashed red potatoes; a juicy Berkshire pork chop with herbed spaetzle, red-wine braised shallots, and mustard greens in an Armagnac-chestnut sauce; and herb-roasted organic chicken with honey-roasted cipollini onions and black truffle-fingerling potato hash. Fine cheeses and luscious desserts. Try the Humboldt Fog goat cheese and the Cabrales blue; the warm cinnamon doughnuts and blood orange cheesecake.

La Tavola, 183 W. Main St., Sayville, NY 11782; (631) 750-6900; latavolasayville.com; Italian; $$–$$$. La Tavola has made-by-hand, country style to go with its flavorful cooking. Come for the rice balls with fennel sausage and provolone cheese; the watermelon-and-feta salad with olives; bucatini tossed with tomato-basil sauce; linguine with white or red clam sauce, and gnocchi Bolognese, made with potatoes and ricotta. Chicken scarpariello, with sausage, red peppers, onions, roasted potatoes, oregano, and red-wine vinegar, is very good; so is the house's chicken parmigiana. Shell steak with chimichurri sauce brings in a zesty taste of South America. At lunch, look for the spin on a lobster roll; the BLT with applewood-smoked bacon, tomato jam, arugula, and garlicky aioli; and any pasta special. New York–style cheesecake, crème brûlée, and chocolate mousse cake are the challengers to the cannoli, gelati, and biscotti.

Le Soir, 825 Montauk Hwy., Bayport, NY 11705; (631) 472-9090; lesoirbayport.com; French; $$–$$$. Reborn after a major fire, the new Le Soir is brighter and more modern, in style and at table. This is one of the few traditional French restaurants left on Long Island, so you should visit for the bubbling, buttery, garlicky escargots Bourguignonne; country pâté, local duck a l'orange, braised sweetbreads with mushroom-and-Calvados sauce, filet mignon with sauce Bordelaise, and sole meuniere. Le Soir has accommodated to reality with fresh pasta, but it includes "pulled duck confit." The poached bay scallops in butter sauce and the crab cakes with celery root remoulade diplomatically go beyond Gallic. But if cassoulet is one of the cool-weather specials, don't miss it. The classic casserole of southwest France made with meat and beans is even rarer than restaurant kitchens that fly the tricolor.

Mitsui, 1 W. Main St., Bay Shore, NY 11706; (631) 630-9890; mitsuisushi.com; Japanese, Sushi; $$–$$$. This sleek, modernist corner restaurant does a good job with Japanese fare, cooked and not. The selections aren't all the usual stuff, either. Try the green-vegetable gyoza, beef sashimi with garlic sauce, or deep-fried oysters with sweet-sour sauce. Chicken tatsuta age, deftly fried, and soft-shell crab, skillfully sautéed with garlic and butter, both are fine. Spicy tuna tartare with a quail egg, the lobster-tempura roll, and a tart, flavorful fluke usuzukuri are recommended. The Fire Island roll brings you to the beach with tuna and salmon, rolled with shrimp, crab, and avocado; the Summer in Alaska, if not Denali, then wherever tuna, salmon, smoked salmon, and avocado lead. The salmon-skin and shrimp-tempura rolls are satisfactory. Stay with the approach and have banana tempura for dessert.

New Peninsula, 55 W. Main St., Bay Shore, NY 11706; (631) 666-8811; newpeninsula55.com; Chinese, Japanese; $$–$$$. Stone lions greet you. A koi pond ripples. And on the plate, New Peninsula links China and Japan. It's done with some care, so you won't consider the experience a duck vs. tuna grudge match. There are some Thai dishes to spice things up along the way. Better appetizers: chicken satay, chicken Soong lettuce wraps, scallion pancake, cold noodles with sesame sauce, fried soft-shell crab, beef negimaki, tuna tataki, and the shrimp-and-vegetable tempura. Crisp, whole sea bass in ginger sauce; grey sole with black bean sauce; shredded duck with ginger and scallions; and "tangy and spicy" lamb are solid main courses. The familiar General Tso's chicken, chicken with peanuts or cashews, Lake Tung Ting shrimp, and shrimp with lobster sauce have their place, too. The range of sushi and sashimi is respectable, covering all the basics, including good, conical hand rolls.

Nonnina, 999 Montauk Hwy., West Islip, NY 11795; (631) 321-8717; nonninarestaurant.com; Italian; $$–$$$. The "little grandma" for whom Nonnina was named must have quite an appetite. The 2-level, contemporary Italian restaurant prepares delicious small plates and you'll down a lot of them. Especially flavorful are the combinations 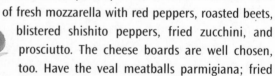 of fresh mozzarella with red peppers, roasted beets, blistered shishito peppers, fried zucchini, and prosciutto. The cheese boards are well chosen, too. Have the veal meatballs parmigiana; fried calamari Rhode Island, translated as marinara picante; clams casino; and tender octopus drizzled with olive oil and lemon juice, and paired with cherry tomatoes and red onion. The small pizzas are worth sharing, particularly the meatball pie with ricotta and tomato and the ramp pesto treat with spicy sopressatta and goat cheese. Sample the ricotta cavatelli Bolognese and the bowtie pasta with almond-ramp pesto and pecorino cheese, too. Leading main dishes include the Long Island duck breast with confit-and-potato hash, a pistachio-parsnip puree, rhubarb, and an elderflower-spurred reduction—not the usual stuff. Nonnina carefully prepares chicken parmigiana and shrimp oreganata, too.

The Pie at Salvatore's, 120 E. Main St., Bay Shore, NY 11706; (631) 206-1060; salvatorescoalfiredpizza.com; Pizza, Italian; $–$$. The south shore outpost of the Port Washington staple, The Pie is Islip's main pizza parlor. The Neapolitan pie that emerges from the coal-stoked, brick oven is excellent; the white pie, just as appealing. Contrarians may pick the clam pie or the Caesar salad pie. If, for some reason, you're here and not feeling pizzalicious, then the manicotti and the meatball hero may be considered. The eggplant parmigiana and baked ziti have their fans, too.

Roots Bistro Gourmand, 399 Montauk Hwy., West Islip, NY 11795; (631) 587-2844; rootsbistrogourmand.com; Eclectic, New American; $$–$$$. Taking the bistro concept to a remarkably creative level, Roots Bistro Gourmand becomes an exciting place to dine. Under Executive Chef Philippe Corbet and Chef James Orlandi, the kitchen is a laboratory for mixing old and new. The result: sparks. Have one of the house's superb cocktails and then plot your course. The chef's tasting menus make it easier. But look for the risotto lollipops with duck confit, mint-pea puree, gruyère, Parmesan, and espelette-and-cucumber yogurt. Or take in the tempura-fried zucchini blossoms with sheep's-milk ricotta, caramelized onion, and garlic, and tarragon-and-warm-heirloom-tomato salsa. Pan-seared striped bass is complemented by charred and concentrated watermelon; pan-roasted local duck benefits from a honey-lavender glaze, braised daikon, and English-pea puree.

The vegetable pot-au-feu is grand. The oyster po' boy gets a flavorful facelift with Sriracha mayo, pickled red onion, frisée, and tomato confit. Consider the ceviche of the week or the lobster BLT at lunch. And celebrate with spiced Ecuadoran dark chocolate mousse or apricot pie with pistachio cream. See the recipe for **Spring Vegetable Pot-au-Feu** on p. 339.

Satelite Pizza, 799 Montauk Hwy., Bayport, NY 11705; (631) 472-3800; satelitepizza.com; Italian, Pizza; $$. The giant cheese pie at Satelite Pizza is roughly 32 inches or 40 slices. But you can be a very content customer with almost any pizza here. The stuffed vegetable number, with broccoli, spinach, eggplant, and mozzarella; and the stuffed meat production, with ham, sausage, pepperoni, and mozzarella, are grand. Likewise, the white pie, Grandma pie, and basic Neapolitan-style pizza. Unlike the giant one, however, it will be difficult to add a full-length inscription in garlic knots. The hard-core crowd that resists pizza will be happy

with the hero sandwiches, chicken or eggplant parmigiana, Gorgonzola and Greek salads, garlic bread, pepperoni pinwheels, and, of course, zeppole to feel as if attending a private street fair. Pasta-tarians can stick with baked ziti, manicotti, stuffed shells, or lasagna.

Siam Lotus, 1664 Union Blvd., Bay Shore, NY 11706; (631) 968-8196; siamlotus.us; Thai; $$. For decades, Siam Lotus has been among Long Island's Thai standards: an understated little restaurant with big flavors and wide appeal. They skillfully prepare all the familiar fare, from chicken satay to pad Thai. But consider the excellent frogs' legs with Thai basil or with garlic and chile sauce; deep-fried Siamese duck; outstanding deep-fried whole red snapper, also with garlic and chiles; superior curries, whether red, green, or mussaman, with chicken, beef, or pork. Curry puffs with chicken and potatoes are cooled with a cucumber salad. Fried, tofu-wrapped crab rolls are sparked with zesty peanut sauce. Beef salad is emboldened with spicy Thai herbs and lime juice. There are many luncheon specials in the mix-and-match category, with beef, chicken, pork, or shrimp sauté. Siam Lotus sends out impressive soups, too, improving on the usual versions of spicy shrimp soup, chicken soup with coconut milk, and bean curd soup with minced pork and scallions.

Takara, 1708 Veterans Memorial Hwy., Islandia, NY 11749; (631) 348-9470; takarasushili.com; Japanese, Sushi; $$. It's easy to miss this shopping-center spot. But sushi fans must be diligent. And Takara provides rewards. After soba or seaweed salad, miso mushroom soup, or tempura udon, put chopsticks to work on an appetizer of sliced beef with ponzu sauce, baked scallops with roe, or chicken negimaki. Sauteed or deep-fried soft-shell crab, fried chicken, and Spanish mackerel tataki in garlic sauce with red pepper are fine, too. But Takara is mainly about sushi rolls, the showier the better. Very good: otaku, a California roll with cooked scallops; Oz, with cooked spicy tuna, chopped shrimp, and avocado; United, with tuna, salmon, yellowtail, and avocado. The UFO roll lands with salmon, tuna, yellowtail, and radish, but no rice. The Tiger's Eye looks at you with fried smoked salmon, tuna, and salmon. And the Black Dragon brings together shrimp tempura, eel, and avocado in harmony. Go with a group and you'll come up with an exceedingly colorful table. The kitchen prepares nigirizushi, too.

Tellers: An American Chophouse, 605 Main St., Islip, NY 11751; (631) 277-7070; tellerschophouse.com; Steak, American; $$$–$$$$. Tellers is in its 15th year, serving superior steaks and seafood in a remarkably refurbished, high-ceiling, former bank building. It's the cornerstone of the Bohlsen Restaurant Group. The bar area is clubby and cozy; the main dining room, a grand space. The old bank vault now is the wine cellar. Start with a slab of thickly cut black-pepper bacon, house-cured, shiny from a sweet horseradish glaze. Balance it with a shrimp or crabmeat cocktail, sashimi of tuna, the seafood tower, a Caesar salad or, surprisingly, a delicious braised-brisket risotto. Then: the 21-day, dry-aged rib eye, a trimmed, imposing cut of beef that tastes terrific; the reliable porterhouse for two; or a fine New York strip steak. The house burger is predictably first-class; the roasted chicken with cornbread stuffing and the vivid, spicy pan-fried Millennium Lobster with whipped potatoes, the best rivals for the beef. On the side: creamed spinach, roasted brussels sprouts with pancetta, housemade Tater Tots, and scalloped Parmesan potatoes. The fudge layer cake and cinnamon-streusel cheesecake with blueberry-citrus sauce wrap things up. There will be doggy and kitty bags. See the recipe for **Millennium Lobster** on p. 347.

Thai Angel, 1812 Veterans Memorial Hwy., Islandia, NY 11749; (631) 348-2555; thaiangelli.com; Thai; $$. Subtle and sharp, Thai Angel alights with vibrant flavors and an inviting manner. The dining room is neatly appointed; the food, deftly prepared and presented. Start with Thai spring rolls with ground chicken, served with plum sauce; curry puffs with potato and chicken; or the crisp wontons, also with chicken and Thai herbs. There are a lot of mix-and-match main courses, with a choice of beef, pork, chicken, shrimp, or tofu. Try the pork with sautéed ginger; the beef with hot sweet basil. Prettily plated crisp scallops in spicy Thai basil sauce and whole red snapper wrapped in a banana leaf and grilled are winning selections. Steamed striped bass in ginger-and-scallion sauce is a balanced, light, satisfying entree. Enjoy either striped bass or red snapper deep-fried and capped with chile-and-Thai-basil sauce; or with red or green curry. Tamarind-honey duck and orange duck are the big birds. Fried banana for dessert.

High Steaks

Here are 7 ways to enjoy a great steak on Long Island.

Sirloin at Blackstone Steakhouse in Melville

Filet mignon at Bryant & Cooper in Roslyn

Romanian at Frank's Steaks in Jericho and Rockville Centre

Kansas City strip at J. Michaels Tuscan Steakhouse in Northport and Oyster Bay

New York strip at Mac's Steakhouse in Huntington

Porterhouse at Peter Luger in Great Neck

Bone-in rib eye at Tellers: An American Chophouse in Islip

Tula Kitchen, 41 E. Main St., Bay Shore, NY 11706; (631) 539-7183; tulakitchen.com; Mediterranean; $$. You're taking a short cruise at Tula Kitchen, which reaches many ports along the way. The informal, amiable restaurant brings you in with very good Mediterranean spreads, from baba ghanoush to hummus and grilled pita bread. Spinach pie with refreshing tzatziki, roasted red beets with almonds and yogurt, sesame-seared tuna with garlicky potatoes and wasabi sauce, and shrimp tacos with roasted garlic slaw show some flair. For lunch, try the Tula cobb salad, with either grilled chicken or shrimp; the grilled chicken Reuben; or the turkey burger with feta. Tula Kitchen offers tasty vegetarian options, too, from a Reuben made with tempeh and tempeh teriyaki, to seared seitan and a lentil bean burger. The desserts show variety: baklava, dark chocolate truffles, chocolate-peanut-butter-tofu pie, a brownie sundae, a root beer float, and a Key lime pie named for Hemingway. Could be Ernest or Mariel.

Tullulah's, 10 Fourth Ave., Bay Shore, NY 11706; (631) 969-9800; tullulahs.com; New American, Tapas; $$–$$$. Downtown Bay Shore is far removed from the hipster precincts of Brooklyn, but Tullulah's imports some of the skinny jeans and irony-laden style to the suburbs. The restaurant is a three-in-one, from the cafelike front space to the spackle-exposed back room and the lean, packed bar between them. Bring your fedora. Chef-Owner Steven Scalesse prepares very savory small plates, which you'll down with first-class local brews and well-chosen wines. The charcuterie-and-cheese board, highlighted by hot dry Calabrian sausage and nine-month aged Manchego, is a good way top start. Likewise, the sliced chorizo sausage complemented by brown sugar–glazed apples and Sriracha aioli. Nutty, sweet pan-seared scallops arrive with French green lentils and chive cream; a trio of fried oysters with fennel-fern aioli, Sriracha aioli, and a spin on mignonette. Baked cauliflower is enriched with aged cheddar and a crumble of brussels sprouts; monkfish "osso buco" with fennel, tomato, carrots, celery, and littlenecks. Desserts are minor. But those jeans have to fit.

21 Main, 21 Main St., West Sayville, NY 11796; (631) 567-0900; 21main.com; Steak, American; $$–$$$. Here's a steak house for the family. The service is accommodating and the dining room's style suggests an upscale home. The crab cake and St. Louis–style ribs are good. Crumbled goat cheese showers the roasted beet salad. The raw bar offers briny oysters and tender clams. The shrimp and crabmeat cocktails are dependable. And you can veer slightly Asian with the house's sashimi of tuna. The big steak is a 38-ounce, bone-in rib eye, 21-day dry-aged. The porterhouse and the sirloin also are notable. Or try the double-cut lamb chops; the skirt steak with chimichurri, sweet cherry peppers, chorizo, and caramelized onions; cedar-planked wild salmon, and a well-steamed lobster. Pancetta boosts the creamed spinach. For dessert, sample the crème brûlée, apple crisp with vanilla ice cream, or, just for the special effects, the liquid-nitrogen ice cream "frozen to order."

Verace, 599 Main St., Islip, NY 1175; (631) 277-3800; veracerestaurant.com; Italian; $$$. The Italian contributor to the Bohlsen Restaurant Group, Verace is recommended from antipasti to dolci. The striking, high-ceiling spot is eye-catching for the visuals, but just as easily for the plates of Italian cheeses and cured meats. The pizzas also are excellent: Gorgonzola dolce with pear and mozzarella; fig and prosciutto with ricotta and a balsamic-vinegar reduction; the "biancoverde" with pesto, mozzarella, roasted peppers, and arugula; and the purist's Margherita. For pasta, pick the gnocchi Piedmontese with taleggio cheese and herbed bread crumbs, linguine with white clam sauce, the cavatelli Bolognese, ricotta lasagna, or a knockout spaghetti alla carbonara. Grilled branzino, chicken saltimbocca, and slow-cooked pork with mustard are fine secondi. And allow for the house's meatball, caponata, and Asiago-onion bread openers. There are panini at lunch, too, headed by a spin on the Muffuletta and the meatball parmigiana. Any time, be sure to order a side of creamy polenta, baked with Parmesan cheese.

View, 3 Consuelo Pl., Oakdale, NY 11769; (631) 589-2694; lessings .com; American; $$–$$$. View has come back looking fine after the extensive damage from Superstorm Sandy. The waterside restaurant keeps the appeal of the site and continues to send out some very good food to accompany it. Try the raw oysters, shrimp cocktail, crab cocktail, yellowfin tuna tartare, or, for something different, the Beijing duck tacos. Pan-seared local diver scallops, with a lobster-white truffle risotto and citrusy gastrique, are buttery and tasty. The fish-and-chips features Montauk fluke. Roasted halibut and steamed lobster continue the theme. For the landlocked, the braised short rib with a sweet-parsnip puree provides an autumn preview year-round.

Coyle's Homemade Ice Cream, 509 Main St., Islip, NY 11751, (631) 617-5014; and 75 Howells Rd., Bay Shore, (631) 666-2229; Ice Cream; $. Find an empty stool or commandeer a booth. Cool off with the soft-serve specials, especially on buy-one-get-one-free Wednesday or on "shake day" Tuesday. Coyle's also is popular for waffle cones, root-beer floats, smoothies, and Italian ices. The ice-cream flavors to keep in mind, and in cone, include "holy cannoli," which underscores the versatility of the pastry; banana-Oreo; Mississippi mud; chocolate-raspberry; strawberry cheesecake; coconut cream; and cotton candy. Any of them would enrich a banana boat that could lead an armada. Expect about 60 flavors, so plan on more than one return visit. Don't overlook the hot fudge, wet walnuts, cherries black and red, or the virtues of M&Ms.

Irish Coffee Pub, 131 Carleton Ave., East Islip, NY 11730; (631) 277-0007; irishcoffeepub.com; American; $$–$$$. Many catered affairs and plenty of Irish coffee mark the venerable pub, an old-fashioned and polished operation that burnishes its image year after year. Visitors return for the shepherd's pie filled with beef and vegetables under the potato lid, fish-and-chips, and, of course, corned beef and cabbage not only on St. Patrick's Day. Cream of potato soup, beef-barley soup, shrimp cocktail, a smoked salmon platter, and clams casino royale, with no apology to Ian Fleming, are typical selections. The turkey club, onion-crusted salmon O'Brien, and bacon-wrapped filet mignon are dependable. Chicken Cork refers to the county, not the texture. It's all served in friendly fashion. Everyone pretty much gets what he or she expects. And the Irish coffee itself is well made.

Island Mermaid, 780 Bay Walk, Ocean Beach, Fire Island, NY 11770; (631) 583-8088; islandmermaid.com; Seafood; $$. You're on the waterfront at Island Mermaid and that's about all you need to know. Enjoy a cocktail and the sunset under the umbrellas. There's live entertainment, too. At table, the choices take in corn-and-crab chowder, matzo ball soup, fish tacos, grilled octopus salad, crabmeat salad, crab cakes, and grilled yellowfin tuna with jicama slaw. Sushi rolls broaden the possibilities. The pan-seared sea scallops arrive with creamed corn, fingerling potatoes, and pistachio pesto, for a New American tangent. The skirt steak with chimichurri sauce and the roasted chicken with buttermilk biscuits head the landlocked alternatives. And if you make it to dessert, the cinnamon spice doughnuts and the blondie sundae will do.

Matthew's Seafood House, 935 Bay Walk, Ocean Beach, Fire Island, NY 11770; (631) 583-8016; matthewsseafood.com; Seafood; $$. Matthew's has been a Fire Island staple since 1974. The appeal of the place stems mainly from the waterfront deck and bar at Great South Bay, with attractions such as Margarita Madness and 2 for Thursdays lobster tails. The cold lobster platter amounts to a signature dish here. And the lobster roll has a hint of tarragon aioli, as well as lettuce, tomato, and potato chips for company. Regulars go for clams and oysters on the half shell, shrimp and lobster cocktails, steamers, and Buffalo chicken wings. The kitchen prepares a seafood cobb salad, too. Swordfish, grilled or broiled; broiled jumbo shrimp; chicken, either fried or roasted; and a "fishermen's stew" in a garlicky tomato sauce are the standard main courses. They'll all seem fine after that first margarita.

The Snapper Inn, 500 Shore Rd., Oakdale, NY 11769; (631) 589-0248; thesnapperinn.com; Seafood; $$–$$$. Water views have been the reason to dine at the Snapper Inn. They're the first thing anyone discussing the sprawling establishment is apt to talk about. On a sunny, summer afternoon and at twilight, it's a good-looking perch. The food is acceptable, from the raw bar to the fried calamari and steamed littlenecks; the swordfish on spinach and the steamed lobster to prime rib and filet mignon. The inn is popular for catered affairs, and you may spot a party in progress.

T.J. Finley's, 42 E. Main St., Bay Shore, NY 11706; (631) 647-4856; tjfinleys.com; American; $–$$. T.J. Finley's has a succinct motto: "No crap on tap." This is a serious venue for beer drinkers, with more than 85 well-chosen selections available in the woody, exposed-brick establishment. Check when it's L.I. pint night for some local brews, and when cask ales, unfiltered and excellent, are being poured. The suds extend to the food with the housemade "stout" chili, made with beef and beans. "Bottle caps" are cheeseburger sliders. They also offer the pulled-pork variety, pulled-pork quesadillas, a hanger-steak sandwich on garlic bread, a rendition of cobb salad, more than enough burgers, and, of course, beer-battered onion rings.

Specialty Stores, Markets & Shops

Dean's Seafood, 19 Degnon Blvd., Bay Shore, NY 11706; (631) 969-0587; deansseafood.com; Seafood Market. To go by the numbers, Dean's catch usually takes in about 50 finfish, 6 shellfish, and a dozen crustaceans. If you're looking for turbot or pompano, Dungeness crab or blue crabs, in addition to lots of local swimmers, Dean's is your place to visit in Islip. There's a take-out menu of prepared foods, too, including baked clams, steamers, seafood salads, soups, sandwiches, and broiled, steamed, or fried dinners. Fried fish also is available by the pound.

Frank & Maria's Italian Pork Store, 10 W. Main St., Bay Shore, NY 11706; (631) 665-0047; sicilianmarket.com; Specialty Market. In addition to being a very good pork store, F&M's stars with panini and assorted take-out. The Parma panino, which holds a breaded chicken cutlet, prosciutto, sun-dried tomatoes, and arugula, and the Rustic, with fresh mozzarella, roasted peppers, basil, and plum tomatoes, are grand. Bring home meat loaf, veal with peppers and onions, sweet sausage with broccoli rabe, and pork chops stuffed with spinach, red peppers, and mozzarella. The rigatoni Bolognese and rigatoni puttanesca also are candidates.

Stanley's Bakery, 68 E. Main St., East Islip, NY 11730; (631) 581-1230; stanleysbakery .com; Bakery. Stanley's has been baking since 1948. It's one of the town's essential spots for crumb buns and jelly doughnuts, Linzer tortes and rugalach, almond crescents and all sorts of cakes. The bread basket includes semolina, ciabatta, rye-pumpernickel, onion rye, 6-grain, challah and more. Breakfasters will find egg dishes and mini-pastries, among other reasons to eat early.

Zenway Natural Food Market, 47 E. Main St., Bay Shore, NY 11706; (631) 665-3050; zenwaymarket.com; Specialty Market, Delicatessen. Those seeking the organic and the gluten-free, juices and lunches, and a very even-tempered style might consider Zenway a landmark. All visitors should enjoy the Zenergizer, a mix of apple, carrot, and parsley; Restore Yourself, with cucumber, parsley, lemon, and spinach; and the aptly named Zen Cleanse, which does the job with apple, cayenne, lemon, and ginger. The kale and quinoa salads also are good, as is the selection of teas.

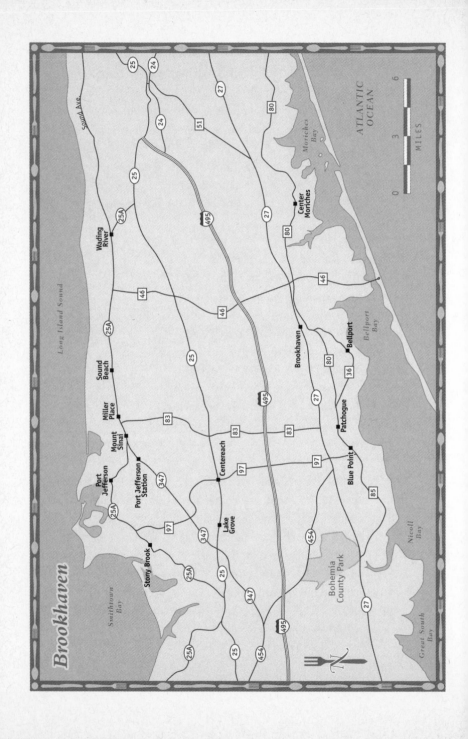

Town of Brookhaven

The Town of Brookhaven is 531 square miles. That means all of Nassau County could fit into it with about 78 square miles left over.

North to south, it goes coast-to-coast, bordered by both Long Island Sound and the Atlantic Ocean. In total area, land and water, Brookhaven is the biggest town in New York State.

The earliest known residents were Native Americans, specifically the Setaukets and the Unkechaugs. In the mid-17th century, English settlers arrived and bought land from the tribes. They named the first settlement Setauket.

In addition to Setauket and Brookhaven, the town's communities include Bellport, Blue Point, Center Moriches, Centereach, Coram, East Moriches, Eastport, Farmingville, parts of Holbrook and Lake Ronkonkoma, Lake Grove, Mastic, Middle Island, Miller Place, Mount Sinai, Old Field, Patchogue, Poquott, Port Jefferson, Port Jefferson Station, Ridge, Rocky Point, Selden, Shirley, Shoreham, Sound Beach, Stony Brook, and part of Wading River.

Brookhaven takes in part of Fire Island, including Point O Woods, Cherry Grove, and Fire Island Pines.

Stony Brook University and Brookhaven National Laboratory are situated in the town of Brookhaven. Students and professors are never limited to their cafeterias.

Alexandros, 1060 Route 25A, Mount Sinai, NY 11766; (631) 928-8600; alexandrosrestaurant.com; Greek; $$–$$$. Alexandros is close to the Acropolis of Greek restaurants in Nassau or Suffolk. The rustic, unaffected establishment confidently prepares the classics and wanders into other territory, too. It's also a very good steak house. The Greek spreads are excellent, especially taramosalata, skordalia, and melitzanosalata, or roe, potato-garlic, and eggplant dips. Grilled octopus, herbaceous and smoky, similarly stands out. Grilled squid, fried zucchini, baked kasseri cheese, and Greek meatballs are fine. Moussaka and pastitsio both shine. Oven-baked lamb with orzo in tomato sauce does, too. Whole fish, notably red snapper, is perfectly grilled, as are swordfish and tuna. The porterhouse, New York strip, rib eye, filet mignon, and skirt steaks sizzle on cue. On the side, go for steamed dandelion greens, lemon roasted potatoes, and mashed potatoes. The familiar Greek desserts are well made, from baklava onward.

Amici, 304 Route 25A, Mount Sinai, NY 11766; (631) 473-2400; amicirestaurant.org; Italian; $$. Unpretentious, no-nonsense, and beloved by regulars, Amici is everyone's neighborhood Italian restaurant. Many diners already are sure about what they want before opening the door. The likely candidates may include baked clams oreganata, eggplant rollatine, roasted red peppers and mozzarella, and Buffalo-style fried shrimp with hot sauce and blue cheese. Farinaceously, there are at least 10 types of pasta available in almost 20 preparations. Mix and match until you're satisfied, but allow for a taste of rigatoni Amici, with ground beef, ricotta, prosciutto, onions, and mushrooms. And there's the full range of parmigianas. In order: eggplant, chicken, shrimp, veal. Good alternatives are the chicken-and-hot sausage scarpariello and the flounder oreganata. Have cheesecake, too.

Avino's Italian Table, 108 S. Country Rd., Bellport, NY 11713; (631) 803-6416; Italian-American; $$–$$$. Whether you're at the patio clam bar on a summer afternoon or inside when it's chilly, Avino's satisfies with uncomplicated Italian-American specialties and a welcoming manner. The patio bar's appeal includes baked clams, clams finished with chorizo and fennel, crisp fried oysters, and Blue Points on the half shell. There also are food salads, sandwiches, and wraps, among them a lobster roll, a mahimahi fish taco, and an oyster po' boy. In the dining room, try the fried eggplant tower held together with ricotta, roasted tomato, and mozzarella; roasted diver scallops with corn pudding; and the tuna tartare. "Nana's pasta bowl" is loaded with gravy, and completed with a mega-meatball and/or sausages. The meatballs and sausage also boost the lasagna. Orecchiette with crumbled sausage, broccoli rabe, white beans, garlic, onion, and olive oil is a soulful main course. That also applies to the pan-roasted chicken with sweet-potato hash and the Creole stew with chicken, ham, shrimp, sausages, peppers, onions, and rice.

The Bellport, 159 S. Country Rd., Bellport, NY 11713; (631) 286-7550; bellport.com/thebellport; New American; $$–$$$. The traditional country house that's home to The Bellport is full of contemporary cuisine. Relaxed and reliable, this is an airy, adroitly run place. Chef Taylor Alonso's menu changes often. Crisply coated oysters play off a summery sauce of fresh corn. Crunchy and tender buttermilk fried chicken arrives with a savory mushroom fricassee and chive-mashed potatoes. The restaurant's pâté delivers a taste of country living, French division. Both the meaty and the vegetarian chili are recommended. Same for the roasted-beet and Caesar salads, the bison burger, and the jumbo lump crab cakes. Pan-roasted chicken is excellent, in a broth spiked with ginger, floating radicchio, and endive. Cider-brined, grilled pork chops are sparked by a stirring barbecue-espresso sauce, collard greens, and a potato-and-cheese croquette on the side. Sweet-potato gaufrettes back the rich, marinated and grilled rib eye steak. Linger over coffee and a blueberry cobbler.

Bobby's Burger Palace, 355 Smith Haven Mall (Route 347), Lake Grove, NY 11755; (631) 382-9590; bobbysburgerpalace.com; American; $–$$. Bobby Flay's chainlet opened its first Long Island branch here. The burgers are good, particularly the Bobby Blue, with blue cheese, lettuce, and tomato; the Crunchburger, with double American cheese and potato chips; the Miami, with ham, swiss cheese, pickles, mustard, and mayo; and the Napa Valley, with fresh goat cheese, watercress, and Meyer lemon honey mustard. The main competition for the burgers is the "griddled cheese deluxe," with 5 cheeses, tomato, and bacon. Sweet potato fries and beer-battered onion rings are good sides. The milk shakes and malteds have the added treat of nostalgia. You can update them with flavored bourbon, vodka, or rum. There also is a Bobby's Burger Palace at 630 Old Country Rd., in the Roosevelt Field Mall, Garden City; (516) 877-7777.

BrickHouse Brewery, 67 W. Main St., Patchogue, NY 11772; (631) 447-2337; brickhousebrewery.com; American; $$. BrickHouse actually is more of a beer fave, but the bar food is acceptable and the joint can be a good time all around. First things first: Hurricane Kitty, a hoppy IPA; Street Light blond ale; Nitro Boom Stout, precisely that; Boy's Red, which packs more than a nice hue; and Main Street Coffee Porter, with an assist from the local Roast Coffee and Tea Trading Company. The brews are served in a building that goes back to the 1850s. That stout fuels the house's respectable chili. "Brewers sausage" also is an apropos choice, served with apple sauerkraut. The version of jambalaya may not send you to the Big Easy, but it does have sufficient heat to call for a pint. Blue Point oysters, littleneck clams, and the shrimp cocktail are basic here. So are beer-battered fish-and-chips, barbecued ribs, and for the Bavarian adventurer, sauerbraten with red cabbage, potato dumplings, and gingersnap gravy.

Chachama Grill, 655-08 Montauk Hwy., East Patchogue, NY 11772; (631) 758-7640; chachamagrill.com; New American; $$–$$$. Elmer Rubio's shopping-center restaurant must rank among the more modest-looking, first-class kitchens around. His food is consistently impressive, served with care in a very welcoming dining room. He prepares savory lobster bisque and a refreshing gazpacho; tender rack of pork with vanilla-scented sweet potatoes and pineapple chutney; juicy rack of lamb with a goat cheese–potato gratin; a fine seafood risotto with lobster, shrimp, and mussels; and splashy yellowfin tuna with patatas bravas, olive relish, and ancho chile aioli. At lunch, enjoy the tortilla wraps; in season, heirloom tomato salad with arugula, avocado, grilled asparagus, and blue cheese. Rubio's sweets take in warm rice pudding with caramelized banana, coconut flan, and tiramisu. Chachama Grill is a find.

The Fifth Season, 34 E. Broadway, Port Jefferson, NY 11777; (631) 477-8500; thefifth-season.com; New American; $$–$$$. Fresh and refreshing, the Fifth Season is a bright spot near the harbor in Port Jefferson. The fare, naturally, is seasonal and the execution stylish. Order the lobster bisque with tarragon crème fraîche, roasted beets with smoked blue cheese and pickled red onion, and the smoked local duck breast with pickled peaches. The roasted corn-and-ricotta ravioli have an endless-summer taste. Pan-seared, day-boat sea scallops are enriched with corn, chorizo, and scallion grits; the pan-seared local duck breast, from a Bing cherry–ruby port reduction. The American Kobe beef burger is juicy. The lobster roll enhanced with shaved fennel, the fluke po' boy, and the Painted Hills filet mignon sandwich with blue cheese also make for a fine lunch. Try the cornmeal cake with grilled peach, blueberry compote, and sweet-corn whipped cream. Labor Day always seems far away.

La Volpe, 611 Montauk Hwy., Center Moriches, NY 11934; (631) 874-3819; lavolperestaurant.net; Italian; $$. La Volpe and the adjoining Anton Pizzeria ensure plenty of good eating. The restaurant has some kitschy touches and whimsy in the decor, which includes understandable reverence for Sophia Loren. You'll be fond of the eggplant parmigiana, fried calamari and zucchini, and salad of arugula, fennel, red onion, and radishes. The spaghetti with sardines goes its own way with the addition of peas and light tomato sauce, but it tastes good, even if it doesn't appeal to purists. Also flavorful are the bucatini all'Amatriciana, cavatelli alla Norma with fried eggplant and ricotta salata, and orecchiette alla Barese, sautéed with ground sausage and broccoli rabe. The grilled shell steak with peppers, onions, and plum tomato sauce is a slightly more refined riff on steak pizzaiola. Be sure to order sautéed escarole on the side. The wood-burning oven yields satisfying pizzas, including the diavolo, with spicy salami; and the 4-cheese, with fresh mozzarella, Gorgonzola, fontina, and provolone. Cannoli for dessert.

Lombardi's on the Bay, 600 S. Ocean Ave., Patchogue, NY 11772; (631) 654-8970; lombardisonthebay.com; Steak, Seafood, Italian; $$$. This offshoot of Mamma Lombardi's focuses on red meat more than red sauce. But there are a few pastas to quell any rebellion. The waterfront restaurant is on a site remembered for an exceptional and elegant French restaurant, Louis XVI. Little remains to remind anyone except some etched glass, which may be gone by now, too. Here, start with hot sausage and peppers, grilled octopus, or a lobster cocktail. The plate of cured meats is good, too. The steaks include tender porterhouse for one or two, bone-in rib eye, bone-in New York strip, filet mignon, and marinated flank steak. The pork loin giardinera with arugula and tomatoes and the steamed lobster are tasty alternatives. And you shouldn't forget about the rigatoni with Mamma's meatballs. At lunch, you can have a lobster roll. Mamma's cheesecake and cannoli are available, along with an ice-cream sundae.

Lombardi's on the Sound, 44 Fairway Dr., Port Jefferson, NY 11777; (631) 473-1440; lombardisonthesound.com; Italian; $$–$$$. The north shore scion of Mamma Lombardi's is situated at the Port Jefferson Country Club at Harbor Hills. It's more restrained in the design, but just as hearty at table. The baked clams and the stuffed mushrooms are satisfactory. Calamari salad and Parmesan cheese with olives also are worthwhile starters. Rigatoni all'Amatriciana, perciatelli with eggplant and tomato sauce, and the baked pastas all evoke the original. The main courses are familiar, too, and reliable, especially the pork braciola, pork chops with vinegar peppers, and chicken parmigiana. For lunch, you may order the "classic country club burger" and "classic cobb salad" before being influenced by the cavatelli with chicken meatballs or the eggplant parmigiana. Fortunately, the desserts are assuredly Mamma's.

Mamma Lombardi's, 400 Furrows Rd., Holbrook, NY 11741; (631) 737-0774; mammalombardis.com; Italian; $$–$$$. The bedrock of the Lombardi empire, Mamma Lombardi's is a major red-sauce restaurant. The kitschy decor is just what you'd want here. Have the baked clams and the octopus salad, pasta piselli and minestrone, genuinely fired-up penne arrabiata and zesty linguine puttanesca, spaghettini with escarole and white beans and baked lasagna with meat sauce, mozzarella, and ricotta. Also: perciatelli all'Amatriciana and penne with eggplant and tomato sauce. The combo of chicken and sausage campagnola, with vinegar peppers; chicken parmigiana;

and eggplant rollatine are naturals. But consider the tender tripe Neapolitan style, the pork braciola, center-cut pork chops with hot cherry vinegar peppers and potatoes, or pork chops pizzaiola. Shrimp fra diavolo makes its deal with the devil and can be ignited to your liking. Ricotta cheesecake, cassata, and cannoli are the finales.

Mirabelle Restaurant and Tavern, 150 Main St., Stony Brook, NY 11790; (631) 751-0555; lessings.com; French, New American; $$–$$$$. Mirabelle was for many years the leading French restaurant on Long Island. Chef Guy Reuge's cuisine, however, has expanded so that his stellar establishment is equally New American. Housed in the Three Village Inn, it's an outstanding kitchen at work in an historic venue. The dining rooms, expertly managed by Maria Reuge, provide a stage. The major change initiated last year was to focus on a farm-to-table approach, emphasizing the seasonal and the local. That said, you still will be able to order Mirabelle's greatest hits, which include the exceptional Duck Mirabelle, with duck breast and confit of leg, and Reuge's tasting menus. Some additions: fluke steak with saffron potato and herb velouté; tagliatelle with lobster sauce, crab, and shrimp; and a delightful Long Island fish soup. The ginger-almond tart, a Mirabelle classic with caramel sauce and Chantilly cream, is superb. Mirabelle's menu is available throughout the Inn, including what had been the separate Mirabelle Tavern. The Tavern's more casual fare still is available. And service is attentive, friendly, excellent. See the recipe for **The Duck Mirabelle** on p. 341.

Orto, 90 N. Country Rd., Miller Place, NY 11764; (631) 473-0014; restaurantorto.com; Italian; $$–$$$. The eastern and more countrified relative of Kitchen A Bistro in St. James, Orto is just as imaginative and full-flavored. The setting is very much like a bucolic home, with several seating areas and an understated style. Eric Lomando's creative cookery does the rest. Some highlights from the ever-changing menus include garganelli pasta in a pork ragù, pappardelle Bolognese, semolina-fried chicken, braised beef short ribs with a potato puree, farro salad with roasted beets, tomato-braised meatballs, coppa with peaches and fennel, shrimp with creamy polenta, eggplant Parmesan, lasagna Bolognese, and hake with a puree of corn with tomatoes and basil. The best way to enjoy Orto is via the 4-course, fixed-price approach: 3 savory courses and 1 sweet. The lemon-ricotta cheesecake and the chocolate-almond cake have that fourth slot covered.

Pace's Steak House, 318 Wynn Lane, Port Jefferson, NY 11777; (631) 331-9200; pacessteakhouse.com; Steak, American; $$$. The scion of Pace's Steak House in Hauppauge, this restaurant emphasizes the staples, with Italian additions. The dining area seems clubbier than its relative's. The food, however, is largely similar. Begin with a shrimp cocktail or with raw oysters, nibble on a Caesar salad, or share the tomatoes and onions. The fresh mozzarella and red peppers are good, too. The steaks include a porterhouse for one or two, New York shell steak, filet mignon, and the tomahawk rib eye for a heroic appetite. The steaks are better without any marinating. Alternatives: a lean, grilled double-cut pork chop with applesauce; herb-crusted rack of lamb; and lobsters, which commence at 2 pounds and are recommended steamed. Side orders to remember are the mashed potatoes and sautéed spinach. Linguine, with white or red clam sauce, and rigatoni with tomato-basil sauce are the leading pastas.

Pentimento, 93 Main St., Stony Brook, NY 11790; (631) 689-7755; pentimentorestaurant.net; Italian; $$–$$$. Dennis Young's creative, full-flavored, excellent Italian restaurant is constantly evolving. And it has never been better than it is at the moment. His seasonal menus contain layers of experience and a sense of authenticity. The dining room, stylish and restrained, is a very pleasant place to spend an evening or two or 20. You could easily pick and choose at random and have a first-class meal. Some of the winning dishes are the arancini, or rice balls, stuffed with mozzarella; fried shishito peppers with sea salt; fried chickpea fritters; the piquillo pepper packed with goat cheese and chives; grilled housemade Berkshire pork and fennel sausage with pickled red onions; snappy fusilli Calabrese ignited with great housemade nduja salami; subtler shrimp-and-chive ravioli; pork chop Milanese; and a Sicilian vegetable stew with eggplant, peppers, zucchini, and more.

PeraBell Food Bar, 69 E. Main St., Patchogue, NY 11772; (631) 447-7766; perabellfoodbar.com; New American; $$. PeraBell Food Bar, pubby and personable, garners quite a crowd for happy hour. But go for the restaurant, too. The eclectic fare encompasses good spiced pork empanadas and a tuna tartare pizza with pickled cucumbers; Thai-glazed short ribs with crisp rice noodles and mango slaw and mussels Basquaise, with roasted chorizo, peppers, onions, and garlicky tomato broth. Midday, the cobb salad with chicken, grilled chicken panino with pesto, and the hefty burger compete with the turkey-and-vegetable chili, beef sliders, and the baked macaroni and cheese with bacon and chives. Lobster BLT sliders, the watermelon-and-feta salad with olives and onions, and the duck breast atop sautéed chard and vegetable couscous also complement the flowing beverages. Expect draught beer specials when the football game is paramount.

Porters on the Lane, 19 Bellport Lane, Bellport, NY 11713; (631) 803-6067; portersonthelane.com; American; $$–$$$. Sitting on the porch at Porters for lunch is a leisurely, enticing way to spend an afternoon. The homey, friendly restaurant is livelier at dinner, but you'll be cosseted anytime. Sample the shellfish cocktails and the raw bar. Go for the New England–style clam chowder. Or begin with the cleverly constructed scallop BLTs, with a trio of shellfish appropriately layered and helped with lemon aioli. The small tuna tacos, with sesame-ginger dressing and mango salsa, are good, too. The kitchen composes a butter-poached, dill-mayo-seasoned lobster roll and a fine crab cake sandwich on a brioche bun. The lobster macaroni and cheese could make you revisit the concept. The "Gorgonzola smothered" flatiron steak and the pan-seared salmon Dijonnais are flavorful main courses. The apple Betty in a jar, New York–style cheesecake, and hot fudge brownie with vanilla ice cream are basic Porters.

Public House 49, 49 E. Main St., Patchogue, NY 11772; (631) 569-2767; publichouse49.com; New American; $$. Public House 49 contributes to the spirited rebirth of Main Street in downtown Patchogue. The food is dependably good and the nightlife dance-driven. Before moving to the music, sidle over to small plates, which include ale-steamed littlenecks with chorizo, garlic, and tomato; pulled pork nachos with guacamole and pico de gallo; tuna tartare; hummus; and tempura shrimp lettuce wraps. There are tasty sandwiches and burgers, from the Reuben and "BBQ rib" ciabatta to the cheeseburger and the "continental burger" with pork belly and a fried egg. For bigger appetites: beer-braised beef short ribs with shiitake mushrooms, Chinese cabbage, scallions, and fried garlic; roasted chicken with wild mushrooms, tomatoes, and mashed potatoes; and seared tuna with soba noodle salad. The smoked pork nachos and macaroni and cheese with smoked bacon and caramelized onions highlight lunch.

Red Tiger Dumpling House, 320 Stony Brook Rd., Stony Brook, NY 11790; (631) 675-6899; redtiger1320.weebly.com; Chinese; $–$$. Red Tiger roars into town with Shanghai-style soup dumplings. The steamed pork soup buns and the steamed crabmeat-and-pork versions are full-flavored and worth risking any overheating after the first bite. Both have a hint of ginger. The crystal shrimp dumplings and chicken dumplings with scallion and ginger also are recommended. The kitchen prepares satisfying pork-and-vegetable pot stickers, pan-fried scallion pancakes, and rice noodles with chicken or beef. Post-dumplings, you may sample General Tso's chicken, diverting cumin chicken, double-cooked pork, spicy beef Sichuan-style, and shredded potato with hot pepper. Red Tiger has fine vegetarian fare, starting with that hot potato, and including eggplant with garlic sauce and crisp spring rolls. It's a modest spot with great appeal.

Ruvo, 105 Wynn Lane, Port Jefferson, NY 11777; (631) 476-3800; **ruvorestaurant.com; Italian; $$–$$$.** The Port Jefferson branch of Ruvo is cozier and warmer than the original in Greenlawn. The Italian fare is interrupted with New American dishes, but both are very good. Try a prosciutto flatbread with arugula, Gorgonzola, fig jam, and pine nuts; or the Maryland crab-and-roasted-corn cakes, accompanied by a braised lentil salad. Rice balls have gusto courtesy of fennel sausage and sharp provolone; the arugula salad, some personality from casaba melon, goat cheese, and pistachios. The housemade gnocchi are light and in a fine Bolognese sauce; orecchiette, bolstered by fennel sausage, broccoli rabe, cherry peppers, roasted garlic, and olive oil. Crisp roast duck flies in with a peach-apricot gastrique and a mix of farro and wild rice. If this seems un-Ruvo, head for the "Ruvo classics"—cavatelli and meatballs, eggplant rollatine, and chicken Parmesan included. The mascarpone cheesecake and tiramisu are in Port Jefferson as well as Greenlawn.

Spicy's, 501 Station Rd., Bellport, NY 11713; (631) 286-2755; **Barbecue; $–$$.** Spicy's is about as basic as it gets, with good barbecue and well-worn looks. You're not coming here or to the Riverhead branch for ambience. But the chopped pork and beef barbecue mix, barbecued chicken, pork ribs, and chicken wings can hook you. The housemade chili is husky and blunt. Fried oysters and clams are satisfactory. But Spicy's is about 'cue. On the side: cornbread, macaroni and cheese, collard greens, baked beans, cole slaw, with sweet potato pie for dessert. In Riverhead, Spicy's is situated downtown and on the riverfront, in a former diner building, stainless-steel variety, that dates to the 1950s, at 225 W. Main St.; (631) 727-2781.

Yao's Diner, 2503 Middle Country Rd., Centereach, NY 11720; (631) 588-2218; yaosdiner.info; Chinese; $$. Just when you think the eclipse of Chinese cooking on Long Island is nearly total, Yao's Diner comes through with its casual, informed Chinatown side trip. This frills-free operation has a fondness for the heat of Sichuan and the fare of northern China. But Yao's is right for kung pao chicken, fried sweet-and-sour pork tenderloin, sautéed shredded beef, and sautéed lamb with scallion. The braised meatball and braised pork, fried fish with cumin, braised prawns, deep-fried crabs in hot chili oil, and sautéed crabs with ginger and scallion each are distinctive and very good. Yao's also prepares flavorful vegetable dishes: fried potato chips, sautéed eggplant in garlic sauce, dry-fried string beans, "hand-ripped" cabbage, sautéed lettuce in oyster sauce, sautéed snow bean sprouts with chopped garlic—all fine. On a cool night, warm up with a soup: West Lake beef, shredded pork with pickle, fish with sour cabbage.

Zan's Kosher Delicatessen, 135 Alexander Ave., Lake Grove, NY 11755; (631) 979-8770; zansdeli.com; Delicatessen; $–$$. Fressers have some searching to do in Suffolk. Fortunately, there's Zan's. This is your destination for matzo ball soup, stuffed cabbage, stuffed derma, fried kreplach with sautéed onions, 3 kinds of knishes, and above all, the overstuffed sandwiches. Hot pastrami and hot corned beef are the pillars; hard salami and brisket hold things up, too. Best are the mix-and-match productions. Choose 2 or 3 meats and prepare for a feast. The "deli double" combines corned beef and pastrami on junior rolls.

Hot, open sandwiches count here: brisket, roast beef, roast turkey with gravy and cranberry sauce. And the omelets, with potato pancakes for company, are recommended.

Landmarks

Carnival, 4900 Nesconset Shopping Plaza, Port Jefferson Station, NY 11776; (631) 473-9772; carnivalrestaurant.net; Italian; $$. An informal restaurant and pizzeria, Carnival has an ardent following. The food is straightforward; the prices, moderate; the result, satisfaction. Good openers: escarole and cannelloni beans, calamari salad, fried zucchini, garlic bread with mozzarella. Pasta piseli, pasta e fagioli, and pasta with lentils lead the soups. Better pastas: baked lasagna, stuffed shells and manicotti, perciatelli with eggplant and plum tomato sauce, linguine puttanesca, orecchiette with broccoli rabe and sausage, and whole-wheat spaghetti primavera. Follow any of them with sausage and peppers pizzaiola, chicken or eggplant parmigiana, chicken rollatine, shrimp fra diavolo, sole Livornese, calamari marinara, or tripe Napoletana. Stay with the fundamental pizzas: Sicilian, white, Grandma, fresh mozzarella, or stuffed vegetable. And Carnival knows how to make a hero sandwich.

McNulty's Ice Cream Parlor, 153 N. Country Rd., Miller Place, NY 11764; (631) 474-3543; Ice Cream; $. McNulty's typically offers 40-plus flavors, from the classic to the out-there in its little shop. The establishment suggests the Long Island now vivid mainly in memories. Maybe it's the comparative minimalism of the place in the era of supersizing everything. No slick salesmanship or just-get-their-attention antics. You owe yourself at least a scoop, maybe a sundae, and probably a few pints to bring to your freezer at home. The specials change by the week and sometimes by the day. Peanut butter and Nutella could stoke a rivalry. And any flavor that includes a brownie is automatically high on the list. McNulty's makes very good ice cream cakes, too, pegged to holidays, special events, your fancies. The youthful staff is eager. How could they not be?

Tiger Lily Cafe, 156 E. Main St., Port Jefferson, NY 11777; (631) 476-7080; tigerlilycafe.com; Sandwiches, Smoothie Shop; $. Self-described as a "funky, creative space for musicians, artists, and great food lovers," Tiger Lily Cafe is creative and fun. The freshly squeezed juices, juice cocktails, fruit smoothies, soy smoothies, and energy shakes are the lures, with the cappuccino bar, sandwiches, and salads playing along. Have a Greek salad wrap, a vegetarian sandwich, or a cheese combo. The melted, sharp Vermont cheddar with tomato and the melted havarti with bacon and sliced tomato, on multi-grain rolls, are fine. So's Shaharazade, a union of hummus, grated carrot, mesclun, and sprouts in a wrap. There are several dishes with meat, too, including the grilled chicken and roasted vegetable sandwich and the smoked turkey wrap. The carrot-apple-ginger and the apple-pear-carrot juices are apropos accompaniments, maybe with a shot of organic live wheatgrass.

WAVE Seafood Kitchen, 25 E. Broadway, Port Jefferson, NY 11777; (631) 928-5200; danfords.com; New American; $$$. WAVE Seafood Kitchen is the restaurant at Danford's Hotel and Marina, perched harborside, with water and ferry views. The hotel was refurbished under new management. And the restaurant has benefited from a new kitchen. Good choices: a ceviche tasting, soft-shell crab tempura with watermelon and avocado, New England clam chowder, raw oysters and clams, the shrimp cocktail, steamed lobster, and grilled swordfish with a ragout of quinoa and more plus tomato-orange jam. Landside, the double-cut pork chop with red wine sauce is a satisfying alternative. At lunch: the lobster roll on toasted challah, seafood cobb salad, and fish-and-chips. The old-fashioned vanilla milk shake and "death by chocolate," a 4-layer cake with chocolate-dipped strawberry, compete for your attention, but the black-and-white gelato sandwiches may win out.

Specialty Stores, Markets & Shops

C'est Cheese, 216-B Main St., Port Jefferson, NY 11777; (631) 403-4944; cestcheesepj.com; Cheese. This charming cheese shop also has a menu of sandwiches and salads to complement the fromage. The grilled cheese section deserves special attention, whether you're drawn to the Capra, with goat cheese, greens, and fig preserves; the Big Blue, with blue cheese and raspberry-cranberry relish; or the Classic, accurately described as "lots of melted cheddar, nothing else." The tasting of 7 cheeses and the plate of salumi also are recommended. Craft beers and boutique wines are available to accompany the dishes. You'll find about 100 cheeses for sale. Pick a few for your in-house tasting. The farmstead American cheeses are particularly fine and well chosen, and there are many notable French choices. It's a ripe stop any time of day.

Dolce Momenti Bakery, 315-D Main St., Holbrook, NY 11741, (631) 509-1898; and 717 Route 112, Patchogue, NY 11772; (631) 758-8667; dolcemomentibakery.com; Bakery. The 2 branches of Dolce Momenti offer innumerable ways to sweeten your day. The Italian-American bakery prepares fine pastries, from sfogliatelle and St. Joseph's to cupcakes and lobster tails; plus Danish, almond boats, chocolate crumb squares, Linzer tortes, doughnuts, and hamentashen. The cakes include cassata, with a cannoli-cream filling; checkerboard cake; strawberry shortcake; and red velvet. And in addition to the banana cream, Boston cream, coconut custard, lemon meringue, pumpkin, and apple pies, Dolce Momenti makes a hearty pizza rustica. The rainbow cookies vie with rugalach, the pignoli with butter cookies. The bakery also makes good breads, among them semolina and challah.

Hoptron Brewtique, 22 W. Main St., Patchogue, NY 11772; (631) 438-0296; hoptronbrewtique.com; Specialty Market. Local craft beer is at the center of Hoptron Brewtique, where you'll dive into suds, find the stuff to make your home brew, and generally revel in the pleasures of the 16 taps. You also can have a light meal at one of the communal tables or in a seating area at the front. Overall, it's an educational as well as imbibing experience. You can purchase well-selected beers and fashion your own 6-packs. From the snack bar, try the soft pretzels, a cheese plate, grilled cheese with tomato and bacon, maybe some popcorn. Some locals to taste: Barrier Brewing Barnacle Brown Ale, Port Jeff White Beach Wit witbier, Spider Bite Eye Be Use, Montauk Eastbound Brown, Barrage Brewing Insane Summer Ale. The bottles and cans to-go list is impressive, with more than a single choice from first-class breweries such as Allagash, Anchor, Dogfish Head, Goose Island, Lagunitas, Left Hand, North Coast, Ommegang, Rogue, Smuttynose, Southern Tier, and Troeg.

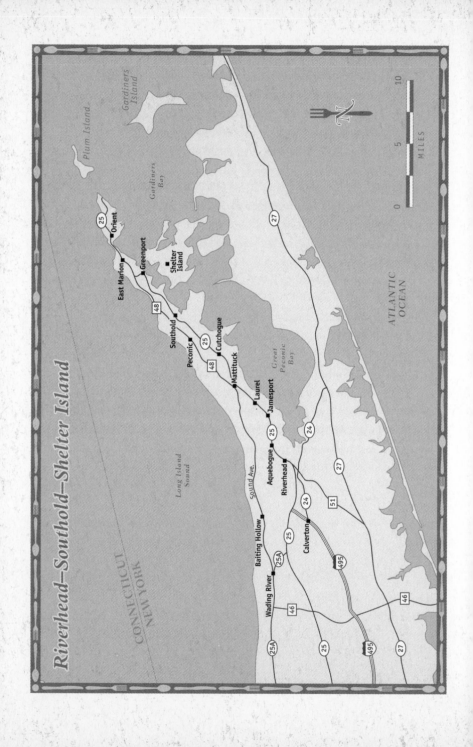

Towns of Riverhead, Southold & Shelter Island

Riverhead is at the mouth of the Peconic River. And it's a town with an appetite. The North and South Forks start just beyond.

At first, Riverhead was part of the Town of Southold, which with Southampton deems itself the first English settlement in New York. The New Haven settlers got things going in 1640. Riverhead split from Southold in 1792.

The Town of Riverhead includes Aquebogue, Baiting Hollow, Calverton, Jamesport, Northville, part of Wading River, part of Manorville, and the hamlet of Riverhead itself. In the hamlet is Polish Town, which was started by Polish immigrants in the early 1900s and continues to celebrate the heritage. Riverhead was home to farmers and eventually shipbuilders.

About 20,000 of the 35,000 acres of Suffolk County devoted to agriculture are in Riverhead. There are many farm stands. And it's also where Long Island wine country begins.

Southold was bought by settlers from the Native American Corchaugs and was a major farming area. Later, Greenport would become a significant whaling port. The Town of Southold includes the village of Greenport, the hamlet of Southold, Laurel, Mattituck, Cutchogue, Peconic, East Marion, and Orient.

Shelter Island, situated between the twin forks, was acquired from the Manhanset Native Americans in the 1600s by sugar merchants from Barbados. Shelter Island Sound and Gardiner's Bay surround it. About one-third of the island is owned today by The Nature Conservancy.

Tourism is a fruitful industry in Riverhead, Southold, and Shelter Island. Visit and you'll immediately see why. Come thirsty.

Foodie Faves

A Lure, 62300 Main Rd., Southold, NY 11971; (631) 876-5300; alurenorthfork.com; Seafood; $$$. Tom Schaudel's seafood enterprise steams lobsters on the site that for decades was occupied by Armando's Seafood Barge. Much more contemporary these days, the restaurant overlooking Peconic Bay still is, yes, a lure for anyone interested in very good grilled swordfish, now with Thai green curry, or local flounder, currently macadamia-and-coconut crusted. The casual pleasures take in a fish taco with guacamole, tomato salsa, and chipotle aioli; a ceviche of bay scallops, with accents of coconut and passionfruit; and yellowfin tuna tartare. Linguine with clams: recommended. And both the steamed lobster and the "knuckle sandwich" lobster roll are excellent. For the rebellious, there's a tasty burger as well as a flatiron steak. Desserts include a Catapano Farm goat-cheese-and-ginger tart and a warm plantain roll.

A Mano, 13550 Main Rd., Mattituck, NY 11952; (631) 298-4800; amanorestaurant.com; Italian; $$–$$$. A smart, casual trattoria-style spot, A Mano is good for wood-oven-fired pizzas, pastas, salads, and light main courses. It's one of chef-restaurateur Tom Schaudel's carefully calibrated establishments. The pizza topped with Catapano

Farm goat cheese, olives, tomato, and rosemary is pleasing. The slowly simmered meatballs with ricotta, tomato, and basil and the charred octopus with fingerling potatoes, capers, red onion, grapes, and olive vinaigrette are satisfying appetizers. Linguine with clams receives professional treatment, too. The marinated and grilled pork chop with polenta and pepperonata and the rib eye steak with roasted potatoes and roasted garlic are among the better entrees. Olive oil and almond cake with roasted local peaches heads the sweets. But it's hard to resist Schaudel's trademark chocolate-bag sundae, here naturally "Il Sacchetto di Cioccolato."

Cliff's Rendezvous, 313 E. Main St., Riverhead, NY 11901; (631) 727-6880; cliffsrendezvous.com; Steak, American; $$–$$$. Cliff's Rendezvous is about the marinated steak, which materializes nearly black. You have to like this sort of thing. The marinade imparts a distinctive character to the broiled beef, whether New York shell steak, porterhouse, or filet mignon. If you're not set on it, consider the steak burger. Precede any of them with the shrimp cocktail, raw oysters, creamed herring, or clam chowder, red or white. Cliff's also may have broiled bay scallops and fried soft-shell crabs. And if you're an immediate fan, you also may visit Cliff's Elbow Room, 1549 Main Rd., Jamesport; (631) 722-3292, and Cliff's Elbow Too, 108 S. Franklinville Rd., Laurel, (631) 298-3262.

Dark Horse, 1 E. Main St., Riverhead, NY 11901; (631) 208-0072; darkhorserestaurant.com; American; $$–$$$. Dark Horse rides into town with a sense of place, a few quirks, and some very good food. The restaurant is decorated with nostalgia, sentimental items, and broad-ranging tastes. It's associated with neighboring Tweed's, but feels contemporary by comparison. Bison stampede here, too. Sample the bison pâté or the charcuterie selection, the shrimp cocktail or the raw shellfish. At lunch: a bison pastrami sandwich, bison chili, a Beijing duck wrap, a grilled multi-cheese sandwich on local Polish rye. Short ribs, sirloin steak frites, crisp confit of duck leg with polenta and creamed spinach, and the lentil-and-potato stew impress at dinner. Cheesecake and Key lime pie vie for best dessert.

18 Bay, 23 N. Ferry Rd., Shelter Island, NY 11964; (631) 749-0053; 18bayrestaurant.com; Italian, New American; $$$. The restaurant 18 Bay moved to Shelter Island from Bayville and became a dining-out destination once more. It's a lovely country restaurant, precisely appointed, with excellent service and a relaxed style that masks a focused, meticulous kitchen. Elizabeth Ronzetti and Adam Kopels create a market-driven, 4-course meal that changes each week. Decision-making: minimal. Dine on the veranda or inside for a brief vacation. Dinner will be defined by a quartet of antipasti, a pasta course, a choice between 2 main courses, and 2 desserts. Some of the exceptional dishes are bluefish crudo; Peruvian-style fluke ceviche; grilled lamb meatballs with sweet onions; carrot soup with dill pesto; cauliflower soup with almond pesto; kale salad with toasted walnuts, pancetta, and a fried quail egg; rotollo pasta with ricotta, chard, and truffle butter; goat's-milk ricotta cannelloni; spaghetti alla chitarra with littlenecks; tagliatelle with lobster, peas, and preserved lemon; sautéed halibut with patty pan squash; and desserts such as almond cake with amaretto cream, olive oil and fig cake with lemon-scented cream, a peach-and-cherry cobbler, and a chocolate affogato with biscotti.

Erik's, 43715 County Road 48, Southold, NY 11971; (631) 765-6264; eriksinsouthold.com; Breakfast, Lunch; $–$$. Simple and to the point, Erik's serves breakfast until 11 a.m., ensuring that everyone has a shot at the fresh pastrami hash and eggs, huevos rancheros, whole grain pancakes, and the "loaded" egg

sandwich. In this company, it's unlikely you'll stick with oatmeal, even with brown sugar or honey. If you're at this tight little operation midday, there are burgers, a pulled-pork barbecue sandwich, deep-fried clam strips, a fried filet of sole sandwich, panini, and housemade soups and chili. After a long drive or a longer night, there are mornings when Erik's seems like an oasis.

First and South, 100 South St., Greenport, NY 11944; (631) 333-2200; firstandsouth.com; American; $$. One of Greenport's high-spirited hangouts, First and South is recommended for very good, informal food and for beer, served in a cozy, comfortable old building. The chowder with smoked cod and clams and the spiced-paprika chicken wings are  snappy opening acts. You'll want some spicy or sweet pickles, cheese fries with farmhouse cheddar and Sriracha mayo, and the soft pretzel. Striped bass crudo elevates the conversation, matched by the whole, roasted porgy with corn and fava beans. Skirt steak with German potato salad and string beans is juicy. And the clam-strip hot dog offers the definite regional topping. The Belgian waffle and BLT omelet highlight brunch with an East End spin on bangers and mash, with chicken-and-apple sausage, buttermilk-mashed potatoes, and a poached egg.

Grana, 1556 Main Rd., Jamesport, NY 11947; (631) 779-2844; granajamesport.com; Pizza; $$. Wood-fired, brick-oven pizza makes Grana the obligatory stop for Neapolitan-style pie on the North Fork. Each pizza is recommended without hesitation. The Rosa Bianca comes in first just because it's so rustic and proprietary, with local potatoes, red onion, Parmesan cheese, and rosemary. But think also about the full-flavored possibilities of fig, caramelized onion, and Gorgonzola as toppings. The Jamesport pizza brandishes fresh mozzarella, tomato sauce, salami, and kalamata olives to fine effect. And the namesake pizza delivers the goods with fresh mozzarella, Parmesan cheese,

THE NORTH FORK

The North Fork is home to most of Long Island's vineyards and wineries, and many appetizing restaurants. Here are 5 sharp tines.

First and South in Greenport, for snacks, small plates, and supper

Modern Snack Bar in Aquebogue, for old-fashioned, homey dishes

The North Fork Table & Inn in Southold, for New American elegance and great desserts

Noah's in Greenport, for superior seafood in a sleek setting

Scrimshaw in Greenport, for creative New American food and a water view

garlic-herb ricotta, and arugula. The Margherita is very good. For those doubting both the concept of the clam pie and the virtue of adding cheese to shellfish, Grana's ridiculously tasty production provides assurance with each garlicky bite.

The Hellenic Snack Bar & Restaurant, 5145 Main Rd., East Marion, NY 11939; (631) 477-0138; thehellenic.com; Greek, Seafood, American; $$. The Hellenic may give you the last acceptable meal on the North Fork before you head to the Connecticut- and casino-bound ferries. Respectable choices at the casual restaurant: moussaka made with ground beef; pastitsio with haloumi and Parmesan cheeses; and appetizers such as red beets with skordalia, stuffed grapevine leaves, saganaki made with kefalograviera cheese, and a platter of taramosalata and melitzanosalata. Better specials may include broiled octopus, cauliflower croquettes, bluefish stew with spinach and tomatoes, broiled whole fluke with fresh garlic, broiled whole porgy the same way, fish-and-chips made with cod, leg of lamb stewed with Merlot-and-tomato stock, and stuffed eggplant. Kataifi, phyllo with almonds and walnuts, and rice pudding are fine. But that toasted cheese babka could convert you. The Hellenic serves breakfast, with eggs, Belgian waffles, pancakes, and French toast.

Jamesport Manor Inn, 370 Manor Lane, Jamesport, NY 11947; (631) 722-0500; jamesportmanor.com; (631) 722-0500; New American; $$$. The rebuilt and reborn Jamesport Manor Inn is a country charmer. Following a blaze in 2005 that leveled the by-then Addams Family–style building, the inn was brought back with handsome woodwork and very good food. A fish-scale mansard roof, dormered windows, and elegant trim once more identify it. The menu changes each day. You may be fortunate enough to be here for the Peconic Bay oysters mignonette and the jumbo lump crabmeat and pear tomato salad; pan-roasted striped bass with wild mushroom risotto; and seared tiger shrimp with polenta and watercress and radicchio salad. The lobster BLT, on toasted brioche with lemon-tarragon aioli, boosts lunch. Ricotta cheesecake, cinnamon-dusted rice pudding, a Valrhona dark chocolate terrine with pistachios and crème anglaise, and the gelati are the better desserts.

La Maison Blanche, 11 Stearns Point Rd., Shelter Island, NY 11965; (631) 749-1633; maisonblanchehotel.com; French; $$$. The pretty, summery hotel hosts an equally pleasant restaurant that plays a mostly French theme. Neither brasserie nor bistro, it's a relaxed and relaxing hybrid. The escargots with garlic butter are plump; the mussels marinière, flavorful; and the fried goat cheese croquant with pesto and greens, an appetizer for all tastes. There's more verve to the endive salad, with bacon and blue cheese. The kitchen presents a tender steak

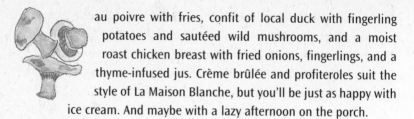 au poivre with fries, confit of local duck with fingerling potatoes and sautéed wild mushrooms, and a moist roast chicken breast with fried onions, fingerlings, and a thyme-infused jus. Crème brûlée and profiteroles suit the style of La Maison Blanche, but you'll be just as happy with ice cream. And maybe with a lazy afternoon on the porch.

La Plage, 131 Creek Rd., Wading River, NY 11792; (631) 744-9200; laplagerestaurant.net; New American; $$$. Across from the beach is La Plage, romantic and removed, except for the roving eye of the unopened Shoreham power plant. Chef Wayne Waddington's food glows on its own. His salads are refreshers, from the tomato, ricotta salata, *haricots verts,* and fennel combo to the gold and red beet number with goat cheese. His pastas include savory English pea and mint ravioli with lamb shoulder ragu and pappardelle with shellfish and chorizo sausage in a spicy tomato sauce. Pork tenderloin and pork shoulder are paired with sweet corn and a bacon-and-sage risotto; delicate squash and shishito peppers accent the achiote-grilled swordfish with sweet butter sauce. And the duck leg confit finds a foil in chive risotto and mushrooms. The spiced pumpkin cheesecake with pumpkinseed brittle, the warm chocolate-banana bread pudding, and the housemade ice creams and sorbets aren't captives of the calendar.

Michael Anthony's FoodBar, 2925 N. Wading River Rd., Wading River, NY 11792; (631) 929-8800; michaelanthonysfoodbar .com; New American; $$–$$$. You're tucked away here, in for some very good food at Michael Anthony's bright, fresh, idiosyncratic restaurant. The presentations are eye-catching, course after course. Years ago, he juiced up the dining room at the Dering Harbor Inn. The FoodBar is never dull, whether you're eating pickled colossal shrimp with lemon yogurt and carrot; octopus with black olive–fennel slaw; crisp oysters with hot-and-sour cabbage; Parmesan custard with grilled apricot, speck, and honey; coconut prawn curry; or dill salmon with kimchee fried rice. The hanger steak is spurred by Ubriaco-cheese cream and paprika chips; rigatoni, with a rustic tomato-and-lamb ragu. This is a kitchen that needs elbow room to go with a very restless imagination. From the GrillBar: a T-bone or porterhouse steak, best accompanied by creamed spinach and mashed potatoes.

Noah's, 136 Front St., Greenport, NY 11944; (631) 477-6720; chefnoahs.com; Seafood, New American; $$–$$$. Chef Noah Schwartz's sleek, precise, slightly industrial and hugely appealing small-plate and seafood restaurant is a must-eat in Greenport. He was the last chef at the Seafood Barge and among the first to redefine the East End fish house. Schwartz stars with Long Island clam chowder, barbecued local oysters, tuna tartare, Shinnecock sea-scallop ceviche, and a fabulous warm lobster roll with shaved fennel, fries, and house-made pickles. His rendition of a local bouillabaisse boasts a savory saffron-fennel broth. Pick the grilled sardines with piquillo peppers, lemon aioli, and basil; the jumbo lump crab cake with snow pea, mango, and vinegar slaw; and the local-catch fish-and-chips, made with Greenport Harbor Brewing beer batter. Be sure to sample the crab-stuffed deviled eggs, gruyère cheese puffs, and crisp Tasmanian red crab tacos. On land: Crescent Farm duck barbecue, braised pork belly pot stickers, filet mignon sliders on toasted brioche, and the grilled hanger steak with scallion-mashed potatoes. See the recipe for Noah's **Long Island Clam Chowder** on p. 331.

The North Fork Table & Inn, 57225 Main Rd., Southold, NY 11971; nofoti.com; New American; $$$–$$$$. When this restaurant opened in 2006, dining out on the North Fork changed for good.

Chefs Gerry Hayden and Claudia Fleming created an instant landmark: a gracious, refined, and outstanding destination devoted to local ingredients, organic produce, and impeccable taste. Hayden was a veteran of Aureole; Fleming, of Gramercy Tavern. Hayden was diagnosed with Lou Gehrig's disease in 2011. Although no longer the day-to-day cook, he oversees the kitchen and menu preparation. Fleming makes the memorable desserts. Typically, the seasonal menu may include dishes such as creamed celery root soup, Peconic Bay fluke crudo with grapefruit and ginger, a warm salad of crisp duck confit with a poached pullet egg and chanterelles, truffle-crusted Casco Bay hake, pancetta-wrapped loin of monkfish, Berkshire pork tenderloin wrapped with bacon and refreshed with fennel salad, and a white truffle risotto. Fleming's sweets may range from a chocolate-caramel tart to upside-down apple tart, a coffee-toffee ice cream sandwich to pear crepes. See the recipe for **Chocolate Caramel Tartlettes** on p. 343.

Pizzetteria Brunetti, 103 Main St., Westhampton Beach, NY 11978; (631) 288-3003; pizzetteriabrunetti.com; Italian, Pizza; $$. Neapolitan pizza purists and looser pizzatarians find paradise here. The choices: Margherita with housemade mozzarella, San Marzano tomatoes, basil, sea salt, and extra-virgin olive oil; Margherita Piu, with mozzarella di bufala, cherry tomatoes, basil, sea salt, and the olive oil; marinara, with the buffalo mozzarella, San Marzanos, cherry tomatoes, basil, sea salt, and olive oil; four-cheeses, with mozzarella di bufala, fontina, ricotta, burrata, and roasted garlic; vongole, with fresh shucked clams, herb-butter sauce, and parsley; mushroom-and-onion, with sautéed shiitakes, caramelized onions, goat cheese, thyme, and honey-truffle oil; "spezie" with sautéed broccoli rabe, broccolini, hot sausage, hot peppers, chile-pepper-infused olive oil, and burrata; a meatball-topped pizza with sheep's milk ricotta, fior de latte mozzarella, basil, and San Marzanos; the Parma, with aged Parmigiano Reggiano, arugula, prosciutto di Parma, and a balsamic vinegar reduction; and the "verde misto," finished with a fig puree, greens, cherry tomatoes, Gorgonzola cheese, red onion, and that balsamic reduction. Artichoke, asparagus, and pear-and-apple pizzas make seasonal appearances.

theRIVERHEADPROJECT, 300 E. Main St., Riverhead, NY 11901; (631) 284-9300; theriverheadproject.com; New American; $$$. Dennis McDermott's remarkable restaurant is in a converted 1960s bank building, low-slung and sleek as a *Mad Men* set. Chef Lia Fallon's cooking is very much up to date, with a stylized tomato tartare with whipped feta; kale salad with paprika vinaigrette, manchego cheese, and Marcona almonds; addictive shrimp-and-crab fritters with sweet corn and summer-herb aioli; and crunchy, tender fried chicken with pineapple-cabbage slaw, grilled avocado, and sweet tangerine honey. Her charred yellowfin tuna with Sichuan-spiced aioli, cucumber kimchee, and chilled sesame rice noodles, and lamb curry with sweet-spicy tomato chutney and toasted-cumin yogurt are layered with flavor. Nibble on fried olives with lemon aioli to get started. Midday: shrimp tacos, a riff on bibimbap with chile-garlic sauce, a civilized hamburger, or omelet with lobster or asparagus. The peach crumble and the panna cotta are just as rich.

SALT Waterfront Bar & Grill, 63 S. Menantic Rd., Shelter Island, NY 11964; (631) 749-5535; saltshelterisland.com; Seafood, American; $$–$$$. Situated at the Island Boatyard and Marina, SALT spreads to include restaurant and bar, both jammed in summer. Chef Darren Boyle cooks dishes that call for a chaser and a light breeze, inside or out. Enjoy the raw bar, the duck wings, steamed mussels in an aromatic ouzo-fueled broth, a bowl of clam chowder, calamari salad with a spicy sauce remoulade or fried calamari, and the beet salad, with feta cheese and watercress. The blackened bluefish taco, steamed littlenecks, and espresso-rubbed steak are blunt and good. Pulled-chicken sliders have a Caribbean kick. The hamburger is rivaled by its vegetarian counterpart. A room for wine tasting adjoins the restaurant, fueled by Jamesport Vineyards.

Scrimshaw, 102 Main St., Greenport, NY 11944; (631) 477-8882; scrimshawrestaurant.com; New American; $$$. Chef-Owner Rosa Ross's charming restaurant amid the wharf buildings offers a water view on 3 sides and excellent cooking in between. It's a bright, comfortable, cosseting establishment, with fine service and genuine personality. Ross expertly prepares delicate zucchini blossoms stuffed with herbed goat cheese; housemade, steamed, Cantonese-style dumplings; roasted striped bass with miso sauce and sticky rice; seared diver scallops with yuzu sauce and lemon-risotto cakes; grilled basil-garlic jerk chicken; and Crescent Farm duck breast with either peach or orange sauce. Her crisp spring roll with duck confit and Scrimshaw chowder with clams, leeks, potatoes, and cream are both delightful. At lunch, try the lobster roll, fish taco, salmon cakes, or cobb salad with turkey. Very good desserts.

Sunset Beach, 35 Shore Rd., Shelter Island, NY 11965; (631) 749-2001; sunsetbeachli.com; French, New American; $$$. No establishment on Shelter Island divides opinions as sharply as Andre Balazs' Sunset Beach. If you're a fan, it's a local spin on Saint-Tropez and a romantic, tres hip escape with Veuve Clicquot umbrellas; if you're not, it's the exact reason why Shelter Island is going tout Hampton and in the wrong direction. What's not in dispute is that the beachside location is lovely and the food pretty good. It's the sort of restaurant that calls for the shellfish plateau and the raw vegetable salad, the tuna tartare with soy vinaigrette, and the Bouillabaisse de Sunset, with Peconic Bay scallops the star ingredient. And look for the charred "cauliflower steak," accented with Thai green curry, for diners not enthused by steak frites. Hélas.

Tweed's Restaurant & Buffalo Bar, 17 E. Main St., Riverhead, NY 11901; (631) 237-8120; tweedsrestaurantriverhead .com; American; $$–$$$. Situated in the vintage John J. Sullivan Hotel is Tweed's, where the roaming buffalo make their last stop. The colorful restaurant specializes in dishes such as grilled bison kebab, bison hanger steak, bison filet, bison T-bone, carpaccio of bison, and bison burgers. They're all lean, juicy, and good. If you're not ready to dig in yet, the combo of seared local duck breast and leg confit finished with a blackberry reduction may get your attention. So will the rack of lamb with a panko-Dijon mustard crust, and the appetizer or main course of Peconic Bay scallops. The hotel has been at this address since 1896. Early on, it was the local stop for politicians and assorted wheeler-dealers. The buffalo head on the wall of the restaurant is said to be the last bagged by Theodore Roosevelt.

Landmarks

Claudio's Restaurant, 111 Main St., Greenport, NY 11944; (631) 477-0627; claudios.com; Seafood, American; $$–$$$. The historic establishment dates to the 19th century and the arrival of Manuel Claudio, from a Portuguese whaling ship. It has had many personalities over the years, including French cuisine and, as with other harbors, a reputed route for bootlegging during Prohibition. But today this is primarily a seafood house aimed at the widest audience, with an enviable location. Best advice is to focus on the steamed lobster or the lobster roll, the lobster BLT, or the Pipes Cove oysters. The waterside empire of Claudio's also includes the casual Claudio's Clam Bar, for the raw and the cooked as well as linguine with clams, and family-style Crabby Jerry's.

Cooperage Inn, 2218 Sound Ave., Baiting Hollow, NY 11933; (631) 727-8994; cooperageinn.com; American; $$–$$$. Homey American cooking is the hallmark of Cooperage Inn, a country-style establishment that's especially popular from Halloween to New Year's. It's all decorated for the holidays and puts on an old-fashioned show. The kitchen offers good chicken potpie with a puff-pastry crust, meat loaf with hunter gravy, a marinated and grilled pork chop with sweet apple chutney, a lobster bake, panko-crusted local fluke and local corn, a garlicky Kansas City steak with roasted corn and frizzled leeks, and, for a millennial spin, duck leg confit with a beet-and-arugula salad and peppered goat cheese and sesame-seared tuna carpaccio. Desserts are more traditional: coconut cream pie, Key lime pie, rice pudding, warm banana bread pudding, and a Davis Peach Farm peach Melba.

The Coronet, 2 Front St., Greenport, NY 11944; (631) 477-6669; coronetrestaurant.com; Luncheonette, Soda Fountain; $–$$. Friendly, uncomplicated Coronet has crowned the corner of Front and Main since 1949, keeping customers blissfully removed from current events, incremental news, multitasking, and the perpetual interruption of the cell phone. The turquoise booths and soda fountain each contribute to the image of time gone by. The place is open from 6 a.m. to 4 p.m., during which time your preferred choices could be buttermilk, blueberry, strawberry, banana-walnut, or chocolate-chip pancakes; malted Belgian waffles; challah French toast; cereal; and later, a roast turkey club sandwich, grilled cheese, chicken salad, a corned-beef Reuben, a BLT, Greek salad, pulled pork, or meat loaf. The ice-cream sodas are good. So are the floats, the rice pudding, and the chocolate pudding.

The Cutchogue Diner, 27850 Main Rd., Cutchogue, NY 11935; (631) 734-7016; cutchoguediner.com; Diner; $–$$. Just by its appearance, the Cutchogue Diner says come in. The structure is a memory of 1941 that stays open till 3 p.m. Early, it's a bacon-and-eggs kind of place. Or make that eggs and kielbasa. There are the elemental 3-egg omelets, and pancakes, waffles, and breakfast sandwiches. Later, the fare moves toward burgers in 7 variations; grilled cheese 6 ways; a BLT; a tuna melt, meat loaf, fried flounder, salads, and fried chicken in a basket with fries. Ice cream and pies for dessert. Have a cup of coffee and audition for *Dayhawks*.

Jamesport Country Kitchen, 1601 Main Rd., Jamesport, NY 11947; (631) 722-3537; northfork.com/catering/jck.htm; American, Italian; $$. This country kitchen is a modest and moderately priced place, prettily appointed. The better choices include salmon cakes, Long Island duckling with cranberry-pear relish, grilled rack of lamb, and at lunch, crisp duck wings, Manhattan-style clam chowder, omelets, salads, sandwiches such as pesto chicken and fresh mozzarella with grilled peppers and tomatoes on focaccia bread, or an unadorned hamburger.

Jedediah Hawkins Inn, 400 S. Jamesport Ave., Jamesport, NY 11947; (631) 722-2900; jedediahhawkinsinn.com; New American; $$$. In this beautifully restored and remade 19th-century Italianate Victorian, chefs have come and gone frequently. Who'll be there when you are may not be known until just before. But generally, the advice is to stay local with your selections, from duck wings and seared duck breast to striped bass and today's catch. The olive oil cake, chocolate marquise, and lemon parfait deserve to become regulars.

Lobster Roll Northside, 3225 Sound Ave., Riverhead, NY 11901; (631) 369-3039; lobsterroll.com; Seafood, American; $$. The North Fork relative of the Lobster Roll in Amagansett, Northside began in 1999. The style isn't quite as summery as the original, but the food is similar. Raw clams, the big baked clam "stuffie," a shrimp cocktail, and crisp puffers, or blowfish, are the popular openers; the lobster salad roll, the key main course. You can branch out with the blue-claw crab cake roll, tuna steak roll, flounder filet roll, fried clam strip roll, or fried-oyster po' boy roll. Once done rolling, consider the fish-and-chips made with cod, steamed lobster, or the charbroiled shell steak, ordered rare if you'd like it medium.

Modern Snack Bar, 628 Main Rd., Aquebogue, NY 11901; (631) 722-3655; modernsnackbar.com; American; $$. Modern Snack Bar endears itself with the kind of straightforward home-style cooking that has kept it full since the Truman era. Inside, the decor is spare and timeless; the service, openhanded; and the appeal genuine. It stands nobly against the relentless spread of trendlets. Enjoy sauerbraten and roast turkey dinners, Peconic Bay scallops, and crabs in season; maybe pot roast, loin of pork, stuffed cabbage, meat loaf, fried chicken, lobster salad, or roast Long Island duckling with stuffing. Allow for pie, definitely apple, coconut custard, chocolate cream, and lemon meringue. And turnips. Yes, mashed turnips. Bring home a couple of quarts. If you don't eat them today or tomorrow, freeze them to be thawed in time for Thanksgiving dinner.

Old Mill Inn, 5775 W. Mill Rd., Mattituck, NY 11952; (631) 298-8080; theoldmillinn.net; Seafood, American; $$–$$$. The original tidal mill went up here in 1812. Now, the restaurant that overlooks Mattituck Inlet is a good place for calamari salad, a cobb salad with shrimp, pan-seared Montauk swordfish, and steamed lobster. Alternatives: fish-and-chips, pan-seared local duck breast, pan-seared crab cakes, and a tuna burger with horseradish-and-wasabi dressing. The dry-aged, Niman Ranch New York strip steak, with either horseradish or olive tapenade, also is a suitable main course. Linger over a drink and watch the birds and the fishing boats go by. You'll feel far removed from the fray of the day.

Ram's Head Inn, 108 Ram Island Dr., Shelter Island, NY 11965; (631) 749-0811; shelterislandinns.com/ramshead; American; $$$. The Ram's Head goes back to 1929, a center-hall colonial with a view of Coecles Harbor and beautiful sunsets. You're on Ram Island, a causeway from Shelter Island and a light year from suburbia. Don't be surprised if there's a wedding under way on the property. The 17-room inn is that kind of destination. Dining here, consider the spring-pea-and-sorrel soup with lobster dumplings, Pipes Cove oysters mignonette, pan-seared sea scallops with lemony beurre blanc, pistachio-crusted rack of lamb, roast chicken with cipollini and morels, or the grilled Block Island swordfish. The banana version of tarte Tatin and cherries jubilee are about right for dessert at the Ram's Head. Be prepared. It's more than likely that you'll want to stay over.

Star Confectionery, 4 E. Main St., Riverhead, NY 11901; (631) 727-9873; Breakfast, Luncheonette; $–$$. This corner luncheonette is from another era, in its look and its style. Regulars come for the cheeseburgers, a BLT, open-face hot turkey and roast beef sandwiches, and the series of salads, from chicken to shrimp and tuna. Fish-and-chips and fried flounder are standards. Almost no one leaves without sampling the homemade ice cream. There are definitely enough flavors to satisfy a small army. Star Confectionery is a memory bank filled with summertime. Enjoy a root beer float and watch the decades pass by as effortlessly as leaves falling in October.

Aldo's, 105 Front St., Greenport, NY 11944; (631) 477-6300; aldos.com; Coffee, Biscotti. That almost says it all. Aldo Maiorana's establishment is about those two things, each exceedingly well made. Barista Maiorana sells earthy and mild Bali Blue Krishna, organic Guatemalan, super Sumatra Madheling, and the always appealing Ethiopia Yirgacheffe. His own Orient Espresso blend mandates an investment. So do the biscotti, either almond or almond dipped in dark Belgian chocolate.

Braun Seafood Company, 30840 Main Rd., Cutchogue, NY 11935; (631) 734-7770; braunseafood.com; Seafood Market. Braun was established in 1928 as an oyster processor and is a respected source for fresh fish and frozen fish, albacore to whiting. This is the seafood market where you may find that elusive wahoo, blowfish, or skate; the essential lobster, scallop, or oyster. You may walk away with lump crabmeat salad, fried clam strips, fish-and-chips made with cod, fresh tuna with mango salsa, fresh swordfish with horseradish mayo, and some very good ideas for tomorrow's dinner. Braun's Seafood 2 Go is its informal dining spot.

Briermere Farms, 4414 Sound Ave., Riverhead, NY 11901; (631) 722-3931; briermere.com; Farm Stand, Bakery. Briermere is an exceptional farm stand. But you should visit for the extraordinary pies, jams, and jellies. These are among the best pies anywhere: apple crisp, blueberry crumb, strawberry-rhubarb, raspberry-peach, raspberry-cherry, blackberry, and the sensational peach cream, strawberry cream, and blueberry cream pies that should be eaten as soon as possible. The unbeatable jams are peach and strawberry. But you also can enjoy beach plum, blueberry, and seedless raspberry. Outstanding cookies include the flourless oatmeal, chocolate chip, peanut butter, and, frankly, whatever else is ready to go. Also, there are very good breakfast breads and other morning treats. In the fall, as Thanksgiving nears, Briermere opens a separate line for apple pie. Stay on the main one and pick up a pumpkin pie, too.

Catapano Dairy Farm, 33705 North Rd., Peconic, NY 11958; (631) 765-8042; catapanodairyfarm.com; Dairy, Cheese. The North Fork's chevre central, Catapano Dairy Farm makes tangy, creamy goat cheeses courtesy of its group of approximately 80 diligent, dutiful producers. They make up to 6,000 pounds of cheese each year. Try the fresh, soft cheese; herbed chevre; whole-milk ricotta; aged, hard goat cheese; a modestly aged Gouda; a blue cheese; and both goat-milk yogurt and goat-milk fudge. You'll find Catapano Dairy cheeses used at some of the region's better locally oriented restaurants. You can try the farm's picnic special, which includes cheese, crackers, utensils, napkins, water, and that goat-milk fudge. Catapano also sells goat's milk beauty products including aloe-and-verbena soap and oatmeal-and-honey soap.

Junda's Pastry Crust & Crumb, 1612 Main Rd., Jamesport, NY 11947; (631) 722-4999; Bakery. Little Junda's packs plenty into its bakery, but the mandatory purchase is the wonderful apple strudel, fresh, crisp, and all you want it to be. The general style here is eastern European. That means very good babkas, plus muffins, scones, crumb cake, jelly doughnuts, custard-filled doughnuts, frangipane tarts, chocolate Linzer hearts, butter cookies, even black-and-white cookies. And it's the right bakery to invest in pfeffernusse. Junda's PC&C is housed in an historic building that goes back to the 18th century. You'll think some of the recipes do, too.

Magic Fountain, 9825 Main Rd., Mattituck, NY 11952; (631) 298-4908; magicfountainicecream.net; **Ice Cream.** At what once was a Dairy Queen, superior ice cream has been made for decades. What distinguishes and defines Magic Fountain is the number of more exotic flavors, all as well made as the more familiar stuff. Come here for lavender, olive oil, kulfi, fig-and-date, coconut-jalapeño, chocolate-chile, licorice, gingerbread, goat cheese, cinnamon bun, pomegranate-blackberry, and rainbow cookie. The banana split and assorted sundaes are ample and memorable. And they make first-class fruit smoothies. Custom cakes are popular, too.

Maple Tree BBQ, 820 W. Main St., Riverhead, NY 11901; (631) 727-2819; mapletreebbq.com; **Barbecue, Caterer.** It's easy to miss Maple Tree. But you'll be looking for good barbecue, western, southern, and then some. Super sandwiches include the combo of Texas brisket, the Tar Heel with North Carolina pork 'cue, coleslaw, and cheese. And there's a grilled pastrami Reuben with sauerkraut and swiss cheese. Arrive for breakfast and enjoy egg sandwiches and pastrami hash. For catering, the south is represented by grand North Carolina pulled pork, Texas barbecued beef burnt ends, St. Louis ribs and, for variety, southern fried chicken. West: smoked brisket, beef ribs, triangle steak. On the side, basics include macaroni and cheese, smoked beans, sweet potato fries, and cornbread. Sweet potato pie and pineapple upside-down cake are the notable desserts.

The Salamander General Store, 38 Front St., Riverhead, NY 11944; (631) 477-3711; salamandergreenport.com; **Take-out, Specialty Market.** This store, known as Salamander's, stars with fried chicken and light meals. Worth it: chicken potpie, Buffalo-style chicken wings, fish-and-chips, cobb salad, grilled Korean-style beef or pork with scallions, and an oyster roll with cornmeal-crusted oysters, tomatoes, greens, and coleslaw. The Tunisian sandwich with hummus, tomato, olives, cucumber, and green salad also is good. Lots of tasty pies, cakes, cookies, ice cream. And home cooking ingredients, if you're sufficiently inspired. But be sure to leave with some of that fried chicken, and maybe some Japanese duck katsu, too.

Snowflake, 1148 W. Main St., Riverhead, NY 11901; (631) 727-4394; snowflakeicecream.com; Ice Cream. Scoop for scoop, Snowflake produces the best ice cream on Long Island. Stu Feldschuh's devotion and skill make this an essential stop for anyone who reveres soft-serve ice cream, loves fresh flavors, and is fanatical about quality. His peach, strawberry, and blueberry sundaes are in-season classics. His malteds taste the way malteds must taste in paradise. And always consider the "monster shake." Terrific waffle cones, too. There's a flavor-of-the-week that's invariably worth tasting. Some of the superior regulars: peach, black raspberry, creamsicle, banana split, maple walnut, chocolate chip, French vanilla, and the fudgy, chocolatey Peconic Swamp Thing. The soft-serve is in vanilla, chocolate, and a twist of the two. Be sure to stock up on the magnificent flying saucers and brown bonnets, better than any that you remember. In summer, Snowflake also makes 5 or 6 sorbets.

Southold Fish Market, 64755 Main Rd., Southold, NY 11971; (631) 765-3200; Seafood Market. The catch(es) of the day could make you stop frequently at Southold Fish Market. It's always an impressive haul, much of it from local fishermen and destined for the tables of local restaurants. On a late summer day, the selection may include striped bass, bluefish, blackfish, flounder, fluke, and weakfish, as well as swordfish and tuna. The market also offers prepared food, which you may eat in or take out, and a raw bar.

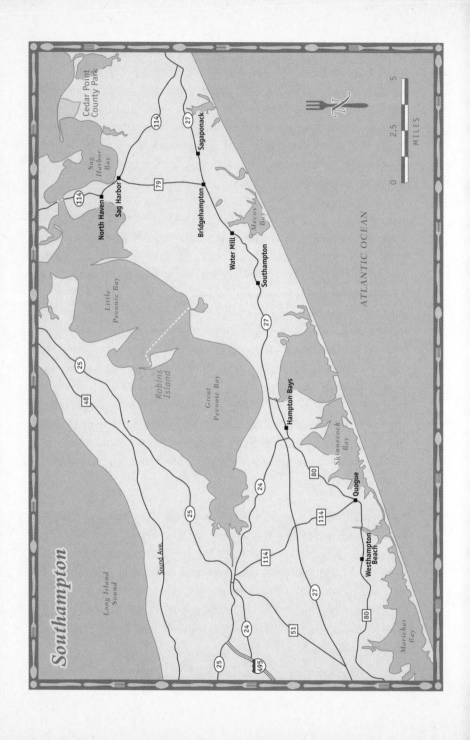

Southampton

Cedar Point
County Park

ATLANTIC OCEAN

Sag Harbor Bay

114

27

Sagaponack

114

79

North Haven

Sag Harbor

Bridgehampton

Mecox Bay

114

Water Mill

Southampton

Little Peconic Bay

27

25

Robins Island

Great Peconic Bay

48

Hampton Bays

Long Island Sound

24

Shinnecock Bay

80

25

114

Quogue

Sound Ave.

114

Westhampton Beach

27

51

80

24

25

495

Moriches Bay

MILES

0   2.5   5

Town of Southampton

In 1640, Puritans established the first English colony in the state in Southampton.

By last year, Calvin Klein had spent a decade and $75 million designing and building a home on Meadow Lane.

The Puritans acquired the land from the Shinnecocks. Settlers farmed and fished. It would become a colony of sweet corn and potatoes, and the very big catch of the day.

During the last century and the current, Southampton became a summertime playground. The name conjured images of blazers and pearls. That eventually would give way to sleeker, more casual affluence. Old Money becomes New Money. The beachside mansions remain—unless they're torn down and replaced with others.

In addition to Calvin Klein, notable residents include George Soros, David Koch, Howard Stern, Kelly Ripa, and the widow of artist Roy Lichtenstein. Meadow Lane and Gin Lane are synonymous with residential wealth.

Estates behind privet hedges, however, reflect only one aspect of the town. The Town of Southampton, incorporated in 1894, includes the village of Southampton, Sag Harbor, Bridgehampton, North Haven, Quogue, East Quogue, Sagaponack, Westhampton Beach, Hampton Bays, and Water Mill.

You'll eat well everywhere.

Almond, 1 Ocean Rd., Bridgehampton, NY 11932; (631) 537-5665; almondrestaurant.com; French, New American; $$$. At the corner of Ocean Road and Montauk Highway is the Hamptons' best bistro Americain. From the tin ceiling to the subway tiles, the service to the food, it's *le vrai choses*. The buzzing dining room is expertly run by Eric Lemonides. And chef Jason Weiner's treats include citrus-cured sardines with a smoked-gazpacho vinaigrette; grilled octopus salad with romesco sauce, pickled spring onions, and marinated artichokes; eggplant 3 ways, featuring caponata, baba ghanoush, and croquettes; and scallop-and-fennel crudo. The marinated hanger steak frites is excellent; likewise, the dry-aged New York strip steak au poivre. Savor the Berkshire pork chop Milanese; juicy roast chicken with crushed potatoes; Montauk fluke with fennel confit, fregola, bacon, and a spin on clams casino; yogurt-marinated breast of lamb, with hummus, tabbouleh, eggplant chips, preserved lemon, and harissa; and an outstanding hamburger. The chocolate pot de crème is a sensational sweet, balanced with salted almonds.

B. Smith, 1 Bay St. (Long Wharf), Sag Harbor, NY 11963; (631) 725-5858; bsmith.com; Seafood, American; $$$. Entrepreneur, actress, model, and media personality Barbara Smith operates a restaurant in Manhattan's theater district. This is the summery home for her enterprise, situated ideally on Long Wharf at the harbor. It's an attractive, waterside perch to examine yachts and contemplate affluence. Enjoy the raw bar, lobster chowder, crisp curried oysters, crab croquettes, and smoked-trout salad with watermelon and frisée. Better main courses are the roast chicken paired with an Asiago cheese potato gratin; grilled lobster with lemon butter; steamed

HOT HAMPTONS

Navigating the restaurant scene from Westhampton Beach to Montauk will require patience and persistence. These 7 tables are worth the effort, the wait, the traffic, and the cost, even on a summer Friday.

Almond in Bridgehampton

Fishbar in Montauk

Nick & Toni's in East Hampton

The Palm at the Huntting Inn in East Hampton

The Plaza Cafe in Southampton

Starr Boggs in Westhampton Beach

Topping Rose House in Bridgehampton

lobster with drawn butter; sautéed Montauk fluke with olive oil–glazed asparagus and tomato confit; and barbecued ribs, accompanied by sweet corn, onion rings, coleslaw, and a snappy sauce. At lunch, try the lobster salad with vegetables and red-pepper aioli, grilled tuna salad niçoise, the oyster po' boy, or the pulled pork sandwich.

Bay Burger, 1742 Bridgehampton-Sag Harbor Tpke., Sag Harbor, NY 11963; (631) 899-3915; bayburger.com; American; $–$$. When the burger toppings are listed on a sign that's shaped like a whale, you know you're in Sag Harbor. No Ishmael burger or Queequeg fries, but definitely a good, summery stop for casual eating in or taking out. The beef burger and the fish burger via cod are menu leaders. The vegetable patty is made with black beans and brown rice and roasted vegetables. Not bad, either. The turkey burger stays moist even with all white meat. Grilled cheese with cheddar and American, the BLT, and the Buffalo chicken sandwich are the main alternatives. And Bay Burger bakes its own buns each day. Joe & Liza's ice cream is the local treat waiting at the end of burgermania. Joe and Liza Tremblay opened Bay Burger in 2007. Their super ice cream is available on the South and North Forks and a few points west.

The Beacon, 8 W. Water St., Sag Harbor, NY 11963; (631) 725-7088; beaconsagharbor.com; Seafood, American; $$$. Sunset seen from The Beacon could justify a cover charge for entertainment. The airy, whitewashed restaurant has a wonderful site, with a water view to complement the solar show. The food is very good, too. Try Executive Chef Sam McCleland's fish tacos with salsa verde; braised pork belly with a soft corn tortilla, grilled pineapple, and mustardy barbecue sauce; duck rillettes with pickled red onions; or steamed mussels, finished with garlic white wine and more. Halibut baked in parchment with sun-dried tomatoes leads the seafood, along with sesame-crusted tuna with napa-cabbage-and-jicama slaw. The grilled sirloin burger with pommes frites and housemade pickles provides the competition for the grilled strip steak and the pork chop Milanese. For lunch: a panino of fresh mozzarella, tomatoes, and pesto; lobster salad; or that burger. Blood orange sorbet and almond cake are fine desserts. The Beacon is a David Loewenberg–Kirk Basnight production.

The Bell & Anchor, 3253 Noyac Rd. (Mill Creek Marina), Sag Harbor, NY 11963; (631) 725-3400; bellandanchor.com; American; $$$. The newest from Loewenberg and Basnight is this sleek, bright, and superior restaurant that takes a long look onto Mill Creek Marina. McCleland is executive chef; David Liszanckie, chef. Their stellar fare includes a delicious version of lobster Thermidor; a surf-and-turf of butter-poached lobster and claws and grilled filet mignon; pan-seared local tilefish with caramelized brussels sprouts and fennel cream; and a grilled Duroc pork chop with mascarpone polenta and grilled asparagus. Start with the knockout P.B. & O, a combo of crisp pork belly, oysters, and invigorating kimchee ready to be wrapped in lettuce leaves; a brandade of salt cod with potatoes and garlic that could lead to a Provençal reverie; the lobster cobb salad; and a Caesar salad rising to emperor status with prosciutto di Parma. The lobster garganelli pasta with corn, basil, and saffron cream also is recommended. Carrot cake, a brownie sundae, and madeleines with salted-caramel sauce are sufficiently rich desserts.

Bobby Van's, 2393 Montauk Hwy., Bridgehampton, NY 11932; (631) 537-0590; bobbyvans.com; Steak, American; $$$. Bobby is long gone. So are James Jones, Truman Capote, Willie Morris, and other habitués of the original Bobby Van's. Only the photos, the memories, and the address remain. Now, it's a chainlet of steakhouses in New York City, Washington, and here. You can eat in the vintage dining room or be very alfresco watching the crawl of eastbound traffic. The original, established in the year of Woodstock, still has some of the old charm. And you'll eat well sticking to shellfish cocktails, salads, and raw oysters before cutting into the sirloin or the filet mignon. Some other options are the fluke meuniere, pan-roasted chicken, and, at lunch, a lobster BLT or a lobster roll, a Cuban sandwich, or a burger with fries. But the distance between the old Bobby's and the new is, well, from here to eternity.

The Coast Grill, 1109 Noyac Rd., Southampton, NY 11968; (631) 283-2277; thecoastgrill.com; New American; $$–$$$. Looking onto Wooley Pond situated at Peconic Marina, The Coast Grill gives you a charming, country setting. The traditional country restaurant keeps the style of decades departed. But the food can be very much of the moment. Executive Chef Brian Cheewing presents a balanced, enticing table. The raw bar sampler is a good way to start, with Peconic Pride oysters and littlenecks, plus cocktail shrimp and sesame-pepper seared tuna. The crab cake is meaty; and the local duck confit, lushly paired with braised lentils, sun-dried cherries, shaved apple, and a Duck Walk port wine reduction. The kitchen prepares excellent steamed lobster; fine pan-roasted fluke with toasted farro, local spinach, and a tapenade of 5 olives; fat seared Montauk sea scallops with black-truffle butter; and a thick, tender broiled filet mignon with red-wine sauce, crumbled Maytag blue cheese, grilled asparagus, and smashed potatoes. The chocolate-and-banana bread pudding and the salty caramel ice cream sundae induce lingering.

The Cuddy, 29 Main St., Sag Harbor, NY 11963; (631) 725-0101; thecuddy.com; New American; $$$. You're advised that the name of this gastropub, which debuted last year, reflects a safe and comfortable little place. That's the kitchen's goal and it keeps with the theme. You might be able to recite part of the menu without seeing it: Caesar salad, heirloom tomatoes and buffalo mozzarella, beet salad, steamed mussels, yellowtail tartare, St. Louis ribs, steak frites, roasted chicken, and The Cuddy burger. Try the Painted Hills hanger steak frites, boosted by chimichurri sauce. Green tomato chutney and scallion waffles enhance the main course of fried chicken and waffles. The pan-roasted striped bass finds good company in basil fregola and a lemon–sweet pea puree. With any course, get the cheddar-and-Parmesan biscuits and the grits with tomato jam. The orange–olive oil cake and the strawberry-coconut bread pudding are heartening desserts. Naturally, The Cuddy makes very fine cocktails, lemonade, and iced tea.

Estia's Little Kitchen, 1615 Bridgehampton-Sag Harbor Tpke., Sag Harbor, NY 11963; (631) 725-1045; estiaslittlekitchen .com; American, Mexican; $$. Colin Ambrose began this mouthful of a restaurant in 1998, succeeding the original Estia in Amagansett. The cozy spot can barely contain all of Ambrose's eclectic flavors.

His crab tostadas with guacamole, grilled-shrimp tacos, and tortilla soup with a feta cheese and avocado garnish are tasty starters, as are the roasted-beet-and-goat-cheese salad and the Mexican sweet corn. Potato-crusted flounder, arroz con pollo, pan-roasted chicken with mashed potatoes, and the hanger steak Azteca, with guajillo-spiced potatoes and spinach, are very satisfying dinner dishes. Lunch sandwiches, salads, tacos, and platters are reliably tasty. So are the breakfast courses, including omelets and burritos. Chocolate pudding, flan, tres leches cake, bunuelos with ice cream—your call.

Fresh Hamptons, 203 Bridgehampton-Sag Harbor Tpke., Bridgehampton, NY 11963; (631) 537-4700; freshhamptons.com; New American; $$$. Veteran East End chef Todd Jacobs's new restaurant moved into the meticulously designed, former site of Southfork Kitchen with a commitment to local ingredients, healthful food, and a fondness for vegan variations. The bonac clam chowder with littlenecks is a very good opener, rife with dill. Salads are uniformly well made, from the one with raw organic kale and hemp seed hearts to the generous Greek salad. Jacobs's small plates include a raw "Fresh" summer roll with vegetables in a collard-greens wrap. Just as good are fried zucchini blossoms stuffed with goat cheese and crisp, baked organic kale chips with sea salt and olive oil. Of course, the raw bar has first-class choices, among them Peconic Pride oysters. Wasabi-spurred skate with ginger beurre blanc and pan-seared porgy with epazote and chile-lime beurre blanc are winning main courses. Same goes for the grilled, Moroccan-spiced hanger steak and the house hamburger. The list of vegetable side dishes is challenging but fun.

Golden Pear, 99 Main St., Southampton, NY 11968; (631) 283-8900; goldenpearcafe.com; Breakfast, Lunch; $–$$. The informal cafe has become a Hamptonian mainstay. It's the kind of place where diners already have a good idea about what they want, starting with coffee, espresso, and cappuccino. The keys to the menu: omelets, oatmeal, a waffle, scones, croissants; soups, sandwiches, and wraps; main dishes such as turkey meat loaf, chicken potpie, macaroni and cheese, a quiche of the day. There are other branches at 111 Main St., Sag Harbor, (631) 725-2270; 2426 Montauk Hwy., Bridgehampton, (631) 537-1100; and 34 Newtown Lane, East Hampton, (631) 329-1600.

little/red, 76-C Jobs Lane, Southampton, NY 11968; (631) 283-3309; littleredsouthampton.com; French, New American; $$–$$$. From the owners of red/bar brasserie, The Bell & Anchor, and others comes little/red, a small, sharp cafe-restaurant that lightens up this part of downtown Southampton. Share a board of cured meats and pâté, dip a spoon into the vibrant yellow tomato gazpacho, try the glistening tuna tartare, and turn Gallic with *frisée aux lardons* capped with a poached egg. The heirloom tomato-and-watermelon salad with ricotta salata also is worth ordering. Main courses from Executive Chef Bob Abrams include a really good grilled cheese sandwich with roasted duck, braised cabbage, mustard, and, surprisingly, brie; the hanger steak with mashed potatoes enriched by Camembert; the generous bistro burger with pommes frites; fish-and-chips with lemon-tarragon aioli; and herb-roasted chicken with honey-glazed carrots and a rich potato salad. The desserts are required eating, especially the sweet corn cake with fresh local peaches and sauce and caramel-swirl gelato, the banana pudding trifle, a brownie sundae, and the butterscotch pot de crème with tart cherry biscotti.

LT Burger in the Harbor, 62 Main St., Sag Harbor, NY 11963; (631) 899-4646; ltburger.com; American; $$. The horseshoe-shaped bar and the white subway tiles give LT its look, star chef Laurent Tourondel its initials and cachet. Burgers and fries are his media here, in many forms and potato buns. The LT Backyard takes everything seriously, with grilled hickory-smoked bacon, cheddar, and the house sauce; the standard, lettuce, tomato, onion, and pickle. Smashed Smoke includes Spanish onion, Mecox cheddar, peppered bacon, and "sweet catch-up." Precede your burger with chili and cornbread, New England–style clam chowder, or an heirloom tomato and bacon salad with fresh ricotta and spicy aioli. Fry-wise: the sweet potato, the waffle, the skinny, or smoked-Gouda laden. The Kobe beef hot dog from Snake River Farms gives the burgers some competition. A vanilla or chocolate shake has the proper affinity; the Valrhona chocolate hot fudge sundae, dibs on dessert.

Muse in the Harbor, 16 Main St., Sag Harbor, NY 11963; (631) 899-4810; museintheharbor.com; New American; $$–$$$. Following Chef Matthew Guiffrida guarantees very good food, and plenty of fun. His fare never is dull. In what years ago was a service station, Guiffrida turns on the ignition with his tuna "ménage a trois," featuring ahi tuna tartare, a blackened tuna lollipop with candied wasabi crust, and seared tuna with seaweed salad. Not ya Mama's Meatballs is a 4-way appetizer, with Asian-style in sweet-and-sour sauce, Italian with tomato sauce and shaved Parmesan cheese, Thanksgiving with a cranberry and caramelized Vidalia onion compote, and Swedish, as you'd expect. They're playful and flavorful. Horseradish-and-Gorgonzola-crusted strip steak, grilled swordfish with charred-corn chow chow and Israeli couscous tabbouleh, and wasabi au poivre duck with grilled sweet potato hash and cranberry-duck confit are edible entertainments. Guiffrida also offers grilled strip steak and finfish, but why bother?

Nammos Estiatorio, 136 Main St., Southampton, NY 11968; (631) 287-5500; nammos-hub.com; Greek; $$$–$$$$. What for a long time was the Post House and for too long Nello Summertimes, now is this professional, spacious Greek restaurant. Have zucchini and eggplant chips. And pick a sampler of rich Greek spreads, such as taramosalata and melitzanosalata; saganaki, or pan-fried kefalograviera cheese; a generous Greek salad with barrel-aged feta; tender, grilled octopus with onions, peppers, and capers; pan-fried feta cheese with a sesame-seed crust and wine-poached figs; grilled lamb chops with a couscous salad and tomato gravy. Most important, however, are whole, char-grilled fish. The Mediterranean catch may include *fagri,* like a pink snapper; *tsipoura,* or royal dorado; *lavraki,* or sea bass; and from the United States, red snapper and Arctic char. You'll see them displayed regally on ice. *Loukomades,* akin to doughnuts, with honey, cinnamon, and ice cream; walnut sponge cake; baklava; and Greek yogurt with thyme honey and nuts are the desserts.

Osteria Salina, 95 School St., Bridgehampton, NY 11937; (631) 613-6469; osteriasalina.net; Italian; $$$. Although Osteria Salina is named for an Aeolian island near Sicily, it doesn't really have all that much to do with Sicilian cuisine. But the restaurant is sunny and summery, very Hamptons, and quite good. The Sicilian dishes include caponata, the eggplant relish, in a restrained version; bucatini con le sarde, or pasta with sardines, that will appeal to diners who prefer mildness to boldness; and mezzi-rigatoni with eggplant, tomatoes, basil, olives, and mozzarella. The ripe tomato salad uses Sicilian olive oil; the crab cake, citrus aioli; charred octopus, parsley pesto; and a timballo of salmon, cucumber and avocado. Try the grilled swordfish, caponata on the side, and the jumbo shrimp, with some verve from the backing of pine nuts, raisins, and orange zest. They offer pancakes and steak-and-eggs for breakfast; a lobster roll and a burger "Americano" at lunch.

Page at 63 Main, 63 Main St., Sag Harbor, NY 11963; (631) 725-1810; page63main.com; New American; $$–$$$. Page at 63 Main is a lovely restaurant on a summer afternoon, all bright and warm, windows open and alfresco tables available. The handsome building itself dates to Sag Harbor's whaling era. Chef Humberto Guallpa brings everything up to date with his aromatic, enticing clam chowder; Montauk tuna tartare with sesame oil and ginger–sweet chile sauce; steamed pork dumplings in miso broth; and an ample crab cake with daikon radish slaw. Guallpa also prepares a savory paella with seafood, chicken, and chorizo sausage, and duck with grilled green tomato, roasted sunchoke, and piquillo pepper jam. Anyone remembering the opening fare at Page will hope for a return of the hefty lobster roll and the sweet-pea ravioli in carrot broth.

Pierre's, 2468 Main St., Bridgehampton, NY 11932; (631) 537-5110; pierresbridgehampton.com; French; $$$. Pierre's brings a Saint-Tropez accent to downtown Bridgehampton, with the French food but just as important the sensibility. Colorful, festive, relaxed, and not too concerned about dollars and euros, the place just asks you to stay and enjoy. The pleasures include grilled sardines escabeche and a Thai-inspired mussel soup with curry, coconut milk, and roasted banana. The lobster salad with fresh mango suits the surroundings, along with a frisée-and-endive salad with Fourme d'Ambert cheese. Lobster, steamed, broiled, or fricassee, enriches the proceedings. So does the duck breast a l'orange with a mousseline of parsnips. Try a croque monsieur at lunch; *oeufs en meurette* or French toast at breakfast. Valrhona chocolate mousse, profiteroles with vanilla ice cream and chocolate sauce, a vacherin with raspberry ice cream, and tropical fruit sorbets all suit Pierre's.

The Plaza Cafe, 61 Hill St., Southampton, NY 11968; (631) 283-9323; plazacafe.us; Seafood; $$$. The Plaza Cafe is the big fish among Long Island's seafood restaurants. Chef Douglas Gulija remade the stellar restaurant a couple of years ago, with marvelous results that improved on the original, refined establishment. It has kept a warm, openhanded style all along. Gulija's essentials include superb lobster-and-corn chowder; seared local squid with piquillo peppers, hummus, kalamata olives, and a sherry vinaigrette; and fluke sashimi with lemon confit and a jalapeño-yuzu emulsion. His instant classics: the lobster-and-shrimp shepherd's pie with shiitake mushrooms, corn, and a chive-potato crust; the grilled Montauk swordfish "chop," with potato-spinach ragout and carrot-chive broth; soy-acacia honey-marinated black cod with an edamame puree and yuzu vinaigrette. They're nearly equaled by sautéed halibut, with a Peruvian potato puree and lobster "succotash," and the sautéed local striped bass with quinoa salad, roasted tomato oil, and avocado vinaigrette. Although seafood is his hallmark, Gulija also excels with a superb duck via sliced breast and barbecued confit of leg, with a corn crepe, tomato-corn salsa, and a foie-gras-based sauce, and pesto-crusted rack of lamb with ratatouille and goat cheese tart. Desserts: a cherry trio, with clafoutis, ice cream, and compote; crème brûlée with local peach compote; a strawberry-theme showcase with swirled ice cream and buttermilk biscuit; white chocolate cheesecake with strawberry compote and chocolate ice cream. See the recipe for **Lobster-and-Shrimp Shepherd's Pie** on p. 332.

red/bar brasserie, 210 Hampton Rd., Southampton, NY 11968; (631) 283-0704; redbarbrasserie.com; French, New American; $$$. Très Hamptonian, red/bar is part local hangout, part visitors' restaurant, mostly very good. It's an early contribution from the Fresno, little/red, and Bell & Anchor people. And the food has kindred style. Some recommendations: crisp, fried smelts with aioli and lemon; char-grilled octopus with warm chickpeas; Montauk fluke crudo; endive-and-watercress salad with stilton cheese and sliced pear; grilled Brandt beef strip steak in a red-wine reduction, with potatoes dauphinoise;

and on a chilly night, beef Bourguignonne, which may not remind you of a trip to Burgundy, but definitely evokes Southampton. Profiteroles with bittersweet chocolate sauce and toasted almonds, the apricot-and-almond tart, and an irony-free baked Alaska, with vanilla ice cream, tropical fruits, and "flaming rum," are the major sweets.

Sant Ambroeus, 30 Main St., Southampton, NY 11968; (631) 283-1233; santambroeus.com; Italian; $$$–$$$$. The Hamptons' offshoot of the Manhattan and Milan restaurants, Sant Ambroeus has been well established in Southampton for more than 20 years. The design is naturally elegant, with ivory banquettes, striped chairs, polished wood, and refined, expensive food. Dinnertime calls for a salad of thinly sliced artichokes, with arugula and Parmesan cheese; *vitello tonnato,* or veal with tuna sauce; or beef carpaccio, here with mustard sauce. Fusilli with pesto, tagliatelle alla Bolognese, and risotto Milanese define the cuisine. Afterward, perhaps a breaded veal chop Milanese, roasted Dover sole, or roasted duck breast served on kale, with a blood-orange garnish. For dessert, just go to the front of the shop, which you enter to reach the dining room. There are lovely chocolates, tarts, cakes, cookies. But have the superb gelati. They're luscious, from chocolate to fior de latte, lemon to passionfruit, hazelnut to crocantino.

Sen, 23 Main St., Sag Harbor, NY 11963; (631) 725-1774; senrestaurant.com; Japanese, Sushi; $$$. Sit at the handsome sushi bar or at table and order sushi at Sen. The veteran restaurant does make fine small plates of charred shishito peppers, seared sea scallops, panko-crusted fried tofu, and crab-and-shrimp wonton tacos. And you can pick an onion ring "tempura" to go with steak teriyaki, too. But Sen is at its best with nigirizushi and sushi rolls. The duly designated exotic rolls include the tiger, with spicy red crab, tuna, avocado, masago, and tempura flakes, wrapped in seaweed; the lobster, with spicy lobster, avocado, celery, fried onion, masago, and a soy-paper wrap; and the caterpillar, with eel, cucumber, and masago inside and avocado, sesame seeds, and eel sauce outside. The sushi and sashimi of note include fatty tuna, sweet shrimp, sea urchin, surf clam, and sea scallop. They have some vegetable rolls, too. The soba and udon noodles also are good, in broth.

Squiretown, 26 W. Montauk Hwy., Hampton Bays, NY 11946; (631) 723-2626; squiretown.com; American; $$–$$$. Comfortable Squiretown offers you a good bar and a better dining room. The service is friendly and the food good at this smoothly run, often ambitious establishment. Sample the Beet Box, with roasted beet filled with parsnip and celery root purees and crumbled blue cheese; the clam fritters, a Caribbean-inspired treat; braised pork belly with shaved apple; skirt steak with fried yucca and chimichurri; braised beef short ribs with mashed potatoes; or the rib eye steak for two. Sandwiches: pulled pork or crisp fried chicken breast. For dessert, there's Elvis Woulda—peanut butter cream inside chocolate cake, with banana-caramel sauce and marshmallow fluff. It will trigger an outburst of "Hound Dog," if not "Love Me Tender."

Starr Boggs, 6 Parlato Dr., Westhampton Beach, NY 11978; (631) 288-3500; starrboggsrestaurant.com; New American; $$$. When Starr Boggs opened his first restaurant in Westhampton Beach more than 25 years ago, it seemed revolutionary. And it was the best example of New American cuisine on the East End. A few locations later, things have calmed down. The food still is very good, often better. Maybe other spots have just caught up, if not gone beyond. His menu changes regularly. But some of the longstanding hits are his stirring Mediterranean fish soup; a fabulous, thickly cut and baked slab of swordfish with a basil crust; seared, rare ahi tuna; steamed lobster; the crab cake with sauce remoulade and corn salad; grilled flatiron steak; rack of lamb; a combo of seared tuna and spicy tuna tartare; and the local beet salad with goat cheese.

Stone Creek Inn, 405 Montauk Hwy., East Quogue, NY 11942; (631) 653-6770; stonecreekinn.com; Mediterranean, French; $$$. The beautiful Stone Creek Inn is one of Long Island's premier country restaurants. It would be at home in a French province or two. Chef Christian Mir's elegant, seasonal cuisine is seductive. Refresh yourself with the chilled tomato-and-red-beet soup. Savor the grilled octopus with warm fingerling potatoes. Spoon up small cheese ravioli in mussel-and-chive broth. Try Long Island duck meatballs, cut with an apple-cider reduction. Mir's local ode to bouillabaisse catches lobster and mussels, porgy and monkfish, and turns them Marseillaise with rouille. He also sets out a lustrous fluke crudo, with apple, basil, olive oil, and fleur de sel. The lobster chopped salad, with corn, golden beets, and golden tomatoes misses only a ray of sun. The grilled bison rib eye with chanterelles and herbaceous chimichurri could make you understand Buffalo Bill. Sorbets are outstanding, as are almost all the desserts.

Topping Rose House, 1 Bridgehampton-Sag Harbor Tpke., Bridgehampton, NY 11932; (631) 537-0870; toppingrosehouse .com; New American; $$$$. The extraordinary restoration and transformation that led to Topping Rose House restaurant and hotel is about time, persistence, and money. The historic 1840's home of Judge Abraham Topping Rose now houses a great restaurant from *Top Chef* lead judge Tom Colicchio and Executive Chef Ty Kotz. Their monthly menus are tributes to local ingredients, meticulously prepared, with sources listed. You may find fried Montauk oysters in the company of Wagyu beef carpaccio; sweet corn agnolotti with black truffles and leeks; bucatini with clams, chiles, and parsley; roasted fluke with fennel, cipollini, and lobster mushrooms; wild striped bass with eggplant, zucchini, and roasted peppers. Cassandra Shupp's desserts are exceptional: a blueberry tart with peach sauce and lime sorbet; a peach tarte Tatin with honey-crème fraîche ice cream; brioche doughnuts with cardamom sugar and lemon cream; perfect ice creams and sorbets. Topping Rose House is costly—and worth it.

Townline BBQ, 3593 Montauk Hwy., Sagaponack, NY 11962; (631) 537-2271; townlinebbq.com; Barbecue; $$. From the owners of Nick & Toni's and Rowdy Hall in East Hampton is this full-blown barbecue joint, rustic, blunt, and good. Townline offers meaty, Texas-style short ribs and dry-rubbed pork ribs, both essential. The smoked meats are terrific, especially pulled pork, brisket, pulled chicken, and the addictive "burnt ends." In addition to these winners, you can have a mighty fine chili dog or a respectable burger. The sides to consider are collard greens, coleslaw, potato salad, bread-and-butter pickles, and corn on the cob. The health-obsessed can put a fork into the wedge salad or the smoked shrimp. Everyone must have corn bread and hush puppies and maybe a few pickled jalapeños. Townline stays faithful to itself with a fried fruit pie, whoopee pie, the icebox cake, and banana pudding. There's a selection of apropos beers including Shiner Bock, Southern Tier IPA, and Montauk Driftwood Ale on tap.

Trata, 1020 Montauk Hwy., Water Mill, NY 11976; (631) 726-6200; trata.com; Greek, Seafood; $$$–$$$$. The lone remaining Trata is situated in this summer place, where the specialty is whole grilled fish and Greek fare. The seafood is displayed on ice. But the rest of the establishment is more restrained in its design, full of comfortable pillows and light hues. Grilled calamari and Greek meatballs are fine appetizers. The tender octopus with roasted red peppers, onion, and capers improves on them. Crisp zucchini and eggplant chips should be shared by the table before making any major main course decisions. The whole, grilled red *fagri,* a pink snapper from the Mediterranean; *lavraki,* Mediterranean sea bass; tiger shrimp; langoustines; and

American red snapper are typically available, and though expensive, excellent. The braised lamb shank and grilled lamb chops highlight the turf side. Baklava sweetly ends the meal. The fixed-price menu is more limited, but the tab is more modest, too.

Tuscan House, 10 Windmill Lane, Southampton, NY 11968; (631) 287-8703; tuscanhouse.us; Italian; $$$. This corner has belonged to Italian restaurants for a long time. The elegant basilico preceded refined Tuscan House. Lots of polished wood and polished cooking here. You could begin, in season, with whipped salt cod on toasted bread, stuffed zucchini blossoms, butternut-squash tortelli in sage-butter sauce, or fresh figs with bresaola; year-round with crostini capped with either chicken liver or speck and robiola cheese; baked clams or mussels Posillipo; maybe a pizzette with arugula and fontina or Margherita-style. Angel-hair pasta with clams and shrimp; bucatini all'Amatriciana; pappardelle in a veal ragu; pappardelle with wild boar sauce; and orecchiette with broccoli rabe, hot sausage, garlic, and olive oil are among the good pastas. *Brodetto,* a seafood stew; osso buco; and chicken and sausage scarpariello are at the top of the main dishes. Tiramisu and fruit tarts highlight the desserts.

World Pie, 2402 Main St., Bridgehampton, NY 11932; (631) 537-7999; worldpiebh.com; Pizza, Italian; $$. The wood-fired pizzas at World Pie are thin-crust, 4 or 8 slices, and often good. You're better off with the basic tomato-basil-mozzarella number or the Parma, with prosciutto, pesto, mozzarella, and tomatoes. The Tuscan, with rosemary-roasted chicken, broccoli rabe, tomato, and ricotta, and Mr. Tang, defined by Asian-seasoned duck, scallion, cilantro, mozzarella, and goat cheese underscore why purists eat contentedly. Although pizza is the main thing here, you can have tasty brunch or a pie-free dinner, too. The dinner options include chicken Sorrentino, here minus eggplant and with mushroom sauce; tandoori chicken, with hummus, baba ghanoush, and curried couscous salad; or local flounder cooked in parchment with shrimp. Beet salad and tuna niçoise salad, and steamed mussels finished with coconut milk, ginger, and Thai chilies expand the map. Brunch: eggs Benedict and "wood-roasted everything salmon" with cream cheese–stuffed tomato.

Landmarks

The American Hotel, 49 Main St., Sag Harbor, NY 11963; (631) 725-3535; theamericanhotel.com; French, New American; $$$–$$$$. The wine list at the American Hotel has garnered more reverential notices than the food. It's as long as *The Brothers Karamazov* and almost as deep. The volume provides some entertaining reading, but you may prefer a synopsis. The historic building dates to 1846, during the whaling industry's prime time. The restaurant has had so-so, good, and better years; the attitude also varies. But currently all's well. Sample the savory duck-and-chicken-liver terrine, gutsy onion soup gratinée, lush brandade of salt cod, or the raw-bar offerings. Local flounder meunière, steamed or grilled lobster, rack of lamb, duckling with orange sauce, and the sirloin au poivre are headliners. The apple tart, lemony cheesecake, and bananas Foster are vintage.

Candy Kitchen, 2391 Montauk Hwy., Bridgehampton, NY 11932; (631) 537-9885; Luncheonette; $. The Bridgehampton Candy Kitchen started in 1925, and the institution remains a popular destination for all-day breakfast and house-made ice cream. It's also a local hangout, informal meeting place, and easygoing stopover for the eastbound visitor. Everything about the place revels in nostalgia. So, try the grilled

cheese sandwich, maybe an egg dish, coffee, and toast, and be sure to sample a scoop or two. You'll feel good. Baby Boomers may feel younger, too.

Lobster Grille Inn, 162 Inlet Rd. West, Southampton, NY 11968; (631) 283-1525; lobstergrilleinn.com; Seafood; $$–$$$. Lobster Grille Inn succeeded the old Lobster Inn two years ago. The Montauk Highway sign kept the type of lettering and crammed in the new name, perhaps so that you wouldn't think they'd turned into a foam-and-gel molecular hot spot. They definitely didn't and the ground hasn't shaken. Crab-crusted flounder with sweet corn sauce and horseradish-crusted salmon with lemon-chive beurre blanc are as nouveau as it gets. More to the point: well-steamed lobsters with lemon, drawn butter, potato, and vegetable of the day, from 1¼ to 3 pounds or so; a lobster roll or lobster salad; and the lobster bake, with one-half lobster, assorted shellfish, potatoes, and corn. Steamers, fried calamari, shrimp cocktail, and raw oysters are the logical starters. But someone may go for the tuna tacos just to stir things up.

Old Stove Pub, 3516 Montauk Hwy., Sagaponack, NY 11962; (631) 537-3300; Greek, Steak; $$$–$$$$. The sign with the red arrow was turned on again last season by Old Stove Pub's new owners, who also operate Nammos Estiatorio. The countrified, contrarian restaurant was opened in 1969 by the Johnides family, who charred many steaks and chops in the brick walled-in, high heat broiler. They also served some good Greek dishes. And the motto that stood was "when you're fed up with the chic, come to the Greek." Calvin Klein, Jimmy Fallon, Ralph Lauren, and others have cut into the crusty beef. The strip loin, porterhouse, and filet mignon, and the lamb chops, reign. The place has been refreshed but still keeps its quirks, plus shrimp in red sauce with feta cheese, pastitsio, taramosalata, saganaki, and *loukomades,* or Greek doughnuts. Historical note: The roadside sign that sported *Cue* magazine's praise is no more.

Silver's, 15 Main St., Southampton, NY 11968; (631) 283-6443; silversrestaurant.com; Continental; $$$. A fixture for three generations, Silver's is Southampton's lunch headquarters. The restaurant offers refined, well-prepared food in a setting that bespeaks the location. Owner and Chef Garrett Wellins prepares a delectable lobster roll, simple, flavorful, served on a baguette. And at $40, it's perhaps Long Island's priciest. The BLT is excellent, on Eli's Tuscan bread. Same for the "Roman sandwich," with prosciutto, fresh mozzarella, tomatoes, and fresh basil. The charcoal-grilled hamburger on a pepper-sesame brioche roll also is a local winner. Other recommendations include the roast duck leg confit with a salad of greens, white beans, pecans, and grapes; potato-leek soup, borscht, red clam chowder, and the salad of arugula, pears, pecans, and stilton cheese. The chocolate pot de crème and the lemon tart are very good.

Southampton Publick House, 40 Bowden Sq., Southampton, NY 11968; (631) 283-2800; publick.com; Brewery, Pub; $$. This microbrewery and restaurant established itself where Herb McCarthy's Bowden Square was a landmark for half a century. Gary Cooper, Truman Capote, Frank Sinatra, the Gabor sisters, and the Duke and Duchess of Windsor, abdication edition, were among the visitors to the Scotch and steak haunt. Southampton Publick House, open since 1996, suits the address for its consistently well-made beers and upscale pub fare. The meat or bean chili, Imperial Porter–braised short ribs, ale-braised pork shank, cheeseburger, pulled-pork sandwich, fish tacos, sesame-crusted tuna, and ale-battered onion rings, all are very good with the brews. Try the Double White Ale, Burton IPA, Keller Pils, or a sampler. The seasonal productions are especially worth the wait.

Specialty Stores, Markets & Shops

The Blue Duck Bakery Cafe, 30 Hampton Rd., Southampton, NY 11968; (631) 204-1701; blueduckbakerycafe.com; Bakery. The Blue Duck now quacks at 4 locations on the East End, each turning out well-made loaves of bread in numerous styles, assorted rolls, pastries, fruit tarts, cakes, pies, muffins, scones, Danish, turnovers, cupcakes, brownies. It's impossible to leave empty-handed. And you can get a good cup of coffee at the cafe. The Southampton Blue Duck is the original, opened in 1999. The other locations are at 309 E. Main St., Riverhead, (631) 591-2711; 56275 Rte. 25, Southold, (631) 629-4123; and 130 Front St., Greenport, (631) 333-2060.

Cavaniola's, 89 Division St., Sag Harbor, NY 11963; (631) 725-0095; cavaniola.com; Gourmet Foods, Take-out. The prepared foods at Cavaniola's set up your picnic. There are specials such as a Montauk flounder sandwich with roasted garlic aioli and a New Orleans–style Muffuletta, panini, and 4 soups each day. Appealing dishes include pulled-pork sliders, grilled tiger prawns with an herbaceous gremolata, chicken potpie, meat loaf, and crab cakes. Good upside-down cakes, among them apple-and-cranberry and blueberry-and-lemon. The cheese shop has an exceptional selection, and the wine cellar covers almost any dish. Cavaniola's on the North Fork is at 477 Main St., Greenport; (631) 477-6561.

Hampton Coffee Company Cafe, 869 Montauk Hwy., Water Mill, NY 11976; (631) 726-2633; hamptoncoffee.com; Coffee, Take-out. This was an early entry in the local coffee-roasting business, independent and blended up to here. The small-batch java has an ardent following from fans of the certified organic. In addition to the coffee, they do carry Republic of Tea products, Oregon Chai, scones and muffins, Tate's cookies, coffee makers, a grinder, and logo merchandise. There also are branches of Hampton Coffee Company at 749 County Road 39A, Southampton; (631) 353-3088, and 194 Mill Rd., Westhampton Beach; (631) 288-4480.

Java Nation, 112 Maple Lane, Bridgehampton, NY 11963; (631) 725-0500; javanation.org; **Coffee.** In a Diedrich 25-pound roaster, Java Nation declares independence. Beans rule. The coffees are light roast or dark, decafs and blends. The robust choices: Sumatra, Brasil Cerrado, Mexico Altura, and, yes, Java. Lighter roasts are Sulawesi, Ethiopian Yirgacheffe, Sumatra Madheling, Guatemala Antigua, and Colombia Supremo. Call them and you'll get your freshly roasted coffee in 2 days. Have a cup at the little cafe.

Loaves and Fishes, 50 Sagg Main St., Sagaponack, NY 11962; (631) 537-0555; landfcookshop.com; **Gourmet Market, Take-out.** Loaves and Fishes could just as easily be listed under Landmarks. The cooking school: widely respected. The cookbooks are appetizing. And the food at the popular shop has appeal. On a typical week in summer, you might find red gazpacho, borscht, pea-and-spinach, and chicken noodle soups; crab cakes, fried chicken, rotisserie duck, and marinated grilled leg of lamb; deviled eggs, smoked salmon and chive cream in endive, and figs and goat cheese with prosciutto. For dessert, they may have peaches-and-cream layer cake, lemon-blueberry tart, or Key lime pie.

Mecox Bay Dairy, 855 Mecox Rd., Bridgehampton, NY 11976; (631) 537-0335, (631) 219-5714; mecoxbaydairy.com; **Cheese.** Mecox Bay Dairy makes excellent farmstead cheeses. On what used to be a potato farm, a herd of Jersey cows produces at least 5 different ones. Mecox Sunrise is a semi-hard, washed-rind, full-flavored choice; Sigit, savory and aged a minimum of 18 months; Shawondasee, a nutty cheese aged up to 5 months; Atlantic Mist, creamy; an English-style farmhouse cheddar; and a blue cheddar are among them. The dairy and creamery's cheeses are sold at several farm stands, including its own, and at the Village Cheese Shop in Mattituck and Lucy's Whey in East Hampton.

Pepajalefa, 7 Main St., Sag Harbor, NY 11963; (631) 899-4630; pepajalefa.com; International Take-out. The gourmet-to-go Pepajalefa prepares sandwiches, soups, salads, meat and seafood dishes, sides, desserts, and beverages. Taste a croque monsieur, caponata-and-goat cheese, or Moroccan chicken sliders; artichoke soup or vichyssoise; cabbage salad or stuffed cabbage; Indian eggplant salad; brandade or beef Bourguignonne, Hungarian goulash, or pork roast with prunes; sauerbraten or shrimp Saigon; pasta primavera or polenta with mushrooms; magret de canard or sardinas en escabeche; flan, semolina pudding, or chocolate cake. The juices and smoothies are excellent.

Tate's Bake Shop, 40 N. Sea Rd., Southampton, NY 11968; (631) 283-9830; tatesbakeshop.com; Bakery. This is where the cookie always seems the freshest. Tate's has expanded and its cookies are sold at numerous markets and shops. But visit the original and be comforted. The coffee cake, apricot-ginger and raisin scones, macaroons, carrot cake, coconut cake, and chocolate fudge cake are little glories. Double chocolate chocolate chip and oatmeal-raisin cookies will become regular visitors in your kitchen. Brownies, blondies, raspberry squares, and crumb cake are sure to follow.

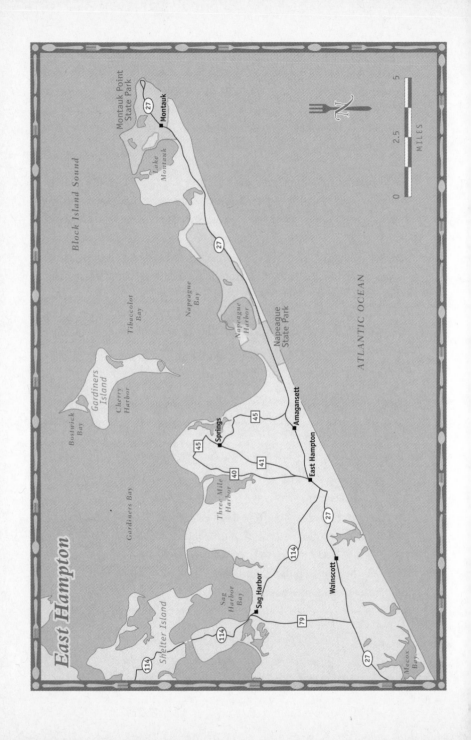

Town of East Hampton

Steven Spielberg is an occasional resident of East Hampton; Jackson Pollock, a permanent one.

This is the Hollywood Hampton, the art Hampton, the Broadway Hampton, the Wall Street Hampton, and above all, the boldface Hampton.

There's the Artists & Writers Celebrity Softball Game for charities, played annually at Herrick Park; the Hamptons International Film Festival; authors night at the public library; maybe Billy Joel driving on Newtown Lane, or Bill and Hillary Clinton dining out.

Pollock painted many of his best-known works here. He was killed in a car crash on Springs Fireplace Road and is buried in Green River Cemetery, with Lee Krasner. Their house and studio is open to the public.

Willem de Kooning, Mark Rothko, Larry Rivers, Robert Motherwell, and Andy Warhol also resided in town. The Rolling Stones immortalized Montauk's Memory Motel. Paul McCartney has dropped in and played at Stephen Talkhouse in Amagansett. Diddy has a party house in East Hampton. Martha Stewart, Calvin Klein, Carl Icahn, Jeff Zucker, Jerry Seinfeld—all neighbors. You could sell homes-of-the-stars maps.

The Town of East Hampton includes the village of East Hampton, Amagansett, Wainscott, part of Sag Harbor, Springs, and Montauk. It was established in 1648, by settlers who crossed Long Island Sound from Connecticut, the first English settlement in New York State.

At first, it was called Maidstone, for the town in England. There are families in East Hampton that go back a dozen generations, traceable to the originals.

Gardiner's Island has been owned by the namesake family for more than 300 years. It was purchased by colonist Lion Gardiner from Wyandanch, sachem of the Montaukett tribe of Native Americans.

Wainscott used to be mostly farmland. Sag Harbor once was a major whaling port. Springs, bordered by harbor and bay, was an artists' colony. Amagansett and East Hampton boast great beaches. Montauk is the end of Long Island—or The End, as bumper stickers proclaim. At the tip is the Montauk Lighthouse, the first in New York, a beacon since 1796. It was designated a National Historic Landmark in 2012.

While on the topic of the historic: Look for Dreesen's doughnuts. Dreesen's Excelsior Market is gone. The doughnuts used to be made by a robotic machine in the front window. Now, they're available in several states—and at Scoop Du Jour on Newtown Lane. And they're the real thing.

More than any other Hampton, this is Foodhampton.

Foodie Faves

Bostwick's Chowder House, 277 Pantigo Rd., East Hampton, NY 11937; (631) 324-1111; bostwickschowderhouse.com; Seafood; **$$.** Whether you're eating outdoors or inside, Bostwick's puts summer on the table. It's sunny, casual, and very good. And the take-out fare ensures a contented day at the beach. Steamers and baked clams are good, as are the clams and oysters on the half shell. Enjoy the New England– or Manhattan-style clam chowders, and the even-better corn chowder. Recommended main dishes include the steamed lobster, with drawn butter, coleslaw, and corn on the cob; the ample lobster roll; broiled sea scallops with lobster sauce; broiled flounder; fish-and-chips; fried oysters with sauce remoulade; the oyster po' boy; and the fish tacos, of which there are at least 5. The lobster taco tops them, with sautéed meat, roasted corn salsa, and chipotle-lime sauce. The rebellious can try the grilled chicken sandwich, with bacon, mozzarella, and basil-tinted mayonnaise. Soft-serve ice cream and a wedge of watermelon are suitable sweets, unless you want to go all out with the "brownie bomb."

Clam Bar, 2025 Montauk Hwy., Amagansett, NY 11930; (631) 267-6348; clambaronline.com; Seafood; $$. On the north side of the Napeague stretch between downtown Amagansett and Montauk, Clam Bar opens its umbrellas and sticks to its ways. The outdoor dining experience here is summer à la carte. If it's pouring, the crowd thins; if it's sunny, you'll have prime-time waiting. Then again, the addicted do cluster near the take-out and ATM counters in light rain, anyway. The cult of the lobster roll brings many here, for a meaty, market-price lobster salad, well seasoned and flavorful, even on the dull bun. You may feel expansive and go for the whole, steamed lobster, too. New England–style clam chowder and spicy crab-and-sweet-corn chowder are satisfying. Lots of frying, with scallops, shrimp, whole clams, clam strips. Grilled tuna, mahimahi, swordfish, and salmon are frequent specials. Sip Blue Point Summer Ale.

Dave's Grill, 468 W. Lake Dr., Montauk, NY 11954; (631) 668-9190; davesgrill.com; Seafood; $$$. Dave's Grill is on Montauk Harbor, docks and fishing boats nearby. It has been cooking since 1988. Eat indoors or out, but be sure to nail a same-day reservation, not always easy, even with repeat dial. The seafood openers include a minty, peeky-toe crab and mango salad; clams casino; mussels with tomato, basil, and garlic butter; and littlenecks on the half shell. Dave Marcley's spin on cioppino, the true San Francisco treat, boasts lobster, scallops, clams, mussels, and squid plus finfish, poached in a tomatoey reduction. He makes a flavorful, warm, buttery lobster roll, accompanied by fries and slaw; and a fine steamed 2-pounder. Lobster stars with pappardelle in a lobster-tomato sauce enriched even more with cream. Add some crunch to dinner with the onion-and-potato crusted flounder. The obligatory dessert is the "chocolate bag," precisely that with fruit, ice cream, and flair.

East By Northeast, 51 Edgemere St., Montauk, NY 11954; (631) 668-2872; eastbynortheast.com; Asian, Steak; $$$. East By Northeast is a big, water-view restaurant with eclectic fare. Not that often will you find Beijing duck tacos challenging lobster sliders, a spicy tuna tempura roll, or chicken wings sparked with Sriracha, blue cheese, and citrusy teriyaki. Tuna carpaccio, comparatively delicate in this company despite yuzu-wasabi, sweet soy, and ginger syrup, is a shining appetizer. You could take a more conservative turn with good shrimp and lobster cocktails and a main-course steamed lobster, with corn and garlic-mashed potatoes. The bone-in Painted Hills rib eye steak and Joka Valley Farm filet mignon are satisfying turfers, with peppercorn or béarnaise sauce. A chocolate pot de crème, the crème brûlée sampler, and cinnamon-sugar churros, in a Lincoln Logs design, with warm chocolate sauce are enjoyable end notes.

East Hampton Grill, 99 N. Main St., East Hampton, NY 11937; (631) 329-6666; easthamptongrill.com; New American; $$$. In 2011, East Hampton Grill moved into the former home of Della Femina, a Hampton mainstay. Dramatically overhauled and refreshed, this member of the Hillstone Restaurant Group immediately established itself as a local star. Hillstone runs restaurants in Palm Beach and Napa Valley. Come to this one for the accurately named "heavenly biscuits," with honey, butter, and rosemary; and other appetizers such as fried oysters with creamed spinach, artichokes, and lemon aioli; tuna tartare, with avocado and deviled egg; and scallop salad with roasted beets, greens, and tomatoes. Chef John McConnell's excellent main dishes include pan-fried Dover sole, with sautéed spinach, whipped potatoes, and sauce remoulade; a juicy prime rib roast; rotisserie chicken with pan juices and tabbouleh; the soft-shell crab version of a po' boy sandwich; and a memorable, freshly ground chuck-and-brisket cheeseburger. The Key lime pie is a Florida side trip.

East Hampton Point, 295 Three Mile Harbor Rd., East Hampton, NY 11937; (631) 329-2800; easthamptonpoint.com; New American; $$$–$$$$. East Hampton Point brings you food with a view and a viewpoint. The very summery restaurant is part of a waterside resort on Three Mile Harbor. Dine on the deck or inside. Chef James Carpenter, a disciple in the slow-food movement, revised and refined the menu in 2013. His hits include roasted wild striped bass with roasted peppers, tomatoes, capers, and herb sauce; day-boat halibut, backed by forest mushrooms, crisp leeks, and a truffled-potato puree; roasted Balsam Farms chicken; lamb meatballs with sheep's milk ricotta *gnudi,* similar to unenclosed ravioli; a juicy, grilled maple-soy marinated Berkshire pork chop given a springtime accent with ramp butter, seasonal greens, and a potato puree; and a seafood stew, dubbed "EHP bouillabaisse," with shellfish, calamari, and fluke in a stirring tomato-saffron broth, all finished with aioli. The notable starters include a savory Provençal-style fish soup with tomato-fennel broth, shrimp, and halibut; and mussels with smoky tomato broth. The mixed-berry shortcake and sticky toffee date cake go in different directions, each successfully.

Fishbar, 467 E. Lake Dr., Montauk, NY 11954; (631) 668-6600; freshlocalfish.com; Seafood; $$–$$$. Chef Jennifer Meadows's unpretentious, evocative spot looks onto Lake Montauk and goes beyond it. Her octopus escabeche with crisp plantains and grilled lemon; deviled crab with red pepper and scallions; and jalapeño-pepper-and-corn fritters with a chile-and-lime remoulade are savory beginnings. And the New England clam chowder carries a hint of Nantucket, which informs and inspires Fishbar. Follow any of them with the combo of scallops and razor clams, with crisp chorizo, olives, dried tomatoes, fava beans, beets, and more; the pan-seared tilefish in a lemon beurre blanc, with a garlic-and-potato "confit"; seared, Cajun-spiced yellowfin tuna with jicama slaw; marinated and grilled monkfish, spurred by house-dried tomatoes, braised radish, and lavender cream. Montauk fish tacos arrive with tomato salsa, avocado salsa, sour cream, and chipotle pepper slaw. The Fishbar lobster roll, with tail and claw meat, is best with coleslaw, a pickle, and fries. Key lime pie provides a sweet-tart finish. Fishbar also operates Bliss Kitchen, a coffee-and-sandwich shop that's pleasant for breakfast and take-out, at 732 Montauk Hwy. in downtown Montauk; (631) 668-8206.

Fresno, 8 Fresno Pl., East Hampton, NY 11937; (631) 324-8700; fresnorestaurant.com; New American; $$$. Fresno has been attracting Hamptonians since 2004 with the type of New American cooking that's aimed at a broad audience. The sky-lit dining area and landscaped patio have summery appeal, too; the zinc bar, more than seasonal. The menu changes often. But some dishes to seek include Chef Gretchen Menser's red and yellow watermelon salad with feta; octopus with chickpeas, piquillo peppers, ribbons of potato, and a zesty tomato broth; braised pork osso buco with mascarpone-laced polenta and a gremolata made with cherry and pistachio; the grilled hanger steak with pommes frites and an arugula salad; and the hamburger with more of those pommes frites. The warm toffee cake with bourbon-caramel sauce and vanilla gelato; and the Key lime parfait, with honey crème fraîche, lime curd, and whipped cream, make up for the restraint of the salads.

Harbor Bistro, 313 Three Mile Harbor Rd., East Hampton, NY 11937; (631) 324-7300; harborbistro.net; New American; $$–$$$. Harbor Bistro is one of the fairly priced restaurants in a very pricey town. The family-owned spot also offers diners a classic water view complete with sailboats and grand sunsets as a backdrop for Executive Chef Damien O'Donnell's dependably first-rate food. O'Donnell is as eclectic as he is careful, bringing in unexpected pairings with panache. His colorful repertoire includes a flavorful, kataifi-crisped lobster bundle and lobster bisque, rigatoni Bolognese and halibut with Indian spicing, tuna sashimi and sesame-seared yellowfin tuna, hibachi salmon and pistachio-crusted tilapia, a 5-spice Long Island duck breast and a Jamaican jerk pork tenderloin. The charbroiled rib eye steak fits in, too. And chimichurri-shrimp tacos add their own spark. Desserts: warm almond cake, a peach-and-blueberry cobbler, berries and sabayon, flourless chocolate cake, and a crème brûlée with Nutella.

The Harvest on Fort Pond, 11 S. Emery St., Montauk, NY 11954; (631) 668-5574; harvestfortpond.com; Mediterranean; $$$. The Harvest on Fort Pond has had a few lives, the latest veering Mediterranean. The comfortable restaurant does give you

a water view, seasonal fare, and some space to roam while waiting for your table. The calamari salad, shining from red-pepper vinaigrette; and the salad of endive, watercress, apple, pecans, and

Gorgonzola cheese, with some balance, are good ways to begin. Steamed mussels, with garlic and parsley, and charbroiled oysters also are flavorful starters. Your main courses may include moist pork tenderloin, with apple-apricot chutney, watercress-pine nut salad, and cured ham, or grilled chicken with garlic-mashed potatoes. Swordfish "piccata" is inviting, in the company of sautéed spinach, olives, capers, and cherry tomatoes. The official "Harvest burger," with bacon, Gorgonzola, and garlic fries isn't bad, either.

Inlet Seafood, 541 E. Lake Dr., Montauk, NY 11954; (631) 668-4272; inletseafood.com; Seafood; $$–$$$. Inlet Seafood was started by six commercial fishermen in 2006, and the restaurant still is devoted to the day's catch. After all, it's a spin-off of Montauk Inlet Seafood, a major packer and shipper. Visit for Montauk Pearl oysters on the half shell and Prince Edward Island mussels steamed with white wine and garlic; sushi such as sliced yellowtail and jalapeño, a spicy lobster roll wrapped with kombu seaweed paper, the FM Station Roll with salmon, tuna, yellowtail, avocado, and 2 types of roe; and nigirizushi, especially maguro tuna, fluke, salmon, and yellowtail. Cooked main courses: flounder oreganata, pan-seared sea scallops with sweet-potato puree and rainbow chard, pan-seared and teriyaki-glazed salmon with soba noodles, and an either steamed or broiled lobster. They have a lobster roll with slaw and hand-cut fries at lunch. The root-beer float, Key lime pie, warm brownie with vanilla ice cream, and strawberry shortcake are good ways to wrap up.

La Brisa, 752 Montauk Hwy., Montauk, NY 11954; (631) 668-8338; tacombi.com; Mexican; $. La Brisa comes to Isla Larga from Manhattan, with a branch opened last summer in The Plaza downtown. The breakfast-lunch-dinner taqueria has Mexican roots, but also a vaguely Miami vibe, a dash of hipster Brooklyn, and the direct connection with Tacombi from Elizabeth Street. They prepare good tacos 3 ways made with local fish, thin-sliced grilled steak tacos with caramelized onions and salsa verde, pork tacos with radish and onion, and roasted-vegetable tacos. Begin the day with breakfast tacos with chorizo and avocado or with pico de gallo. But La Brisa sounds more than one note, with chilaquiles, pancakes, a bean-and-avocado tostada, very good ceviche, and toasted corn with lime and chipotle mayonnaise. And the curved windows provide a fine view for Montauk boulevardiers.

La Fondita, 74 Montauk Hwy., Amagansett, NY 11930; (631) 267-8800; lafondita.net; Mexican; $–$$. Exceedingly informal, with some outdoor seating, La Fondita specializes in counter-ordered tacos, burritos, quesadillas, and tostadas. The nachos supreme will make you smile, too, as will the freshly made guacamole. Specifically, try the Baja-style fish taco, with chipotle mayonnaise and shredded cabbage; and the burrito packed with cod, the same mayo, rice, cabbage, and pico de gallo. Sandwiches on Portuguese rolls provide the competition, especially the chorizo number and the grilled chicken version. On the side: Mexican corn, off the cob, with queso fresco, red peppers, onions, cilantro, mayo, and chili powder. Flan and tres leches cake are the main sweets. Jarritos sodas and fresh fruit drinks highlighting watermelon, tamarind, and lime top the beverages unless you're up for a Corona. From the owners of celebrity haunt Nick & Toni's.

The Living Room, 207 Main St., East Hampton, NY 11937; (631) 324-5006; careofhotels.com; New American, Scandinavian; $$$. When c/o The Maidstone took over what for almost a century had been The Maidstone Arms, the Swedish owner remade the old place, making it greener and retooling the restaurant to include Scandinavian and Nordic fare amid the nouvelle dishes. In 2013, under Chef Mathias Brogie, you could nibble on horseradish-cured gravlax or sea-scallop carpaccio with apple-cucumber salad and a bleak-roe-and-jalapeño citronette. Enjoy *raraka,* a delectably crisp potato cake, and herring with pickled onion and Västerbotten cheese. Bleak roe with brioche sticks, sour cream, and red onion is very appetizing. So is *rabiff,* or steak tartare with beetroots, red onion, horseradish, and an egg yolk. Go local with grilled Montauk black sea bass. Grilled lobster: very good with a salad of raw fennel, celery, carrot, and radicchio; rivaled by marinated rack of lamb with spicy carrot and fiddleheads. And the Swedish meatballs with lingonberry jam, pickled cucumber, cream gravy, and potato puree could have been served in *Fanny and Alexander.* Apple-cranberry crisp and Swedish ginger cake are apropos.

Navy Beach, 16 Navy Rd., Montauk, NY 11954; (631) 668-6868; navybeach.com; New American; $$–$$$. On the strip between Fort Pond Bay and Fort Pond, Navy Beach puts its tables on the sand. The casual, nautically themed beach restaurant also has indoor dining and imbibing, but seating a backstroke from the water is irresistible on a sunny afternoon. The cooking is mostly coastal. Very good choices include clam-and-corn chowder with bacon and chives; grilled octopus with chorizo, fingerling potatoes, Serrano peppers, and smoked paprika; shrimp-and-corn fritters; a Dungeness crab cake with orange-and-fennel salad; ceviche of fluke, shrimp, and scallop; and miso-marinated cod. From the land, try the crunchy, tender buttermilk-fried chicken with a drizzle of spicy honey, plus slaw and cornbread; "Yunnan" ribs heated with chilies and sweetened with caramel; and a fine cheeseburger, with cheddar, housemade pickles, and bacon-onion marmalade. The Parmesan-dusted fries, charred shishito peppers, and "Mexi corn" with queso fresco are lively sides.

Nick & Toni's, 136 N. Main St., East Hampton, NY 11937; (631) 324-3550; nickandtonis.com; Italian; $$$–$$$$. This is the Hamptons' true boldface restaurant, a celebrity magnet for Hollywood and Washington names, with Broadway and Wall Street regulars, too. But Chef Joseph Realmuto merits the columns and the name-dropping for his excellent Italian cooking, served in a country-style dining area where each table is coveted. On a Saturday night in summer, it's the toughest reservation in town. If you snag one, nibble on the zucchini chips, prosciutto involtini with charred ricotta salata, seared tuna loin with caponata, or the watermelon salad. Then sample Realmuto's outstanding penne alla vecchia bettola, in a spicy oven-roasted tomato sauce; airy ricotta gnocchi with roasted red peppers, green onion, and fontina cheese; or spaghetti tossed with jumbo lump crabmeat, cherry tomatoes, arugula, and toasted bread crumbs. Main dishes: seared Berkshire pork with roasted peaches; pan-roasted scallops with a puree of truffled corn, mushrooms, and golden tomatoes; or the wood-oven roasted whole fish of the day. The blueberry-mascarpone tart, roasted local peach with rose-crème fraîche sorbet and vanilla meringue, and the mint-chocolate cake with garden-mint gelato, cocoa nib, and chocolate curls, are wonderful. See the recipe for **Penne alla Vecchia Bettola** on p. 336.

The Palm at the Huntting Inn, 94 Main St., East Hampton, NY 11937; (631) 324-0411; thepalm.com; Steak, Seafood; $$$–$$$$. The national enterprise, with high-power dining rooms in Manhattan, Washington, and other major cities, turns positively bucolic at this address. The vintage white building also holds some of summer's most-sought tables for beefeaters. But lead off with the big crabmeat cocktail, shrimp cocktail, or shrimp Bruno, sautéed with mustard sauce. Pick on a Caesar salad or, naturally, hearts of palm. Contemplate veal Milanese or veal parmigiana; or linguine with clam sauce, red or white. Then, get serious. The New York strip, bone-in rib eye, and filet mignon are thick and excellent. The epic Nova Scotia lobsters start at 3 or 4 pounds and are on a par with the beef. The sticklers have swordfish and crab cakes to debate. On the side, the fundamentals: hash browns, baked potato, potatoes au gratin, creamed spinach, fried onions. Who has room for dessert?

Rowdy Hall, 10 Main St. (Parrish Mews), East Hampton, NY 11937; (631) 324-8555; rowdyhall.com; Bistro/Pub; $$. Have a very good brew and a better meal at Rowdy Hall, which effortlessly combines the most appealing qualities of bistro and pub. The stylish, informal spot off Main Street comes from the owners of Nick & Toni's. Here, sample bracing onion soup and New England clam chowder, kale and beet salad, a Roquefort cheese and toasted walnut salad with Boston lettuce and endive, buttery escargots and lush duck rillettes, the serious Rowdy burger, fish-and-chips made with cod in a Guinness stout batter, and steak frites. The meat loaf elevates homey, and the lunchtime croque monsieur and croque madame are amply cheesed and terrific. Swordfish niçoise brings a spirited taste to midday, too, accented with white anchovies, niçoise olives, fingerling potatoes, and a hard-cooked egg. Vegetarian and beef chili: both recommended. The Halsey Farm apple cobbler, warm bread pudding with bourbon sauce, chocolate-brownie sundae, and chocolate layer cake are suitably rich. Good root-beer float, too.

The 1770 House, 143 Main St., East Hampton, NY 11937; (631) 324-1770; 1770house.com; New American; $$$$. The historic inn has hosted many restaurants, most very good. The current one is excellent, under Chef Michael Rozzi. Dine in the elegant, main room or spend a summer evening at the patio tables, which surround a fountain and are circled by tall hydrangeas. Service is exceptional. The menu changes frequently. Recommendations are many: Montauk striped bass with lobster sauce, local peas, and gaufrette potatoes; roasted day-boat halibut with smoked local scallions, fava beans, red mustard greens, and wild mushrooms; spicy calamari with linguine in a sauce with cherry tomatoes, tasso ham, and marjoram; crisp-skinned roasted chicken with green garlic jus, local rainbow chard, and parsnip puree; a Painted Hills strip steak with herb-and-olive oil, baby spinach, and buttermilk onion rings, among others. Desserts may include ricotta cheesecake with hazelnut crust and blueberry compote, tres leches cake with coconut sorbet, and a fresh strawberry bouche with vanilla whipped cream and orange vin cotto. You'll want to stay over—and can.

668 The Gig Shack, 782 Main St., Montauk, NY 11954; (631) 668-2727; 668thegigshack.com; Seafood; $$. Loose and playful, 668, etc., has surfer-dude style, spilling onto Main Street and the patio with a little good food, a lot of music, and enough humor for you to channel your inner beach bum. Montauk is a resort town, and the idiosyncratic, quasi-Caribbean, partly southern-California, semi-Margaritaville breakfast-lunch-and-dinner-plus-drinks kind of joint has its laid-back niche, at least until the jamming and overcrowding starts. Fish tacos are the populist choice. Blacken the catch of the day, frequently fluke, add sweet mango salsa, crisp slaw, and a house-made tortilla, and you have the "signature dish." Sometimes they offer a respectable lobster roll, a lobster slider, ginger-coconut-driven Thai mussels, seafood paella, smoky-sweet ribs, tuna taquito, pork tacos, and, always, guacamole and chips. Key lime pie is the obvious dessert.

Smokin' Wolf, 199 Pantigo Rd., East Hampton, NY 11937; (631) 604-6470; smokinwolfbbq.com; Barbecue; $$. Arthur Wolf, who mastered barbecue at the departed Turtle Crossing, relocated near the old site and serves the same stuff. The hardwood-smoked barbecue is very good. The very informal joint excels with eat-in and take-out, southwestern, and 'cue. Salads, sandwiches, wraps, and quesadillas are available. The essentials: smoked brisket and ribs; pulled pork, chicken, and duck; roasted chicken; and combination barbecued meat platters. Dissidents can be satisfied with the broiled or fried fish tacos and spice-rubbed grilled salmon. Tasty sides include the garlic-mashed potatoes, red potato salad, mashed sweet potatoes, macaroni and cheese, collard greens, and cole slaw. The Thai chicken wrap with peanut sauce and the fajita wrap with chicken, steak, or shrimp are among the alternatives. The chili is respectable, too. And you can pick a quinoa or arugula salad. But stay focused.

Sotto Sopra, 231 Main St., Amagansett, NY 11930; (631) 267-3695; letseat.at/sottosoprahamptons/menu; Italian; $$$–$$$$. Modern and very Hampton, Sotto Sopra touches on enough Italian and East End tastes to fit in with flair. The stylish spot took over the site of Exile. Sotto Sopra prepares light and good salads, with the requisite goat-cheese-and-beets and Caesar; tasty antipasti such as cured meats and cheeses; and smoky, thin-crust pizzas, including the spicy-sausage-topped diavola and the provolone-prosciutto-arugula disc. The housemade pastas are highlights, among them short-rib agnolotti, spinach-and-ricotta ravioli, and ricotta gnocchi with butter, sage, and tomato. Main dishes include saltimbocca, an espresso-rubbed rib eye steak, moist grilled swordfish, and a riff on cioppino, with grouper, salmon, calamari, and shellfish in lobster stock. There's a tasting menu, too, but the whole table has to order it.

South Edison, 17 S. Edison Dr., Montauk, NY 11954; (631) 668-4200; southedison.com; Seafood, American; $$$. Summertime is a main course at South Edison, from the raw bar to the drinks bar. You're a short walk from the beach. The modern, bright dining room is a good stop for fried belly clams, olive-oil-braised baby octopus tacos, a spicy BLT chalupa, or lobster brioche buns, elevated rolls with drawn butter. Follow them with the grilled local striped bass, black-and-blue local sea scallops, the buttermilk-braised crisp chicken with bacon cornbread, or grilled lobster with couscous, mustard greens, frisée, and oyster mushrooms. The smoked fingerling potatoes, fried olives with piquillo pepper goat cheese, and kale chips are the right accompaniments. For dessert: blueberry shortcake with buttermilk biscuit, pineapple-coconut upside-down cake with passionfruit sorbet, an espresso float with coconut sorbet, and the salted caramel ice cream bar with Valrhona devil's food cake.

Swallow East, 474 W. Lake Dr., Montauk, NY 11954; (631) 668-8344; swalloweastrestaurant.com; New American, Small Plates; $$. The buoyant, noisy, and very good relative of comparatively serene and cozy Swallow in Huntington, this sprawling restaurant and bar presents live music on weekends and full-flavored cooking every day. The docks are directly behind and you'll see fishermen at work. Your work should include the chilled lobster roll on a buttery bun; the cantilevered yellowfin tuna BLT with rare tuna and wasabi aioli; refreshing ceviche; a delicious salad of golden and red beets with ricotta and local honey; and tacos with striped bass, roasted corn, tomato, scallions, and lime crema. Shrimp and grits: equally good, with cuts of chorizo and grape tomato in the hominy; and the marinated and grilled Wagyu skirt steak. Beer-battered asparagus fries with a lemon-and-mustard aioli are tasty bar food, with a Montauk Brewing Co. Driftwood Ale. Finish with lemon-curd cheesecake or Nutella bread pudding.

Zakura, 40 Montauk Hwy., Amagansett, NY 11930; (631) 267-7600; zakurasushi.com; Japanese, Sushi; $$–$$$. Straightforward Japanese fare defines Zakura, an eatery that's modest by Hampton standards but generally good. Pick gyoza and shumai, beef negimaki and tatsuta age, miso soup and seaweed salad. Usuzukuri, tuna tataki, and spicy salmon tartare also are commendable. The standard teriyakis and tempuras are available. The better route is sushi, either nigirizushi or special rolls. The Old Montauk roll features shrimp tempura; the

Green River, soft-shell crab; and the namesake production, spicy lobster tempura, asparagus, lettuce, and a topper of spicy salmon. A la carte, pick fatty tuna, yellowtail, fluke, or mackerel. The sushi-and-sashimi platters for one or two could probably feed twice as many. For dessert, Zakura fried cheesecake, ice cream, and, going one for three, bananas.

Zum Schneider, 4 S. Elmwood Ave., Montauk, NY 11954; (631) 238-5963; zumschneider.com/MTK; German; $$. Beer, wursts, schweinebraten . . . Montauk? This unlikely and very festive communal establishment from Sylvester Schneider is the way-east relative of his East 7th Street stalwart in Manhattan. After the May Pole blast to start the season, this is like having a second Oktoberfest in July. The Bavarian beer house style is both entertaining and welcome. Hoist a beer from Hofbräuhaus Traunstein and bite into a soft pretzel with mustard, roasted pork shoulder in dark-beer-tinted gravy with potato dumplings, bratwurst with sauerkraut, crisp pork belly, wiener schnitzel, and the pan-roasted sirloin in red-wine sauce. Thinly sliced radish with swiss cheese and pickles, potato dumplings with sauerkraut, and herring in yogurt-cream sauce also are offered. On the side, try the Bavarian cabbage salad. Figure on the German pancake or apple fritters for dessert. And maybe postpone that surfing adventure at Ditch Plains for a day.

Landmarks

Duryea's Lobster Deck, 65 Tuthill Rd., Montauk, NY 11954; (631) 668-2410; duryeaslobsters.com; Seafood; $$. What started as a wholesale seafood business almost eight decades ago has boasted a minimalist outdoor dining spot for more than 20 years. The great view of Fort Pond and Gardiner's Bays could make you order anything. But stay with the lobster roll or the steamed lobster, both defining.

Maybe precede them with a crab cocktail, steamed littlenecks, or New England–style clam chowder. The most contrarian diner can pick a hamburger or a hot dog. Duryea's does a brisk take-out business, so you may head home with a perfectly steamed lobster as the ultimate souvenir of Montauk; or have one sent ahead via Express Mail. Duryea's seafood market keeps the choices manageable and good.

Gosman's, 500 W. Lake Dr., Montauk, NY 11954; (631) 668-5330; gosmans.com; Seafood; $$–$$$. Gosman's Dock, with its restaurants and shops, is associated with Montauk almost as much as lobster and lighthouse. It's a tourist site that started in 1943 as a source for fish markets; the first eatery was devoted to chowder and lobster. Now, the main restaurant is erratic, but they can steam or broil a lobster; and the lobster bake for two, with mussels and clams in the supporting cast, is popular. More casual is the Inlet Cafe, where lobster also is a big draw, as are the chowders and clams, baked or raw; and the Clam Bar itself is acceptable for a lobster roll, fish sandwiches, wraps, or hot dogs. Gosman's Topside bar offers a fine harbor view and dishes similar to those at the restaurant. And there's always the fish market, which sells retail as well as wholesale. You can take home a cooked lobster, local finfish, and shellfish.

The Lobster Roll, 1980 Montauk Hwy., Amagansett, NY 11930; (631) 267-3740; lobsterroll.com; Seafood; $$. What started as a clam shack began its journey to landmark status in 1965. The big, illuminated sign says, LUNCH. You won't miss it, on the south side of the Napeague stretch. Behind are sand dunes and the ocean. On the rustic tables: good lobster rolls, tempura-fried puffer fish, clams on the half shell, fish-and-chips made with cod, fried calamari, fried flounder sandwiches, pecan-crusted flounder, and for the dissenters, grilled cheese, a hot dog, or a hamburger. If the regular-size lobster roll seems too costly, consider the lobster salad slider instead. Shrimp salad and yellowfin tuna salad continue the theme. The warm lobster roll, with drawn butter, is a rich alternative to the basic salad. Lobster Roll Northside, opened in 1999, is situated on the North Fork, at 3225 Sound Ave., Riverhead; (631) 369-3039.

Montauk Yacht Club, 32 Star Island Rd., Montauk, NY 11954; (631) 668-3100; montaukyachtclub.com; New American; $$$. The restaurants at the Montauk Yacht Club have undergone many changes. Currently, Gulf Coast Kitchen is the main one. The bright, summery, and, yes, coastal-theme dining room benefited from a fairly recent overhaul. Among the better selections: a striped-bass trio, ceviche, crudo, and smoked; heirloom tomato salad; cream-fueled clam chowder; fluke in cartoccio with caramelized fennel, herb butter, tomatoes, chickpeas, spinach, and white wine; gnocchi Bolognese; the "lobster bake"; and prosciutto-wrapped chicken with garlic-mashed potatoes, kale, and spicy tomato sauce. The more casual Hurricane Alley is good for chowder, a lobster roll, fish tacos with cod, tuna niçoise, salads, sandwiches, smoked chicken, pulled pork, and smoky meat loaf sliders.

Specialty Stores, Markets & Shops

Amagansett Farmers Market, 367 Main St., Amagansett, NY 11930; (631) 267-3894; elizabar.com; Specialty Market. Eli Zabar, the baron of bread and the force behind E.A.T. gourmet deli and cafe, Eli's Vinegar Factory, and TASTE restaurant in Manhattan, runs the sprawling Amagansett market. He has significantly improved it. The 3,000-square-foot market, on the north side of Montauk Highway and east end of downtown Amagansett, started in 1954. Zabar operates it in partnership with the nonprofit, conservation-minded Peconic Land

KICKING UP COCKTAIL HOUR:
LONG ISLAND ICED TEA

Long Island iced tea has found immortality in episodes of *Gilmore Girls* and *The Simpsons*, in a song by Cadillac Moon, and in the slightly hazy memory of too many hangovers.

This cocktail was created by Robert Butt in 1972 at the always controversial and long-gone Oak Beach Inn. He was taking part in a bartenders' contest. The drink's impact was, and is, immediate. Few cocktails pack as much alcohol.

The recipe contains 1 ounce each of 5 white spirits: gin, vodka, white rum, white tequila, and triple sec, plus up to 1½ ounces of sour mix and a splash of Coca-Cola for that bit of color, all shaken and poured into a tall glass.

It unquestionably does not contain tea.

But you may garnish it with a slice or wedge of lemon.

Trust. It now includes a retail farm stand, which stresses what's local; bread baked on site; cheeses; a butcher shop; breakfast pastries and coffee; a soup-and-salad bar; plus prepared foods. You'll also find plants and flowers. Call ahead and they'll gather the items for your shopping list. There's a terrace for your impromptu picnic.

Amagansett Wines & Spirits, 203 Main St., Amagansett, NY 11930; (631) 267-3939; amagansettwine.com; Wine, Liquor. This has been the toast of the Hamptons for more than three decades, with a solid selection of wines and spirits. Moreover, special attention is given to the bottles of local wineries. Almost as important, it's a user-friendly shop, oriented toward value. Browse away. Amagansett Wines also has a

tasting room with some serious vino available. Staff members know what they're talking about and can guide you in the right direction as well as make recommendations about pairing wine with food, wine regions, and more.

Breadzilla, 84 Wainscott NW Rd., Wainscott, NY 11975; (631) 537-0955; breadzilla.com; Take-out. Stuck in traffic? Lunchtime? Turn onto Wainscott Northwest Road and make a Breadzilla stop. They make some of the best sandwiches around, and offer other fine baked goods. The listing changes each day. But a few of the regulars to remember are: grilled cheese with avocado and bacon; coconut-curry, pan-seared halibut filet with Asian slaw on a grilled squishy roll; the lobster roll; the Cuban sandwich, with roast pork, smoked ham, swiss cheese, pickles, and mustard on grilled sourdough; the fundamental meatball parmigiana; the crisp duck quesadilla; the spicy tuna salad with Monterey Jack cheese and pickled jalapeños on 8-grain bread; and the Hippy Dippy, a union of cheddar, avocado, tomato, carrots, and alfalfa sprouts on toasted honey-wheat bread. The gazpacho, avgolemono, and vegetarian green split pea soups also are tasty.

Citarella, 2 Pantigo Rd., East Hampton, NY 11937; (631) 537-5990; citarella.com; Gourmet Market. From the Upper West Side, the Upper East Side, and Greenwich Village, Citarella brings an exceptional selection of fresh and prepared foods to the Hamptons. No one will ever be short of balsamic vinegar and there will never be an extra virgin olive oil crisis. Citarella carries outstanding baked goods, cheeses, meats, fresh seafood, smoked fish, deli products, fresh ravioli and pastas, sauces, and for that special party-fundraiser-extravaganza beyond the gates and hedges, truffles, foie gras, and caviar. Rotisserie chicken and steamed lobsters, too. There also is a smaller branch of Citarella at 2209 Montauk Hwy., Bridgehampton.

coffee 'tauk, 83 S. Elmwood Ave., Montauk, NY 11954; (631) 668-7007; nycoffeetauk.com; Coffee, Gelati. Here's the way to wake up in Montauk. coffee 'tauk caffeinates with skill, whether you're a cappuccino, macchiato, latte, or espresso person. The Fishermen's Blend, with the jolt of an aggressive alarm clock, is the most sought after, available solely here, with customers clearly on a quest to find it. The hot cocoa also is good and you can sip a satisfying iced coffee or peach iced tea. There are some baked goods, in the muffins and crumb cake categories. Kale chips and gourmet oatmeal expand the edibles. The gelati from Il Laboratorio del Gelato are, of course, exceptional, thereby making this a hangout even if you're not addicted to java or Wi-Fi. The yogurt parfait seems popular with the fedora set. coffee 'tauk is also a pleasant gathering place, the earlier the better, if for some workaholic reason you need to conduct quick business before retiring to the beach. The shop's coffee-cup-stain symbol underscores the artsy style of the joint.

Joni's Kitchen, 34 S. Etna Ave., Montauk, NY 11954; (631) 668-3663; jonismontauk.com; Take-out. Joni's came with the millennium. Montauk regulars will add it was a long time coming. You're a short walk from the beach, so stop in for sandwiches, salads, breakfast items, fruit smoothies, juices, and whatever else you'll need to stock the cooler before spreading out on the sand. Favorites: Curry Up, or curried chicken salad with mango chutney, pineapple, and greens, in a tortilla; Love, Peace and Chicken, with brown rice, black beans, avocado, Monterey Jack, salsa, and sour cream, also in a tortilla; the Soprano, or mozzarella, tomato, basil, greens, and olive oil on olive bread; and the Zen Rabbit, with greens, tomato, avocado, olives, onion, shredded carrot, and goat cheese. Early in the day, try homemade granola with bananas and yogurt; or "jaffles," grilled sandwiches with breakfast ingredients of your choice. Fine juices and coffees.

Levain Bakery, 345 Montauk Hwy., Wainscott, NY 11975; (631) 537-8570; levainbakery.com; Bakery. Levain Bakery goes east from Manhattan's west side. This second Levain bakery arrived in 2000, in effect following the summertime migration. The cookies, cakes, tarts, and breads are excellent and you'll pay for the quality. Some favorites: the rustic, folded-over fruit tart; lush lemon loaf cake; sour-cream coffee cake; the plain brioche and the cinnamon brioche; oatmeal-and-raisin scones; Valrhona chocolate rolls; the crusty baguette; and the country boule. The cookies include a very rich dark-chocolate chocolate chip; and a more modest chocolate chip with walnuts. The baguette with butter and jam makes for a good, quick start for continental breakfast on the run. Know that they run out of the breads early.

Mary's Marvelous, 207 Main St., Amagansett, NY 11930; (631) 267-8796; marysmarvelous.com; Specialty Market. Visit for breakfast, lunch, or to gather the goods for take-out eating. Mary's Marvelous prepares superior salads, sandwiches, panini, and bigger dishes such as chicken potpie, lasagna, and turkey meat loaf. Breakfast includes arepas, egg dishes, steel-cut oatmeal, and bagels, with or without smoked salmon. Very good cookies: Mary O's, hazelnut pistachio biscotti, coconut macaroons, oatmeal-raisin, chocolate chip. Also, try the pecan squares, coconut cupcakes, chocolate-and-salty caramel tarts. There is a second branch of Mary's Marvelous at 105/107 Newtown Lane, East Hampton; (631) 324-1055.

Red Hook Lobster Pound, 34 S. Etna Ave., Montauk, NY 11954; (631) 668-5683; redhooklobsterpound.com; Take-out. Red Hook east is the offshoot of Red Hook on Van Brunt Street in Brooklyn.

But it's very much at ease at The End, and gives a symmetry to the island-wide love of lobster. The specialty is lobster rolls, in 4 varieties: Maine-style, with mayo; Tuscan-style, in a basil vinaigrette; and Connecticut-style, served warm and buttery, with lemon, each on a top-split grilled hot dog bun; and the Bikini Roll, gluten-free on Bibb lettuce. They're all excellent. The lobster BLT, with good bacon, is terrific. Also: shrimp rolls, finished with garlic-tarragon mayo; tuna melt with fresh, local tuna; a Berkshire pork-and-bacon hot dog; lobster macaroni and cheese; New England clam chowder; shellfish and haddock bisque. At the same site is Sweet'tauk, where you can buy lemonade sweetened with agave nectar to accompany your roll. The Meyer lemon, watermelon-cucumber, and peach–Thai basil drinks are refreshing accompaniments.

Red Horse Market, 74 Montauk Hwy., East Hampton, NY 11937; **(631) 324-9500; redhorsemarket.com; Gourmet Market, Bakery, Caterer.** The superior fresh mozzarella made by Pasquale Langella alone makes Red Horse Market a necessary stop. He's a cheese artist. You'll also enjoy the specialty pizzas, Sicilian or Neapolitan style, particularly with toppings such as the handmade mozzarella, fresh basil, escarole, roasted peppers, and arugula. The market has very good pastries and cookies, crullers and doughnuts, pies and cakes, cupcakes and muffins, breads and rolls, and holiday specials from stolen to babka to Yule logs. The butcher shop, seafood selection, and fresh produce are first-rate. And to energize you, the barista bar prepares serious espresso, cappuccino, latte, and iced coffee. Red Horse offers a breakfast buffet, lunch, and dinner. The barbecued brisket benefits from a snappy dry rub and is available in a sandwich or by the pound.

Springs General Store, 29 Old Stone Hwy., Springs, NY 11937;
(631) 329-5065; springsgeneralstore.com; Bakery, Cafe, Caterer. The
store started in 1844 and was Springs' first post office. The gas pumps in
front are nostalgic reminders of what things used to look like. Come for
the breakfast and lunch menus, which offer egg sandwiches, burritos,
pancakes, French toast, muffins, scones, and croissants. Satisfying
espresso, cappuccino, juices, smoothies; deli sandwiches and combos,
burgers and specials such as chili, gazpacho, melon-and-berry soup,
turkey meat loaf, and cobb salad. It's a pleasant gathering place, where
you may find live music, jamming, and socializing.

Stuart's Seafood Market, 41 Oak Lane, Amagansett, NY 11930;
(631) 267-6700; stuartsseafood.com; Seafood Market. Definitely a
catch-of-the-day stop, Stuart's is a wholesale distributor and a popular
spot for prepared foods. It began in 1955 as a packing station. You'll
find plenty of flounder and fluke, striped bass and swordfish, bluefish
and tuna, colossal shrimp and scallops, clams and oysters. And there
are many, many lobsters. They'll cook yours to order, for a rich to-go.
The prepared fare hauls in cedar-planked salmon, sesame-seared tuna,
smoked whitefish pâté, fish cakes, crab cakes, lobster cakes, and salads.
The catering ranges from clambakes to pig roasts. See the recipe for
Clam Pie on p. 335.

Wineries & Vineyards

In the fertile land that for centuries yielded potatoes, Long Island's grapevines took root. And in the last 40 years, more than 60 producers have raised a glass of their own.

Wine has been made for centuries in what's now New York State, by the first settlers from Europe in the 1600s and by the well-established farmers of the 19th century. Grape growing is farming, with a harvest to be poured.

The modern era of winemaking on Long Island began in 1973, when Louisa and Alex Hargrave bought a farm in Cutchogue. They established the Hargrave Vineyard, and with it the vine-to-wine industry in the well-drained, coarse soil of the North Fork.

Cutchogue is on Long Island's North Fork, which extends from Riverhead to Orient Point. The North Fork is the sunniest area of New York State, with the longest growing season. Long Island Sound, Peconic Bay, and the Atlantic Ocean are "moderating influences." The two forks have microclimates that the Hargraves and their successors found ideal for vinifera grapes, the species of Chardonnay and Cabernet Sauvignon.

The original vineyard continues to produce grapes and yield wines for Castello di Borghese, which bought the Hargrave Vineyard.

All the stories, however, haven't been that upbeat. Several wineries failed over the decades, too. The casualties included the Bridgehampton Winery, the Mattituck Hills Winery, and Le Rêve.

Today, 3,000-plus acres are devoted to grapes. The area produces more than 500,000 cases of wine each year. To put that last statistic in some context, the E. & J. Gallo Winery, the world's largest, annually produces 60 million cases under its many labels. It makes the entire Long Island wine trade seem like a boutique operation.

But the East End, taking in the North and South Forks, is the state's newest viticultural area.

The first significant and successful vintage year was 1988, followed by 1993, 1995, and 1997. Some of the reds from these years are drinking well now. There has been a run of fine vintages since 2000. Reds from 2005 stand out and 2010 was a great year all-around.

Harmony Vineyards is in Head of the Harbor and Loughlin Vineyards in Sayville, in central Suffolk. But almost all the East End's wineries are on the North Fork. Three are on the South Fork, in the Hamptons. Many are open to visitors. Some offer tours. Tastings abound, with prices depending on the choice of wines. Many Long Island wines are available at the Empire State Cellars Tasting Room at the Tanger Outlet Center in Riverhead.

These are among the best ones to visit, with some recommendations about what wines to taste or buy.

Grape Nuts: Visiting Wineries

Bedell Cellars, 36225 Main Rd., Cutchogue, NY 11935; (631) 734-7537; bedellcellars.com. Bedell Cellars grew in a potato field bought by Kip Bedell in 1979. The first vintage appeared in 1985. The winery currently is owned by film executive Michael Lynne of New Line Cinema. He was a producer of the *Lord of the Rings* trilogy. In addition to making excellent wine, Bedell also exhibits art at the winery. Bedell's labels have displayed works by Chuck Close, Ross Bleckner, Eric Fischl, Barbara Kruger, and April Gornik. A Chuck Close daguerreotype of grapes identifies Musée, an outstanding, plummy, cassis-driven red blend of Merlot clones, Cabernet Sauvignon, Petit Verdot, and Syrah that's Bedell's rich, complex top wine. At $90, it's close to the peak of Long Island prices, too. The winery makes some of Long Island's best Merlot, a remarkable Syrah, and a crisp, lush white blend called Gallery. Taste Red and Taste White also are recommended blends. In addition, look for the Bedell sparkling rose. For a less-expensive introduction to the winery, there are the house's First Crush red and white wines. Bedell also owns Corey Creek Vineyards on Main Road in Southold; (631) 765-4168; coreycreek.com.

Castello di Borghese, 17150 Rte. 48, Cutchogue, NY 11935; (631) 734-5111; castellodiborghese.com. Castello di Borghese is the winery that succeeded the original Hargrave Vineyard on Alvah's Lane. The Hargraves sold the winery in 1999 to Marco and Ann Marie Borghese. Borghese is a down-to-earth Italian prince. The Borgheses have expanded the Hargrave repertoire. The winery produces exceptional Burgundy-style, estate and reserve Pinot Noir; stirring Cabernet Franc; Cabernet Sauvignon; Merlot; a red-blend Meritage of Cabernet Sauvignon, Merlot, and Cabernet Franc; and elegant Chardonnay. Allegra is an inviting dessert wine made with frozen grapes. The more modest wines include Petit Chateau, a Merlot–Cabernet Franc blend; Chardonette, a steel-fermented Chardonnay; and Fleurette, a dry rose made from Merlot. Borghese also sells olives and olive oils from the family estate in Italy. This is an essential stop, both for the first-class wines and for a taste of local history.

Channing Daughters, 1927 Scuttlehole Rd., Bridgehampton, NY 11932; (631) 537-7224; channingdaughters.com. From Walter Channing's dramatic sculptures made from roots and tree trunks to a list of wines that not only includes red, white, and pink but orange, Channing Daughters is a vivid winery. You won't find this kind of experimentation and variety elsewhere. Yes, there's very good Chardonnay, but also Pinot Grigio, Muscat Ottonell, Tocai Friuliano, Blaufränkisch, Lagrein, and much more. The unusual, eclectic, and very appealing white blends are a defining part of Channing Daughters. Dry, multifaceted Mosaico uses 6 grapes; likewise, the golden-orange-tinted Meditazione, a complex and vibrant creation. Additionally, consider L'Enfant Sauvage Chardonnay, barrel-fermented and from 2 vineyards; and the satisfying Scuttlehole Chardonnay. The notables also take in Sylvanus, a citrusy white blend; Pazzo, a fortified and Madeirized wine; Envelope, which stuffs plenty of grapes inside; and the colorful Rosato di Lagrein.

Duck Walk Vineyards, 231 Montauk Hwy., Water Mill, NY 11976; (631) 726-7555. duckwalk.com. Duck Walk, which is owned by Pindar Vineyards of Peconic, also grows grapes in Southold, on the North Fork, but this is the tasting room to visit. It stands out on Montauk Highway like an updated chateau, the building that housed the short-lived Le Rêve winery. Duck Walk makes a full-bodied reserve Merlot, Cabernet Sauvignon, and Cabernet Sauvignon reserve, as well as respectable Sauvignon Blanc and Chardonnay. Its more playful productions include Gatsby Red, a semi-sweet number with a clever label; and Pinot Meunier, an unusual varietal made with one of the grapes used to produce Champagne. And Duck Walk does offer a Brut sparkling wine. Other curiosities: the Vidal Blanc dessert wine, blueberry Port made with Maine blueberries; and boysenberry wine, which includes strawberries. You're also a sip away from the relocated, new Parrish Art Museum. Duck Walk North is on Main Road in Southold.

Jamesport Vineyards, 1216 Main Rd., Jamesport, NY 11947; (631) 722-5256; jamesportwines.com. The history of the Jamesport Vineyards vines goes back to 1981. Now, three generations of the

Goerler family participate in running the place. The winery built a reputation on its standout Sauvignon Blanc. Jamesport has 3 levels of wines, the introductory East End series, the estate series, and the reserve series. Jubilant Reserve, a Cabernet Franc–based blend, heads the reds. Melange de Trois uncorks as a solid, Bordeaux-style red blend, made with Cabernet Sauvignon, Merlot, and Cabernet Franc. Syrah defines the plummy Sidor Reserve, from Mattituck grapes; and there's a dry, well-made sparkling Syrah, too. Jamesport also makes a fine Pinot Noir and a rarity, a Petit Verdot that's inviting with berries. In addition to the Sauvignon Blanc, and a peachy Chardonnay, an expressive white at the winery is the luscious, honeyed, creamy late-harvest Riesling. Non-alcoholic verjus, made with half-ripe Riesling grapes, could be subbed for vinegar. It's a good condiment.

Laurel Lake Vineyards, 3165 Main Rd., Laurel, NY 11948; (631) 298-1420; laurellakewines.com. The white, colonial-style building at Laurel Lake in the low-key hamlet of Laurel has a deck that overlooks the vineyards. It's a pleasing spot where you may linger over a glass, maybe thinking about the joys of a sunny, summer afternoon. The tasting room also boasts a handsome bar. Laurel Lake is situated near wetlands. The winery is owned by Chilean and American investors and the wines are a wide-ranging group. Golden Harvest refers to a honeyed near-dessert wine that has benefited from botrytis. Sparking Moscato is gently bubbly. And the barrel-aged Syrah delivers some power along with plenty of berries. Laurel Lake makes good, balanced, and full-bodied Cabernet Sauvignon, Merlot, and steel-fermented Pinot Noir, plus a slightly floral, notable Cabernet Franc. The creamy, toasty Chardonnay estate-bottled reserve is the headiest of the white varietals.

The Lenz Winery, 38355 Main Rd., Peconic, NY 11958; (631) 734-6010; lenzwines.com. The spare, rustic look of Lenz suggests a lot of restraint. But this winery produces very lively reds and whites, as well as 2 exceptional sparkling wines. Lenz kept the name of former owners, who were local restaurateurs and opened the spot in 1978. Ten years later, they sold it. And Lenz developed into a top-tier winery under their successor Peter Carroll and winemaker Eric Fry. He has made wonderful Chardonnays: barrel-fermented Gold Label and cold-fermented Silver Label. Lenz also has remained one of the leading producers of aromatic, dry Gewürztraminer with trademark notes of lychee and citrus. Lenz's Old Vines series is available to subscribers, but you may be able to pry away a bottle of the the potent Cabernet Sauvignon. Lenz's elegant Merlot has competed favorably against classic Bordeaux. And the sparkling wines are genuinely celebratory. The Pinot Noir–based Cuvée is sought in every vintage. The Cuvée RD, for "recently disgorged," is a terrific wine, rich and effervescent, complex and true.

Macari Vineyards, 150 Bergen Ave., Mattituck, NY 11952; and 24385 Main Rd., Cutchogue, NY 11935; (631) 298-0100; macariwines.com. Macari acquired the former Mattituck Hills Winery, and what used to be Gristina Vineyards and Galluccio Estate Vineyards in Cutchogue, turning the two properties into a dependable source of fine wine. It's a family operation, from Joseph Sr. and Katherine to Joseph Jr. and Alexandra Macari. They emphasize biodynamic farming. The mostly Merlot red blend named Alexandra displays power and finesse. And the singular, opulent, and plummy red blend, Bergen Road, shows Macari at its finest, with complexity and style. Block E designates excellent dessert wines, red and white. Macari also makes commendable Sauvignon Blanc and reserve Chardonnay. One of the initial treats from harvest is the crisp, Chardonnay-based Early Wine. Sette is Macari's all-purpose, workmanlike red blend; and the easygoing, casual Collina series is a bargain-priced group of reds and whites.

Martha Clara Vineyards, 6025 Sound Ave., Riverhead, NY 11901; (631) 298-0075; marthaclaravineyards.com. The Entenmann family, which brought you those often-addictive doughnuts and cakes, owns Martha Clara, named after the mother of Robert Entenmann. It's a visitor-friendly, informal operation, built on what had been the Entenmann thoroughbred horse farm, which still earlier had been a potato farm. The venue is good for tastings and whatever other events they've put on the calendar. In bottle, the big Martha Clara wine is 6025, a powerful red blend made with 6 grapes, primarily Merlot, Cabernet Franc, and Cabernet Sauvignon. At the other extreme is Ciel, a gilded dessert wine, balanced and refreshing, that's half Chardonnay and half Viognier. Martha Clara also comes through with a very good Brut sparkling wine that's about three-quarters Chardonnay, one-quarter Pinot Noir.

Paumanok Vineyards, 1074 Main Rd., Aquebogue, NY 11931; (631) 722-8800; paumanok.com. Paumanok Vineyards ranks among the top 5 Long Island wineries for its high quality and remarkable consistency. Charles and Ursula Massoud have been growing grapes at the former potato farm since 1983. His background in wine stemmed from making it in the expatriate community of Kuwait. Her family ran vineyards in Germany. Now, their son Kareem is the winemaker. The roster of marvelous wines includes Long Island's only Chenin Blanc, a charming white wine associated mainly with the Loire Valley and South Africa, and the grand Tuthills Lane Vineyard Cabernet Sauvignon, always among the leading red wines made on the North Fork. Paumanok excels with Assemblage, an intense but refined red blend, and a late-harvest Sauvignon Blanc that's like a quick trip to Sauternes. The house's dry Riesling and semi-dry Riesling sell out quickly, and the dry rosé is a warm-weather necessity. Also, sample the barrel-fermented Chardonnay and the well-priced, introductory Festival Chardonnay. The older vintages of Paumanok reds are coveted.

Pellegrini Vineyards, 23005 Main Rd., Cutchogue, NY 11935; (631) 734-4111; pellegrinivineyards.com. The Pellegrini Vineyards winery, with 3 buildings arranged to create a courtyard, is one of the more striking destinations along the wine trail. There's also a gazebo in the vineyards. It's a site for weddings and parties as well as winemaking and imbibing. Bob Pellegrini, a corporate designer, offered his first vintage in 1992; the vineyard dates to 1982. Pellegrini has 2 additional vineyards that resulted in more Cabernet Sauvignon. Pellegrini has produced first-rate Merlot, Cabernet Sauvignon, Cabernet Franc, Chardonnay, a refined red blend called Encore, a plummy reserve, and a delectable dessert ice wine, Finale, which is made with Gewürztraminer and Sauvignon Blanc. And Pellegrini makes a delightful, distinctive Petite Verdot. The winery also produces a lower-price, uncomplicated series dubbed East End Select. It includes a "BBQ red" and a rose wine.

Pindar Vineyards, 37645 Main Rd., Peconic, NY 11958; (631) 734-6200; pindar.net. Here's the largest winery on Long Island, an unpretentious, people-friendly place that makes wine at many price points and just as many styles. Pindar, named for the Greek poet, was established by Stony Brook physician Herodotus Damianos. Pindar has what's arguably the best wine tour, informative, thorough and enthusiastic. Pindar's peak is Mythology, an evocative, Bordeaux-style red blend of Cabernet Franc, Cabernet Sauvignon, Merlot, Petit Verdot, and Malbec. It will age well. Pindar also makes a jammy, satisfying Cabernet Franc, peppery Syrah, and another red blend called Pythagoras, a precise and accessible Merlot–Cabernet Sauvignon alliance. In some years, the winery also produces an enticing, concentrated dessert wine made with Riesling and a gutsy Cabernet

Port. Peacock Chardonnay and Sunflower Chardonnay, the former crisp and the latter oaky, are popular picks. Dr. Damianos's son, Jason, runs Jason's Vineyard in Jamesport. Pindar also operates the Duck Walk duet.

Pugliese Vineyards, 34515 Main Rd., Cutchogue, NY 11935; (631) 734-4057; pugliesevineyards.com. Pugliese Vineyards welcomes visitors with warm style and unpretentious and easily enjoyed wines. Over the years, Pugliese also has experimented. Briefly, the winery made Long Island's lone Zinfandel, and it has made a satisfying Sangiovese. The house's sparkling Merlot is another unusual selection. Ralph Pugliese likes to term it "red Champagne." Pat Pugliese has decorated and personalized bottles for years. Dolce Patricia is the name for a sweet sparkling wine. Pugliese also produces a dry Blanc de Blanc and fruitier Blanc de Noir sparkler. The late-harvest Riesling is a fruity dessert wine; the late-harvest Gewürztraminer, one with a touch of tropical fruit. The traditional varietals include Cabernet Sauvignon and Chardonnay, with good reserve wines, straightforward Pinot Grigio, and Riesling. The Sangiovese does have a long-distance taste of Chianti.

Raphael, 39390 Main Rd., Peconic, NY 11958; (631) 765-1100; raphaelwine.com. Raphael is a beautiful winery, built in a style that suggests both the Mediterranean and Napa Valley. It includes a small chapel. John Petrocelli, a builder, clearly has expertise in erecting churches. It's worth wandering around. The view of the vineyard from the back of the winery is enough to make you book an event here. The winery is oriented toward Merlot, and its First Label Merlot is exceptional. The Estate Merlot delivers fine fruit and flavor; and the Estate Cabernet Franc, blackberries and herbs. La Fontana is a versatile red blend, with Merlot, Cabernet Sauvignon, Malbec, and Petit Verdot; La Tavola, a more rustic, everyday red made with Merlot, Malbec, and

Petit Verdot. The rose of Merlot is a spring-and-summer wine, meant for picnics and poolside snacking. Sauvignon Blanc is Raphael's white, fruity and aromatic.

Shinn Estate Vineyards, 2000 Oregon Rd., Mattituck, NY 11952; (631) 804-0367; shinn estatevineyards.com. Barbara Shinn and David Page started in New York as restaurateurs, with Home and Drover's Tap Room in Manhattan. Here, they run a creative, outstanding winery and a bed-and-breakfast, too. Their wines show extraordinary variety: a fruity sparkling Brut; a lively blend of Sauvignon Blanc and Semillon, Haven; Wild Boar Doe, an aromatic red blend; and the standout Nine Barrels Reserve Merlot. If you're ready to spend, look for Grace, a lovely Cabernet Franc–Merlot number, and the even better Clarity, a complex and age-worthy blend of Cabernet Sauvignon and Merlot. The former is about $75; the latter, about $100. The dessert wine, Veil, subtly blends Sauvignon Blanc and Semillon. Coalescence is the citrusy union of Sauvignon Blanc, Chardonnay, and Riesling. Very good Sauvignon Blanc, Chardonnay and Pinot Blanc, too. And Shinn also makes small-batch grappa and brandy. You'll want to stay over.

Waters Crest Winery, 22355 County Rd./Rte. 48, Cutchogue, NY 11935; (631) 734-5065; waterscrestwinery.com. Jim and Linda Waters operate a user-friendly, very welcoming, and very serious winery with a smart staff. Waters Crest produces dependably fine varietals, red and white, plus ripe and rich blends. Go for a tour and then for a taste. Campania Bianco welcomes summer, with a well-balanced blend of Chardonnay, Sauvignon Blanc, and Riesling; Campania Rosso does the same bringing together Merlot, Cabernet Sauvignon, Cabernet Franc, and Petit Verdot for a Bordeaux blend with an Italian accent. The house's Cabernet Franc has excellent varietal character, as does the reserve Chardonnay. The nimble, instantly enjoyable dry Riesling

STILL THIRSTY?

In addition to the wines from these producers, you also should seek:

The Pinot Noir of McCall Wines in Cutchogue; the rosés of Croteaux Vineyards in Southold; the sparkling wines of Sparkling Pointe in Southold; Cabernet Franc and Merlot from Anthony Nappa Wines in Peconic; Cabernet Franc and red blends from Roanoke Vineyards of Riverhead; Chardonnay and Merlot from One Woman Wines in Southold; Pinot Blanc and sparkling wine from Lieb Cellars in Mattituck and Cutchogue; sparkling wine and Merlot from The Old Field Vineyards in Southold; Chardonnay from Sherwood House in Mattituck; Merlot from Gramercy Vineyards in Mattituck; Chardonnay and red blends from Diliberto Winery in Jamesport; Merlot and Mistura red blend from Scarola Vineyards in Southold; Cabernet Franc and red blends from Roanoke Vineyards in Riverhead; Shiraz and red blend from Suhru Wines in Mattituck; Archaeology red blend and Merlot from Clovis Point in Jamesport; and Chardonnay and Old World blend from Mattebella Vineyards in Southold.

amounts to a brief jaunt to Alsace, showing off the charms of northeast France by way of northeast Suffolk. Waters Crest has a small tasting room centered on a barrel-and-marble bar, a slab atop 3 barrels to be exact. It has a more one-on-one look than most of the others. And it ensures at least one flight of reds or whites.

Wölffer Estate, 139 Sagg Rd., Sagaponack, NY 11962; (631) 537-5106; wolffer.com. Wölffer Estate could be dropped into the Tuscan countryside and blend in. The winery's art is on display in the architecture and the land as well as in the bottle. Winemaker Roman Roth and vineyard manager Richard Pisacano put Wölffer in the top tier on either Fork. The winery was established in 1987 by the late Christian Wölffer, venture capitalist, businessman, and oenophile. The current selections are remarkable—as usual. They include superior Chardonnay, Cabernet Franc, and Merlot, especially the Christian's Cuvee Merlot. Roth makes a remarkable Amarone-style red, Claletto; an intense red blend, Fatalis Fatum; and what will be a long-lived cabernet sauvignon, Cassango. Additionally: the Fabiana Botrytis Late Harvest Rose, Noblesse Oblige Sparkling Rose, Trebbiano, Chardonnay, and Sauvignon Blanc. Roth's own label, the Grapes of Roth, is responsible for terrific Merlot and Riesling. Wölffer's verjus and vinegar are worth purchasing, too. Wölffer is a mandatory stop on your wine tour.

Breweries & A Distillery

Condzella's Farm in Wading River started in the 1920s growing vegetables, and it continues to yield asparagus, peas, beans, and more. But its latest crop is hops—the green flower that blooms in beer.

There's definitely a market.

The craft-beer business has grown steadily in New York State, which once had hundreds of thousands of acres growing hops upstate. Now, more than 140 craft breweries operate in New York, at least 10 percent on Long Island. Some have their own breweries, some contract out.

Following is a sampler of breweries, what to look for from the smaller ones, and a lagniappe of a different kind.

What's Brewing—Beer, Here!

Barrier Brewing Co., 3001 New St., Unit A2, Oceanside, NY 11572; (516) 594-1028; barrierbrewing.com. Barrier Brewing's tasting room could overflow with beers. Its notable brews start with Antagonist ESB and go to Zythossaurus Double IPA. In between you'll taste seasonal farmhouse ales, brown and black ales, amber and wheat ales, butternut-squash ale, Belgian-style Dubbel, smoked beer, Kolsch,

Gose, Baltic Porter, and a Czech-style Pilsner. The house's "robust Porter" is named Rembrandt; its Russian Imperial Stout, Morticia.

Black Forest Brew Haus, 2015 New Hwy., Farmingdale, NY 11735; (631) 391-9500; blackforestbrewhaus.com. This pubby restaurant-microbrewery satisfies with a soft pretzel, onion-and-ale soup au gratin, German potato soup, sauerbraten, tafelspitz, and a platter of wursts. The brewery makes a tasty Black Forest Pilsner and Hefe-Weizen wheat beer; toasty Black Forest Amber; a smooth Schwarzbier; and a big IPA.

Blue Point Brewing Co., 161 River Ave., Patchogue, NY 11772; (631) 475-6944; bluepointbrewing.com. Blue Point is the largest craft brewer on Long Island, known mainly for its fine Toasted Lager, which was introduced in 1998. Visit the brewery and try to go on a Saturday for the tour. You may end up buying a keg. Blue Point makes seasonal Oktoberfest and Pumpkin Ale, Winter Ale, Summer Ale, Spring Fling, and many more. Hoptical Illusion, an American-style India Pale Ale, stands out for maximum hop flavor; Pale Ale, for its versatility and easygoing appeal; No Apologies, for its Double IPA earthiness; for taste and exclusivity, the full-bodied, hearty Extra Special Bitter; and for a barley-wine style, strong ale on a January night, Old Howling Bastard. Anheuser-Busch InBev recently bought Blue Point.

BrickHouse Brewery, 67 W. Main St., Patchogue, NY 11772; (631) 447-2337; brickhousebrewery.com. BrickHouse offers a food-friendly selection of brews. They include year-rounders such as the IPA Hurricane Kitty, a nitrogen-charged Nitro Boom Stout, and easygoing BrickHouse Red. Also notable are Street Light, a blonde ale; Main Street Mocha Porter, which adds chocolate and coffee; and Mother Chugga, an English-style amber.

Great South Bay Brewery, 25 Drexel Ave., Bay Shore, NY 11706; (631) 392-8472; greatsouthbaybrewery.com. How do you not smile when the brew is Robert Moses Pale Ale? Or Field 5 Golden IPA? Great South Bay enjoys its very local approach and you'll like the results. Try a flight here. Maybe Kismet Saison, an effervescent, crisp choice on a warm, sunny afternoon; or a hopped-up Massive IPA and Hoppocratic Oath Imperial IPA; or autumnal Splashing Pumpkin Ale. Blood Orange Pale Ale, blended with blood oranges, is lively and calls for a second pint. Snaggletooth Stout, with its chocolatey approach, is a rich, malty selection.

Greenport Harbor Brewing Co., 234 Carpenter St., Greenport, NY 11944; (631) 477-6681; harborbrewing.com. Greenport Harbor is in a converted 19th-century firehouse, near the village's old jail. The brews are just as colorful and very good. Hopnami delivers 4 types of hops in a high-octane, tasty package; the Citrus IPA, part of the Project Hoppiness series, has balance and just enough citrus taste; Black Duck Porter is heady with chocolate and coffee; and Leaf Pile Ale brings in pumpkin for an autumn brew. They also make a French farmhouse–style Rye Saison; and Weesh'd Scotch Ale, a brown ale with a suggestion of caramel.

Long Ireland Beer Company, 817 Pulaski St., Riverhead, NY 11901; (631) 403-4303; longirelandbrewing.com. Long Ireland has a quartet of brews being poured in Nassau and Suffolk. The big one is the smooth Celtic Ale, the ingredients of which include oats and honey. Long Ireland's raspberry wheat beer carries a hint of summer; Pale Ale, a go-with-anything versatility; and the breakfast Stout, low alcohol plus Kenyan coffee and flaked oats. The goal: a cream-and-coffee character, achieved. The Wet Hop Pale Ale is made with hops from Condzella's Farm in Wading River and Wesnofske Farms in Peconic. Long Ireland is available on tap.

Coming Attractions

Whenever you find a brew from Holbrook-based Spider Bite Beer Co., sample it. Spider Bite currently contract brews at Butternuts Brewing in Garratsville, NY. Recommended: Boris the Spider Russian Imperial Stout, toasty, layered and sweet, with a chocolate note; First Bite Pale Ale, amber and light; and Eye Be Use Imperial IPA, gilded, citrusy, and very hoppy.

And look forward to the wider availability of beer from Fire Island Beer Co., which brews its amber Lighthouse Ale upstate; Blind Bat Brewery, a nano-brewery based in Centerport; Barrage Brewing, in Farmingdale; Moustache Brewing Co. and Crooked Ladder Brewing Company, both *in medias res* in Riverhead; and the Vienna Lager, Maibock, Pilsner, and Altbier from Rocky Point Artisan Brewers.

Montauk Brewing Co., 62 S. Erie Ave., Montauk, NY 11954; (631) 668-8471; montaukbrewingcompany.com. Montauk Brewing plans to have its own brewery going this year. There's a tasting room in Montauk, near the movie theater and Primavera pizzeria. The brews currently are being made upstate to Montauk's specifications. The flagship brew is called Driftwood Ale, an Extra Special Bitter that's balanced and very good. Montauk also produces Helmsman Hefeweizen, a modestly hopped wheat ale; malty Arrowhead Irish Red Ale; EastBound Brown Ale, which has a trace of chocolate; Montauk Summer Ale; and OffLand IPA.

Oyster Bay Brewing Co., 76 South St., Oyster Bay, NY 11771; (516) 802-5546; oysterbaybrewing.com. The Oyster Bay Brewing Co. tasting room arrived in 2013. And the comparatively new brewery's line of beers includes a summery wheat ale, a balanced amber ale, an invigorating Pale Ale, and a potent imperial IPA. The brewery expects to make a chocolate Stout and raspberry wheat. They add that their "most important ingredient" is Oyster Bay water.

Port Jeff Brewing Company, 22 Mill Creek Rd., Port Jefferson, NY 11777; (631) 475-2739; portjeffbrewing.com. Port Jeff makes small batches of its brews, ensuring freshness. Made year-round, Schooner Ale is the most popular. It's refreshing, makes no demands, and has a hint of citrus. Port Jeff Porter gets its slight sweetness from local organic honey. Boo Brew is the seasonal pumpkin ale, with more than a suggestion of pumpkin-pie spices. Runaway Smoked Ferry Imperial IPA includes smoked malt. The spring seasonal is Dead Ryes Ryes-N-Bock; the summer, White's Beach Wit. Starboard Oatmeal Stout comes through for the start of cooler weather. Tripel H is the most inviting, a gilded, local tribute to the Belgian tripel.

Southampton Ales & Lagers, 40 Bowden Sq., Southampton, NY 11968; (631) 283-2800; publick.com. Southampton produces a broad range of brews, all very good or better. They include a distinctive, excellent, Belgian-style Double White; a German-style Altbier, malty, hoppy and fruity; Burton India Pale Ale, a dry, English pale ale; unfiltered and lightly carbonated Keller Pils; the lower-calorie Montauk Light; seasonals such as Pumpkin Ale, Imperial Porter, and a zesty, smooth Biere de Mars; and stirring farmhouse ales, which take in the rich, layered Saison Deluxe; Abbot 12, a dark, potent number; and Cuvée des Fleurs, flavored with edible flowers such as chamomile and lavender.

Long Island does have a distillery:

Long Island Spirits, 2182 Sound Ave., Baiting Hollow, NY 11933; (631) 630-9322; lispirits.com. Long Island Spirits distillery makes LiV Vodka, which has a whiff of vanilla and is pretty smooth; Ristretto Espresso Vodka, with chocolate and coffee notes; Sorbetta, potent potato-based liqueurs with macerated fresh fruits in flavors lemon, lime, orange, raspberry, and strawberry; the amber Pine Barrens American Single Malt Whisky, distilled from Blue Point Brewing's Old Howling Bastard; Rough Rider Straight Bourbon Whisky, which has notes of spice and caramel; and Rough Rider Bull Moose Three Barrel Rye Whisky, a velvety, fruity success.

Farm Stands & Festivals

It may seem like an apple and an orange, or around here more like an apple and a strawberry, but the farm stand and the food festival do go together. Besides, everybody gets to eat local.

Long Island is dotted with farm stands, west to east, but especially on the North Fork and in the Hamptons. It's common to see cars full of fresh produce making the return trip west or north. And there are festivals to celebrate fruits, vegetables, seafood, heritage, and history across Long Island from spring to fall.

Farm Stands

Here's a selective list of farm stands where you'll find especially good quality and variety. It's followed by a listing of festivals with notable food.

Balsam Farms, Windmill and Town Lanes, Amagansett, NY 11930; (631) 735-8510; balsamfarms.com. The harvest takes in fruits and vegetables. Highlights include sweet corn, fingerling potatoes, heirloom tomatoes, all peppers, eggplant, sunflowers, pumpkins, artichokes, berries, cauliflower, fava beans, and kale.

Briermere Farms, 4414 Sound Ave., Riverhead, NY 11901; (631) 722-3931; briermere.com. Pies and breads, jams and jellies are standouts, but Briermere also offers very good produce, from apples to tomatoes, apple cider to peach juice. As if you need another reason to join the line.

Davis Peach Farm, 561 Hulse Landing Rd., Wading River, NY 11792; (631) 929-1115; davispeachfarm.com. Davis Peach Farm has more than 80 varieties of peaches, including 6 doughnut peaches alone; 30 varieties of nectarines; 50-plus of plums; and about 30 types of apple from its orchard. And keep in mind plumcots, a cross between plum and apricot; and pluots, 75/25 plum to apricot. Davis also has a farm stand at 284 Boyle Rd. in Port Jefferson Station, at Boyle and Old Town Roads; (631) 509-5033. Davis sells jams, jellies, salsas, cookies, and freshly baked pies.

Gabrielsen's Country Farm, 1299 Main Rd., Jamesport, NY 11947; (631) 722-3259/5847; gabrielsonscountryfarm.com. Nibble on the roasted corn, have some lemonade, head into the corn maze, take a hayride, and before you leave get some apples and pumpkins, or sweet corn and strawberries. The dairy cows are a popular attraction, too.

Garden of Eve Organic Farm, 4558 Sound Ave., Riverhead, NY 11901; (631) 680-1699; gardenofevefarm.com. In addition to hosting the Long Island Garlic Festival, Garden of Eve spreads out with strawberries, heirloom tomatoes, sweet corn, peppers, eggplant, onions, pumpkins, and, of course, garlic.

Golden Earthworm Organic Farm, 652 Peconic Bay Blvd., Jamesport, NY 11947; (631) 722-3302; goldenearthworm.com.

Golden Earthworm is certified organic and a source of fine strawberries, heirloom tomatoes, broccoli rabe, celery root, cauliflower, fennel, parsnips, onions, garlic, eggplant, beets, squash, melons, and potatoes.

The Green Thumb, 829 Montauk Hwy., Water Mill, NY 11976; (631) 726-1900; greenthumborganicfarm.com. The Green Thumb's land has been farmed since the middle of the 17th century. They grow a haul of vegetables, asparagus to zucchini, including many varieties of beans, beets, berries, eggplant, greens, kales, herbs, lettuces, melons, peppers, tomatoes, and winter squash and roots. The farm stand sells cheese from Catapano Dairy Farm and Mecox Bay Dairy and baked items from Tate's in Southampton and Junda's in Jamesport.

Hank's Pumpkintown, 240 Montauk Hwy., Water Mill, NY 11976; (631) 726-4667; hankspumpkintown.com. In addition to the maze games, the roasted corn, and the cider doughnuts, Hank's has wagon rides, a playground, an apple orchard, and enough pumpkin-picking to keep everyone busy.

Harbes Family Farm and Vineyard, 715 Sound Ave., Mattituck, NY 11952; (631) 298-0800; harbesfamilyfarm.com. Harbes Family Farm excels with sweet corn, heirloom tomatoes, watermelons, apples, and peaches. Pick your own berries and pumpkins, visit the Barnyard Adventure, walk into the Spooky Midnight Maze. There's apple picking at the Harbes Farm and Orchard, at 5698 Sound Ave. in Riverhead, where you'll find pumpkin picking, pony rides, and a corn maze; and pony rides, live music, and food at Harbes Family Farm, 1223 Main Rd., Jamesport.

Kerber's Farm, 309 W. Pulaski Rd., Huntington, NY 11743; (631) 423-4400; kerbersfarm.com. The reborn Kerber's is very different from the much-missed original, which was primarily a poultry farm with great turkey and chicken, cooked and not. There was a no-frills farm stand alongside, too. Now, the successor is a bright, airy spot with fruits and vegetables sourced from Long Island, upstate New York, and New Jersey farms. The baked goods have gone upscale, too, with cheddar biscuits, scones, and fruit pies among the highlights. It's all fine quality, tailored to a new audience, and dressed like Amagansett.

KK's The Farm, 59945 Main Rd., Southold, NY 11971; (631) 765-2075; kkthefarm.com. KK's is revered by restaurants and shops and anyone who walks in. The family-run, organic,

biodynamic farm has spectacular produce and plants. KK's pickles, jams, tomato sauce, herbs, fruits, and vegetables are extraordinary. Be sure to invest in KK's heirloom tomato plants, basil, parsley, and cilantro; strawberries, raspberries, blueberries, currants, pears, and figs. The hard-stemmed garlic is great. And the arugula, kale, leeks, beets, peppers, and peas have remarkable flavor. If you only have one stop, this is it.

Latham's Farm Stand, 20055 Main Rd., Orient, NY 11957; (631) 323-3569; lathamfarmstand.com. Latham's is about as far east as you go for tomatoes, arugula, kale, peppers, carrots, beets, and canned or jarred items. Latham has been farming the east end of the North Fork since about 1642. They know the land.

Lewin Farms, 812 Sound Ave., Wading River, NY 11792; (631) 929-4327; lewinfarm.com. Pick your own strawberries, raspberries, blueberries, blackberries, peaches, apples, tomatoes, peppers, eggplant, pumpkins, and gourds and . . . Christmas trees. Lewin also has a corn maze. Try roasted corn here.

Makinajian Poultry Farm, 276 Cuba Hill Rd., Huntington, NY 11743; (631) 368-9320. Fresh turkey, chicken, duck, and eggs are the draw to this farm, which has been preparing for Thanksgiving since

1948. They sell pies, local honey, milk, butter, herbs, cider, and organic vegetables.

Meyer's Farm Stand, 750 Woodbury Rd., Woodbury, NY 11797; (516) 364-1777. Among the westerly locations, Meyer's is on a much-trafficked north-south road. But the selection will make you feel positively bucolic. In season, the tomatoes are sufficient reason to pull over.

The Milk Pail, 1346 Montauk Hwy., Water Mill, NY 11976; (631) 537-2565; milk-pail.com. Great peaches and apples will make you turn quickly to this stand on the north side of the highway. The farm grows 26 varieties of apples. And the apple cider is very good. But those peaches are sensational. Major pumpkins and gourds arrive in September. Off Montauk Highway at Mecox Bay is the orchard for apple picking. The Halsey family has been farming in what's now Water Mill and Bridgehampton for more than 350 years. The country store has been an attraction for more than 30 years.

Richter's Orchard, 1300 Pulaski Rd., Northport, NY 11768; (631) 261-1980. The focus is on apples, pears, and peaches. You'll also like the apple cider at this orchard, which has been flourishing for more than a century.

Rottkamp's Fox Hollow Farm, 2287 Sound Ave., Calverton, NY 11933; (631) 727-1786. This farm is 200 acres. It's particularly good for sweet bicolor corn, tomatoes, cucumbers, string beans, lettuces, beets, potatoes, and asparagus.

Sang Lee Farms, 25180 Sound Ave. (Rte. 48), Peconic, NY 11958; (631) 734-7001; sangleefarms.com. Certified organic Sang Lee overflows with heirloom tomatoes including brandywine, yellow taxi, striped German, white beauty, and green zebra. Plum tomatoes, garlic, eggplants, beans, fennel, squash, and prepared foods such as pickles and soups also are excellent.

Satur Farms, 3705 Alvahs Lane, Cutchogue, NY 11935; (631) 734-4219; saturfarms.com. Owned by Chef Eberhard Müller, formerly of the departed Lutece and Bayard's in Manhattan, and wife Paulette Satur, Satur Farms is a source for chefs, restaurants, and anyone interested in heirloom tomatoes, specialty greens, microgreens, edible flowers, root vegetables, and herbs.

Schmitt's Family Farm, 26 Pinelawn Rd., Melville, NY 11747; (631) 271-3276; schmittfarms.com. Off busy Route 110 is this farm, known for its 7-acre corn maze, pumpkin picking, Halloween haunted house, pony rides, and very good produce. Schmitt's sells vegetable plants, annuals, and perennials, and offers school field trips.

Sep's Farm, 7395 Main Rd., East Marion, NY 11939; (631) 477-1583. Tomatoes and sweet corn are the primary reasons to visit Sep's. The farm stand, a vegetable specialist, also sells fine peppers, eggplant, potatoes, beans, homemade pies, and jams. The farms are in East Marion and Orient.

Wells Homestead, 460 Main Rd., Aquebogue, NY 11931; (631) 722-3796; wellshomesteadmarket.com. Family-owned and operated since 1661, Wells Homestead continues to bud. Although many visitors come here for the annuals, perennials, and vegetable plants, there's also a first-rate selection of fruits and vegetables, homemade pies, and jams.

Wickham's Fruit Farm, 28700 Main Rd., Cutchogue, NY 11935; (631) 734-6441; wickhamsfruitfarm.com. Peaches and apples, strawberries and raspberries, blueberries and cherries, pies and jams are just some of the reasons to visit Wickham's, one of the area's historic farms. Part of the farm dates to 1661. Enjoy a wagon ride into history, to and from the orchards, and a pick-your-own experience.

Windy Acres, 3810 Middle Country Rd., Calverton, NY 11933; (631) 727-4554. Windy Acres excels with the vegetables that will land on your Thanksgiving table, and with Christmas trees, too. Before those, there's the big corn maze and tasty roasted corn. Pick up 30 varieties of apples, potatoes, sweet potatoes, squash, cauliflower, brussels sprouts, homemade pickles, apple cider, candy and caramel apples, and some doughnuts for the road. Also look for berries, peaches, and nectarines. The u-pick pumpkin field is 6 acres.

Woodside Orchards, 729 Main Rd., Aquebogue, NY 11931; (631) 722-5770; woodsideorchards.com. Woodside Orchards offers 27 varieties of apples. And it's a stop for apple cider, cider doughnuts, pies, and honey. Naturally, the pies include apple, apple crumb, honey apple with honey and cinnamon, and no-sugar apple, plus blueberry pie, blueberry crumb, and blueberry-apple. Peach, too. Woodside also sells apple bread, apple butter, jams, candy apples, caramel apples, and cookies, including chocolate chip and apple hermits, which have cranraisins and walnuts. The farm stand is at 116 Manor Lane, Jamesport.

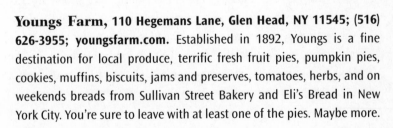

Youngs Farm, 110 Hegemans Lane, Glen Head, NY 11545; (516) 626-3955; youngsfarm.com. Established in 1892, Youngs is a fine destination for local produce, terrific fresh fruit pies, pumpkin pies, cookies, muffins, biscuits, jams and preserves, tomatoes, herbs, and on weekends breads from Sullivan Street Bakery and Eli's Bread in New York City. You're sure to leave with at least one of the pies. Maybe more.

Bayville Waterside Festival, Ransom Beach, Bayville, NY 11709; (516) 317-7729; bayvillechamberofcommerce.com. Seafood is the staple at this annual festival, held in mid-September. There's a food and beverage court, live band music, games, activities, a raffle, arts and crafts, and, if you're inclined, yoga classes on the beach.

Greenport Maritime Festival, Main and Front Streets, Greenport, NY 11944; (631) 477-2100; eastendseaport.org. Oyster shucking, tall ships, arts and crafts, and considerable eating of oysters and clams on the half shell mark the Maritime Festival. A Taste of Greenport at the East End Seaport Museum features food and beverages from local Greenport chefs, restaurateurs, and merchants. Local wines and craft beers are poured at the late-September showcase.

Hard Cider Festival, Peconic Bay Winery, 31320 Main Rd., Cutchogue, NY 11935; (631) 940-7290. Produced by Starfish Junction, this "pour the core" gathering of cider enthusiasts features at least 30 domestic and international hard ciders as well as local brews at a winery. You must be at least 21 years old to enter, proper identification required. The early October festival is held outdoors under tents, rain or shine. Live music performed.

Long Island Apple Festival, Sherwood Jayne Farm, 55 Old Post Rd., East Setauket, NY 11733; (631) 692-4664; splia.com. Sponsored by the Society for the Preservation of Long Island Antiquities, the festival at the farm includes hayrides, apple-relay races, an apple pie baking contest, freshly pressed apple cider, candy apples, apple fritters, apple crafts, and a free apple and tour of the house. Befitting the sponsor, the orchard has trees that are more than 100 years old.

The Long Island Fair, Old Bethpage Village Restoration, 1303 Round Swamp Rd., Old Bethpage, NY 11804; (516) 572-8400; lifair .org. This fair dates to 1842. The annual event, held in late September, includes prizes and blue ribbons for jams, butter, pickles, fudge, and cakes. There's also a home-brew competition. A brass band provides some of the entertainment.

Long Island Garlic Festival, Garden of Eve Organic Farm & Market, 4558 Sound Ave., Riverhead, NY 11901; (631) 722-8777; gardenofevefarm.com. If it doesn't quite transform Riverhead into Gilroy, California, the festival certainly makes the town more aromatic. Buy heirloom garlic varieties and taste garlic bread, fries, and garlic ice cream. Last year's festival included a garlic eating contest. The festival is held in late September.

Mattituck Lions Club Strawberry Festival, County Road 48, Mattituck, NY 11952; (631) 298-2222; mattituckstrawberryfestival .org. This is the big berry, held in June, rain or shine. Strawberry shortcake, strawberry pie, chocolate-dipped strawberries, pristine and ripe ones, they're all here during peak harvest time. Maybe a strawberry daiquiri will go with the roasted corn, funnel cakes, sausages, hamburgers, pizza, ice cream, and other food at the festival.

Mother Cabrini Feast, Grant Campus, Suffolk Community College, Brentwood, NY 11717; (631) 581-8525; mothercabrinifeast .org. The Giuseppe A. Nigro Lodge–Order Sons of Italy in America presents this festival, which include a quarter-mile-long food court, fireworks, live entertainment, and a zeppole-eating contest. After the sausage and peppers, calzones and zeppole, you might have an appetite for the Spanish and Greek fare, too. The festival benefits local nonprofit organizations.

Nassau County Strawberry Festival, Bellmore BOCES School Ground, Jerusalem Avenue at Newbridge Road, Bellmore, NY 11710; nassaucountystrawberryfestival.com. The annual event in late May–early June is sponsored by the Bellmore Lions Club and Bellmore Kiwanis as a fundraiser for the underprivileged. Strawberry cheesecake, strawberry shortcake, strawberry everything, carnival rides, games, and a pie-eating contest.

North Fork Craft Beer, BBQ & Wine Festival, Martha Clara Vineyards, 6025 Sound Ave., Riverhead, NY 11901; (631) 940-7290; northforkcraftbeerfestival.com. Starfish Junction also produces this event, which is a 2-session affair featuring 50 brewers and 100 brews. The August festival includes barbecue from Maple Tree BBQ in Riverhead. No one under 21 years old admitted. Martha Clara hosts Oktoberfest events in September, including German food, music, and beer.

Ompahfest, Plattduetsche Park Restaurant, 1132 Hempstead Tpke., Franklin Square, NY 11010; (516) 354-3131; parkrestaurant .com. The annual celebration of German-American heritage is a lederhosen-and-suds event held in mid-September in the Plattduetsche Park biergarten. German specialties, from bratwurst and knockwurst to pretzels and potato pancakes, are among the highlights, washed down with German brews on tap. Live band music, plenty of dancing.

Oyster Bay Oyster Festival, Theodore Roosevelt Park, Oyster Bay, NY 11771; (516) 628-1625; theoysterfestival.org. Billed as Long Island's biggest festival, this tribute to the bivalve attracts more than 30 vendors. In addition to oysters on the half shell, fried, in stews, and in po' boys, among other ways, you'll be able to sample raw or steamed clams, lobster rolls, seafood gumbo, sausage and peppers, bratwurst, steak sandwiches,

Belgian waffles, roasted corn, funnel cakes, and more. The oyster festival, held in October, attracts 200,000-plus visitors. In addition to the food and the oyster eating and shucking contests, the lures include live entertainment, midway rides, and tall ships. The festival is run by the nonprofit Oyster Bay Charitable Fund to benefit 27 local nonprofit organizations in the Oyster Bay–East Norwich school district.

Pickle Festival, 900 Park Ave., Greenlawn, NY 11740; (631) 754-1180; gcha.info. The Greenlawn-Centerport Historical Association notes that the area once was full of cucumber and cabbage farms and home of a major pickle works. The pickles were destined for New York City. The processing of pickles ended in the 1920s; cabbage, the 1930s. Allen's Pickle Works in Glen Cove has been supplying the pickles for the festival, where you'll also get hot dogs, roasted corn, smoked meats, cheeses, baked goods, and homemade jams and jellies. The festival is held in September.

Polish Town USA Street Fair and Polka Festival, Pulaski Street and Osborne Avenue, Riverhead, NY 11901; (631) 369-1616; polishtowncivicassociation. Held in mid-August, this ethnic festival is a feast for fans of pierogies, kielbasa, stuffed cabbage, and similarly husky, soulful food. Balance these dishes with babkas and fried-dough pastries under a snowfall of powdered sugar. Expect lots of music from polka bands and perhaps the reenactment of a traditional Polish wedding.

Riverhead Country Fair, Main Street, Riverhead, NY 11901; (631) 727-1215; riverheadcountryfair.com. The festivities are along the Peconic River, with lots of vendors, carnival rides, and live entertainment. And there are prizes for the biggest zucchini and the biggest head of cauliflower. The fair includes a vegetable-decorating competition and another for carving pumpkins.

St. Rocco's Feast, Church of Saint Rocco, 18 Third St., Glen Cove, NY 11542; (516) 676-2482; stroccoglencove.com. This celebration has a deserved reputation for delicious food, from sausage and peppers to meatballs and tripe, zeppole and pastries to homemade ice cream and espresso. There's an indoor restaurant as well as an outdoor pastry pavilion. Please see chapter covering Glen Cove.

Recipes

After enjoying a great dish, there's always the temptation to try and recreate it at home. What follows are recipes for 12 of them.

Long Island Clam Chowder

Many chowders are served on Long Island. Noah Schwartz's clam chowder, served at his restaurant, Noah's, in Greenport, is one of the best.

Serves: 4

For the Soffrito:

2 carrots, peeled
1 fennel bulb
2 shallots
5 garlic cloves, peeled

1 cup fingerling potatoes, boiled until tender, halved, and sliced
Olive oil

For the Chowder:

¼ cup flour
¼ cup butter
1 quart clam juice
1 cup heavy cream
8 littleneck clams, washed and steamed open

¼ cup soffrito (see recipe)
½ cup chopped canned clams
¼ cup chopped fine herbs (parsley, tarragon, chervil, chives)
Black pepper to taste

To make the soffrito: Finely chop all vegetables and cook in olive oil over low heat for 10 minutes, or until tender.

To make the chowder: Cook flour and butter together over low heat, stirring often for 10 minutes, forming a golden-colored roux.

Add clam juice and cream and bring to simmer for 20 minutes.

Add remainder of ingredients and return to simmer.

Divide chowder with 2 steamed clams in each of 4 large soup bowls.

Season with black pepper to taste.

Noah's, Greenport (p. 237)

Lobster-and-Shrimp Shepherd's Pie

This dish has been on the menu at the Plaza Cafe in Southampton since the restaurant opened in 1997. Chef Douglas Gulija said it was created by his late wife, Andrea. Gulija had overordered lobster and shrimp. After sautéing the shellfish, Gulija added garlic mashed potatoes and lobster sauce. Andrea, who was raised in Amish country, said it should be called "shepherd's pie."

Serves: 6

- 1–2 shallots, minced
- 4 ounces olive oil, divided
- 1–2 carrots, diced small
- 1–2 celery stalks, diced small
- Fennel tops from 1 head, diced small
- 1–2 garlic cloves, minced
- 2–3 ounces oyster mushrooms, diced
- 6 ears corn, shucked and split

- 16 ounces Lobster Sauce (recipe follows)
- 18 fresh gulf shrimp 16/20, peeled and deveined
- 4 ounces Wölffer Estate verjus
- 8–9 ounces lobster meat, blanched and diced
- Chive-Potato Puree (recipe follows)

For the Garnish:

- 12 potato gaufrettes
- 6 grilled shrimp

- 1 bunch chives, minced

Lightly sauté shallots in 2 ounces olive oil. Add carrots, celery, and fennel, and cook until al dente. Add garlic, mushrooms, and corn.

Add lobster sauce; simmer for approximately 5 minutes and let flavors meld.

Heat 2 ounces olive oil until very hot. Add shrimp and caramelize them. Deglaze with verjus and add lobster meat; remove from heat; the seafood should be slightly undercooked.

Add seafood mix along with pan drippings to lobster sauce mixture, pour into baking dish, and simmer until seafood is opaque at center.

Pipe Chive-Potato Puree on top of seafood and brown under broiler.

Garnish with 2 potato gaufrettes, grilled shrimp, and fresh minced chives.

Lobster Sauce

Yield: About 1 quart

3 lobster heads, gills and shell
    removed
1 stalk celery, sliced
4 tomatoes, quartered
3 shallots, sliced
½ fennel bulb, sliced
10 white peppercorns
5 coriander seeds

10 sprigs thyme
5 sprigs tarragon
2 ounces olive oil
½ cup white wine
¼ cup brandy
1 quart heavy cream
2 tablespoons lobster-shrimp
    glace (optional)

Sweat first 9 ingredients with olive oil for 20 minutes. Deglaze with wine and brandy. Add cream, bring to simmer, and infuse. Strain while trying to extract as much flavor as possible from the lobster heads.

Bring strained mixture back to a simmer and enrich with lobster-shrimp glace. Adjust seasonings and reserve.

Chive-Potato Puree

Yield: Approximately 1½ pounds

4 Idaho potatoes, 90 count,
    peeled, large dice
3–4 cloves roast garlic
6–8 ounces butter, cubed

4–6 ounces milk
3–4 ounces chive oil (puree of
    chives and grapeseed oil,
    infused a day and strained)

Bring potatoes to boil in salted water. When potatoes are done, drain well and force through a sieve. Fold in butter, a couple of pieces at a time. Bring milk to a simmer and slowly add to puree to reach desired consistency. Slowly add chive oil to reach desired taste and color. Portion puree into piping bag.

The Plaza Cafe, Southampton (p. 261)

Whole Fish Baked in Salt Crust

The red snapper or branzino baked in crosta di sale is a signature dish at Casa Rustica, Mimmo and Benedetto Gambino's exceptional Smithtown restaurant.

Serves: 1

For the Fish:

1 whole red snapper or branzino, about 1 ¼ to 1 ½
pounds, gutted, scales on

2 garlic cloves
1 sprig rosemary
Kosher salt

For the Sauce:

2 tablespoons olive oil
Salt and pepper to taste
2 teaspoons fresh lemon juice
Basil and parsley to taste,
chopped

1 teaspoon mustard
3 plum tomatoes, peeled,
seeded, and chopped

Lemon wedge

To prepare the fish: Stuff the belly of the fish with the garlic cloves and rosemary. Place the fish on a sheet pan lined with kosher salt. Sprinkle some water on the fish. Cover the fish with kosher salt and sprinkle with water again. Place fish in a 400°F oven for about 20 minutes.

Meanwhile, make the sauce: Place olive oil, salt and pepper, lemon juice, chopped basil and parsley, and mustard in a small bowl. Add the plum toma-toes and combine with rest of sauce.

Take fish out of oven, crack the salt crust off, and filet it. Place the fish on a plate and put sauce on it. Gar-nish with a lemon wedge.

Casa Rustica, Smithtown (p. 176)

Clam Pie

Travelers on the East End sometimes see a roadside sign advertising clam pies. These savory dishes have their roots in New England and probably Olde England. Charlotte Sasso, co-owner with Bruce Sasso of Stuart's Seafood Market makes this winner.

Serves: 2-4 as a main course; 6-8 as an appetizer

1 medium onion, finely chopped

2–3 stalks celery, finely chopped

2–3 tablespoons unsalted butter

2 tablespoons freshly chopped parsley

6–8 small red potatoes, chopped and steamed until tender

18–24 cherrystone or chowder clams, shucked, drained, and chopped, or put through a food grinder

¼ cup heavy cream

Pie shell with top crust (homemade or bought)

1 teaspoon poultry seasoning

Salt and pepper

1 beaten egg

Preheat oven to 400°F.

Sauté onions and celery in butter until softened. Add parsley and cook for another minute. Add cooked potatoes, clams, cream, and seasonings. Place filling in the pie shell, and top with piecrust. Brush pie with beaten egg. Cut 4 or 5 slits in top to release steam.

Bake for 10 minutes, lower heat to 350°F, and bake 30–35 minutes more.

Stuart's Seafood Market, Amagansett (p. 298)

Penne alla Vecchia Bettola

This zesty pasta is a regular on the menu at Nick & Toni's in East Hampton, where Chef Joseph Realmuto adds to the restaurant's star power. His recipe yields 2 quarts of sauce.

Serves: 6-8

2 (28-ounce) cans peeled plum
    tomatoes
1 medium Spanish onion,
    diced
7 cloves garlic
¼ cup extra virgin olive oil
½ tablespoon red chile flakes

1½ tablespoons dried oregano
1 cup vodka
2 cups heavy cream
4 tablespoons fresh, chopped
    oregano
Grated Parmesan cheese

Set oven to 375°F.

Drain tomatoes through a sieve and crush with hands into an ovenproof 5-quart pot. In a large sauté pan, sweat onions and garlic in oil until translucent over medium heat. Add chile flakes and oregano. Add vodka and let reduce by one-half. Pour onion mixture over tomatoes. Cover with tight lid and place in oven. Cook for 1½ hours at 375°F.

Take out of oven and let sauce cool for 15 minutes. In a blender, puree sauce until a smooth consistency.

To serve, reheat 1 cup sauce with ½ cup cream for each person. Sprinkle with fresh, chopped oregano. Salt and simmer for 5 minutes. Toss with cooked penne pasta and grated Parmesan cheese.

Nick & Toni's, East Hampton (p. 20)

Campagnola Soup

This bracing, artful, pastry-capped multi-bean soup is a mainstay at Stresa restaurant in Manhasset. Chef Ella Rocca's recipe serves four people. Although it begins the meal, you could enjoy Campagnola as a main course or a full lunch.

Serves: 4

½ cup olive oil

6 ounces chopped onions

6 ounces celery

4 ounces dry red kidney beans, soaked

4 ounces dry white cannellini beans, soaked

4 ounces dry chickpeas, soaked

4 ounces dry lentils, soaked

1 cup white wine

1 cup tomato sauce

6 cups chicken or vegetable stock

6 ounces chopped parsley

2 pinches oregano

2 pinches fresh parsley

2 pinches fresh basil

Salt and pepper to taste

Uncooked pastry dough

Parmesan cheese, grated, for garnish

Note: The beans need to be in dry form, then soaked for 12 hours.

In a large pot, heat oil until hot. Add onion and celery and stir until brown. Stir in the soaked kidney beans, white beans, chickpeas, and lentils and mix together with onion and celery. Add wine and stir. Let above ingredients cook for 5 minutes. Add tomato sauce, chopped parsley, and stock, and stir. Salt and pepper to taste. Cook for 1 hour over medium heat, stirring occasionally. Additional broth can be added if required. Stir in oregano, parsley, and basil.

Presentation: Pour soup into soufflé bowls. Coat the tops of the bowls lightly with oil. Cut pastry to cover each bowl with a ¼-inch overlap. Place into oven at 350°F for 5 minutes. Serve with grated Parmesan cheese to taste.

Stresa, Manhasset (p. 26)

Pasta con le Sarde

Pasta con le Sarde is a classic Sicilian dish, one of the most flavorful pastas you'll ever taste. The updated recipe is from restaurateur Benny DiPietro of Benny's Ristorante in Westbury. Bucatini and perciatelli are the pastas most frequently used.

Serves: 4–6

3 cloves garlic, minced
¼ cup olive oil
¼ cup white wine
1 (28-ounce) can peeled San Marzano tomatoes
2 tablespoons tomato paste
¾ pound fresh sardines (if unavailable, canned will do)

¼ cup pine nuts
¼ cup raisins
¼ cup wild fennel
Salt and pepper to taste

For Bread Crumbs:

1 tablespoon olive oil
½ cup panko bread crumbs

Touch of paprika

Sauté garlic with olive oil until slightly browned. Add white wine. Add tomatoes and tomato paste and let simmer for about 15 minutes. Add remaining ingredients and cook on low heat for 25–30 minutes.

For bread crumbs, add oil to medium-hot pan and toast panko crumbs until slightly brown. Add paprika, mix to combine, and remove from heat.

Toss your choice of cooked pasta with the sauce, then sprinkle with the toasted bread crumbs.

Benny's Ristorante, Westbury (p. 8)

Spring Vegetable Pot-au-Feu

Philippe Corbet of Roots Bistro Gourmand in West Islip makes a seasonal vegetable dish that's both light and rich, with layers of flavor. Three elements come together in harmony. And please have that crusty baguette with it for a fourth.

Serves: 4-6

For the Broth:

1 gallon water
¾ bottle white wine
1 bunch thyme
1 bunch rosemary
Black peppercorns, whole

6 large Spanish onions, chopped, divided
2 large carrots, chopped
1 head of garlic, cut in half, but not peeled
Salt

For the Vegetables:

4 baby beets, peeled
4 baby rainbow carrots, peeled
4 heirloom cherry tomatoes
20 fava beans, shelled

4 baby turnips, peeled
8 purple asparagus spears
4 fingerling potatoes, washed

For the Aioli:

2 Russet potatoes, boiled and peeled
8 cloves garlic, minced
3 egg yolks

1 cup extra virgin olive oil
Black pepper, ground

To Serve:

Sel de Guerande

Crusty baguette

To make the broth/stock: To a large pot, add water, wine, thyme, rosemary, and peppercorns. Bring to a boil. Set aside 4 onions. Add 2 chopped onions, carrots, and garlic to boiling mixture. Turn heat down and let simmer for 2–3 hours. Strain and discard vegetables, herbs, and peppercorns. Put remaining liquid back on stove and add remaining 4 chopped onions. Let simmer for 1 hour and then strain. Add salt to taste. Split broth in half. Save one half for serving.

To cook vegetables: Bring half of the broth to a boil. First add beets and let cook for 15 minutes. Add the rest of the vegetables and let cook for at least 15–20 minutes. Check for doneness. Time may vary depending on the size of the vegetables.

To make the aioli: In a food processor, combine boiled, peeled potatoes with minced garlic. Add the egg yolks and mix them completely at medium-low. While food processor is running, slowly incorporate the olive oil. It is important to do it slowly so the mixture emulsifies. Season to taste with black pepper.

To compose the dish: Heat the remaining broth and divide into 4 bowls. Strain cooked vegetables and disperse evenly in bowls. Put aioli on top or on the side. Finish with Sel de Guerande or your favorite finishing salt. Serve with a crusty piece of baguette (optional, but highly recommended).

Roots Bistro Gourmand, West Islip (p. 199)

The Duck Mirabelle

Chef Guy Reuge was served duck in two courses in France, first the breast followed by confit of leg with a crisp salad. He makes his version of it year-round, with seasonal sauces and garnishes. It remains one of Mirabelle restaurant's most in-demand dishes. To make it, you'll need four boned-out Pekin ducks.

Serves: 8

- 4 Pekin ducks, 3½ pounds each
- 4 shallots, cut in half
- 2 heads of garlic, split
- 1 tablespoon black peppercorns

- 4 sprigs fresh thyme
- 2 bay leaves
- 10 juniper berries
- Salt and pepper

Remove the breasts and legs from the duck and trim them well of excess fat and skin, reserving the fat and skin. Remove all fat and skin from the bones and reserve it. Set aside the bones for duck stock.

Using a sharp knife, make crisscross incisions on the skin of the breasts and arrange the duck breasts skin side up on a sheet tray. Refrigerate the breasts uncovered for 2 days in order to dry out the skin.

Season the legs with salt and pepper on both sides, transfer them to a shallow roasting pan, and add the shallots, garlic, peppercorns, thyme, bay leaves, and juniper berries. Refrigerate the duck legs overnight.

Transfer the reserved fat and skin from the breasts, legs, and bones to a saucepan. Add 1 cup of water and bring it to a boil over moderately high heat. Reduce the heat to moderate and cook the mixture until the water is evaporated and the fat is completely melted, cooking the skin down. The melted fat will become golden and clear and the remaining skin crisp. Carefully pass the melted fat through a sieve into a large bowl, let it cool, and refrigerate it overnight.

The next day, melt the fat in a saucepan, pour it over the duck legs to submerge them, and bring it to a boil over moderately high heat. Transfer the roasting pan to a preheated 250°F oven and cook the duck legs for at least 2½ hours, or until they are cooked through and feel soft. The process is called confit. Let the pan cool and refrigerate the legs, keeping them in the roasting pan. The duck legs can be refrigerated for up to a month as long as they are submerged in the chilled fat.

To serve: Remove the duck legs from the fat, placing them skin side down in a shallow roasting pan. Roast the duck legs in a preheated 350°F oven for 35 minutes, or until the fat is absorbed and the skin is crisped.

Season the breasts on both sides with salt and pepper. Sear the breasts skin side down in a hot, dry skillet over medium heat, removing the excess fat from the pan from time to time. Cook the breasts until the skin is crisp and golden and turn them over. Continue to cook the breasts until they are medium rare. Transfer the breasts to a cooling rack and let them rest for 10 minutes before serving. Slice the breasts into 5 or 6 pieces each.

Serve the breasts first with a garnish and sauce of your choice. Follow with the duck leg confit either simply with a small salad or other preparation of your choice.

Mirabelle, Stony Brook (p. 218)

Chocolate Caramel Tartlette

Claudia Fleming's desserts are among the great pleasures of dining at The North Fork Table & Inn in Southold. The decadent Chocolate Caramel Tartlette is one of her best.

Yield: 2 dozen tartlettes

For the Chocolate Tart Dough:

½ cup (1 stick) unsalted butter, softened

½ cup plus 1 tablespoon confectioner's sugar

1 large egg yolk

¾ teaspoon vanilla extract

1 cup all-purpose flour

¼ cup unsweetened Dutch-processed cocoa powder

For the Caramel Filling:

2 cups sugar

¼ cup light corn syrup

½ cup (1 stick) unsalted butter

½ cup heavy cream

2 tablespoons crème fraîche

For the Chocolate Ganache Glaze:

¾ cup heavy cream

3½ ounces extra bittersweet chocolate, chopped

Pinch of fine sea salt, such as fleur de sel (optional)

To prepare the tart dough, in the bowl of an electric mixer fitted with the paddle attachment, cream the butter and confectioner's sugar until combined, about 1 minute. Add the egg yolk and vanilla and beat until smooth. Sift in the flour and cocoa powder and beat on low speed until just combined. Scrape the dough onto a sheet of plastic wrap and form it into a disk. Wrap and chill until firm, about 1 hour, or up to 3 days.

Preheat the oven to 325°F. On a highly floured surface, roll the tart dough to an 18 x 12-inch rectangle, ¾ inch thick. Using a 2½-inch round cutter, cut out 24 rounds of dough and press them into muffin tins or 2-inch tart pans, trimming away any excess dough; prick the dough all over with a fork. Chill the tart shells for 20 minutes.

Line the tart shells with foil and fill with pie weights or dried beans. Bake for 15 minutes. Remove the foil and weights or beans and bake for 5 to 10 minutes longer or until the pastry looks dry and set. Transfer to a wire rack to cool. The tart shells can be made 8 hours ahead.

To prepare the filling, place ½ cup water in a large saucepan. Add the sugar and corn syrup and cook the mixture over medium-high heat, swirling the pan occasionally, until you have a dark, amber caramel—about 10 minutes. Carefully whisk in the butter, cream, and crème fraîche (the mixture will hiss and bubble up so stand back), whisking until smooth. (The caramel can be made up to 5 days ahead and refrigerated). Divide the caramel among the tart shells while still warm (or reheat the caramel in the microwave or over low heat until it is pourable) and let sit until the caramel is set, at least 45 minutes.

To make the glaze in a saucepan, bring the cream to a boil. Place the chocolate in a bowl. Pour the hot cream over the chocolate. Add a pinch of sea salt. Let it sit for 2 minutes. Then whisk until smooth. Pour some of the glaze over each of the tarts while it is still warm. Let the glaze set at room temperature for at least 2 hours before serving.

The North Fork Table & Inn, Southold (p. 237)

Kung Pao Monkfish

Michael Wilson's clever, delicious updates of Asian dishes make Monsoon a culinary storm. Here's how he reinvents and enriches what's usually the name attached to chicken and peanuts.

Serves: 1

- 3 (3-ounce) pieces monkfish, cut like tail
- 4 ounces Monkfish Marinade (recipe follows)
- 1 tablespoon grapeseed oil
- Sufficient canola oil to deep-fry monkfish
- 2 teaspoons ginger, chopped
- ¼ cup celery, chopped
- ¼ cup carrots, chopped and blanched
- ¼ cup water chestnuts
- ½ cup bean sprouts
- 1 tablespoon Chinese chives, chopped
- 1 teaspoon salt
- 1 ounce Chile-Sichuan Sauce (recipe follows)
- 1 tablespoon scallions, chopped
- 1 tablespoon peanuts, chopped and roasted

Marinate monkfish pieces for at least 2 hours in Monkfish Marinade.

Deep-fry monkfish in canola oil until golden. Finish in the 400 degree oven for about five minutes and hold to rest.

In succession, stir-fry the next 6 ingredients. Finish with the chives and salt. Place vegetables in the bowl and top with the fish. Spoon the Chile-Sichuan Sauce over the fish. Dress the plate with the scallions and the peanuts.

Monkfish Marinade

Yield: 2 portions

- 1 teaspoon baking soda
- ½ cup cornstarch
- 1 teaspoon white pepper, ground
- 1 teaspoon salt
- 1 egg white
- 2 tablespoons rice vinegar
- 1 tablespoon sesame oil
- ¼ cup water
- ¼ cup Shaoxing wine

Combine all and stir.

Chile-Sichuan Sauce

Yield: 1 pint

¼ cup Shaoxing wine
½ cup chili bean paste
¾ cup sweet chili sauce
4 tablespoons oyster sauce

¼ cup rice vinegar
1 tablespoon sesame oil
6 tablespoons Sichuan Oil
(recipe follows)

Cook the alcohol out of the wine, letting it come to a boil. Combine all ingredients and reserve.

Sichuan Oil

Yield: 1 pint

2 pieces star anise
3 ounces chili oil
1 ounce annato seed

1½ ounces Sichuan
peppercorns
16 ounces vegetable oil

Combine all ingredients and heat over a low flame for 10 minutes to infuse the flavors. Steep the aromatics until cool and strain through a chinois. Chill.

Monsoon, Babylon (p. 162)

Millennium Lobster

This lobster dish originated at Tellers: An American Chophouse in Islip and has appeared at other restaurants in the Bohlsen Restaurant Group, including Prime in Huntington (p. 142) and H2O Seafood Grill in Smithtown (p. 180).

Serves: 1

1 (2-pound) lobster
3 tablespoons Millennium
   Flour (recipe follows)
3 tablespoons butter
1 tablespoon vegetable oil
1 tablespoon garlic, chopped
½ teaspoon chili flakes
1 tablespoon shallots, chopped

2 teaspoons lemon juice
4 ounces clam juice
Salt to taste
2 tablespoons basil chiffonade
¼ pound butter, unsalted
4 ounces mashed potato

Cut lobster in half lengthwise. Evenly dust lobster with Millennium Flour. In a large sauté pan, heat the 3 tablespoons butter. Saute the lobster, cut face down, until lightly golden. Turn lobster over and finish cooking in 350°F oven for 10 minutes.

While the lobster is cooking, heat the oil, garlic, chili flakes, and shallots and cook until lightly colored. Deglaze with lemon juice and clam juice. Add salt, basil, and ¼ pound butter and reduce by one quarter over high heat, emulsifying sauce.

Place hot mashed potatoes in center of the plate. Wedge the lobster into the mashed potatoes and pour the sauce over the lobster.

Millennium Flour

Yield: 1 serving

2 ounces granulated garlic

2 ounces onion powder

2 ounces Cajun seasoning

8 ounces all-purpose flour

1 ounce chili powder

1 ounce cayenne pepper

In a large container, mix all ingredients. Strain all through a sieve. Store in an airtight container.

Tellers: An American Chophouse, Islip (p. 201)

Appendices

Appendix A: Eateries by Cuisine

La Marmite, 32
Oak Chalet, 54
Plattduetsche Park Restaurant, 66
Pumpernickel's, 150
Rialto, 24
Silver's, 270
Villa d'Este, 64
The Village Lanterne, 168
Vitae, 149

Creole
Big Daddy's, 75

Crepes
Fresco Creperie & Cafe, 115

Delicatessen
Andel's of Roslyn (Kosher), 30
Ben's Kosher Delicatessen, 9, 75
Kabanos Polish Deli, 171
Pastrami King, 55
Zan's Kosher Delicatessen, 223
Zenway Natural Food Market, 209

Diner
The Cutchogue Diner, 242

Eclectic
Lola, 20
Maroni Cuisine, 136
Roots Bistro Gourmand, 199, 340
Vinoco Wine Bar & Tapas, 29

French
Almond, 252
The American Hotel, 268
Aperitif, 41
Bar Frites, 7
Bistro Cassis, 123
Bistro Citron, 10
Brasserie Cassis, 77
Brasserie Persil, 43
Chez Noëlle, 30
Kitchen A Bistro, 181
La Maison Blanche, 235
Le Soir, 197
little/red, 258
Mirabelle, 218
Pierre's, 261
red/bar brasserie, 262
Stone Creek Inn, 265
Sunset Beach, 240

Fusion
Perfecto Mundo, 185

Gastropub
The Brass Rail, 76
Heirloom Tavern, 83
Sapsuckers, 145

German
The Currywurst Company, 115
Oak Chalet, 54
Plattduetsche Park Restaurant, 66
Prost Grill & Garten, 58

Japanese

Nisen Sushi, 184
Roppongi Sushi Restaurant, 164
Sen, 263
Shiki, 165
Show Win, 145
Sushi Ko, 62
Takara, 201
Wansuapona Musu, 93
Zakura, 289

Latin
La Casa Latina, 18
Perfecto Mundo, 185

Luncheonette
Candy Kitchen, 268
The Coronet, 242
Henry's Sweet Shoppe, 109
Hicksville Sweet Shop, 96
Laurel, 118
Munday's, 150
Star Confectionery, 245

Mediterranean
Abe's Pitaria, 114
Bistro Etc., 11
The Harvest on Fort Pond, 281
Kitchen A Bistro, 181
Stone Creek Inn, 265
Tula Kitchen, 203

Mexican
Besito, 9, 122

Chichimecas, 79
Estia's Little Kitchen, 256
Gold Mine Mexican Grill, 130
La Brisa, 282
La Fondita, 283
Los Compadres, 135
Oaxaca, 139

New American
Acacia, 121
A Mano, 230
Almond, 252
The American Hotel, 268
Aperitif, 41
The Argyle Grill & Tavern, 167
Babylon Carriage House, 159
Bar Frites, 7
Barney's, 74
The Bellport, 213
Black & Blue Seafood
    Chophouse, 124
The Brass Rail, 76
Brasserie Cassis, 77
Brasserie Persil, 43
Butterfields, 174
Cafe Red, 175
Cafe Testarossa, 78
Cedar Creek American Bar &
    Grill, 104
Chachama Grill, 215
City Cellar, 13
The Coast Grill, 255
CoolFish Grille & Wine Bar, 79

Appendix B:
Dishes, Specialty
Stores & Producers

Messina Market, 99
Springs General Store, 298
St. Rocco's Bakery, 111

Caterer
Iavarone Bros., 69

Cheese
Babylon Cheese Cellar, 168
Catapano Dairy Farm, 247
C'est Cheese, 226
Ideal Cheese & Wine Cafe, 155
Mecox Bay Dairy, 272

Chocolatier
Bon Bons Chocolatier, 151
The Chocolate Duck, 97
Kron Chocolatier, 36
Lazar's Chocolate, 37

Coffee
Aldo's, 246
coffee 'tauk, 295
Georgio's Coffee Roasters, 170
Hampton Coffee Company Cafe, 271
Java Nation, 272

Dairy
Catapano Dairy Farm, 247
Mecox Bay Dairy, 272

Fairway Market
Maple Tree BBQ, 248

Messina Market, 99
The Purple Elephant, 156
Red Horse Market, 297
Springs General Store, 298

Gourmet Market
Cavaniola's, 271
Citarella, 294
Curds & Whey, 98
Fairway Market, 35, 98
Gemelli's Fine Foods, 169
Grace's Marketplace, 35
Iavarone Bros., 69
Kitchen Kabaret, 36
Loaves and Fishes, 272
Messina Market, 99
Razzano's, 110
Red Horse Market, 297

Ice Cream/Gelato
Baci Gelato, 34
Coyle's Homemade Ice Cream, 206
Hicksville Sweet Shop, 96
Itgen's Ice Cream Parlour, 69
Leonetti Pastry Shop, 37
Magic Fountain, 248
Marvel Dairy Whip, 70
McNulty's Ice Cream Parlor, 224
Sant Ambroeus, 263
Snowflake, 249

Italian Market
Ceriello Fine Foods, 34

Index